Design History and Culture

This student-friendly text provides a comprehensive exploration of the methods and approaches employed within design scholarship, drawing upon influences from history, art history, anthropology and interdisciplinary studies such as science and technology studies and material culture studies.

Drawing connections between these methods and the evolving landscape of design, the book expands design culture beyond traditional outcomes to encompass areas like design for social innovation, digital design, critical design, design anthropology and craftivism. Additionally, the book introduces novel theoretical frameworks to facilitate discussions on contemporary designers' work, including new materialism, object-oriented ontology and decolonization.

This comprehensive overview of methods and approaches will enable students to select the most appropriate methodological tools for their own research. It is an ideal guide for both undergraduate and postgraduate students in design, design culture, design history, design studies and visual culture.

Javier Gimeno-Martínez is an associate professor of Design Cultures at the Vrije Universiteit Amsterdam. His research interest encompasses the crossovers between design scholarship and other disciplines within the humanities and the social sciences. He is the author of *Design and National Identity* (2016).

Design History and Culture
Methods and Approaches

Javier Gimeno-Martínez

Routledge
Taylor & Francis Group

LONDON AND NEW YORK

Designed cover image: Cover image composition: Kylièn Sarino Bergh.
Cover images: Housewife using a strain machine - Vintage property of
ullstein bild Published in: Wir Hausfrauen 2:2, photo by Dorothea von der
Osten/ullstein bild via Getty Images; chair - Salt Research via Flickr.

First published 2025
by Routledge
4 Park Square, Milton Park, Abingdon, Oxon OX14 4RN

and by Routledge
605 Third Avenue, New York, NY 10158

Routledge is an imprint of the Taylor & Francis Group, an informa business

© 2025 Javier Gimeno-Martínez

British Library Cataloguing-in-Publication Data
A catalogue record for this book is available from the British Library

ISBN: 978-0-367-70628-9 (hbk)
ISBN: 978-0-367-70629-6 (pbk)
ISBN: 978-1-003-14728-2 (ebk)

DOI: 10.4324/9781003147282

Typeset in Times New Roman
by Taylor & Francis Books

Contents

Figures

Table

Acknowledgements

This book is the outcome of my teaching in the MA Design Cultures. Running this MA, teaching this course and supervising students' theses are extremely rewarding experiences. The amount of detail in which these methodologies need to be elaborated has been the product of years of teaching and of conversations with both colleagues and students, to whom I am extremely grateful. I am especially indebted to the Design Cultures team that is currently composed of Joana Meroz, Cyril Tjahja and Jane Tynan. Working with you is a true luxury. Furthermore, I am indebted to my colleagues at the Arts and Culture division. Being in this environment has stimulated my interest in delving into the frameworks of art, media and architecture studies. The goal of this book is rooting design scholarship in the field of the humanities, partly because of working within this context. I am particularly grateful to Ingrid Vermeulen, who shared with me her fascinating research on the development of art schools in the seventeenth century. The research behind this book has been possible thanks to a grant from the interfaculty Research Institute for Culture, Cognition, History and Heritage of the Vrije Universiteit Amsterdam (CLUE +) through which I could appoint the then MA student Marthe Oosting to help me for a few months. Another enthusiastic MA student, Kylièn Bergh helped with the cover of the book when I was unable to decide. Finally, I would like to thank my partner Rudi Meulemans for helping me envision this book. For his conversations, his care and for reading and re-reading the different chapters. Many thanks for making this a better book and mine a happy life.

Introduction

Since 2010, I have taught the course "Methods of Design Analysis: The Meanings of Design" at the Vrije Universiteit Amsterdam within the MA Design Cultures. Structuring this course has been a journey of discovery. I searched for a book to guide me but could not find any. Therefore, I had to read and re-read the design scholarship, understand what my colleagues had done from a methodological point of view and finally, look for the formulations of those methods both within and outside design scholarship. I noticed that this exercise was not only beneficial for my teaching but also for my research.

Since this MA is embedded in a Faculty of Humanities, I benefitted from conversations with colleagues with different disciplinary backgrounds. It was also clear that my course and this book had to look for connections with both well-established and novel academic discussions. A journey through literature from the humanities and the social sciences made me understand the complexities behind methods and approaches and the reasons behind using one or the other. That is how the idea of this book emerged. This is the book that I have been looking for. A book that would equip the reader with the academic skills to both identify and implement approaches and methods properly. A book that presents a selection of methods and approaches and elaborates on their theoretical foundations, making the reader aware that methodologies have a disciplinary background that cannot be ignored. At the same time, a book that would look at the practice of design and explore the scope and limitations of those methods and approaches for the study of design today.

Why this book? And why now?

I have been trained both as an industrial designer and as an art historian and am particularly sensitive to the importance of the work of designers as well as the relevance of a proper academic knowledge. I enjoy scrutinizing how artefacts are made and how they can gain cultural relevance by participating in academic debates. Design history, design studies, design philosophy and design culture studies have succeeded in defining a field of study, that is, a subject of investigation that has been defined as "design." Albeit this field

DOI: 10.4324/9781003147282-1

might be in constant expansion and redefinition, design has found its place among the visual arts, media and architecture. Penny Sparke notes that "what was still in the 1990s a relatively recognizable, definable discipline, complete with a set of sub-disciplines – product design, fashion, graphics, interior design, landscape design, etc. – has become unrecognizable" (2016: 2). If design had been artefact-based, either material or visual, there is a myriad of new understandings of the practice of design in which the artefact is less important than the processes involved. Take, for example, design for social innovation, craftivism, critical design or biodesign. Moreover, technical and social debates are changing the way designers work. New technologies have generated other forms of design based on the Internet, artificial intelligence and mobile technologies and opened up debates about post-humanism. On the other hand, social changes point to new understandings of non-binary gender identities, decolonization and climate crisis. Therefore, this book will examine the validity of these methods and approaches to face these new situations.

The methods used to study this field come from different disciplines. This has resulted in a rich multidirectional study of the field of design in which all perspectives from production to mediation or consumption, meet. Chiefly art history but also cultural studies, material culture studies, science and technology studies, sociology and anthropology have provided methodological tools for the analysis of design. As design scholar Guy Julier candidly acknowledges:

> Design cultures is scary. The specialist in design cultures has to move through many academic fields. If this new discipline includes the study of the production, mediation, circulation and regulation of design, she or he must be an expert in psychology, management, technologies, politics, cultural studies and be a historian, an economist, an anthropologist, philosopher, sociologist and geographer. In addition to these, he or she has to be visually, materially and spatially literate.
>
> (Julier 2011: 1)

As a result, the theoretical foundations of design scholarship are dispersed. Design history and design culture run the risk of becoming distanced from their methodological origins. Therefore, the goal of this book is to identify widely employed methods and approaches for the academic study of design, discern their theoretical foundations and disciplinary origins and examine their use within design history and design culture.

But what is the point of exploring the methodological foundations of such a hybrid discipline? In the introduction to *The Culture of Design*, Julier declares his fear of "methodological orthodoxy not least because the variations by which design cultures are constituted and performed demand flexibility and inventiveness in their study" (2014[2000]: xvi). I agree that listing all the possible methods and approaches can be an endless task. Nevertheless, reflecting on the most used can open up new research avenues and consolidate the theoretical foundations of design scholarship, precisely characterized by its interdisciplinarity.

Perhaps, the next question to answer would be "why now?" If design scholarship has survived without a strong methodological foundation, why do we need it now? The answer lies in the increasing complexity of design scholarship, developments in the humanities and the changes in the practice of design. Design scholarship is expanding from design history and design studies to design culture studies and design philosophy. Accordingly, methods and approaches for the academic study of design are indeed expanding. Far from being static, there is undeniably an evolution in how these more traditional approaches and methods have been used. There are new theoretical frameworks, for example object-oriented ontology or new materialism, which come to add albeit do not substitute long-standing ones such as post-structuralism. This book gives an account of both new and long-standing methods and approaches, related to various theoretical frameworks.

Furthermore, there are challenges within the humanities and the social sciences that require design scholarship. Advances in the digital humanities and the environmental humanities make clear that design scholarship is a substantial part of these disciplinary groups and that it needs a strong methodological foundation to face these challenges. Therefore, this book will integrate these debates and reflect on how design scholarship participates in them.

Selecting methods and approaches

Methods have internal requirements. Are we aware, for example, of the different kinds of case study research that exist? Is the typological approach outdated? Are designers' monographs condemned to a heroic approach? What is the difference between structuralist and post-structuralist object analysis? This book offers an analysis of those theoretical foundations, acknowledging their origins and their evolution, evaluating how they have been used within design analysis and exploring possible challenges. The disciplinary origins of each method and approach gives the possibility to demonstrate their global past. The reflection on their challenges helps elucidate possible directions for their future. Furthermore, the very definition of design is also evolving. As a result, artefacts previously studied within anthropology and the decorative arts are now part of the design scholarship.

When deciding how to structure this book, I looked at the methods and approaches that have been extensively used within design scholarship. Then, I reflected on what design scholars might need to implement them. Therefore, I decided to focus on methods and approaches that process evidence and not on those that gather evidence. The reason is that the former need to be adapted to the field of design and the latter less so. Thus, this book will not deal with archive research, bibliometrics or geographic information systems. These are all valid methods for gathering evidence for design scholars. Their application may not vary significantly within design scholarship or other fields and there are likely other standard manuals explaining these methods. Conversely, evidence processing methods are closely tied to specific disciplinary backgrounds, requiring at least a minimal translation when employed by design scholars. For example, this book does not provide guidance on conducting interviews but instead focuses on oral history and ethnography – both methods that involve interviewing.

Every method and approach is eligible for a wide-ranging – yet limited – number of research questions. For example, ethnography involves a genuine interest in a sample group as the research focus. Probably, the same group will be less helpful in shedding light on how designed objects have been conceived, produced and manufactured. To achieve that goal, other methodologies and other sample groups are more appropriate. Such observations help both researchers and students understand the possibilities that methods and approaches offer.

This book structures methods and approaches for design history and design culture studies because these disciplines engage with methods and approaches more intimately than other fields of design scholarship. This book does not aim at creating a divide between the different directions in which design scholarship has developed – they all contribute to the academic understanding of design. It is at times difficult to distinguish between design history and design culture studies since they both flow seamlessly. If design history has a long tradition, I see design culture studies as stemming from it to develop a more intimate connection with recent history and partly with theory. When looking at design culture scholars, they have also been active or are still active in both fields, as, for example, Guy Julier or Kjetil Fallan.

The precedents of this book are scarce; there is only one chapter in John A. Walker's *Design History and the History of Design* (1989) that discusses the most used methods and approaches in design history. Fallan's book *Design History: Understanding Theory and Method* (2010) extends this list with another three methodologies derived from science and technology studies. Both books are outstanding, but the former is too outdated and the latter too limited regarding scope. Along with these two examples, there have been very brief accounts of the methodological foundations of design history and culture by Gregory Votolato and more recently by D.J. Huppatz (Votolato 1998: 251–279; Huppatz 2018). They have mapped existing methods and approaches but as a brief overview, which is difficult for an in-depth analysis. From the methodology manuals outside design scholarship, I would highlight Gillian Rose's book *Visual Methodologies* (2016) in that it embraces material research along with visual research methodologies and it has been useful as long as design can be analysed according to the parameters of art.

It is striking how methodological trends can change in a short period of time. Methods and approaches might seem invariable and there is indeed a strong foundation in all of them. At the same time, they evolve and transform to adapt to changing realities. A periodical update of methodological trends within design scholarship is therefore most necessary. Take, for example, the influence of science and technology studies on design scholarship. Fallan predicted that actor–network theory (ANT) and script analysis would play a central role in design history in his 2010 book *Design History: Understanding Theory and Method* (2010: 66–89). Its influence had recently reached a peak at the 2008 Design History Society Annual Conference in Falmouth entitled "Networks of Design" in which Bruno Latour (1947–2022) was one of the keynote speakers. Design history was said to be one of the new audiences of science and technology studies and, according to Fallan, some of the most important theoretical perspectives and frameworks informing and transforming design history stem from it (Fallan 2010: 103). However, as Fallan himself acknowledged, "there are only few who have made anything of it" (2010: 77). Looking back, ANT has been pivotal as a theoretical framework and has influenced other frameworks ranging from object-oriented ontology to new materialism. As a method, script analysis has been important within design scholarship but has not become "central."

In 2018, D.J. Huppatz discussed the lack of impact of ANT methodologies on design history, arguing that, even when these methods are potentially useful, Fallan did not offer much guidance about how to use them and they do not offer solutions to the most pressing challenges of the discipline (Huppatz 2018: e35). One could expect that it is within design culture studies that ANT has had the most impact since Fallan advocated for it and Guy Julier similarly introduced ANT in his *The Culture of Design* (2014[2000]) as has been included in Ben Highmore's *The Design Culture Reader* (2008). As Julier said, understanding ANT is considering "the 'things between' as much as the things themselves" (Julier 2014[2000]: 234). This seemed promising since design culture studies connect cultural studies and social sciences (Julier 2014[2000]: 245). Nevertheless, in the recent volume that seeks to consolidate the foundations of design culture, *Design Culture: Objects and Approaches* (Julier et al. 2019), there is little mention of ANT.

These reactions should not distract from the fact that far from losing momentum, the influence of ANT has been integrated in other trends that connect with debates around the Anthropocene and the pluriverse. ANT reflects on the importance of the material as connected to humans and nonhumans and initiated a non-anthropocentric vision of the world that questioned the divide between culture and nature. Therefore, it has impregnated recent design scholarship mostly regarding design anthropology and sustainability.

Regarding material culture studies, they are rooted in different fields such as museum studies, anthropology, philosophy of science and archaeology. For example, material culture studies have been pivotal to the formulation and dissemination of consumption studies in the 1980s – a particular interpretation of material culture studies that had its impact on design history. Furthermore, material culture studies have influenced social and cultural historians, too (Grassby 2005; Auslander 2005). The historian Leora Auslander refers to the relevance of objects as non-linguistic sources when she argues that people's relation to language is not the same as their relation to things, and that what they express through their creation and use cannot be reduced to words. Therefore, artefacts can also act as sources of history distinct from written records (Auslander 2005: 1017).

The influence of material culture studies in the broader sense – beyond consumption studies – on design scholarship is evident in Judy Attfield's *Wild Things: The Material Culture of Everyday Life*. In her book, Attfield uses the term "thing" as standing for "the basic unit that makes up the totality of the material world" (2000: 9) and proposes going beyond the framework that confines design scholarship to the work of professional designers, to reach out at "how people make sense of the world through physical objects" (2000: 1). The book places design against the backdrop of material culture, viewing design as a subgroup of distinguishable objects. According to Attfield, design is "just one type of 'thing' among the collectivity of material culture in general" (2000: 29). But how then can design be distinguished from other types of similar artefacts? In *Wild Things*, the field of design is defined basically as the artefacts that have traditionally been studied by design historians. A second differentiating characteristic for design according to Attfield is "things with attitude" (2000: 20). It is however difficult to discern which artefacts have more attitude than others. The subjectivity and arbitrariness of this defining characteristic itself demonstrates the difficult divide between design and portable, functional artefacts at large.

Terminology

All approaches to material culture share a commonality in designating their study objects as "artefacts," signifying items crafted by humans. The term "artefacts" specifically denotes the material aspect of material culture studies and is generally favoured over alternative terms like "objects," "things," "goods," "products" and "commodities." The preference for this term in material culture studies could stem from various reasons. For instance, "objects" brings to mind the Platonic and Kantian dichotomy between subject and object, suggesting the subordinate nature of the latter. Currently, the dichotomy between subjects and objects is increasingly challenged, especially since the dissemination of ANT. "Things," on the other hand, refers to objects independent from the subject and has been used in philosophy, most notably by Martin Heidegger (1889–1976) (1971: 163–186). However, its extended use in everyday language makes this term less suitable for academia. "Goods" and "products" for their part intrinsically involve an exchange value. Similarly, the term "commodities" is related to "goods" since it evokes exchange value and is closely linked to capitalist market relations; but it is even more specific since it designates a particular moment in the life of an artefact, namely when it becomes involved in an exchange (Woodward 2007: 15). The term "artefacts" appropriately recalls artificiality, an intrinsic cultural character and a source of knowledge in itself. Moreover, this term is less common in everyday language and its use is, therefore, less clouded. It denotes greater independence from humans than "objects," more specificity than "things" and a broader range of social meanings than "goods," "products" or "commodities."

This book will use these terms accordingly, regarding whether the method or approach under discussion is inserted within one or other academic tradition. I will favour "artefacts" when discussing methods and approaches related to material culture studies, "commodities" when discussing Marxist-inspired approaches and "goods," "objects" and "things" indistinctively according to each author discussed. For example, the anthropologist Igor Kopytoff writes about the cultural biography of things and I will use this term when discussing his work. In other cases, I will use the more generic "object" and also "artefacts" as a category that encompasses material, visual and spatial objects.

The scope of design history and design culture studies has been acknowledged by their output that ranges from product design to fashion, from professional designers to the work of amateurs and from recent to historical accounts. Attempts to achieve this goal have stemmed from design historians close to the field of material culture studies, craft and non-Western design. For example, the book *Global Design History* (2011) edited by Glenn Adamson, Giorgio Riello and Sarah Teasley studies subjects ranging from fashion to websites, and from the Renaissance to the present day. The authors distance themselves from a design history centred on modernization and industrialization – which has produced a historiography based on North America and Europe – to present evidence of design as a wider and more complex phenomenon. If designed artefacts, in general, are the object of study, then there is little sense in reducing the scope of the field to one or another subfield. The challenge lies in embracing the totality of artefacts belonging to design, delimiting its extension towards other fields such as architecture or art, and at the same time acknowledging their overlap. This book, therefore, aims to offer a comprehensive perspective on how to implement methods and approaches within design scholarship integrating all practices.

Content

This book aims to help readers in the selection of methodological tools. To achieve this aim, it makes a distinction between methods and approaches. The difference between the two resides basically in the fact that methods offer minimal instructions on how to process evidence to answer a specific research question. For example, oral history is a method, since it offers steps to follow when decoding interviews. Approaches, on the other hand, do not offer specific steps to follow but reunite research that shares the same perspective and therefore can be compared. One example is gender studies, which gathers research dealing with the construction of gender categories. In that sense, approaches are compatible with different methods. For example, there can be one piece of research on gender that has been conducted through the use of oral history and another piece of research on gender that has been conducted using discourse analysis.

Both methods and approaches are methodological tools and should not be confused with theoretical frameworks. The former two clarify *how* to do research and what other researchers are doing similarly. The latter offers an understanding of *what* concepts mean and how they are interrelated. There might be methods that are strongly connected to theoretical frameworks, for example Chapter 1 explores a close-reading method that is structuralist and Chapter 2 another that is post-structuralist. Understanding reality from different perspectives has an impact on the method itself, but they both remain the same method, that is, close readings. Similarly, an approach is compatible with different theoretical frameworks, that will define different ways of interpreting evidence. For example, gender studies based on psychoanalysis would deal with evidence differently than gender studies using structuralism as a theoretical framework.

Methods are grouped under the first part of the book and approaches under the second. Both parts focus on the design object itself, the intrinsic processes in which design is produced, mediated and consumed and the contexts in which these processes take place. This book thereby enables readers:

- to create order in the design literature. This book allows classifying texts – whose content might be multifarious – according to their methodological similarities;
- to identify possible perspectives at hand depending on one's research goal;
- to position themselves in the field. Readers will find the methodology that fits them best and thereby develop their own academic voice.

Each chapter discusses either a method or an approach and examines, from a methodological point of view, examples from design scholarship that have made use of them. Each chapter is illustrated with examples and structured along four recurrent sections:

1   "Origins" studies the theoretical and disciplinary roots of each method and approach.
2   "Development" explores how each method and approach has developed until being appropriated by design history and design culture.
3   "Implementation" reviews how each method and approach has been used in design literature.
4   "Challenges" questions how contemporary design practice and recent theoretical insights can evidence shortcomings in each method or approach.

The selection of the examples from design scholarship in each chapter is rather illustrative than comprehensive. Each chapter conducts an in-depth analysis of a few, chosen examples because of their representativeness. Similarly, the chapters will not offer extended instructions on the implementations of methods that can be found elsewhere. They aim to introduce the use of specific methods and put forward the basis for their understanding and implementation.

Part I
Methods

1 Close readings I

Structuralism

Jules David Prown's method of artefact analysis is rooted in an art historical context. It is built upon a clear structuralist foundation, conceptualizing artefacts as cultural releasers, which grant researchers access to specific cultures. This method unfolds in distinct, well-defined steps aimed at enhancing perceptual skills. It places importance on both internal evidence, derived from the observation and manipulation of objects, and external evidence in the form of written records. Consequently, it facilitates the development of fresh insights into a particular artefact. However, this method comes with both strengths and risks. Internal evidence, stemming from observation and manipulation, should not be treated as absolute facts but rather as opportunities to formulate hypotheses to be later substantiated with the use of written sources. Despite originating in the early 1980s, this method still holds relevance today, as evidenced by its adaptation to the field of dress in 2015 by Ingrid Mida and Alexandra Kim.

Origins: Objects as indexes of culture

The everyday can be pivotal to understanding culture, since designed artefacts are repositories of valuable cultural information. But how can this information be disclosed? Hammers, bridges, posters and paintings require different analytical approaches. An adequate method of inquiry extracts the most information from each artefact. To achieve this aim, close readings of artefacts are key not only because they serve to generate descriptions of artefacts but also because they open up interpretive avenues. Their goal is not just to describe what the researcher sees but to acknowledge the relevance of these observations for new lines of inquiry.

In the 1960s, scholars and critics turned to structuralist and semiotic approaches. Structuralism allowed them to state that observations on particular cultural products were representative of the society at large. Semiotics argued that those products were releasers of cultural meaning and that, by implementing methods typical of linguistics, scholars were able to interpret them. When approached as acts of social communication, scholars realized

DOI: 10.4324/9781003147282-3

that objects were able to release information that other methods were unable to disclose. Regarding this, Judy Attfield noted that

> [u]nless we can go beyond a static, object-based approach based on an aesthetic analysis, it is not possible that there is a dynamic dimension of symbolic representation in artefacts which is more akin to language and which can be used to articulate a material world.
>
> (Walker 1989: 220)

One of these scholars was Jules David Prown (b. 1930), an art historian who specialized in eighteenth-century painting and material culture in general. From his initial formalist training, he evolved towards the implementation of structuralism and semiotics to develop his own theoretical approach to object analysis. This shift occurred when he was a student in the Winthertur Program in Early American Culture at the University of Delaware between 1954 and 1956. One of his instructors, Anthony Garvan (1917–1992) claimed that "objects embody culture and can be so studied," which according to Prown opened up new research perspectives other than formalism and iconography. Within an art historical take on material culture studies, Prown proposed a method applicable to any artefact created by humans. Up until then, formalism and iconography had championed object analysis in art history. They answer chiefly questions such as "What are the formal considerations leading the creation of this work?" or "What is the meaning enclosed in the symbols used?" Even as both questions are significant, they proved insufficient for design, first and foremost because these methods prioritize aesthetics and ignore functionality, which is essential for a great number of designed artefacts.

Prown's structuralist method understands objects as intermediaries that reflect the beliefs of individuals and by extension the society that made, commissioned, purchased or used those objects. He claims that material culture studies imply "that objects made or modified by man reflect, consciously or unconsciously, directly or indirectly, the beliefs of individuals who made, commissioned, purchased, or used them, and by extension the beliefs of the larger society to which they belonged" (1982: 1–2). The word "reflect" in this sentence is pivotal, since structuralism considers artefacts chiefly as tangible materializations of the abstract concept of culture.

Before going further, a definition of material culture both as a discipline and as a field will help understand Prown's goal when formulating this method. Unlike other authors, Prown uses the term "material culture" to denominate the discipline and "artefacts" as the field or object of study. He states that material culture is the study through artefacts "of the beliefs – values, ideas, attitudes, and assumptions – of a particular community or society at a given time." The term "material culture" has been frequently used to refer to the artefacts themselves, to the body of material available for such study. Prown refers to the evidence simply as "material" or "artefacts" (1982: 1). In this context, the significance of artefacts lies in their role as a means "through" which culture can be studied, emphasizing their function as a conduit rather than an ultimate objective.

In his initial position as an art historian, Prown's option for the use of "artefacts" instead of "works of art" extended the range of study objects from art to ordinary objects. Artefacts have an inclusive character since they involve material production superseding categorizations of high and low culture or art and design. The core aspect of an artefact is therefore its artificial character, its opposition to nature. In other words, the study of material culture might include a hammer, a plow, a microscope, a house, a painting or a city and it would exclude trees, rocks, fossils, skeletons. However, the border between the artificial and nature is not clear-cut. Prown clarifies that a carefully stacked pile of rocks could be regarded as an artefact, since it is not merely untouched nature but rather nature altered by humans (Prown 1982: 2). Furthermore, Prown's definition of artefacts differs from other authors in terms of scale, since he considers cities as artefacts, too. Other material culture scholars would disagree with considering large-scale, immovable objects as artefacts. For example, the sociologist Ian Woodward defines artefacts as something chiefly portable and greater units such as cities as networks of artefacts rather than as artefacts themselves (Woodward 2007: 14).

In terms of disciplinary and methodological premises, Prown's method is clearly delineated. Its chief premise is that artefacts evidence the presence of human intelligence at the time of creation (1982: 1–2). They represent the moment in which they were created and contribute to the understanding of that specific period. Alongside, three auxiliary premises drawing from determinism, structuralism and semiotics underpin this core premise. First, Prown's *determinism* argues that every effect observable in or induced by the artefact has a cause. Hence, to comprehend the culture of a specific era (the cause), researchers can utilize the artefact (the effect) as a means to achieve that understanding. Second, establishing a proper connection between cause and effect involves adhering to the structuralist assertion that the configuration and properties of artefacts align with patterns both in the mind of the individual creator or creators and in the society to which they belonged. This implies that our findings on particular artefacts go beyond the individual intentions of the producer and, in cultural terms, extend to the broader societal context. The third premise is the *semiotic* principle that artefacts "transmit signals which elucidate mental patterns of structures" (1982: 6). The implementation of semiotics allows the researcher to interpret those signals, thereby disclosing the cultural meaning of those artefacts.

Development: Jules David Prown's "affective approach"

If close readings are interpretations of artefacts, for which culture are they meaningful? For the originating culture or for the researcher's culture? The answer would be for both. Prown's method places artefacts as originating in a specific culture and therefore as a firsthand experience for the researcher.

Moreover, it defends close readings as interpretations conditioned by the researcher's mind. In Prown's own words, artefacts

> can yield evidence of the patterns of mind of the society that fabricated them, of our society as we interpret our responses – and non-responses – and of any other society intervening in time or removed in space for which there are recorded responses.
>
> (1982: 6)

Accordingly, drawing from artefacts instead of from written documents serves two goals. The first is that there might be no written evidence of a culture's beliefs since they are so "generally accepted that they never need to be articulated" (1982: 4). Indeed, we cannot expect to find written records of all important cultural convictions of a society. Moreover, the work of the cultural researcher, as Prown states, is to get at hidden beliefs. Not only have certain cultural patterns escaped documentation in written form, but individuals may also be unaware of them, making it the responsibility of the researcher to uncover these patterns. The workings of the human mind are not entirely comprehensible to the individual, necessitating the interpretation of researchers (1993: 3).

Firsthand access to artefacts is key to properly implementing this method since it starts with a detailed analysis of artefacts based on observation and manipulation, also described as an "affective approach." It is not sufficient to analyse the artefact's shape, but also how it works, how it feels and what connotations it awakens. This "affective approach" requires the researchers to approach the object with their senses. Regarding this, Prown states that

> the best way for investigators to get at the configuration of that belief, to make contact with the producing culture, is through close analysis of the object itself first, apart from its context, to discover mutual commonalities – what we share with those who made and initially viewed or used the object.
>
> (1997: 26)

Researchers are advised to initially observe the artefact and subsequently engage in manipulation. While observation is a common aspect in both formalist and iconographic analyses, physical manipulation distinguishes Prown's method. Thereby, this method is particularly suitable for design, since it allows for a discussion not only of the visual characteristics of a given artefact but also its functionality. This part of the analysis increases the knowledge of the artefact through firsthand experience of the artefact itself, inspiring new insights, ideally other than those acquired by reading about the specific artefacts.

After the initial observation and manipulation, researchers need to write down their findings, which is not just a way of recording them but an opportunity to reflect on them. Reflection is the next stage in the interpretative process. Prown states that when examining an artefact, our perceptions need to be converted into words, "to say what you see, even if only to yourself, in order actually to see it" (1996: 23). In his words, writing is seeing; it brings the researcher to a state of consciousness that supersedes our everyday, inattentive relation to artefacts. If the researchers' goal is to disclose the cultural dimension of an artefact, then they need to engage with the artefact and reflect on the culture at large in which it was produced.

When writing down, the researchers make use of internal evidence and gradually incorporate external evidence (1982: 7–12). Initially, there are three stages based solely on internal evidence posing an increasing level of complexity, that is, description, deduction and speculation (Table 1.1). It starts with the description of the object, and is subdivided into three stages:

- The substantial analysis deals with the tangible aspects of the artefact, including its physical dimensions, material composition and the arrangement of its constituent elements.
- The content analysis aims to interpret explicit representations. This stage is always relevant to graphic design or objects that feature images on their surfaces but may not apply to featureless artefacts.
- The formal analysis delves into the form and structure of the artefact.

Table 1.1 Summary of Prown's method. Own elaboration

Description: what can be observed in the object itself.

- Substantial analysis: physical dimensions, material and articulation
- Content: reading of overt representations
- Formal analysis: object's form and configuration

Deduction: the interaction between the object and the perceiver.

- Sensory engagement: the sensory experience of the object
- Intellectual engagement: what it does and how it does it
- Emotional response: the emotions that a particular object may trigger

Speculation: moves completely to the mind of the perceiver.

- Theories and hypothesis: summing up what has been learned from the internal evidence of the object itself and developing theories that might explain the observations
- Programme of research: developing a programme for validation. This shifts the inquiry from analysis of internal evidence to the search for and investigation of external evidence

Investigation of External Evidence

After the description, the deduction follows, in which the interaction between object and perceiver is key. Likewise, the deduction is subdivided into three sub-stages:

- Sensory engagement involves the exploration of the artefact's sensory experience.
- Intellectual engagement requires the researcher to delve into the functions and mechanisms of the artefact.
- Emotional response refers to the emotions that a specific artefact may evoke in both the observer and others.

The last of the three stages is speculation, in which the analysis moves completely to the mind of the perceiver. There, the first step is formulating a hypothesis. Summing up what has been learnt from the internal evidence, the researcher concentrates on the aspects that deserve further research. This sub-stage finishes with the development and implementation of a programme of research that would validate this hypothesis, shifting the inquiry from internal evidence to the search for and investigation of external evidence. Only after thorough observation, are researchers ready to incorporate external evidence, once the artefact has been understood in depth and firsthand.

The gradual implementation of the distinct stages allows for a direct approach to artefacts without being influenced by pre-existing interpretations. The outcomes from the initial three stages serve as sources of inspiration to formulate an original hypothesis, encouraging researchers to think creatively and explore cultural interpretations of artefacts that deviate from dominant narratives, opening up new interpretative possibilities. Nevertheless, while the findings from internal evidence may be innovative, they remain speculative and require validation through external sources to lend credibility to the research. In this regard, Prown's method unfolds as a progression from the specific to the general, from the physical to the mental and from the material to the cultural.

Implementation: Formulating a hypothesis

Good examples of the implementation of Prown's method are in the edited volume entitled *American Artifacts: Essays in Material Culture* (Prown and Haltman 2000), which includes a collection of analyses by Prown's students who applied his method to different objects ranging from 1970s lava lamps to Amish quilts. One remarkable essay in this collection is Amy B. Werbel's analysis of a 1930s aluminium food mill manufactured in the USA composed of a sieve, a blade-shaft and a wing nut at the bottom that assembles the two (Figure 1.1). Werbel starts describing the artefact in detail, even the traces of use, concentric scratches towards the base that suggest the rotations of the blade. This method allows her to pay attention to those elements that have been replaced and repaired. The food mill possesses a straightforward yet

Figure 1.1 A food mill in use. Vintage property of ullstein bild. Published in: *Wir Haus-frauen* 2:2. Photo by Dorothea von der Osten/ullstein bild via Getty Images

effective mechanism, with its entirely metallic appearance associating it with technical devices. The essay continues deducing its use according to the traces left, the material used and the articulation of the different elements. This artefact is appropriate for the preparation of soft meals for children during weaning. The "affective approach" makes salient that this artefact displays quite a technical appearance despite its daily use, combining a contradictory very professional look with a homely character.

Werbel then moves from internal evidence to external evidence, looking for the justification for this odd combination. In doing this, she connects with the professionalization of housewife activities in North America in the 1930s, finding evidence of increasing nutrition advice for mothers that did not stem from family circles but from nutrition professionals. The authority of house-wives, as it had been understood until then, became suddenly questioned. The mother's own notions on this matter had to be placed aside and replaced by professional advice, deriving from specialists and aiming to be scientific. This incursion of the realm of science in the home was spread through publications in a period that coincided with the circulation of prepared vegetable meals in cans for babies. Werbel concludes her analysis by affirming that this food mill symbolized the perpetuation of the traditional maternal role, wherein mothers nurture their children through homemade food rather than relying on ready-made options. Simultaneously, it marked a departure from the past by embracing a modern, sanitary and technological approach to food preparation. The efficiency of this device surpassed that of traditional methods involving a strainer and a spoon (2000: 229–241).

Following Prown's method, Werbel starts with observable characteristics of the object such as a technological appearance and traces of actual use as a kitchen accessory to prepare baby food. From these observations, she can formulate the hypothesis that this artefact presents some contradictory features, such as a scientific appearance and a home-cooking use. This observable contradiction is confirmed by the contemporary literature about baby feeding as a modern, medical issue.

Formulating a hypothesis could be deemed the most demanding aspect of this method. This phase involves transitioning from observations to a research question, which is then subjected to testing against external evidence. Nevertheless, this step is key. In Werbel's chapter, observing that the appearance of a mundane object reflects a transitional period in the role of women at home, engages with the cultural background of the researcher. The more the researcher knows about gender roles in the 1930s USA, the easier it will be to interpret this artefact and place it in this narrative. If, as mentioned above, writing is seeing, then knowing is seeing, too. Formulating a hypothesis is a personal eureka moment. It depends indeed on the researcher's knowledge and creativity to come up with a significant narrative. In the case of Werbel's, the reward of a sophisticated hypothesis is evident. An artefact that would be speechless suddenly encapsulates the epoch in which it was made. Its aesthetic and functional contradictions correspond to the abrupt discontinuity of traditional values around motherhood. The researcher brings the reader from visible characteristics of objects to hidden cultural patterns.

When implementing Prown's model, it is crucial that the various stages are interconnected, seamlessly transitioning from one to another, moving fluidly from observation to interpretation, from internal evidence to external evidence. The discoveries made in one stage should somehow foreshadow the questions posed in the next. Werbel's conclusions flow logically from the initial observations. Her original observations about the material and use of the artefact are linked to her hypothesis and her conclusion. In that sense, there is a careful balance between the relevance of the internal evidence and the external evidence and both need to be intimately linked when using this method. A lack of connection between the different stages would lead to conclusions that do not stem from an "affective approach" or fail to link specific observations with broader cultural beliefs.

Valerie Steele, herself a former student of Prown, has advocated for the use of this method. She argues that surviving examples of clothing are valuable sources that can complement and even contradict written and visual sources, often used by fashion historians. Steele observes how myths persist in the fashion industry without being substantiated or challenged with evidence. For example, the acceptance of the myth of the 30-centimetre waist in late nineteenth-century dresses, a notion supported by references to journalistic sources from that era. Her own conclusion, after measuring herself a good number of corsets in several collections, is that these tiny waists were an exception rather than the norm (1998: 332). In that sense, Steele adds a recommendation when proceeding with the deduction stage making clear how common or how peculiar the artefact under scrutiny can be. She recommends comparison with other similar artefacts belonging to the same category (1998: 330). In Werbel's case, for example, the researcher might need to know if the use of aluminium was extensive or if the food mills worked differently in previous decades.

A more recent example of the adaptation of Prown's method for the study of dress is Ingrid Mida and Alexandra Kim's *The Dress Detective* (2015). Similar to Steele, this book draws on Prown's method, albeit leaning more towards his "affective approach" rather than its structuralist framework. The authors prioritize a meticulous firsthand analysis of artefacts over the belief that objects reveal concealed cultural beliefs. In essence, their focus is on generating observations and substantiating them with external evidence, with less emphasis on uncovering unconscious beliefs shaped by the cultural patterns of a particular society. While Prown's method maintains a balance between speculation and facts, Kim and Mida demonstrate a clear preference for the factual. Their method reflects a time when structuralism had lost its authority in academia, and its foundations were being questioned by post-structuralist alternatives.

Significantly, the different stages of Prown's method are reformulated in Mida and Kim's variant. Starting with the first stage "description," which they replace with "observation." They argue for a "slow approach to seeing," which involves both taking notes and sketching (2015: 28, 35–36). The second stage changes from "deduction" to "reflection" and is rather a continuation of the first but based on "thoughtful contemplation." Mida and Kim justify this change because deduction apparently implies cultural and personal biases and identifying them can be "confusing to researchers" (2015: 29). They encourage the researchers to write down their personal biases towards the garment but at the same time to look at the context and start gathering external evidence in the form of textual material, such as diaries or letters, and visual sources, such as photographs and illustrations. In this case, the use of external evidence comes earlier than in Prown's original, somehow curtailing the potential of the "affective approach" when implemented on its own. Similarly, the last stage changes its name from "speculation" to "interpretation." It reunites the descriptive and the emotive/sensorial observations of the preceding two stages. Mida and Kim argue that this leap toward the formulation of a hypothesis can be problematic for students since there is no clear prescription on how to interpret the clues. Drawing from the researchers' own experience and from theory can help to overcome this difficulty. Furthermore, the authors acknowledge that there is a necessary component of creativity in formulating a good hypothesis (2015: 31).

The examples in *The Dress Detective* are very much connected to existing sources in a straightforward way – much more than in Werbel's example. For example, an analysis of an early nineteenth-century pelisse – that is, a women's coat with long sleeves open at the front that reached to the ankles – observes the presence of military adornments (Figure 1.2). Mida and Kim contrasted this fact with secondary sources, acknowledging thereby the inspiration of women's dress in military uniforms since the eighteenth century but reaching a peak during the Napoleonic Wars (2015: 100). After reading Werbel's analysis of the 1930s food mill, their interpretation reads less insightful. Perhaps the researcher could have gone further in studying the role of women in politics or their appropriation of a typically masculine realm such as the army and military uniforms. As it stands, their hypothesis reads very acceptable as an interpretation but less adventurous and therefore somehow obvious. Prown's goal of reaching the hidden beliefs of a culture through the study of artefacts can admittedly result in far-fetched interpretations, but too-evident hypotheses do not seem to capitalize on the potential of this method.

Challenges: Looking "through" artefacts or "at" artefacts?

This section explores discussable and unresolved aspects in Prown's method. Take, for example, his definition of artefacts as cultural intermediaries, the advantages and disadvantages of cultural distance between researchers and artefacts and his categorization of artefacts.

Considering artefacts as **cultural intermediaries**, as this method suggests, implies looking "through" them while at the same time looking "at" them. Both perspectives hold significance for design scholars, engaged as they are in studying both artefact-based and culture-related aspects. Nevertheless, for design scholars, designed artefacts are not only instruments but also subjects of study in their own right. In other words, artefacts are not mere sources but a study object in themselves.

Prown gives the example of art history being both a discipline and a field. Art history develops its own disciplinary view and at the same time is genuinely interested in artworks as its subject of investigation. Conversely, material culture is a discipline, not a field and sees artefacts therefore only as a vehicle to understand culture and not as an object of study. However, like art history, design scholarship is interested in the field of design as an object of study. Therefore, the question arises: to what extent is a method based on material culture studies fully relevant for design?

This is most striking because Prown's method studies artefacts very precisely, conceding as much importance to them as to contextual aspects. He states that material culture is interested in the motive forces that condition behaviour "specifically the making, the distribution, and the use of artifacts" (1982: 6–7). After reading this fragment and studying the method, it seems as if object and context are indissolubly related. The very impossibility of

Figure 1.2 Pelisse, probably American, circa 1820. Designer unknown. Photo by Heritage Art/Heritage Images via Getty Images

separating the two is what makes material culture studies such a manifest influence on design scholarship.

Despite this, it seems clear that Prown's method considers the artefact itself mainly and foremost as a source rather than as an object of study. But what kind of source and how is it different from written sources? Prown distinguishes between internal and external evidence, artefacts and written sources, indexes and documents. Are artefacts as indexes better qualified to interpret culture because of their firsthand experience? Or are written sources as documents better placed because of their objectivity? Prown considers that artefacts are historical evidence but disappointing as communicators of historical facts, which are better transmitted through textual documents (1993: 3; 1982: 16). This statement seems to discredit artefacts in favour of written sources. Nevertheless, he also states that artefacts are internal evidence, and that material culture would be unable to interpret cultural biases through written records alone (1993: 11). Since documents are intentional, conscious expressions of belief, they can never suffice when getting to the unintentional cultural meanings of a specific culture. In that sense, artefacts are better placed.

Prown's categorization of indexes and documents is not a hierarchical one where one supersedes the other. Instead, it underscores the comparable significance of internal and external evidence, acknowledging the complementary nature of both. He contends that reality is not solely discernible in factual information and contextual data, nor solely in the mind of the observer, but in the interplay between the observer and the artefact (1996: 26). Consequently, he advocates for collaborative research wherein both internal and external evidence contribute with their respective roles.

These observations lead us to other concepts proposed by Prown that are equally open to debate, such as the significance of **cultural distance**. In essence, the question arises: to what extent should researchers be immersed in the culture they are studying, and does this either enhance or hinder cultural analysis? Does being part of the studied culture better equip researchers to unravel unrecorded cultural assumptions, or does it not? In his quest for objectivity, Prown seems to oscillate between positions articulated by the anthropologist Claude Lévi-Strauss (1908–2009) and the art historian Arnold Hauser (1892–1978). He follows Lévi-Strauss when saying that researchers are better placed to study foreign cultures than their own. Paradoxically, the deep knowledge of one's own cultural structures would impede rather than facilitate their analysis. In a different culture, researchers can better identify biases that might be overlooked due to their common occurrence in their own culture (1996: 24–25). On the other hand, he diminishes its significance by aligning with Hauser, who argues that once aware of the issue, researchers can actively counter their own subjectivity and thereby aim for objectivity. The awareness of one's own biases "is a large step in the direction of neutralizing the problem" (1982: 4–5).

Cultural differences influence a fundamental aspect of Prown's method, namely his "affective approach," which he contends is transcultural. Prown asserts that an "affective approach" to artefacts aims to attain the objectivity characteristic of the scientific method, as it provides a means to overcome the distortions resulting from our specific cultural standpoint. Equally crucial, it brings to light the otherwise imperceptible, unconscious biases inherent in our cultural perspective (1982: 5). This method relies on the common human experiences shared by researchers and individuals from the studied culture. In this sense, Prown argues that the neurophysiological apparatus of human beings has evolved slowly over time (1993: 232). Further, he defends that it is common to all humans how we "experience the physical world – our experience of gravity, for example, and of innumerable binary oppositions: day/night, open/closed, wet/ dry, etc" (1996: 22).

If the "affective approach" is transcultural, then the cultural background of the researcher should be of little relevance. The theoretical foundation of this method shows a double attitude towards cultural distance. If researchers need to be aware of their distance towards the originating culture, they can also rely on a common sensorial experience. In this method, the "affective approach" unlocks through the senses the primary information that the artefact can release. Prown considers that stage as based on neurophysiological commonalities. This stage triggers a mental interpretive work in which the cultural distance does play a role. Prown considers that material culture is based on interpretations but under no circumstance should assign "intentionality or even awareness to the fabricating culture" (1982: 10). The "affective approach" can be transcultural but results in interpretations, not facts. When validated by external evidence, these interpretations become academically acceptable. The question remains about why aspire to develop a scientific method when the research outcome remains an interpretation.

The last topic for discussion is his **categorization of artefacts**. In this aspect, Prown moves between normativity and relativism, more specifically in his definition of art. Across his work, he repeatedly stresses that "artefacts" is an inclusive term that unites all the facets of the artificial in their capability to serve as cultural releasers. On the other hand, Prown introduces a certain hierarchy within this inclusivity. In that sense, his classification ranges from "art" to "devices" depending on the grade of intentionality attached to each category. He considers art as the most intentional, conscious expression of belief and therefore presents similar problems of liability as written documents. Prown continues by saying that the distinction between art and artefacts is that artefacts "do not lie" (1993: 5). It is unclear if art is one more category under artefacts or places itself outside, since he seems to dissociate art from other kinds of artefacts (1982: 3). This dissociation becomes even greater when he elaborates on the function of art, according to him "to communicate – whether to instruct, record, moralize, influence or please" (1993: 5).

Prown problematically states that because utilitarian devices such as card tables, teapots, hammers or telephones have specific functional programs, then "the variables of style through which the program is realized are unmediated, unconscious expressions of cultural values and beliefs" (1993: 5). While it is accurate that tradition can shape the form of designed artefacts and formal variations may align with prevailing stylistic trends, it is untenable to argue that designers are unaware of their choices or that design lacks the capacity to "instruct, record, moralize, influence, or please." In this context, design appears to align with various categories of Prown's artefacts, including art.

Furthermore, and contradicting his normative characterization of art, Prown relativizes its definition. Sometimes, he defines art as a permanent category based on essential, defined traits (1982: 12–13). Elsewhere, he states that art is not permanent but open to definition and that many cultures do not have a special category of objects identified as art. He states that "art is what we say is art, including ethnographic and technological objects not created as art, but which have been aestheticized by being placed in museums or other special collections" (1993: 2). So, if art is easily characterized, how is it that its definition is context-bound?

In sum, Prown's method presents certain statements that warrant careful examination. Viewing artefacts as indexical sources is characteristic of this method but the outcome of the analysis goes beyond this consideration offering in-depth analysis of the artefact itself. Werbel's analysis is a good example of this. Nevertheless, Prown considers artefacts as a particular indexical source for two reasons: they can be approached with the senses, and therefore unbiasedly, and they offer trustworthy cultural information. The challenge arises when Prown links the credibility of artefacts directly to various typologies. Typologies lack cohesiveness and may not align with consistent levels of intentional, conscious expression of belief. The true intentions reside in the designer's mind rather than within the object itself.

2 Close readings II
Post-structuralism

Structuralist and post-structuralist close readings serve different aims. The theoretical foundations of both approaches are radically different and involve different understandings of the relationship between the artefact and the cultural context, the agency of humans and artefacts and the influence of the former on the latter. Both theoretical frameworks explore the connection between artefacts and societies, but if the first focuses on the aesthetic and symbolic qualities of an artefact, the second focuses rather on its functional performance. After studying a structuralist method in Chapter 1 – in which artefacts are considered as intermediaries between culture and researcher – this chapter explores another take on object-centred analysis in which the artefact is rather seen as a mediator of human relations. A post-structuralist model of close readings, Madeleine Akrich's "de-scription," which is inserted in actor–network theory, proposes to read an object as embodying a script. The task of the analyst is to de-script the object and translate it into words.

Origins: Technology and society

Actor–network theory (ANT) explores how artefacts contribute to articulate societies. Its origin within the social sciences is a factor to consider. If artefacts are evidently relevant for design scholars, they have been less so for sociologists. The stress on their importance might seem overstated for a design readership but considerably pioneering for sociologists, whose chief focus has been people rather than artefacts. Even as ANT seems to explain technology, its impact is even more visible in the conceptualization of society. The main theorist of ANT, the sociologist Bruno Latour, for example, calls for a reconsideration of social accounts. He claims that morality cannot be measured in a society without considering how artefacts condition human behaviour (Latour 1992: 227). In that sense, this account is relevant for design, since it discloses how design is injected with moral values and how artefacts condition human behaviour.

Latour's work diverges from the social constructionist approaches that were dominant in the philosophy of sciences. Antecedents of this theory formation can

DOI: 10.4324/9781003147282-4

be found in the social construction of technology (SCOT), enunciated by Trevor Pinch (1952–2021) and Wiebe E. Bijker (b. 1951), and in Thomas Hughes' idea of "systems." The former challenges technological determinism, stating that the success or failure of technological advances did not reside in the quality of the invention, but in how society constructed them. Quality and novelty have not been the primary justification for technical advances, but society and technology mutually influence each other – they are not separate analytical units. On his part, Thomas Hughes (1923–2014) argues that the spread of inventions depends on how they relate to existing systems. When clarifying the emergence and dissemination of an invention, one should look not only at the invention in itself but at how it connects with other existing developments. Thus, the use of lamps, for example, cannot be measured on their own but rely on the spread and supply of electric current (Law 2009: 143). If SCOT linked the reasons for the spread of artefacts to society, then Hughes did the same with the pre-existence of other artefacts.

The most straightforward way to comprehend ANT is by defining its constituent terms: actors, networks and theory. Latour defines **actors** as "entities that do things" (1992: 241). This is an overarching term for all the participants in a given action without distinguishing between objects and subjects, humans and nonhumans. As long as an element has agency in making an action possible, it belongs to the same category as the other actors. This category is all-encompassing but not infinite since it excludes both humans and nonhumans that are not significant or do not contribute to a specific action, that is, that do not have agency (Latour 2005: 130). Agency, another pivotal concept within ANT, is not the same as free will or intentionality. The next quote offers a nuanced explanation of this apparent paradox:

> This, of course, does not mean that these participants "determine" the action, that baskets "cause" the fetching of provisions or that hammers "impose" the hitting of the nail. Such a reversal in the direction of influence would be simply a way to transform objects into the causes whose effects would be transported through human action now limited to a trail of mere intermediaries. Rather, it means that there might exist many metaphysical shades between full causality and sheer inexistence. In addition to "determining" and serving as a "backdrop for human action", things might authorize, allow, afford, encourage, permit, suggest, influence, block, render possible, forbid, and so on.
>
> (Latour 2005: 71–72)

Agency is granted as soon as an actor participates in and therefore conditions a specific action, but actors do not need to be the motor behind that specific action. In that sense, ANT sophisticates the interaction between technology and society, between humans and nonhumans beyond a subject–object divide.

Both humans and nonhumans participate in and constitute the **network**, which the connections between the actors configure. As the sociologist John Law states, this term is used in the absence of a better one, rather as a metaphor than as a well-suited option, similar but not exactly the same as an actual net. Regarding this, Latour says that

> a network is not made of nylon thread, words or any durable substance but is the trace left behind by some moving agent. You can hang your fish nets to dry, but you can't hang an actor-network: it has to be traced anew by the passage of another vehicle, another circulating entity.
>
> (Latour 2005: 132)

Thus, in the action "hitting a nail in the wall," the actors would be: a human, a hammer, a nail and a wall. These actors are all connected to each other in a network which is defined by the translation of flows between them. Fetching the hammer, stroking the hammer against the nail, the nail penetrating the wall. After the action is finished, this specific network disappears and the actors are free to reconfigure other networks.

Paradoxically, the heterogeneity of actors involved and their similar role within a network, homogenizes their importance, which is a pivotal difference between ANT and technological determinism or social constructivism. Technological determinism would grant the success or failure of an invention to its intrinsic quality and how it improves previous similar inventions. This vision will consider that the nonhumans, and not the humans, resolve their own evolution. Conversely, social constructivism would put the responsibility on humans, stating that only humans have the status of actors (Akrich 1992: 206). Thus, the conceptualization of actors and networks as mutually constituent negates pre-existing dominant frameworks by acknowledging the agency of nonhumans.

Yet, what kind of **theory** is ANT? John Law states that it is actually a method, rather than a theory. Regarding its methodological premises, ANT combines ethnomethodology and semiotics. It makes use of ethnomethodology since it draws from the observation of how actions hold or collapse. For this, an observation of reality is necessary. In that sense, it shares Prown's claim of holding firsthand contact with the artefact, which might mean that ANT is only applicable to the study of observable networks and therefore of no use in the study of design from the past. Ideally, observation is intrinsic to ANT but Latour allows the use of external evidence such as archives in the study of actions happening in the past. He studied, for example, the intricacies of the investigation and success of scientist Louis Pasteur (1822–1895) without obviously being a firsthand witness (Latour 1993[1984]).

The second methodological premise is semiotics, which seems again to coincide with Prown's method. Nevertheless, ANT's interest in semiotics is not in how objects can be interpreted as texts, as for Prown, but in how meaning emerges through the interaction between artefacts in the same way that words acquire meaning when interacting with each other in a sentence. Law explains this point by stating that "entities take their form and acquire their attributes as a result of their relations with other entities" (Law 1999: 3).

Regarding this, Law lists ANT's three pillars stating that there is "semiotic relationality (it's a network whose elements define and shape one another), heterogeneity (there are different kinds of actors, human and otherwise), and materiality (stuff is there aplenty, not just 'the social')" (Law 2009: 146).

Accordingly, ANT proposes *how* something happens but does not strive to explain *why* something happens; it is "descriptive rather than foundational in explanatory terms" (Law 2009: 141). Accordingly, ANT will not provide a background on which to start a discussion in the sense that Prown might do. It does not state how artefacts necessarily relate to culture, for example, since every network is different and responds to different motivations.

The differences with a structuralist approach become even more clear when stating how ANT positions itself as a product of post-structuralism. First, Law explains that ANT does not "say anything positive on any state of affairs," since it does not explain the links between the elements of the network. It evidences their connections but the reasons for them to emerge are not fixed. It is not that artefacts always "reflect" culture, as Prown would defend (Law 2009: 143). Second, ANT is rather a theory about how *not to* study things. It positions itself against a subject–object dichotomy, technological determinism and social constructivism. Therefore, it does not consider that there is something outside the artefacts being called "culture" that exists independently from them. Moreover, it is not just a means to map networks; the conceptualization of reality in networks implies a way of looking at the world. Third, ANT is not a structuralist science since it implies that the social and the technical are embedded in each other; that culture shapes and is shaped by cultural objects.

Albena Yaneva expands on this when stating that ANT does not try to unveil hidden meanings of design – as Prown would do – but mediates social relations. In her study of a door lock at her university department, she states that rather than "being an intermediary that would 'express,' 'reify,' 'objectify' or 'reflect' university policies, the institutional order and rules (thus serving as a mirror of institutional life), the lock acts as a mediator that constitutes, recreates and modifies social relationships." Along these lines, she seems to challenge all the issues that Prown defended. She concludes that "design functions socially; the social is not outside it, at a cosmic distance from its objects. It is in the objects' world" (Yaneva 2009: 278). In that sense, artefacts do not reveal but constitute culture.

Development: Madeleine Akrich's "script analysis"

I notice that my students often have difficulties in accepting that artefacts can "do" things. This proves how the object/subject divide is embedded in a Western way of speaking and thinking. Artefacts are normally perceived as passive elements and therefore in contradiction with ANT vision. Ordinary language falls short in describing how actors interact in a network and, for this reason, ANT develops a specific jargon to precisely describe socio-technical interactions (Akrich 1992: 206).

The first step towards a proper understanding of ANT is discerning what artefacts actually do. Latour proposes that "every time you want to know what a nonhuman does, simply imagine what other humans or other nonhumans would have to do were this character not present" (Latour 1992: 229). Thus, the agency of a scarf becomes salient when imagining wearers needing to cover their neck with their own hands. What a poster announcing an exhibition "does" is revealed when thinking that someone should be 24 hours a day shouting the staging of that specific event instead. This is what ANT's language calls "delegation" (also displacement, translation, shifting) – the functions that humans delegate in artefacts to serve us.

Nevertheless, when some agency has been delegated to artefacts, this mere act implies the translation of some power to these artefacts. From all the possibilities of covering a neck from the cold, the scarf is, perhaps dominant, but is only one of them. Because a scarf is a consolidated way of neck-covering, it creates expectations that this artefact would be made out of soft materials. Neck-covering artefacts made out of rigid materials would be considered appropriate to cure neck injuries rather than to keep someone warm. The same can be said of a poster or of any other artefact that has become the most obvious of a typology. From that moment, artefacts impose expectations on humans. This property is called "prescription" and is defined by Latour as "the moral and ethical dimension of mechanisms" (1992: 234).

Collateral to this prescription is the suitability of artefacts to serve some users better than others. As Latour wrote, artefacts "have to thoroughly organize the relation between what is inscribed in them and what can/could/should be pre-inscribed in the user" (Latour 1992: 237). So, exhibition posters tend to display written messages, making their decoding problematic to illiterates. It is in those moments when the arbitrariness of delegation is most evident, since artefacts do not adapt to every user, but users have to adapt to them, sometimes more easily and sometimes more abruptly.

Prescription can present itself as an imposition and therefore as an opportunity for rebellion. Users can "write it off." The imposition of ways of behaving can result in rebellion towards the original design. In some cases, the writing-off might be caused by a manifest disconformity with the original design and the morals it might convey. For example, in late nineteenth-century Finland under Russian occupation, subversive attitudes were expressed through using postage stamps upside down. If initially intended to celebrate the Russian Empire, these postage stamps were "written-off" and subverted (Raento and Brunn 2005: 145).

Artefacts relate not only to humans but also to other artefacts, defining the limits of the setting, which ANT calls "circumscription." According to Latour and the sociologist Madeleine Akrich, circumscription is "[t]he limits that the setting inscribes in itself between what it can cope with – the arena of the setting – and what it gives up" (1992: 261). Latour gives the example of computers, that are circumscribed by the plugs, the screen, the disk driver or the user's input, anything that allows the artefact to perform the action and is not the artefact itself (Latour 1992: 237). As artefacts become more complicated, their circumscription becomes more sophisticated and some artefacts are impossible to be conceived without considering their circumscription. Take, for example, Facebook. There is the graphic interface, the devices to consult and submit input, the Internet connection and the Internet network, the user viewing but also the necessity of other users submitting text and images, since Facebook requires multiple users to work. Thinking of circumscription goes against a misleading idea of the autonomy of artefacts and confirms the necessity of thinking in terms of networks.

One last concept deserving attention is "re-inscription," which refers to the gradual redesign of a specific object. In that sense, the resulting design is not a static solution to a specific problem but a negotiation through time of the original design and the antiprogrammes that prompt its redesign. Latour states that every piece of an artefact "becomes fascinating when you see that every wheel and crank is the possible answer to an objection" (Latour 1992: 247).

A good example of a re-inscribed design is the graphic identity of the Catalonia Autonomous Government in 1981, which revived a former emblem designed in 1931 by the architect Bartomeu Llongueras (1906–1994). It depicted an oval coat of arms with four red bars on a yellow background. At the four corners, two laurel leaves turned the oval form into a rectangular one (Figure 2.1). Josep M. Trias'

Figure 2.1 The coat of arms of Catalonia situated between the regional flag of Catalonia, right, and the Spanish national flag, left, in the assembly hall at the Catalan parliament in Barcelona, Spain. Photographer: Lourdes Segade/ Bloomberg via Getty Images

design team developed the implementation guide and variations of the logotype in the visual identity manual published in 1985. This sign joined pictographic features with pictorial ones. As pictograms, it used only one colour but nevertheless, the peripheral laurel leaves insinuated an external light source, as they were illuminated in a "naturalistic way." In 1996, the same design team updated the manual with no substantial changes. However, the designers retouched the laurel leaves. As their shadows made the logo slightly asymmetrical, external graphic design offices sometimes implemented the logo wrongly and, as a result, it could be seen in the public sphere upside down. The wrong utilization of the logo led to an update in 1996, which depicted the laurel leaves as illuminated in a "non-naturalistic" way in order to achieve a completely symmetrical logo. This means that the shadows of the laurel leaves were even at their outer edges and, as a result, the logo looked exactly the same after being rotated 180 degrees (Figure 2.2). This alteration was welcomed since it improved the communicative efficiency of the logo, something arguably impossible to imagine in 1981, when fidelity to the 1931 version was key (Gimeno Martínez 2016: 119–120).

All these terms contribute to understanding ANT's way of looking at reality. In terms of a specific method for the analysis of artefacts and suitable for design scholarship, Akrich developed what she called "de-scription." This close-reading method is based on the idea that artefacts prescribe behaviour and morals to users, through a "script" that the artefact itself conveys and is in-scribed in the artefact by the designer. Using film-related vocabulary, a

Figure 2.2 A ballot box that was used for the illegal Catalan independence referendum in 2017, displays the logo of the Catalan Autonomous Government. Photo credit: JOSEP LAGO/AFP via Getty Images

script defines the actions of the different actors. It orchestrates what happens in the setting. Unlike when actually reading a script, users decode artefact scripts without noticing, made possible through a tradition of using artefacts.

Scripts are put there by the designer, whom Akrich and Latour compare with the "scriptor," a concept that the linguist Roland Barthes (1915–1980) formulated in his essay "The Death of the Author" in which he questions traditional notions of individual authorship (Akrich and Latour 1992: 259–260). He argues that texts are multidimensional spaces where different writings "blend and clash" (Barthes 1977[1968]: 146). Accordingly, the alleged originality of texts transforms into multiple references to other texts. The author is not a source of originality but a mere scriptor.

In terms of artefacts, their design is conditioned among others by the expectations of the user, the available materials, the processes of fabrication, mercantile international relations, the manufacturer's commission, the existence of similar artefacts, their function and tradition but also the forecasting of a future use that advances future conditions of use, whether that is prolonging the current conditions or deviating from the norm. This is what Akrich labels "script" or "scenario" (Akrich 1992: 208).

Thus, de-scribing artefacts is not the same as using them, since de-scribing involves an analysis that is absent when using the artefact. When using an artefact, the attention of the user is oriented towards solving an action, but not to how a specific artefact works and what it facilitates. Akrich and Latour acknowledge that de-scribing only happens in some situations, such as when dealing with a new artefact, when the artefact does not work as expected, when there is a deliberate experimental breaching or, as in our case, when the analyst reconstructs the use of a given artefact through archival research, observation or thought experiments, what Akrich and Latour have labelled "the historical situation" (Akrich and Latour 1992: 259–260). In this sense, once the analyst knows how a designer operates, it will be easier to revert the roles, since de-scribing is reverting the process of designing.

Implementation: How to read scripts

Yaneva (2009) de-scribes a staircase at her university that leads to the lecture theatres on the upper floors and analyses what is the "vision of the world," or script, injected in this design. It is a wide staircase with a low inclination angle and a wooden handrail. These characteristics are consciously inscribed in the staircase by the designer and prescribe a specific behaviour to the users. The width of this staircase allows the casual coming together of colleagues and students, having enough space to start small conversations or to formulate and answer questions. The low inclination makes the ascension easy, facilitating these short encounters. The wooden touch of the handrail facilitates the user to lean for a long period of time because of its warm, soft touch (2009: 274–275). This results in this staircase facilitating socialization between the users of the university. If the staircase was narrower, with a higher inclination or the handrail made of a cold material, the opportunities to socialize would be less spontaneous and more limited.

In her analysis, there is ethnomethodology, since it is based on Yaneva's firsthand experience and observation, and there is semiotic relationality, since the handrail and the steps of this staircase acquire meaning as they interact with each other and the users. A wooden handrail does not allow socialization per se but acquires this property when placed in a wide staircase in a context like a university where relations between users happen formally in the lecture theatres and can extend beyond those spaces informally. Moreover, Yaneva's analysis makes use of ANT jargon reformulating relationships of agency between humans and nonhumans.

What makes this analysis post-structuralist? A structuralist, Prownian analysis of this very staircase would be very different and look rather into the aesthetic characteristics of this staircase than into its functionality. It would look into how this object encapsulates the culture of the period, that is, how this artefact represents the spirit of the times and the society in which it was made. Looking at the staircase from this perspective, what becomes evident is that the staircase is extremely unadorned. The steps of this staircase are made of stone and the handrail has a structure of iron on which the wooden elements rest. The shape of the different elements is based chiefly on the properties of the different materials. There are no elements that denote status or luxury, which might point towards a society in which democratic values dominate. It would be very different if this staircase was made out of luxurious materials such as marble, if it was decorated and, even more so, if there were two independent staircases, one for the students and another for the tutors. These observations would lead to the formulation of a hypothesis pointing towards the correlation between democratic values and unadorned forms. The implementation of the research programme would reach out to external sources substantiating this correlation between democratic values and unadorned interiors especially regarding public buildings in general and universities in particular.

So, two close readings of the same artefact would serve different ends depending on their structuralist or post-structuralist framework. When implementing a method, it is not sufficient to follow the steps proposed but to participate from the theoretical framework in which they are formulated. A structuralist close reading would formulate questions related to cultural aspects such as "how does this artefact reflect ideological values of a specific society?" but not "how does this artefact facilitate socialization?" A post-structuralist ANT-based close reading would do the opposite.

There are examples in which a method has been implemented just following the steps but without participating in the theoretical framework. Chapter 1 mentions how Mida and Kim adapted Prown's analysis in their *The Dress Detective* (2015), obviating its structuralist character. Similarly, in the case of script analysis, there are examples in which ethnomethodology and semiotics might be present but not sufficiently balanced. One example is Marit Hubak's analysis of car ads for women (1996). There, Hubak implements script analysis separating two dimensions of the script according to Akrich, that is, the physical script and the socio-technical script. The physical script is embedded in the tangible characteristics of a specific design, put there by the designer. The socio-technical script is the connotations that a specific design acquires by its mediation through, for example, marketing, advertisement and media coverage (Akrich 1995). The former is rather explored through ethnomethodology and the second through semiotic relationality.

Hubak's research aims to explore "a symbolic side of private motoring ... namely car marketing and advertisement" (1996: 171). This interest in the symbolic already presents problems since it seems better placed in a structuralist tradition, even when Hubak makes it explicit that the method used is Akrich's script analysis (1996: 175). Indeed, this research makes use of ethnomethodology in the form of interviews with advertisers and car importers and there are semiotic readings of different gendered car ads. The ethnography is rather a confirmation of how ad agencies see cars not just as functional elements but also as symbolic. The semiotic analysis reads the ads as texts, as a Prownian analysis would do, but does not look for semiotic relationality, as Yaneva does or Law proposes.

Hubak's book chapter finishes by acknowledging that it analysed "the relationship between the car as a means of transport and its additional symbolic properties," that it has given examples of "how gender is presented in car advertisements" and that "advertisements also portray understandings of society" (1996: 196). Again, this emphasis on the symbolic is little connected to ANT. All these inconsistencies, related to both the research question and the method, result in an analysis that paradoxically explores the symbolic but uses a post-structuralist method, employs semiotics but in a structuralist sense and makes use of conventional human/nonhuman relations instead of ANT interactions reflected in its specific jargon.

If Hubak's is a methodologically impeccable semiotic analysis of car ads, but inadequate as a fully-fledged ANT analysis, the next case is a good ethnographic analysis of hospital beds, but only partially connected to ANT. Søsser Brodersen, Meiken Hansen and Hanne Lindegaard (2015) studied two models of robotic beds used for disability care through script analysis, to "investigate *how* the artefacts (beds) and the multiple users go through a mutual adaptation process in their daily practice, and how this adaptation varies in different cases " (emphasis in the original). Their research responds to the question "how does the scripting of beds affect the beds' use and the different users?" (2015: 16) and their conclusion states that one of the two models, the RotoFlex, is a better choice since it allowed the user to get in and out of bed independently (2015: 28). This study is indeed valuable to test these two models but does not achieve any conclusion beyond conventional ethnographic research.

The connection between the social and morality, present in ANT's writings, is absent in this article. For example, Latour and Akrich's script analysis of the key of a hotel room reflects how the heavy weight attached to the keys will force the user to comply with the rules and leave the key at the hotel desk (Akrich and Latour 1992: 259–260). Yaneva's analysis of a staircase expands on how the wooden railway facilitates small chats on the staircase (2009: 274). The semiotic relationality that explores the agency of some actors when interacting with others, has not been developed in this article about robotic beds that presents a competent but conventional ethnographic research.

A third example is Trine Brun Petersen's study of the one-piece snowsuit for children in the Nordic countries, which has been on the market since the 1960s (2021). Her account is a script analysis that exhaustively tells the story of this garment considering how different factors such as climate, new fibres and pedagogic regimes instead of only an innovative company or a single designer contributed to its popularity (2021:12). Researching a single product by inserting it into its context is something made possible not only by ANT but by other methods also, for example cultural history or John A. Walker's production–consumption model. In Petersen's article, all the contextual elements are well-explored but remain as a *context* that surrounds the trajectory of the *object*, that is the snowsuit. An ANT network, in which object and context dilute, precisely questions such hierarchy.

Challenges: Object-oriented ontology and the pluriverse

The understanding of objects as defining social rules, typical of ANT, seems more revolutionary for sociology than for design scholarship. Nevertheless, ANT and script analysis when properly implemented can open up new insights for design history and design culture studies since they invite the superseding of the object–subject divide.

First, de-scription can be used to analyse how the performativity of an artefact is co-defined by both the designer and the user. In that sense, Akrich defines how the script of an artefact must be seen as "decisions about what should be delegated to a machine and what should be left to the initiative of human actors" (1992: 216). The designer predicts possible uses and inscribes them in the design of an artefact. In general, users manipulate artefacts accordingly but that is unpredictable. The design of an artefact is a negotiation between the designer and the prospective user. The artefact's qualities are a consequence, not a cause, of collective action (Latour 1987: 258). According to Kjetil Fallan, this principle incites design history to be more attentive to consumption, appropriation, domestication and use. Design and use are therefore not inextricably linked to each other but shaped through negotiations which take place in networks (Fallan 2010: 70).

Second, de-scription can distinguish between the actual technological design of an artefact and its interface. Users manipulate computers and cars appropriately without knowing how they actually work. Artefacts have an internal technological design that does not present itself overtly to the user. They are designed not only to work well but also to be properly manipulated.

Designs are therefore black-boxed or, according to Latour, they are "science in action" (Latour 1987: 258). Artefacts generate meanings at different levels, either for a car engineer or a car driver (Fallan 2010: 70). Hence, when designing and utilizing artefacts, it is essential to account for a black-box element, as they are employed based on a combination of knowledge, conviction, and trust.

Third, design occurs within heterogeneous networks involving commissioners, manufacturers, providers, trend watchers, technology experts and designers, among others. They all might have different goals and be affected by different situations of economic, social or strategic nature. Regarding this, Latour speaks about the inside and outside of science and that both need to be studied simultaneously (Latour 1987: 153–156, 258). De-scribing an artefact involves following these conflicts of interest and considering design as a product beyond the triad of functionality, aesthetics and symbolism. Latour gives the example of the development of the diesel engine. Rudolf Diesel (1858–1913) was confident at the start that all fuels would work in his engine and that all possible users would be interested in his more efficient engine. However, most fuel producers rejected his engine and consumers lost interest (Latour 1987: 259). Any failure can be studied as a result of conflicting interests, emerging from power struggles between different networks instead of from moral questions or intellectual disputes (Fallan 2010: 71). Furthermore, this angle facilitates a design history that treats all sorts of non-conformist design and ideals analytically on a par with their confirmed and well-known counterparts, as products of negotiations, either successful or unsuccessful.

The framework that ANT proposes and that object-oriented ontology further elaborates has been useful in reconsidering the role of design within society. ANT has developed from the observation that humans construct their knowledge and reality through and with nonhumans. In addition, these interactions do not only take place within established societies but in the natural world. The anthropologist Arturo Escobar elaborates along these lines on ontological design in his book *Designs for the Pluriverse: Radical Interdependence, Autonomy, and the Making of Worlds* (2018[2016]). The ontological turn pays attention to a myriad of factors that deeply shape what is experienced as reality, but that social theory has barely tackled. Factors such as artefacts, nonhumans, matter, and materiality (soil, energy, …), emotions, spirituality, and many more. The ontological turn requires connecting nature and culture back together and moving away from oppressing dualisms (2018 [2016]: 139). Particularly in design, this calls for a move towards collaboration and co-design.

But why should design be considered ontological? Artefacts define ways of being. Designers design artefacts and these artefacts design the world. According to Escobar, due to the pressure of globalized capitalism, the world is slowly *deworlding*. Thus, to *reworld* involves the elimination or redesign of not just structures, institutions or technologies but the human ways of thinking and being. He refers to Tony Fry who calls for a redesigning of the human being because we are the ones causing unsustainability (2018[2016]: 118).

Escobar argues for a new paradigm within design, which is more user- and human-centred, far from its destructive connection with capitalism and liberal politics. To do this, designers should move away from modernist, sexist, dualist and racist ideologies and work towards a world where many worlds fit (2018[2016]: 47). Therefore, Escobar proposes a shift away from the universe towards the pluriverse: a world that goes beyond the dualisms existing in Western modernity, such as the divide between nature and culture, the divide between us and them – West and the Rest, the moderns and the nonmoderns, the civilized and the savages, which is also known as the colonial divide – and the divide between subject and object – mind/body dualism. These dualisms create a disconnection since they are always hierarchical and excluding (2018 [2016]: 93). As Escobar claims, it is not possible to live in a world where humans are separated from nature. To dissolve those dualisms, Escobar argues for a move towards nondualist rationality, in which ANT's lack of hierarchy between humans and nonhumans resonates.

Object-oriented ontology is directed towards designers, calling for a creative engagement with each other and the Earth. Nevertheless, design scholars can contribute to disclosing the nondualist nature of design. In this context, describing acquires an ethical dimension in itself. ANT's emphasis on morality relates to the cohesion of social groups, which are composed of humans and nonhumans but finally, as a concept, morality affects humans solely. In that sense, ANT acknowledges that nonhumans have agency in defining societies, but humans are those who either benefit or suffer from the interaction with nonhumans. In pluriversal thinking, both humans and nonhumans are both creators and either beneficiaries or victims. For that, Escobar draws from the work of postcolonial feminists such as Gloria Anzaldúa (1942–2004), who proposes to move from a dualist to a nondualist vision that acknowledges the kinship among humans and nonhumans (2018[2016]: 201). The ethical dimension of de-scribing is precisely its capacity to reveal this kinship and to change ways of thinking, showing that design is not only responsible for creating ways in which humans relate to each other but also how they relate to the planet.

As Akrich and Latour claim, ordinary interaction with artefacts does not necessarily prompt a nondualist consciousness; their dualist ontological character is revealed in specific situations, such as when the analyst reconstructs the use of a given artefact – "the historical situation." Therefore, nondualist de-scriptions of artefacts following ANT disclose nondualist visions of the world. De-scribing not only reveals the morality that the artefact imposes on society but is in itself an ethical practice. Regarding this, Escobar quotes Anzaldúa when stating that "When you relate to others, not as parts, problems, or useful commodities, but from a connectionist view, compassion triggers transformation" (2018[2016]: 201).

Escobar's account encapsulates the main aspects of ANT in general and of de-scription in particular. It claims for the suppression of a dominant dual thinking in terms of humans and nonhumans in favour of network thinking. Object-oriented ontology considers design as an active mediator in shaping the world rather than as passive intermediary. However, it goes further than ANT in promoting a nondual thinking that not only demonstrates how humans and nonhumans shape societies but demonstrates a responsibility of humans towards nonhumans.

3   The life cycle of objects
Tracking design

Design can be analysed chiefly in two ways: one is a synchronous approach, much like what has been discussed in the previous two chapters, and the other is a diachronic approach, which involves tracking its lifespan from the point of creation to its eventual use by consumers. Studying the life cycle of objects from their production to their consumption has been at the core of Marxism, arguing that this analysis brings transparency to opaque capitalist modes of production. Other authors see different possibilities. For anthropologists, among which Mary Douglas and Igor Kopytoff, tracing the life cycle of an object helps understand the culture in which it was embedded. Within design history, John A. Walker's production–consumption model, embedded in a social history perspective, came to reconsider the different stages involved in the life of design products. Its linear character has been challenged by other models that explore the interaction between the different stages in a nonlinear way.

Origins: The commodity as a category

Biographies about individuals are familiar to most people. As the literary critic and biographer Hermione Lee describes, they are about either living or deceased people, and usually are meant to tell someone's life story. However, Lee also states that biographies do not necessarily have to be about a person but can also be about an animal or a thing, for example (Lee 2009: Chapter 1). Different theoretical frameworks value the biography of objects for different reasons. In general, the object's biography is valued as it reveals cultural mechanisms that have to do with the circulation of that object. The biographical stages are often defined by how the object develops its exchange value.

The philosopher Karl Marx (1818–1883) analyses the material world focusing on the commodity as its fundamental unit. For him, the term "commodity" holds a distinct meaning that terms like "artefact," "thing" or "object" would not fully capture. Marx employs "commodity" to denote objects that possess a monetary value and are exchangeable. Beyond this, he envisions the commodity as embodying capitalist relationships. First, because

DOI: 10.4324/9781003147282-5

they are products of human labour within the capitalist framework, commodities represent exploitative practices. Second, commodities propagate a distorted consciousness among exploited social classes, diverting their attention towards consumption, and consequently overshadowing their exploited status within the capitalist system. Consequently, commodities lead to a dual alienation both from one's own labour activity and from the outcome of one's labour. The more a worker produces, the further they are estranged from the products of their labour (Marx 1975[1844]: 326).

Marx's interest however does not lie in the commodities' nature as material constituents of culture or in the interactions between individuals and objects as for Prown or for ANT authors. The closest that Marx approaches material culture is when acknowledging that gaining a thorough understanding of human existence requires comprehending the intrinsic nature of commodities. This comprehension entails an awareness of the alienation encapsulated in artefacts, or commodities for Marxists. Thus, in the act of shaping the objective world through commodities, humans truly demonstrate their essence as individuals. As a result, they can observe themselves within a world that they collectively shape (Marx 1975[1844]: 329).

Marx's elaboration of the commodity theory contends that the object of consumption in capitalism is not as transparent as it appears. Originally straightforward, tangible articles or goods – like iron, baskets or clothing – transform when they become a commodity and embody a singular social substance: human labour (Marx 1954[1867]: 76). At first glance, the commodity might seem "a very trivial thing, and easily understood." Its analysis shows however that it is, "in reality, a very queer thing, abounding in metaphysical subtleties and theological niceties" (Marx 1954[1867]: 76). For Marx, this opaqueness encapsulates the alienation intrinsic in consuming.

In formulating a theory of exploitation and alienation, Marx established the most influential framework for comprehending commodities, centred on the study of relations and methods of production. There have been some positions within Marxist thinking that expanded the initial Marxist ideas during the initial three decades of the twentieth century. The philosopher György Lukács (1885–1971) explores the inefficiency of Marx's account in illuminating the persistent spread of capitalism. He addresses why the marginalized classes did not revolt to emancipate themselves, something expected in Marx's analysis. Instead of focusing on the Marxian logic behind class struggle, Lukács directs his explanatory focus towards culture, which he sees as a potential obstruction to the collapse of capitalism. He arrives at the conclusion that culture, permeated by dominant ideology, hinders radical socioeconomic transformation (1971: 86).

Like Marx, Lukács' analysis confers on the commodity an opaque ideological role. Similarly, Lukács argues that penetrating the facade of the commodity leads to understanding capitalism itself. However, in contrast to Marx, Lukács primarily focuses on the processes of commodification as cultural, rather than economic, obstacles that hindered significant societal transformation. In other words, engaging in the consumption of goods and services without considering their origins distracts from the awareness of social inequalities. It could be proposed that for Lukács the act of shopping, symbolizing the allure of consumer culture on a wide scale, triumphed over revolutionary ideals (1971: 83).

The cultural critic Curtis Marez offers an illustrative example of a Marxist analysis of design (2009: 473–477). The Homies are popular collectable plastic figurines, standing at around five centimetres in height, that portray the predominantly Latinx residents of a fictional community (Figure 3.1). These figurines represent numerous historical and contemporary demographic shifts that occurred alongside the "dotcom boom" from 1995 to 2001. This "boom" consisted of a stock market bubble related to substantial increases in Internet usage and the swift escalation of the value of emerging online businesses (Castells 2003: 103). Originating in 1998, they draw inspiration from the illustrations of their creator, David Gonzales, who fashioned numerous characters after individuals from his place of origin, San José in California, a city that lies in close proximity to Silicon Valley.

Nearly 200 Homies characters exist, each assigned a name and a brief biographical description detailing their profession, personality and relationships with other characters. For example, Gordo the Chef is a cook with his own "Mexican cuisine television show. He adds chile and jalapenos to everything he makes (and a dash of tequila). He discusses exciting recipes on a daily basis" (Homies website "Gordo the Chef" 2023). While the majority of Homies depict Latinx individuals, there is a modest yet notable assortment of Asian characters, and even a more substantial representation of Black characters, such as B-Boy, who

> rolls around with the hip-hop record producer Payday from Payday Record Label. He has the gift of the gab and everyone likes him. He thinks he can talk anyone into anything. It is his job to try and sign some of the hip-hop talent coming out of the Barrio.
>
> (Homies website "B-Boy" 2023)

Marez's analysis of the Homies explicitly aligns with dialectical materialism, the foundational theory of Marxism. He elaborates on how the Homies symbolize labour relationships inherent in the history of the Internet age, since they both are a critique and participants of this industry (Marez 2009: 475). In contrast to a dominant emphasis on the immateriality of the Internet industry, the Homies prompt us to reassess the physical exploitation of marginalized migrant workers. On the other hand, because of their small size, the Homies replicate the miniaturization logics of cell phones and computers. Furthermore, the prepackaged figurines, encased in transparent plastic, mirror the blister packs that encase computer disks and microchips (Marez 2009: 474).

Regarding their production, the Homies display a "Made in China" imprint on their backs. Thereby, they adopt a strategy similar to numerous companies in the information technology sector that outsource their manufacture to zones along the Chinese coastline, aiming to tap into cost-effective labour (Marez 2009: 474). Marez explains that in doing so, Gonzales positions his creations on the fringes of the new economy, closely emulating some of its core strategies.

Figure 3.1 The Homies figurines, depicting Gordo the Chef, in the plastic ball, and B-Boy with open arms in the middle. Photo by Steve Campbell/Houston Chronicle via Getty Images

This involves marketing the Homies online and likely capitalizing on the efficiency of "just-in-time" production facilitated by the Internet (Marez 2009: 475). Thereby, the Homies simultaneously adopt the production methods linked to the information technology sector in Silicon Valley.

There are numerous angles to study these figurines. Marez's Marxist approach takes them as primary objects of capitalism, unveiling their essence as commodities by examining how they are intricately woven into systems of production and consumption. This analysis illustrates how objects fundamentally manifest the human labour that generated them. When interpreted as a commodity, ultimately any object epitomizes human exploitation and the fundamental erosion of human creativity and identity (Woodward 2007: 85). Reconstructing the life cycle of a particular commodity in a Marxist tradition contributes to recognizing the queerness of commodities, as per Marx's perspective, or their "phantom objectivity," as outlined by Lukács.

Development: Cultural approaches to material culture

In contrast to Marxism, cultural anthropology focuses on the cultural aspects of consumption objects, emphasizing their social, cultural and emotional dimensions. While the biographies of these objects are still influenced by their circulation and whether or not they acquire exchange value, cultural anthropology interprets this process in a broader cultural context, rather than being strictly confined by its economic nature. More specifically, the anthropologist Mary Douglas (1921–2007) along with the economist Baron Isherwood (b. 1945), redress the Marxist approach that castigates consumption and consumerist tendencies as "greed, stupidity and insensitivity to want" (1996 [1979]: vii). Douglas acknowledges that even goods originated in the system of capitalist production "carry social meanings" and, as resources for thinking, commodity objects make "visible and stable categories of culture" (2000 [1966]: 38). Though goods "come from" the economy, in order to understand their attractions and meanings they need to be conceptualized autonomously, separate from economic frameworks (Douglas 2000[1966]; Douglas and Isherwood 1996[1979]).

Douglas and Isherwood provide a systematic treatment of goods as cultural props. In the preface to their book *The World of Goods* (1996[1979]), they assert that: "goods are neutral, their uses are social; they can be used as fences or bridges." Their core argument is that goods are resources for thinking, demarcating and classifying. Consumption, for them, is about meaning-making. They state that consumption becomes the social system itself: the actual means for constituting the self, society and culture, with each episode or consumption event being merely one part of the process of building culture (Douglas and Isherwood 1996[1979]: 49)

A good example of how consumption constitutes culture is the essay on the cultural biography of things by the anthropologist Igor Kopytoff (1986). Kopytoff argues that commodities are not exclusive products of capitalism but are universal. Selling and buying, either monetarized or as barter, are not only specific acts of capitalist societies, therefore, neither are commodities (1986: 68). Moreover, he maintains that being a commodity is not an all-or-none state of being and he maps processes of commodification, singularization and recommodification. Things can enter and exit the category of commodity. A specific thing can be a commodity at the moment of purchase, then it gets singularized by acquiring a personal meaning as a personal possession. In some cases, it can become a commodity again if sold again after use. Kopytoff maintains that the only time when the commodity status of a thing is beyond question "is the moment of actual exchange" (1986: 83). The general point is that things are never culturally fixed, but always in the process of being and becoming.

This dynamic of commoditization and singularization is the basis of the cultural biography of things. Kopytoff argues that things, not just people, have social lives. When something has been commodified, and is thus a commodity, it can be exchanged for something that is deemed of similar value. However, things can be singularized, which is the exact opposite of when a thing is a commodity (1986: 68–70). For a thing to be singular means that it is pulled out of the sphere of commodities. Singular things cannot be traded because they either have an incalculable value or they are worth very little. Kopytoff says that sacralization can be achieved by singularity but that singularity does not guarantee sacralization. He states that being a non-commodity "does not by itself assure high regard, and many singular things (that is, non-exchangeable things) may be worth very little" (1986: 74). Giveaway leaflets for example are not sacralized but are not commodities either, since they are distributed for free.

Both culture and individuals can ensure that something becomes singularized (1986: 73–77). Kopytoff stresses the different interpretations and meanings that things can have in their "biography" as a result of an interaction between the individual and society. Drawing from the anthropologist Margaret Mead (1901–1978), he explores how culture decides which biographies are successful and which are not. Kopytoff translates Mead's way of looking at society through the "career" of things (1986: 66). He gives the example of a Renoir painting ending up in an incinerator (1986: 67). Considering this fact as "tragic" is significant of the value of art in Western society today. It is actually the reaction towards the fact and not the fact itself that is meaningful. The fact of incinerating a painting can be experienced differently by some as a success and by others as a failure in an iconoclast period, or as an act of censorship or as an unfortunate accident. Thus, valuations of "success" and "failure" reflect the cultural values of a given society, or of specific groups within that society.

Kopytoff argues that in complex societies, their publicly recognized commoditization operates side by side with innumerable schemes of valuation and singularization devised by individuals and groups. These schemes stand in unresolvable conflict with public commoditization as well as with one another (1986: 80). He gives the example of a statue of the film character Rocky

Balboa. A controversy erupted in Philadelphia when some groups proposed to place a statue of Rocky, the fictional boxing hero, at the entrance of the Philadelphia Museum of Art. This museum served as both a symbol of the local elite and an artistic hub, but also the place where Rocky used to train in this film series, ascending and descending the long stair leading to the museum entrance. The statue, originally from the *Rocky* movie set, held deep meaning for the working-class Italian-American community in South Philadelphia, signifying ethnic, class and regional pride. However, those connected to the museum saw it as mere junk, sparking a heated debate intertwining issues of identity, value and aesthetics. Art Museum officials and the municipal Art Commission opposed the idea, pointing to the commercial nature of this statue and questioning its artistic quality. In a compromise, the statue was located on the steps of the Philadelphia Museum of Art for a few months, then moved to the Philadelphia Sports Complex about four miles south of the city centre. Later, the statue found its home not far from the museum but not at its entrance (1986: 81–82). What is deemed worthy of display beside a museum is contingent and specific to particular societies at given moments. Crafting a biography of the commoditization and singularization of this statue unveiled the valuation of art within that particular cultural context.

Like Marxism, this cultural approach acknowledges objects in general to be central to the constitution of society and culture, and maintains that in order to understand the contours of culture even the most banal or trivial objects need attention (Woodward 2007: 107–109). For the rest, the cultural approach to objects is almost the complete opposite of Marxism. While the Marxist approach obliterates the possibility of finding meaning in objects other than the embodiment of exploitive capitalist relations, the approach of cultural anthropology presented by Douglas, Isherwood and Kopytoff admits a myriad of other possibilities.

Cultural studies incorporated the linguistic turn exploring the mechanisms behind representation (du Gay et al. 2013[1997]). The role of consumption in creating individual identity has been thoroughly integrated into the "circuit of culture" that Paul du Gay, Stuart Hall, Linda Janes, Anders Koed Madsen, Hugh Mackay and Keith Negus introduced in the book *Doing Cultural Studies: The Story of the Sony Walkman* (2013[1997]) and that focuses on the relation between representation and culture. As the authors themselves describe it, the book's main purpose is "to set up an approach to the study of 'culture,' using the Walkman as a case study" (2013[1997]: 11).

Drawing from Mary Douglas' ideas on consumption, Du Gay's "circuit of culture" uses the biography of an object as a means to learn how culture works (2013[1997]: 2). This circuit maps processes in which meaning is produced and circulated. The Sony Walkman is located within five elementary underlying junctions: representation, identity, production, consumption and regulation. Its biography reveals how it articulates these various elements and questions of design, production and meaning are mentioned at various points. The "circuit of culture" engages with the creative role of consumption, which resonates in the work of cultural approaches such as Kopytoff's but expands the twists in an object's biography beyond commoditization and singularization.

The "circuit of culture" takes the form of a five-point star enclosed within a circle, creating direct connections among all five constituent elements, each positioned at the points of the star. Du Gay warns that it does not matter where to start, because to be completed an analysis needs to go the whole way round. Each part is intended to reappear in the next (2013[1997]: 4). The result is a diagram that considers all the different stages as simultaneous, revealing the complexity of the relation between the stages but without following the diachronic logic of Kopytoff's models. For Du Gay, the trace that an object's life leaves in a culture is more important than the life of the object itself.

Implementation: Design in diagrams

Studying the life cycle of products has been rooted originally in Marxism and later incorporated into both anthropology and cultural studies. In the field of design scholarship, two examples elaborate their own vision of the intertwinement between production, distribution and consumption. The first is John A. Walker's production–consumption model, a method for design historians first introduced in 1989, strongly influenced by social history and later further adapted to the field of visual culture in 1997 (Walker 1989; Walker and Chaplin 1997). The second is Guy Julier's "domains of design culture" diagram, which claims to represent "the bigger picture of design culture" (2014[2000]: 16). It explores the intersections between the concepts of value, circulation and practice to be implemented in design culture studies (Julier 2006: 72–76).

As Walker explains, one of the first tasks of design history was to decide on the object of study: what is actually "design"? (1989: 22) The answer to this question is ambiguous, says Walker, since "design"

> can refer to a process (the act or practice of designing); or to the result of that process (a design, sketch, plan or model); or to the products manufactured with the aid of a design (designed goods); or to the look or overall pattern of a product ("I like the design of that dress").
>
> (1989: 23)

Walker stresses that, even though objects are important for the design historian, the object of study for design history is not just the object itself. He states that the only way to develop a complete understanding of design, is through mapping "the relationships between all various elements involved," proposing thereby a processual definition of "design" (Walker and Chaplin 1997: 69; Walker 1989: 58).

To help define "design," Walker creates a model that covers the production, distribution and consumption of design (1989: 67). The production stage is twofold, comprising both design and manufacture, and according to Walker is primarily stimulated by consumers through their needs and desires. First, the design process leads to either a final design or a prototype. Second, the manufacturing process transforms the design or prototype into a designed good. After being designed and manufactured, objects are marketed and advertised, brought to trade fairs, exhibitions, design institutions or design centres, and eventually packaged and transported to warehouses and shops. The stage of distribution puts the designed goods in the context of retailing, bringing products to the consumers. Finally, the consumer interacts with the previously produced and distributed products (Walker 1989: 70; Walker and Chaplin 1997: 67, 73, 74).

Walker specifically mentions that the model is based on a Western, capitalist society with industrial production in mind, in which the process of design is separated from the manufacturing of the object (Walker and Chaplin 1997: 68–69). This emphasis on capitalism, might give the wrong idea that Walker follows the Marxist tradition fully. If it was so, this diagram would be only useful to disclose the labour encapsulated in designed objects and to reveal the misleading nature of commodities, such as in Marez's analysis of the Homies. Indeed, Walker's processual vision of design can serve to generate a Marxist analysis but can also lead to many more ends. As the architectural historian Bruno Giberti observed: "Walker claims to be a materialist, but he talks like a social historian" (1991: 54). Walker's diagram shows that design is a process embedded in social relations, and it is the historian's job to unravel these connections. He is therefore interested in design within society. His social history perspective might originate in but supersedes strict Marxist perspectives.

The stage of consumption reverts through feedback loops in the other stages, defining a cyclical model. Walker notes that even though production and consumption are "distinct," they are interdependent since production is needed to have consumption and consumption is needed to have production (Walker and Chaplin 1997: 65). The most influential consumption-related aspect is what Walker calls "public for design (needs, tastes)" that comprises the demand for new products. It has an impact on all the other stages, informing marketing (distribution), research and development (manufacturing) as well as the educational training of designers and the client's brief (design). The other consumption aspects are less influential since they only revert to one stage. The conservation of design in museums and private collections informs only the resources that inspire the designer (design) and the recycling of materials reverts to the material resources (manufacturing) (Walker 1989: 70).

Walker's model is both unidirectional and cyclical. It is unidirectional because the three stages have an "irreversible temporal sequence," which follows the consecutive order of production, distribution and consumption (Walker and Chaplin 1997: 65). A horizontal middle axis accentuates the linearity of the diagram and the sequential progression of each stage. It is cyclical because of the feedback loops that originate in the consumption stage. Even when this model is cyclical, Walker notes that the word "cycle" is somewhat misleading because it implies exact repetition, which in fact never occurs. Multiple cycles take place simultaneously and successively. Every new cycle is slightly or even dramatically different because of a changing socio-economic environment, technological innovations and the introduction of new media and culture (Walker and Chaplin 1997: 74).

The consumption stage is pivotal for the transition from a linear to a cyclical model. Despite that, Walker's consumption is social rather than personal, based on demand, conservation and recycling instead of the construction of identities. The mutual influence of the different parts is more limited than in the "circuit of culture" in which each stage contributes to rethink the others. Furthermore, if Walker's model maps the physical actions involved in design, the "circuit of culture" is rather focused on symbolic processes.

Guy Julier proposes two diagrams to understand design culture, the first is nodal and the second systematic. He defines design culture as engaging with the interrelationships of designers, production and consumption with the design artefact – which can be an object, an image or a space. Design culture explores how each of these nodes affects the other (Julier 2006: 72). Julier's diagram positions artefacts at the focal point of analysis, akin to Walker, rather than placing culture at the centre, as Du Gay does. The artefact takes a central position and is inscribed within a triangle. Production, consumption and designers are situated at each vertex of this triangle. The diagram forms connections between these four elements. As a result, he combines the social historical bias of design history, present in Walker's production–consumption model, with the interest in creative practices of consumption derived from cultural studies, present in Du Gay's "circuit of culture" (2006: 73).

Under the influence of design research and design studies scholars, Julier replaced this nodal scheme with a systematic scheme, presenting a revised conceptual framework for design culture that covers the dynamics and effects of material and immaterial relationships that are articulated by and through the artefacts (2006: 74). His diagram changes from a triangle to three intersecting circles, each representing the domains of value, circulation and practice. "Value" involves the origination of new products and product forms, but also their value augmentation. "Circulation" refers to straightforward elements underpinning and shaping the productive processes of design culture – including available technologies, environmental and human factors – as well as non-material elements such as existing knowledge networks, legislation, political pressures, economic fluctuations and fiscal policies. "Practice" involves routinized behaviour that is both individually enacted but also socially observable. Consumption, therefore, is a part of practice (2006: 74). The outcome is a diagram grounded in production (value), distribution (circulation) and consumption (practice), similar to Walker. Each of these aspects is conceptualized as processes rather than stages, aligning with Du Gay's perspective.

The intersection of the three circles demonstrates the multiple dependence between the components, without prioritizing any of them. Julier takes branding as a paradigmatic indicative of design culture's multidimensional qualities, both material and symbolic, arguing that in branding, the commodity and the sign appear as one (2006: 67). For him, branding reflects the growing interdisciplinarity of design, since it integrates product, graphic and interior design in order to create coherent and complete design solutions. Branding further explains the design profession's increased integration with marketing, management and public relations (2006: 75).

If Walker's diagram concentrates on a life-cycle model with subsequent steps following each other, Julier eliminates its diachronic character and focuses on the interaction among the elements rather than on the periodization of the different stages. Design culture, for Julier is not only about the different agents involved, but about the practices that each of them plays and how they are influenced by each other. Julier's diagram replaces Walker's linear directionality and progression with the simultaneous occurrence of various processes, giving priority to interactions rather than their sequential nature. Julier's diagram represents a life cycle that unfolds simultaneously across multiple dimensions, akin to how an individual's life can hold different meanings for various people. For instance, one person may be a friend to someone, a mother to another and a colleague to yet another. The overlay of these diverse dimensions shapes a multi-voiced biographical account of that specific individual.

Challenges: The prosumer and the object's afterlife

There are consumption practices that not only inform but interfere with the other stages of the object's biography. They are not based on cyclical or systemic diagrams but include hybrid, mutant entities that simultaneously activate different stages. Practices like "prosumption" – or the hybridization of producers and consumers –, do-it-yourself (DIY) practices, craft consumerism and mass customization give rise to these mutant entities, half consumer, half something else, who shape the afterlife of objects. They reconduct the biography of objects enabling them to resuscitate, to transfigure and to be reborn.

These hybrid consumers add complexity to the distinction between production, distribution and consumption, present in the abovementioned models. "Prosumption" can be found in customization business services as well as in DIY practices (Knott 2013: 46). Prosumption allows for a de-skilling of design which enables the non-specialist to gain agency through direct involvement and allows the average consumer to configure the material world. Thus, consumers shape and influence the products they own, which allows them to "appropriate, re-accent, re-articulate or trans-code" and thereby design mass-produced objects to their own requirements (Knott 2013: 47).

The furniture company Ikea is an example of a system where consumption is deeply integrated with production. Since its beginning in 1943, Ikea has primarily branded its products as cost-efficient, well-designed and functional. Because Ikea aims to provide "a range of home furnishing products that are affordable," it has developed several business strategies to make its products as cost friendly as possible (Ikea Official Website "The Ikea Concept" 2023). Ikea usually designs, manufactures, distributes and sells its products as kits; separate components which, when correctly assembled, form a finished item (Figure 3.2). For customers to be able to assemble the furniture pieces themselves, Ikea de-skills the assembling process to such an extent that non-specialists can assemble the products themselves. Helping manuals provide the necessary instructions. Depending on the purchased product, Ikea also includes specific sets of assembly tools, for example the "hexagon key L-shape." Along with the manual and tools, the kits are "equipped with all the required screws, fittings, brackets, and pre-measured pieces of timber with holes in the right place" so that assembling the products is as straightforward and fast as possible (Knott 2013: 59).

The Ikea DIY model is only one of the many possibilities in which the distinction between designers, producers and consumers blurs. Paul Atkinson proposes four different ways in which DIY can be characterized: "essential DIY," "pro-active DIY," "reactive DIY," and "lifestyle DIY." For the current analysis, "essential" and "pro-active" DIY are key. "Essential DIY" fits in with Ikea DIY seamlessly, consisting of "home maintenance activities carried out as an economic necessity or because of the unavailability of professional labour, and which often involve the following of instructional advice from manuals" (Atkinson 2006: 3). Just as this definition suggests, Ikea focusses on the economic benefits of DIY, but also emphasizes the personal customization that it offers. According to the Ikea website, a home is a place "where everything looks the way you want it to, works the way you need it to ... without costing a fortune" (Ikea Official Website "Ikea Ideas" 2023).

Along with the "prosumption" activities introduced by Ikea, top-down, bottom-up initiatives bring the participation of consumers even further. "Ikea hacking" has been developed through the website "Ikeahack.net," which has been run by Jules Yap from Malaysia since 2006. The Ikea hack website provides suggestions and ideas for those who want to "hack, personalize, [and] repurpose Ikea products into the very thing [they] want" (Ikea Hacker Website 2023). Consumers are invited to become "designers" as they change and combine Ikea objects into completely new products (Knott 2013: 59).

Ikea hacking goes beyond prosuming, as the consumer not only assembles furniture, but is both the maker and designer of a product, a notion which has recently been labelled as the "craft consumer"; a consumer who "brings skill, knowledge, judgement, passion and a motivation for self-expression" (Campbell 2005: 23). This activity fits in with Atkinson's definition of "pro-active DIY," consisting of "activities which contain significant elements of self-directed, creative design input, and which might involve the skilled manipulation of raw materials or original combination of existing components," a type of DIY which is often motivated by personal pleasure and/or financial gain (Atkinson 2006: 3). "Essential DIY" differs from "pro-active DIY" in that the former is usually performed through the use of direction manuals and

Figure 3.2 Swedish showroom decorator Marit Schjetne assembles a *Lack* table at Ikea's outlet in North York (Canada). Photo by Keith Beaty/Toronto Star via Getty Images

originated by necessity while the latter is rather a preferred choice resulting in a creative outcome (Atkinson 2006: 3; Rosner and Bean 2009: 1).

Hacking transforms the original plans of the designer and producer, changing the planned course of an object's life. Ikea hacking means a variety of things. In some cases, Ikea hackers propose to "fix" or "remake" broken Ikea products so that they can be used again. A hack post on the Ikea *Nisse* chair proposes a way to repair this chair by using a washing line to make a corded makeshift seat and backrest. The result prolongs the life of this chair (Ikea Hacker Website 2023). Along with offering fixes for broken Ikea products, Ikea hacking involves purchasing Ikea products with a predetermined intent to redesign, combine or change the objects into new repurposed products. A practice that Ikea products facilitate, since many share similar measurements, materials and assemblage tools. The "Platonic Sun" hack shows a redesign of a product beyond Ikea's prescription. It consists of numerous Ikea *Lampan* lamps which are assembled together to form one large new customer-designed lamp. The craft consumer or pro-active DIY in general and Ikea hacking in particular, alter the lifespan of objects, granting them a rebirth – in the case of the fix and remake tutorials – or undergoing a transfiguration – in the case of the integral redesign.

Digital technology, such as social media and Web 2.0, opens up other possibilities, allowing customers to design their own individual T-shirts, watches, kitchens, PCs or sneakers online, which the manufacturer can then produce to order (Franke et al. 2010: 126). The consumer not only participates in assembling or transforming a product but also in its design. The consumer not only resuscitates or transfigures, but in this case creates the object. Known as "mass customization," the company provides the consumer with easy-to-use design tools to subsequently tailor the product to these specific requirements (Franke et al. 2010: 126).

Again, Ikea offers examples of mass customization. Though the Ikea store and brand are first and foremost intended to be a physical, bricks-and-mortar retail store, Ikea has developed the online "Ikea Planner Tools," which allow customers to become their "own interior designer" (Ikea Official Website "Planners-Ikea" 2023). The "Ikea Planner Tools" consist of a virtual space where customers can "drag and drop" their choice of virtual furniture and plan, decorate and fit it to specific measurements of the customer's home. Many of Ikea's kitchen and wardrobe products are available to be virtually placed, including flooring and walls, which allows the consumer to create a 3D prototype of their future home interior. This design tool, according to Ikea, makes a customer "just like an architect" (Ikea Official Website "Planners-Ikea" 2023).

Walker's model indicates that there is a wide gap between the "cultural producer" and the consumer as they each have different needs and desires; the two could therefore, not share the same end vision for the product (Walker and Chaplin 1997: 67). However, mass customization allows consumers to decide the measurements, colours and materials, which brings the needs and desires of the consumer closer to those of the producer. The resulting Janus-like characters originate the overlap of functions, bringing different visions closer.

In conclusion, the phases of production, distribution and consumption adequately map the standard biography of objects. Nevertheless, these stages do not correspond to defined profiles and these hybrid practices between consumption, design and production affect these conceptual maps. There is a consumer, a designer and a producer, but they are not necessarily different individuals with different backgrounds and different goals. They can be one and the same person and their agencies can combine, introducing a different layer of complexity to the object's biography. One that not only deals with its synchronic and diachronic issues but with the lack of differentiation between the different individuals shaping an object's life.

4   The comparative method

Differences and similarities

Comparison enhances our ability to describe by highlighting similarities and differences among cases. Its primary purposes include tracing genealogies to identify shared origins, uncovering underlying structures and conducting transnational analyses. Throughout, the emphasis is on pattern recognition. Design scholarship similarly employs comparative approaches. The digital humanities facilitate extensive comparisons, contingent on the digitalization of archives. However, the coding of these archives is not neutral; it shapes available metadata and comparison possibilities. Coding reflects contemporary ideologies and may perpetuate past worldviews. Addressing potentially offensive historical perspectives becomes a challenge in this context.

Origin: Tracking genealogies

Is it possible to compare a T-shirt with, say, a poster? The conventional wisdom in terms of medium specificity is a resounding "no." A T-shirt belongs to the medium fashion, which develops its own particular system. Fashion designers get specific training in fashion schools, where they acquire knowledge about textiles, their materiality and their manipulation. Patternmaking adapts two-dimensional fabric to the three-dimensional shape of human bodies. Conversely, a poster belongs to the medium graphic design for which knowledge of printing and digital techniques is required. The goal of the resulting design is visual and revolves around the communication of a specific message. For the fashion item, the connection with the body is paramount. The poster would favour its communicative aspects.

If we probe deeper, T-shirts and posters might share common dilemmas. Take, for example, the T-shirt "Do You See Us Now?" that the designer duo Botter, composed of Rushemy Botter and Lisi Herrebrugh, included in their Autumn Winter 2019 collection. The garment is an oversized white T-shirt. The slogan "Do You See Us Now?" is printed in a large-size font, which divides the sentence into four lines. The black serif typeface against a white background translates the message directly to the viewer. The text acquires anti-racist connotations when shown on a Black model and most evidently so, when showcased in a period of anti-racial claims prompted since 2013 by the organization Black Lives Matter (Figure 4.1).

DOI: 10.4324/9781003147282-6

Figure 4.1 Botter (Rushemy Botter and Lisi Herrebrugh) present their collection during the fashion show of the 34th edition of the International Festival of Fashion in 2019 in Hyères, France. Photo by Arnold Jerocki/Getty Images

Regarding the poster, take, for example, the *Black Lives Matter/Defund the Police* poster that the designer Ernesto Yerena Montejano created in collaboration with photographer Nance Musinguzi. This poster depicts the face of a Black woman with a braided hairstyle and a blue face mask, looking directly at the viewer. The two slogans of the poster are divided between the upper and the lower part, both in a non-serif font in yellow against a black background. This poster has been available to download for free on Yerena's website since 15 June 2020 (Yerena Official Website 2014) and was widely distributed and seen in the protest of 23 June 2020 that took place in the city of Los Angeles (USA) calling on the board of education to defund school police (Figure 4.2). This protest against police brutality directly criticized the brutal murder of George Floyd, a 46-year-old African-American man, during an arrest in Minneapolis on 25 May 2020.

The medium-specific differences between the T-shirt and the poster might prevent a comparison that presents a few analogies. However, these two artefacts share commonalities. They both refer to anti-racist actions connected to Black Lives Matter, one before Floyd's assassination and the other afterwards. The interest in communication typical of graphic design is present in both artefacts, which display texts prominently. Both the T-shirt and the

Figure 4.2 Ciera Foster, actress and co-founder of Blac 4 Black Lives, poses with the *Black Lives Matter/Defund the Police* poster that Ernesto Yerena Montejano created in collaboration with photographer Nance Musinguzi and Akpos (model). The poster has been available to download for free on Yerena's website since 15th June 2020. Photo by VALERIE MACON/AFP via Getty Images

poster might adapt to the body, an aspect typical of fashion. This is obvious in the case of the T-shirt, but also the poster was "worn" by protesters who held them in front of their bodies during the protests. Comparing can stress differences but also analogies that might pass unnoticed otherwise.

The comparative method analyses two or more systems of relation for common patterns and distinctions. It usually identifies these patterns as products of either a shared genealogy or shared responses to specific historical conditions. For one thing, any descriptive effort, any typology or classification involves comparison. Indeed, even the observation of singular phenomena gains when placed in a comparative perspective (Rihoux and Ragin 2009: xvii).

The humanities use comparison all the time. This is true in explicitly comparative disciplines like historical linguistics or comparative literature. Modern comparativism has been used widely in history but consolidated in the transition from the eighteenth to the nineteenth century as the preeminent method for finding commonalities across an extraordinary range of aesthetic, social and scientific fields of research, from philology to anatomy, from geology to sociology. The literary scholar Devin Griffiths coined this trend as "Romantic comparativism," which he understands as a single movement with differentiated issues, rather than an independent invention of various fields of inquiry (Griffiths 2017: 473).

Philology championed this comparative impulse at the end of the eighteenth century when the philologist Sir William Jones (1746–1794) extended etymological traditions of comparing several languages to understand their evolution and to look for a common source. A judge working for the British East India Company in Bengal (India), Jones compared the etymological and grammatical features of Sanskrit, Latin, Greek and what he termed "Gothick" and "Celtick" (Errington 2008: 49). He recognized resemblances between these languages and praised the structure of Sanskrit deeming it "more perfect than the Greek, more copious than the Latin, and more exquisitely refined than either." He argued that all three languages had a common source that might have disappeared, which is currently known as Proto-Indo-European (Errington 2008: 56; Bod 2013: 190).

These resemblances originated an interest in comparative grammar. The philologist Franz Bopp (1791–1867) developed a comparative metric for grammatical study based on the studies that the philologist Panini compiled in his *Eight Books*, especially his search for the smallest meaning carriers of Sanskrit's word structure (Bod 2013: 284–285). A Brahman from Vedic India, Gandhara, currently Afghanistan, Panini lived between the seventh and the fourth century BCE. His work characterizes a language as a system containing a finite number of rules that can be used to describe a potentially infinite number of linguistic utterances (Bod 2022: 65). Similarly, Bopp's investigation isolates part-for-whole relations between roots and grammatical elements as the core of the true organism of a language (Errington 2008: 78; Griffiths 2017: 479).

For the linguist Henry M. Hoenigswald (1915–2003), Bopp's call for a "comparative dissection of languages" marked the birth of the true comparative method, that is, a method directed not to comparison at large, such as typological comparison, but to establishing **common origins**, the initial of the three objectives for employing the comparative method within the humanities. Thereby, Bopp inaugurated a process whereby original features can be separated from recent ones and that seeks to reconstruct rather than to classify (Hoenigswald 1993[1963]: 55; Griffiths 2017: 478–479). Similarly, the art historian Ittai Weinryb argues that the specific goal of comparativism is to find the Ur-moment, that moment in which objects, or cultures, were connected. He argues that the fundamental aspiration of every comparativist is to find the moment in which comparativism is no longer possible, the moment of sheer basic connectivity between two or more objects (Weinryb 2017: 90).

Comparative philology influenced other sciences. The naturalist Charles Darwin (1809–1882) developed his interest in evolutionary genealogy through comparative studies of barnacle physiology. He acknowledged that his investigation was very similar to the study of comparative grammar (Griffiths 2017: 477). The main difference with comparative grammar is that Darwin looked for the explanation of those changes. Darwin published his theory of evolution in his 1859 book *On the Origin of Species* that provoked a change in theories of evolution from competing explanations to natural selection. In making the case for common descent, he included evidence of homologies between humans and other mammals. Darwin adopted a formal study to discern the relation between widely different forms of life. Thereby, he originated an ecological reading of form and its bearing for the study of humanity and social structures. Darwin read such forms not as carefully engineered correspondences between organism and the world but as a network of adaptation. He studied ecologies as the complex networks of growth and cooperation, competition and death, through which living and nonliving agents interact (Griffiths 2021: 71–73).

Literature, another branch of the humanities, incorporated the comparative method (Griffiths 2017: 489–490). The literary critic Ferdinand Brunetière (1849–1906) implemented Darwin's theory of evolution directly to the study of literature, with genres treated as species evolving according to distinct laws and principles (Melas 2007: 20). A similar interest in transnational classifications of literature characterized the work of Mary Ann Evans (1819–1880), known by her pen name George Eliot, when she reorganized the *Westminster Review* in the 1850s. The contemporary literature section used subject-based divisions in place of national categories, emphasizing her intent to build a "comparative history of contemporary literature" outside the coordinates of national identity (Griffiths 2016: 21)

The first generation of academic programs and journals of comparative literature appeared in the third quarter of the nineteenth century, alive to the tensions between "major" and "minor" kinds of literature and taking full advantage of the possibilities opened up by the transnationalism of their day (Damrosch et al. 2009: xi). The literature scholar Hugó Meltzl (1846–1908) was the editor of *Acta Comparationis*, the first journal of comparative literature, which was to have a global scope confirmed by its ten official languages. The editorial board included scholars from around the globe, with contributing editors from India, Australia, the United States and Iceland, among many other countries. This journal was published for 11 years and disseminated translations and discussions of literature in dozens of languages. In his introductory essay, Meltzl emphasizes "the principle of polyglotism," making a prescient comparison of less-spoken languages to endangered species and emphasizing that comparative literature should give equal attention to the world's folk poetry as well as to major literary masterpieces (Damrosch et al. 2009: 41–42).

A similar interest in scientific principles like Brunetière's lay behind the work of the literature scholar Hutcheson Macaulay Posnett (1855–1927). His book *Comparative Literature* of 1886 interprets the development of literature according to evolutionist theories. Though he admits of regressions, stasis and various indirections, the governing idea of his analysis is the "principle of growth." He treats literature primarily as a social phenomenon influenced by environmental factors, amenable to classification and governed by large processes and general laws rather than as the product of individual genius. Like Bopp, Posnett perceives the role of the scientific comparatist not merely as comparing one object to another, but rather as "tracing the development" of the progress of comparison (Melas 2007: 24).

In line with this perspective on comparativism, a thorough examination of Botter's T-shirt and Yerena's and Musinguzi's poster should extend beyond recognizing their analogies and differences. Instead, it should attribute meaning to these relationships and seek a shared origin. These two designs demonstrate the existence of political design in which the textual gets prominence over the visual. Tracing its origins will involve the comparison to similar examples, such as the graphics of the Black Panther Party in the 1970s or the slogan T-shirts that Katharine Hamnett has designed since 1983 and that included a *Be Anti-Racist* addition in the early 2020s. Reproducing a genealogy of similar examples contributes to reconstructing a trajectory that reveals possible influences among the examples.

Development: Underlying structures and transnationalism

Along with the reconstruction of genealogies, the second goal of the comparative method has been to recognize **underlying structures** (Hoenigswald 1993[1963]: 63). Similarly to Paninian linguistics, these authors demonstrated that an infinite number of phenomena can be covered with a finite number of resources. In showing simple, lawlike behaviour, comparative philology essentially launched the structural project, demonstrating the ability of comparative analysis to elucidate the deep structure of social forms (Bod 2013: 328; Griffiths 2017: 481). Thereby, these authors aimed to crack the code of how communication and culture works.

The philologist Ferdinand de Saussure (1857–1913) outlined a research programme that distanced itself entirely from evolutionary nineteenth-century linguistics. Saussure positions the object of analysis of linguistics not within territories or historical contexts but rather within the realm of human minds, considering them as sociopsychological, that is, cognitive, entities. Accordingly, languages are framed as self-contained systems which are not bound up with any evolutionary force, as Posnett claimed. Saussure's analysis was no longer historical or diachronic, in search of origins, but synchronic, in search of underlying structure (Errington 2008: 155; Griffiths 2017: 481).

Saussure emphasizes the intimate relation between his analysis and comparative linguistics in his *Course in General Linguistics* (1916), characterizing his own method as an outgrowth of comparative study. His linguistics do not search for laws but for relations of differences between linguistic signs of a specific language. What primarily concerned Saussure was the intrinsic structure of language. Forms and meanings were not to be identified with anything external to language. For example, if one wants to describe the form of the English word "bat," then it does not make sense to do this in terms of the sequence of sounds /bat/ and the meaning of "bat" cannot be identified with a certain species because different languages use different words for biological species. Instead, the relation of /bat/ with contrasting words in English should be investigated, such as /kat/, /fat/ and /hat/ (Bod 2013: 287–288).

Vladimir Propp (1895–1970), a literary theorist, applied structuralism to analyse Russian folk tales, aiming to identify a set of rules governing an entire literary genre. In his work *Morphology of the Folk Tale* (1928), he dissected numerous folk tales into smaller parts, ultimately identifying the smallest narrative units, which he termed narratemes. These narratemes, such as "the villain collects information about the victim," represent stable story elements with consistent functions. Propp also identified seven character types, including the hero, villain, helper, donor, dispatcher, false hero and royal personage, which, when combined and recombined, can generate all Russian folk tales. The arrangement of narratemes in a story can be likened to the syntax or grammar of storytelling, akin to the word order in a sentence (Bod 2013: 328–329).

Structuralism inspired the art historian Heinrich Wölfflin (1865–1945), whose ideas were influenced by his father, a renowned linguist and language history scholar (Preziosi 2009[1998]: 117). Wölfflin developed an analytical method based on which the formal features of the work of art were examined, as well as their relationship with the whole and the use of light and colour. He introduced a series of stylistic concepts that he grouped in five pairs of opposites in order to characterize the style transition from Renaissance to Baroque. As in structuralist linguistics, the use of these opposites corresponds to the relations of differences principle (Bod 2013: 315–316).

In terms of subject, Saussure's, Propp's and Wölfflin's work appears to be part of the same tradition. Their primary emphasis is on an analysis of the form and not the meaning. After Propp had been translated into French and English in the 1950s, there was a quest to augment literary analysis with meaning within the structuralist framework. The best-known exponent was the anthropologist Claude Lévi-Strauss (1908–2009), who analysed myths on the basis of opposites such as life versus death, non-life versus non-death and high versus low, not high versus not low. However, Lévi-Strauss's method did not yet provide a system of rules with which these assignments of meaning could be derived (Bod 2013: 330). In the studies of Lévi-Strauss we can identify one important line of influence for Saussure's structuralism, which he applied in anthropological studies of myth, kinship and consciousness.

Lévi-Strauss' ideas can be regarded as anti-phenomenological. He rejected the promise of a subjective basis for interpretation and meaning. In his key works, Lévi-Strauss argued a line of structuralist determinism, meaning that the expressions of the human mind are determined by linguistic laws and semiological systems which are not knowable to everyday actors or non-specialists (Woodward 2007: 64).

A third goal of the comparative method along with the search for origins and structures is a **transnational** perspective that would supersede the nation-state as a unit of study. Meltzl's polyglotism understood the study of comparative philology as foundational to his approach and valued the representation of literature in different languages, thereby maintaining the relevance of the nation-state. In the aftermath of the Second World War, scholars like Erich Auerbach (1892–1957) and Réne Wellek (1903–1995) emphasized the transnational and cosmopolitan aims of comparative literature. Auerbach considered the focus on multiple languages important insofar as it grounded comparative literature's transnational turn in the studied interconnection of literatures. For him, comparative literature should illustrate the specific cosmopolitan dimensions of past and present literatures.

Wellek turned back to Johann Wolfgang von Goethe (1749–1832) for early articulations of a *Weltliteratur* that would be transnational in character. In articulating a version of comparative literature in which comparative philology was largely absent, Wellek also launched a critique against social–scientific approaches to language and literature. Wellek's work emphasized the importance of cosmopolitan humanism over cultural nationalism (Damrosch et al. 2009: 162). His critique takes particular force from the powerful evidence of science's violent applications during the Second World War, from atomic weapons to Nazi racial science with its explicit adoption of Proto-Indo-European as evidence for the long historical superiority of the "Aryan" race (Griffiths 2017: 492–494).

Wellek's critique of nineteenth-century comparative philology gained extraordinary force in the analysis of the literary critic Edward Said (1935–2003), who, along with historians of subaltern studies, identified philology with "orientalism" and the bureaucratic and academic mechanisms by which Western nations pursued colonial administration. Said admitted the powerful attraction of latter-day comparative literature and its ambitious search for a "vast synthesis of the world's literary production transcending borders and languages but not in any way effacing their individuality and historical concreteness" (Said quoted in Griffiths 2017: 493). Similarly, the literature scholar Natalie Melas points out that Posnett's comparativism is imperial in various respects, but not as one might expect in the most obvious or instrumental sense as a pretext or justification for empire. For Posnett, comparison's expansion reaches its highest point in Western empires because of their variety of cultural contact. Comparison itself turns out to be a prominent measure of social progress: the more a society advances – that is, expands and specializes – the more it brings under the purview of comparison (Melas 2007: 20–21). According to Melas, Posnett's comparatism is imperial first of all conceptually in that it is intrinsically expansionist, but most important it is imperial because by definition it can only be available in its most evolved scientific or reflective form to a privileged denizen of empire. The authority to encompass comparatively all the literature in the world is thus reserved implicitly and without argument to the Western scholar because he represents comparison's highest development (Melas 2007: 23).

To go beyond Orientalism and Eurocentrism, the literature scholar Shu-Mei Shih acknowledges that comparative literature has been largely based on the comparison of European literatures among themselves and that Goethe's concept of *Weltliteratur* has been relatively recently reactivated despite its eighteenth-century origin (2015: 431). She proposes to incorporate relational comparison for the study of literature, a methodology stemming from the "connected histories" that the historian Sanjay Subrahmanyam introduced in 1997. Relational comparisons explore microhistorical evidences that are evident to understanding larger patterns. Shih considers the excavation of these relationalities as the ethical practice of comparison, where both marginalized and canonical texts are brought into relation, breaking up the centre-periphery model of world systems theory, since the texts form a network of relations wherever the texts are written, read and circulated (2015: 436).

Implementation: Ornament, archetypes and connected histories

Within design history, a number of major theorists of ornament from the 1850s onwards, sought to reconstruct processes of form genesis, based on the methods of comparative grammar (Labrusse 2010: 97). The parallel between the sciences of language and ornament was also based on their convergence in an interest for the Orient. Similar to the exploration of a Proto-Indo-European language, the items from the Indian decorative industry, primarily from Northern Muslim India following the Mughal tradition, showcased at the London World's Fair in 1851 significantly influenced the adoption of reformist theories of ornament. From this point on, the Islamic culture became a structuring reference for most authors of grammars of ornament and similar works, led by Owen Jones with Nasrid art in Granada in his *Grammar of Ornament* (1856) and Jules Bourgoin with Mamluk art in Cairo in his *Grammaire élémentaire de l'ornement* [Elementary Grammar of Ornament] (1880). The main difference was that the Orient of ornamental theories was predominantly Muslim, while the Orient of languages was essentially Hindu Sanskrit (Sloboda 2008: 225; Labrusse 2010: 97).

For Jones, the origins allow to construct a formal theory of ornament and to validate the universality of the general principles of form and colour by showing that they already appear in non-Western cultures. In its entirety, both in visual representations and written content, the process of theorization aligns closely with formalism. Bourgoin's work involves a reduction to principles, transitioning from the narrative arrangement of adorned images in a specific context to a lexicon of motif-words. This progression includes the juxtaposition of decontextualized ornamental types and culminates in a network of forms conceived through analogy with radicals and inflexions, organized in declensions and conjugations (Labrusse 2010: 102).

On the other hand, Gottfried Semper's *Style in the Technical and Tectonic arts, or, Practical Aesthetics* (1860–63) proposes a theory in which he intends to demonstrate that forms are the product of a combination of many factors. In this case, he looks for the original Ur-types that predate the artistic and decorative expressions of the oldest cultures, in whom they already appear in degraded form. For Semper, art is primarily a technique applied to a material for the fulfilment of a function. He examines therefore the case of a Maori village and a Carib ceremonial hut, developing an evolutionary perspective through a comparative history of styles. According to him, each style is indicative of evolution through adaptation. Focused on examining artistic processes rather than the outcomes, he aims to comprehend the underlying Ur-forms and principles driving the evolution of artistic forms. In this regard, he specifically explores the symbolic function of objects and architectural elements, an area that Jones scarcely addresses. These distinctions significantly shape how each places importance on origins within their argumentative framework (Varela Braga 2020: 38).

The vocabulary of ornamentation seemed, through its link with geometry, capable of escaping history and inviting to apply the universal language of forms to the present. Jones, Bourgoin and Semper wish to establish the primordial nature of aesthetic principles, so that they can serve as material for the development of a new expressive form, that is, for the creation of a contemporary style (Labrusse 2010: 104–105; Varela Braga 2020: 38).

The search for archetypal forms was a common preoccupation of designers in the early twentieth century. According to the architectural historian Adrian Forty, this use of "type" was a counterreaction to the individualized, fashionable taste of mass consumption that produced a flood of new forms and products. Within the Deutsche Werkbund, Hermann Muthesius (1861–1927) and Walter Gropius (1883–1969) argued that after a period of technological development and experiments with form, a standard type-form would emerge that would no longer have to be altered, that even should not be altered anymore. Le Corbusier (1887–1965) aimed for a similar result by "ordering existence," getting rid of all these different tastes and forms by referring to his furniture designs as *objects-types* (Forty 2013[2000]: 307).

The history of the decorative arts has been based on formal analysis, the reconstruction of lines of stylistic influence and the detailed study and classification of processes of making. All of them are attentive to underlying structures and have been grouped under the name of "connoisseurship" (Adamson 2013: 33). *The Dictionary of Decorative Arts*, edited by John Fleming and Hugh Honour in 1984, exemplifies this approach. Objects are described based on their formal qualities, presenting a juxtaposition of modern furniture by designers like Alvar Aalto (1898–1976), Charles Eames (1907–1978) and Marcel Breuer (1902–1981) alongside historical pieces such as Louis XIV sideboards and Gothic Revival chairs by Augustus W.N. Pugin (1812–1852). The "glass" section spans from a second-century Syrian jar to a contemporary Finnish glass bowl by Tapio Wirkkala (1915–1985), organized solely by changes in production techniques. According to Victor Margolin, the inclusion of modern designers is influenced by the pioneering shift towards modern design chronicled by Nikolaus Pevsner (1902–1983) in 1936 and the book becomes sporadic and arbitrary beyond the First World War, when Pevsner's book ends, guided primarily by the formalist principle of "good design" (Margolin 1985: 28–29).

Both design history and material culture have rejected the tools that belong to decorative art history, which were initially developed in the late nineteenth century, but a more inclusive history of design reaching beyond the Industrial Revolution needs to consider those periods and methods, that Glenn Adamson considers deserve reconsideration (Adamson 2013: 37).

As design historians endeavoured to globalize the field of design history from the 1990s, they found the comparative method to be insufficiently implemented. Grace Lees-Maffei observed in 2010 that comparative methods "are generally underused and yet they have the potential to overcome the blunt confines of national borders" (Lees-Maffei and Houze 2010: 468). Similarly, Glenn Adamson, Giorgio Riello and Sarah Teasley observed in 2011 that it is surprising that comparative methodologies are not widely used in design history

> if one thinks about the wealth of studies on different nations – both in Europe and also, increasingly, outside the borders of the Western world – that have addressed implicitly transnational topics such as the professionalization of design, the emergence of specific stylistic vocabularies, or the cultural embeddedness of design.
>
> (2011: 5)

Similarly to Subrahmanyam's connected histories, they argued that the juxtaposition and eventual cross-referencing of existing research is one of the areas of great potential for the study both of design and design history, not only to illuminate cultural similarities and differences but also on ideas of "cultural suitability," attitudes to reproduction and copying, hybridism and the borrowing of conceptual and material language.

In terms of adding a transnational perspective, the comparative method has allowed to grant a place for peripheral design histories, when engaging with canonical narratives. Anna Calvera's "The Influence of English Design Reform in Catalonia. An Attempt at Comparative History" was published in 2002 but stems from a paper first presented in 1994 (2002: 98). This article contests the then-accepted idea that William Morris and the Arts and Crafts movement influenced the Catalan version of Art Nouveau, known as *Modernisme* that ran from the 1870s to 1910. Calvera states that Morris was not very well known at the time that *Modernisme* emerged but his influence arrived rather in the 1890s, and even then Morris was rather a remote cultural reference than a major influence. It was in the reaction against *Modernisme*, known as *Noucentisme*, that these influences were more blatant. Profoundly political, *Noucentisme* extended from 1911 to 1929 and defended a return to classicism and Mediterranean traditions as an antidote to the gothic excesses and the northern artificiality of *Modernisme*. Politicians were looking for forms of production outside the industry and the social problems that it engendered. Stylistically, the Arts and Crafts provided the "sophisticated simplicity" of domestic country living, an example of vernacular comfort, which was less ostentatious than the French examples that were then in vogue, providing a route whereby modern design solutions could be arrived at via the reinterpretation of tradition (2002: 96–97).

The idea of "transnational" was preferred to "global" by Yuko Kikuchi and Yunah Lee as a model to study connections in East Asia. They argue that both concepts transcend the borders of nations, but transnational doesn't necessarily have to be "global"; rather a transnational approach can be used as a supplementary tool for capturing national histories, or for providing a transnational understanding of national history. They consider this transnational approach to be useful, as it builds on knowledge already accumulated, for example in Japanese design history, while bringing out empirical research which can productively be used to write underdeveloped historiographies of, for example, Korean design and Taiwanese design. A transnational take is particularly useful for dealing with cultural dissemination and appropriation, as well as in denationalizing the subject (Kikuchi and Lee 2014: 325).

In its ability to track processes happening both within and beyond the boundaries of nation-states, Harriet Atkinson, Verity Clarkson and Sarah A. Lichtman considered the transnational key. It acknowledges the migration of people, objects and ideas between places and the traces they leave. For that, they opt for the study of how museum and gallery exhibitions, trade fairs and international expositions held between 1945 and 1985 provided the focus for transnational exchanges. Atkinson, Clarkson and Lichtman look through or beyond exhibitions' content, to highlight their role not simply as acts of "exposure" but as something more: as heavily freighted objects of diplomacy, as networks, and as articulators of national values and principles. They suggest that the period between 1945 to 1985 exhibitions acquired a more nuanced political and cultural potency, diversifying and proliferating against a shifting backdrop of broad historical changes and processes including decolonization and globalization becoming locations for the display of "soft power," for the exercise of cultural diplomacy between nations, and as spaces for addressing areas of social or political contestation (Atkinson et al. 2022: 1–3, 6).

Another lens to look at the transnational has been through international design organizations, which are also viewed as venues of soft power by Jeremy Aynsley, Alison J. Clarke and Tania Messell. These organizations enable the amalgamation of national and international influences. They achieve this by advancing designated national design principles, endorsing domestic industries and products, as well as occasionally aligning their processes with ideological political objectives (Aynsley et al. 2022: 5–6). Similarly, Dora Souza Dias explores the nature of cultural exchanges between Western Europe, Anglo America and Latin America, through the lenses of centre-periphery and postcolonial theories, by focusing on a regional conference on graphic design – Icogradalatinoamérica80 – held in Mexico in 1980 and sponsored by a self-proclaimed international council, namely Icograda (Souza Dias 2018: 188). She argues that, in order to move on from Eurocentric narratives it is necessary to not only locate intercultural interactions but also to problematize their outcomes by focusing on their contexts and underlying structures of power. Her investigation demonstrates the negotiations embedded in transnational interactions through an approach that analyses flows between centre and periphery (Souza Dias 2018: 203).

Challenges: The digital humanities and the implications of algorithms

Computational methods have been used for the study of the humanities, in their capacity to compare huge amounts of data. For the study of art, the digital humanities started developing in the second half of the twentieth century. Algorithms from computational image analysis were used to anatomize the use of light and colour, brushstrokes and perspective from different periods. Using extremely detailed digitized scans of paintings, computers can statistically analyse the texture and the use of light and perspective with great precision (Bod 2013: 320).

Some methodologies are, intuitively at least, particularly adaptable to digitalization. One of them has been the connoisseurship techniques of the art critic Giovanni Morelli (1816–1891). Trained in comparative anatomy, Morelli extended his taxonomic classification principles to painting. His method posited that every artist possesses a distinctive style evident in even the smallest details beyond their control. Even when attempting a different style, an artist could be identified by comparing details like ears, noses, hands and various elements in their work. Morelli applied this taxonomy to body parts, clouds, leaves, folds, and brushstrokes, striving to closely match depictions in other paintings. His method relies on examples rather than explicit rules, isolating detailed examples in the artist's style (Bod 2013: 312–314). He came to describe these patterns as *Grundformen*, or "ground forms," and he offered line-drawn examples in his publications (Langmead et al. 2021: §12).

The "Morelli Machine" project ran from August 2018 to January 2019, focusing on extracting facial features like eyes and mouths from a dataset using advanced off-the-shelf facial recognition technology. Initially, faces were extracted, and Google's technology identified 3,205 faces. The researchers produced an Old-Master-Painting mouth extractor, but the results did not cluster these features by artist. The results for eyes were no better. These pre-processed abstract forms, not recognizable mouths, represented the extreme computational abstraction needed for claims about sameness and difference in a computer. The difference is that Morelli's *Grundformen* are not simply dimensional reductions of visual data but form syntheses, that result from human judgement and deliberate analysis of paintings. Computer-generated abstractions employ the computer's abstraction power to generate analogous, dimensionally-reduced representations. The effectiveness of Morelli's method is because it works in tandem with human judgement (Langmead et al. 2021: §55).

Within design history, the digital humanities have been considered as a possibility to connect different archives and go beyond institutional divides (Moriarty 2016: 56). Kjetil Fallan considers the digital humanities as a promising modality for studies that deal with the examination of non-textual material, such as design. He sees the digitalization of design

culture – both as object and as practice – as a terrain with potential to reconnect design history with design practice (Fallan 2019a: 22–23). Similarly, D.J. Huppatz sees the digital humanities as useful for design historians, since the idea of gathering evidence on a large scale and analysis of that data via algorithms may be useful for some studies (Huppatz 2020: e36).

Moriarty recognizes the limits of the archive and argues that the production of connected data depends on the extent and detail of the parent data. There is a great deal in archives and museums that is not yet described digitally or identified in such a way that connections can be established. This means that various things that we know to be the case, through other forms of evidence, are not revealed (Moriarty 2016: 60). For example, Yerena's and Musinguzi's poster *Black Lives Matter/Defund the Police* was acquired by the Cooper Hewit Museum in 2021 in two versions, digital and printed. The object has been tagged as belonging to the two authors and as "digital poster," "2020," "image (computer generated)," and "offset lithograph on paper" (Cooper Hewit Official Website 2023). As such, it will be easy to connect to other works of graphic design like the posters of the Black Panther Party, but more difficult to relate to Botter's T-shirt. The creation of metadata is therefore culturally conditioned and will condition the search among archives.

Coding is a form of worldmaking, proposes the media scholar Matthew Kirschenbaum, in which the coder defines how that world operates (Kirschenbaum 2009). In the context of digital humanities, coding gives the power to create new worlds to model human knowledge and culture. Roopsi Risam and Alex Gil are specifically concerned about how coding needs consideration especially when working with material from communities that have historically been – and continue to be – excluded from the cultural record (Risam and Gil 2022: §16).

Coding can not only represent recent world visions but can also perpetuate old ones. It can include some offensive visual objects (images that are non-canonical, violent and ambiguous) with the potential to cause trauma. The literary scholar Kate Holterhoff analysed this case in a number of museums, among which the Pitt Rivers Museum (Holterhoff 2017: §9). Augustus Pitt-Rivers (1827–1900) classified the collection of Oxford University's museum, founded in 1884 and named after him. In his collection, Pitt-Rivers found types to be an acceptable approach to the organization of ethnographic objects, especially items of which he had little knowledge. When the date or evidence of the use of objects was unknown, Pitt-Rivers suggested that a typology is the best course of action – imitating displaying techniques of archaeology and ancient objects. He saw the logic behind a typology as the true evolution of objects and their natural place in society by allowing different types to coexist much like different species do in nature (Pitt-Rivers 1891: 115–122).

Pitt-Rivers explored the possibilities made available by sorting by type instead of date or geographical location, as was customary at the time, weighing his logic on the fact that a simple form will prevail across time and space. He argued that types are "a tree of progress, and distinguishes the leading shoots from the minor branches" (Pitt-Rivers 1891: 116). In this format, the use of types and subtypes seemed substantial. The anthropologist James Clifford's essay *Collecting Ourselves* makes mention of Pitt-Rivers' typological displays as "developmental sequences" (Clifford 1988: 278). This is in relation to the human development narrative that dominated exhibitions at the time, focused on evolution and the acknowledgement of Europe prevailing over the rest. Similarly, Chris Gosden, Frances Larson and Alison Petch find typecasting objects into cultural groups problematic. Examples such as racial types and barbarism could be offensive to entire groups of people; no matter if a "true" depiction of history through the arrangement of objects is conveyed (Gosden et al. 2007: 108).

The Pitt Rivers Muscum's digital archive embodies both the growth of an anthropological collection and the preservation of nineteenth-century traditions and ideologies. Unlike other institutions, it contains controversial and sometimes offensive content, offering access not only to artefacts but also to letters, manuscripts and photos documenting Pitt-Rivers and his colleagues. The database includes a disclaimer acknowledging the historical context of records. However, disclaimers, akin to trigger warnings, merely notify visitors without engaging or critiquing the past. A troubling example from the archive is sexist, racist letters. While not advocating censorship, Holterhoff questions how hateful artefacts are presented in digital archives. Instead of static records, she argues that archivists could provide specific editorial statements, links to contextual explanations, and metadata labels like "racist" to encourage scholarly critique and conversation. The challenge lies in balancing historical accuracy, ethical presentation and available resources in digital archiving (Holterhoff 2017: §9–12).

In her article, Holterhoff grapples with how digital archivists can effectively use metadata and annotations to categorize and contextualize offensive, particularly racist, objects, aiming to educate the public, promote social justice and facilitate scholarly research. She proposes to go beyond disclaimers to actively supporting and advocating for oppressed groups. Institutions, such as museums and libraries, face challenges in digitizing and providing access to traumatic materials. As digital archives' metadata becomes integral to data mining and digital humanities projects, curators need to assess changes in the value and utilization of their digitized collections. For those involved in creating and maintaining digital archives, the practical and imminent concerns discussed in Holtertoff's article require thoughtful consideration. While adding contextual metadata may be time-consuming and costly, prioritizing problematic materials and viewing metadata as an ongoing process can enable a more sensitive approach to digitization. Taking heed of Tara McPherson's warning about the importance of engaging with fields like gender studies and critical race theory in digital humanities, Holterhoff aims to contribute to scholarly discussions on the role of digital archivists in handling traumatic materials and proposes best practices for utilizing metadata in the pursuit of justice (Holterhoff 2017: §31–32).

5 Case study research

The specific and the general

Conducting case study research involves a thorough examination of existing entities or phenomena, such as objects, individuals, groups, organizations or events. The primary objective is to attain a deep understanding of the subject under investigation and to explore its complexity in the context of a larger discussion. Like all methods, case study research has its inherent limitations. Generalizing the findings is not applicable, as case studies are geared towards precise exploration and comprehensive examination. Even in multiple-case research, the focus remains on the distinctive nature of each individual case rather than on their representativeness. Both single- and multiple-case research methodologies have been employed in design scholarship, each with its unique claims and requirements. The exploratory nature of single-case research and the fragmentary outcomes of multiple-case research are not drawbacks when their relevance is effectively connected to an established debate.

Origin: It is not about representativity but about relevance

In the view of political scientist John Gerring, there exist distinct approaches for acquiring knowledge about house construction. For example, a person could either delve into the specifics of constructing a particular house or analyse the building processes of numerous houses. The former method involves conducting an inquiry through single-case research, while the latter centres around multiple-case research. Both follow different paths to explore the same general subject, that is, the construction of houses (Gerring 2017[2006]: 1).

Case study research is the intensive study of one or a few units for the purpose of understanding complex problems (Gerring 2017[2006]: 28). In the field of design practice, this rationale was followed by the *Arts and Architecture* magazine in 1945 in the organization of its Case Study Houses programme. The best known of these houses might be Case Study House #8 that Charles Eames and Ray Eames (1912–1988) designed in Los Angeles to become their residence. The magazine editor and publisher John Entenza (1905–1984) launched the Case Study Houses programme to

DOI: 10.4324/9781003147282-7

explore the impact of new living standards and technologies generated during the Second World War. It aimed at exploring new attitudes in the work of architects and designers in the post-war era and giving them physical form, "not merely to preview but to assist in giving some direction to the creative thinking on housing being done by good architects and good manufacturers whose good objective is good housing" (Entenza quoted in Neuhart et al. 1989: 49). The Eames house aimed to show how to work with prefabricated materials such as steel H-columns and open-web bar joists. To give stability to the framing, tension rods and turn-buckles added diagonal bracing to the frame. This stable structure was quick to construct, in this case, one and a half days, and provided an example to follow for the practice of building houses with new materials (Neuhart et al. 1989: 109). The Eames residence exemplifies single-case research while, all of them together, the Case Study Houses featured in this programme serve as a notable example of multiple-case research.

Transitioning from design practice to academic research, and particularly within the realm of the humanities, case study research contributes to comprehend preexisting historical contexts or theoretical frameworks. It explores entities and phenomena in their context, without exerting control over the variables that influence their unfolding. This stands in stark contrast to other methodologies such as experiments. The more the research question seeks to explain the "how" and "why," the more case study research will be appropriate (Yin 2018: 32). Case study research is therefore rather qualitative than quantitative. It answers questions related to both unanticipated and expected relationships, such as "how have prefab houses influenced the attachment of owners to their homes?" Conversely, quantitative research would answer questions in which a limited number of variables are involved, such as "are the window openings of prefab houses bigger than in traditional buildings?" (Stake 1995: 41). It is important to clarify that qualitative research does not imply that researchers dismiss objective outcomes. Rather, it signifies the researcher's endeavour to offer fundamental explanations for specific phenomena (Gillham 2000: 7).

For phenomena to qualify as cases, a comprehensive exploration is essential as is their significance to ongoing investigations. Therefore, the selection of a case for study depends on its relevance. The mere presence of copious evidence regarding a specific case does not inherently validate its study (Stake 1995: xi). Determining the relevance of a specific case depends on its connection to the larger discourse in which it is involved. A "typical" case study can effectively address certain research inquiries, whereas in other instances, an "unusual" case may more effectively challenge established notions within history or theory (Stake 1995: 4). The analysis of multiple cases could potentially assume a role akin to quantitative research, given its transformation into a large-N study, contrasting with the small-N approach of single case studies (Gerring 2017[2006]: 10). However, case study research does not align with the principles of sampling research. Consequently, case studies offer depth of analysis but cannot lay claim to rock-solid representativity (Gerring

2017[2006]: 13; Stake 1995: 4). The significance of case study research lies in its exploratory contribution, such as the development of a new theory, or in its refutational potential, when challenging the universal applicability of an existing theory. This diverges from a confirmatory function, which would entail verifying a theory's validity and is beyond the scope of case study research (Gerring 2017[2006]: 23).

In the humanities, case study research has been identified within history in the oral and written chronicles of the sort produced in Ancient Greece by the poet Homer in the eighth century BCE and the historians Herodotus and Thucydides in the fifth century BCE (Gerring 2017[2016]: 3). Drawing on the specific features of the case at hand, these chronicles imparted general lessons on politics, society, human nature or religion. For example, Thucydides explained that history is useful because understanding past events will allow people to know what to expect when similar circumstances recur in the future. The cases served as warnings, analogies and inspiration (Boedeker 2011: 144). These histories not only elaborated on particular events, but also provided the building blocks for a general knowledge of the world, functioning as case studies because of their instrumental character (Gerring 2017[2016]: 3–4). In this manner, these authors abstracted from the particular to the general. Their investigations were not only about the immediate description of a case but the specific studies acquire a relevance that helps understand complex situations.

Case study research has been rather theorized and developed within the social sciences rather than in the humanities, particularly in the domains of anthropology and sociology. The sociologist John A. Creswell sees specific foundational examples in the study of the structure and function of French families by the sociologist Frédéric le Play (1806–1882) in the mid-nineteenth century, in the work of the anthropologist Bronislaw Malinowski (1884–1942) on the Trobriand Islands in the early twentieth century and in the case studies of the University of Chicago Department of Sociology from the 1920s through the 1950s that attempted to illuminate the experience of immigrants established in the United States. In all three cases, the relevance of the considered cases was not their representativeness but their ability to understand the ideal through the real. In the case of the Chicago sociologists, their goal was to pin down abstract issues related to the experience of immigration through the experience of Polish immigrants. Those experiences were not the same for other groups but contributed to a qualitative, tangible understanding of an otherwise too abstract phenomenon (Creswell 2013: 97; Mills et al. 2010: xxxvi).

How to proceed with case study research? Case study research has no fixed routine formulas. The research begins with the definition of the problems or issues to be studied and the development of a case study plan and strategy. Therefore, case studies typically involve collecting a wide range of data through observations, interviews, archival records and written material – protocols also typical of other methods such as ethnography and biographies, for example. The data are then analysed and interpreted to form an understanding of the case. This process is iterative, with new data being collected and analysed as the research unfolds.

Case study research lacks a specifically delineated methodology but draws upon established qualitative techniques. Take the example of ethnography and biographies: what sets case study research apart from these other methods? Much like ethnographies and biographies, case study research might focus on subjects such as individuals, events or groups. However, a distinction arises as case studies entail in-depth examinations and depictions of either a single unit or multiple units, with the aim of constructing argumentative frameworks that extend beyond the presented evidence. This disparity is not rooted in procedural variances, but rather in the overarching research objective. For instance, ethnography delves into the beliefs of a particular culture, and biographical studies aim to comprehend individual lives. To belong to one of these methods, a specific investigation needs to align with these respective objectives. Conversely, case studies are more flexible in their goals and serve a wider variety of research questions. What makes case study research distinctive is the instrumentality of the specific study within the research, in other words how it is relevant to understand a complex phenomenon (Hancock and Algozzine 2006: 9–11). In other words, ethnographic and biographical studies will be legitimately applied to the study of any group or individual, but they become case study research when they prove relevant to understand phenomena beyond the scope of the evidence presented, being housing after the Second World War, immigration or general knowledge of how the world works, as Thucydides intended.

Development: Critical, unusual, common, revelatory and longitudinal

Scholars warn about the abuse of "case study" outside academia. The social scientist Robert K. Yin argues that case studies also exist as an everyday form of exposition, appearing in newsprint, magazines, blogs, videos and nearly every type of popular media. To illustrate this, he mentions the common expressions "Let's write a case study" or "We need to find a case" (Yin 2018: 21). These case studies are not considered as a formal research method, since they do not necessarily follow any explicit research procedures. They might appear frequently as supplementary materials in professional training and practicums, which have been commonly called "teaching cases" with the purpose to present information about practical situations (Yin 2018: 22). Similarly, the sociologist Malcolm Tight observes that calling a piece of research a case study and adding a brief reference to the case study literature may then seem to add credibility. He adds that while, in one sense, "everything is a case (i.e. all individual items may be seen as worthy of analysis), all research is not case study research" (Tight 2017: 38). Taken together, the popular case studies, as well as the teaching-practice case studies likely drive everyday impressions of what constitutes a case study, giving the false impression that "case studies" are a form of supplemental practice material and not an explicit endeavour within academic research.

From the point of view of the humanities, the classification between single-case and multiple-case studies, as described by Yin, might be the most suitable (2018) even when there are multiple classifications of case study research formulated by other social scientists (Thomas 2016; Woodside 2010; Gerring 2017[2016]). The choice between a single case or multiple cases will depend on the specific research. When selecting single-case research, that case should be related to the theory or the historiography that needs to be explored or refuted. A multiple-case study can help when evidence needs to be more compelling. A specific investigation might need several cases to define "how" a specific phenomenon occurs or "why" it happens. It offers a greater variety than a single case.

Yin offers a classification of **single-case** studies in which a case can relate to a specific academic debate (2018: 84). Because case study research is fragmentary, exploratory and refutational rather than comprehensive and confirmatory, it needs to be validated against the backdrop of an existing theory. Take, for example, the fact that prefabricated constructions have been first detected in eleventh-century Europe (Bouet 2015). The chronicle of the medieval poet Robert Wace (1110–1174) detailing the Norman conquest of England circa 1066, as depicted in the Bayeux Tapestry, recounts the construction of the keep of Hastings Castle from prefabricated timber materials (Master Wace 2013[ca. 1175]: 129). However, due to the absence of archaeological evidence and the retrospective narration of the facts, certain scholars cast doubt upon this narrative, questioning the feasibility of transporting such heavy materials using the boats available at that time (Wright 2019: 54). Conversely, other scholars dissent, acknowledging that prefabricated housing was a common practice in the same region around Hastings at a later time and in continental Europe during an earlier part of the same century, thereby asserting the accuracy of Wace's account (Bouet 2010: 92; Higham 2003: 109–110).

The choice for a single-case study might respond to different goals. According to Yin, single cases can be critical, unusual, common, revelatory or longitudinal (2018: 84–87). By conducting **critical** case studies, it becomes possible to determine the accuracy of specific propositions in a theory or to consider alternative explanations. Theories often define a distinct set of circumstances in which their propositions are deemed true. Although a single critical case study may not serve as the cornerstone for developing theories or establishing historiography, it possesses the ability to question the fundamental assumptions that underpin them. Should a case study emerge demonstrating the existence of prefabricated houses predating the eleventh century, it would effectively challenge the notion of these houses being pioneers. In this context, a single case study would suffice. This particular case would indeed qualify as a critical case study, as its purpose would not be to establish an entirely new historical narrative, but rather to question assumptions of previous historiography.

An **unusual** case study deviates from theoretical norms. It can be very similar to a critical case study and in some cases interchangeable in the sense that it questions previously accepted truths. Following the example of eleventh-century prefabricated constructions, an unusual case could be one that shows an example of prefab houses combining traditional construction techniques and prefab materials. It would not be critical to the statement that "prefab constructions first appeared in the eleventh century in Europe" but would present a construction technique that was hybrid and worth documenting, even when minoritarian, to understand the construction of prefab houses in this period.

A **common** case study captures the circumstances and conditions of an everyday situation. For example, there is evidence about the existence of prefabricated constructions in the eleventh century in general but perhaps there might be a specific example that has been documented in greater detail. This example can explain how the different pieces were designed and manufactured and how they were tested and then transported in "kit" form. Moreover, the case can reveal details about the assemblage of the whole and even about the experience of the owners, their motivations and their status. This common case offers details that general accounts do not and therefore would be worth developing. This common case might not represent the way that all eleventh-century prefabricated constructions without exception were made and assembled but neither does it deviate from the established historiography.

Revelatory cases give the opportunity to researchers to observe phenomena previously inaccessible. Take, for example, that after the publication of a study on eleventh-century prefabricated constructions and after developing a common case study, new archaeological or archival evidence becomes accessible where there is evidence of a prefab house that was much bigger than those studied initially. This case is not critical because it conforms to our initial ideas, it is not unusual because it is made fully with prefab materials and it is not common because it was not available yet when formulating our theory. It is, nevertheless, extraordinary because it conforms to a complex example and is therefore worth developing as a case.

Longitudinal cases involve the study of the same single-case at two or more different points in time exposing how certain conditions and underlying processes change over time. Researchers can predict changes at specific moments that can be confirmed with longitudinal case studies. For example, how a prefab house might age depending on the materials used cannot be studied synchronically but diachronically. The same single case can be explored when recently built and at the moment in which those specific materials are expected to present problems of stability and solidity. Longitudinally registering the damage will confirm or refute the hypothesis of the deterioration process.

Within the same academic debate, a **multiple-case** study might explore ways in which eleventh-century prefab constructions were assembled, either with specialized workforce, non-specialized workforce, a mix of the two, with the help of specific machinery, with the participation of animals... This might discern if a prefabricated keep could have been transported by boat from continental Europe to the southern coast of England. In this case, a multiple-case study is preferable, since this research question demands a greater variety of evidence to be answered accurately.

When undertaking multiple-case research, the cases are preferably studied following an analogous logic, replicating the same research steps in each of them for the sake of consistency. Their goal should be either to offer similar results – a literal replication –, or contrasting results – a theoretical replication (Yin 2018: 91). In the case of eleventh-century prefab constructions, a hypothetical investigation might show that they all followed a similar procedure, which demonstrates that prefabrication imposed a standardized way of constructing. In this case, in which the results are similar, there is literal replication. On the contrary, another hypothetical investigation might demonstrate that prefab houses have been adapted to specific locations. This would demonstrate that prefabrication did not involve standardization but allowed personalization and adapted to specific contexts. In this case, in which the results are contrasting, there is theoretical replication.

To sum up, the primary objective of case study research is to identify a case's significance within a particular debate. Consequently, researchers must not only define the case itself but also consider the framework within which the specific case will be analysed. This leads to making a choice between conducting a single-case or a multiple-case study. Multiple-case studies are often favoured for their stronger evidence and perceived robustness compared to single-case studies. However, there are instances where a single-case study can effectively make the intended point, rendering multiple-case studies unnecessary. The very rationales of some case study models, such as the critical case, the unusual case and the revelatory case, are always single-case and would not benefit from a larger study that a multiple-case study might provide (Yin 2018: 91).

Implementation: How to deal with fragmentary evidence

Within design scholarship, single-case study research is abundant both in design history and particularly within design culture. According to Guy Julier and Anders V. Munch, design culture studies distinguish themselves from design history because of their extensive focus on contemporary expressions of design – while still seeking historically informed insights relevant to emerging scholarly inquiries and design practices. Furthermore, design culture studies place a strong emphasis on gaining a profound understanding of design artefacts and their interactions with various stakeholders involved in their creation, functioning and reproduction (Julier et al. 2019: 1). This emphasis on the contemporary, the design practice and the artefacts alongside its aim to contribute to discussions in various related fields – such as business and management studies, human geography, anthropology, media and communications studies, and cultural studies – makes single-case research a good exploratory method.

As mentioned above, a case study should always be a case study of something. In his study on the beverage Fritz-kola – a brand founded in Hamburg in 2002 by the entrepreneurs Mirco Wolf Wiegert and Lorenz Hampel – Mads Nygaard Folkmann explores the strategies of aestheticization employed by this company. Through this case study, he argues for the relevance of aesthetics for design culture studies (Figure 5.1). Nygaard Folkmann's research delves into Fritz-kola and its marketing tactics, examining how aesthetic components and methods of sensory attraction and reflective significance are created through a comprehensive presentation of the product. This involves aspects like visual identity, advertising, store environments and brand spaces. Moreover, consumers play a role in reproducing these elements as they engage with the product and showcase it through their own perspectives on social media (2019: 69).

According to Nygaard Folkmann, aesthetics as a concept for entering, analysing and understanding design has often been marginalized within design history, which primarily promoted the analysis of cultural, social, economic and political contexts for design. As a result, design history affiliated aesthetics with art history and with superficial stylistic changes of form without a connection to context in an attempt for the discipline to distance itself from traditional art-historical approaches. Nygaard Folkmann argues for design culture studies to consider aesthetics as a matter of sociologically based "taste," as a way of describing how the appearance of products makes promises about their performance (2019: 107).

Fritz-kola may not be exceptional as a case of contemporary design culture, adds Nygaard Folkmann. Many other companies operate with the same means for staging their products in settings that inject the products with cultural meaning, carried out in both the physical and the virtual space. Nevertheless, Fritz-kola is an example of how a company in contemporary design culture aims to impose perceptual patterns on consumers by aesthetic means (2019: 108). In summary, this is not a case that deserves attention because of being extraordinary but because, following Yin's classification, it is rather a common case study that provides tangible context for a theoretical proposition that might otherwise be challenging to comprehend. This parallels the role of the Eames house as a demonstration of how to construct with emerging post-war technologies, since this house materialized the initial Entenza's propositions in a specific proposal.

Multiple-case research has been employed, for instance, to delineate emergent national histories of design in works like Tony Fry's *Design History Australia* (1988) and Artemis Yagou's *Fragile Innovation: Episodes in Greek Design History* (2011). Rather than aiming to present comprehensive accounts of design history in Australia and Greece, both authors adopt a fragmentary approach, developing select examples while acknowledging the presence of gaps. They consider their contributions as initial steps towards inspiring future research in the field. At the same time, both investigations explore thereby the methodological shortcomings of canonical design historiographies.

Figure 5.1 Fritz-kola bottle. Photo by XAMAX\ullstein bild via Getty Images

Fry (1988) develops in his book an extensive and sound methodological reflection on the use of case study research as an alternative to canonical design history. The first chapter explores the state of design history at that moment. The second develops the framework of social design and the methodology of case study research as an alternative to canonical design histories. The third implements this method on three case studies. The initial case study explores "The Great White Train," an exhibition train that travelled across Australia during 1925 and 1926. The second study revolves around MacRobertsons, a confectionery company established in Melbourne in 1880, which effectively concluded through a takeover in 1967. Last, the third contemporary example examines Australia's Wonderland, a theme park situated in outer western Sydney. All three deal with the representation of Australianness. The first two cases are examples of what Fry calls economic nationalism and its extension of Australian products. The third is about the recreation of Australian history in a themed park (1988: 82, 129).

Fry argues against the international accounts of the history of design that presume to be a comprehensive narrative but only consider a limited number of powerful countries as guiding forces. They create a few central over-investigated narratives and a periphery of under-investigated or just omitted national accounts. The Australian case, Fry argues, is not separated from the "central" events but at the same time exposes local peculiarities that deserve separate investigation. His aim is not "to write a history of Australian design resembling dominant histories of design" (1988: 14). Fry rejects the construction of a nationalist design history based on products as canonized aesthetic typeforms and designers as heroes. Such a model, he says, affirms marginality and generates fiction (1988: 82). In his eyes, a "true design history" would be a history of everything instead of a partial history of a few aesthetically validated objects mostly from Europe and the USA, and their "heroic" designers (1988: 18). Therefore, he advocates for a social history of design to understand the complexity of the role of design in everyday life, since "nothing which is designed speaks for itself" (1988: 53–54).

Regarding case study research, Fry argues for a design history that values the fragment and does not pretend to be comprehensive. He says that writing history is always a myth, a specific interpretation of the facts. "Real history," "the facts" and "real events" are irretrievable and only known through the media of historical mediation. Myths, therefore, are not untrue but construct certain kinds of representation, through imagination (1988: 82). Case studies for Fry are myths, too, but of a specific kind, produced as an account of focused fragments of the past, "written from the present to infer, prompt and promote a desired future" (1988: 84). Fry's goal back in 1988 was to demonstrate the need for a change of paradigm in design history writing at that moment that would generate a change.

Another example of a similar emerging national history of design structured across a collection of case studies is Yagou's book (2011) divided into seven chapters covering the period between the mid-nineteenth century up to the 2010s – two on nineteenth-century design, two on the inter-war period, two on the post-war period and finally one on references to Greekness in design that extend over all periods. Like Fry, Yagou proposes her work as an alternative to the well-established histories based on aesthetic connoisseurship about certain classes of objects (2011: 2). She clarifies that her book is not intended as a comprehensive history of design within the country. Instead, it provides a broad perspective on the evolution of local design through the examination of specific case studies. Furthermore, she mentions that the resulting synthesis represents a unique and possibly uneven assemblage of cases that somehow exemplify distinct periods (2011: 3). According to her and similarly to Fry's claims, this is not a finalized product but a first attempt to pin down the basic parameters of a neglected academic subject that the author hopes serves as an example for other emerging design historiographies (2011: 3). Yagou's conclusion is that this volume shows "a string of incomplete initiatives and inconclusive efforts" and that design in Greece may be viewed as subject to the difficulties and controversies of Greek modernization (2011: 153–154).

Despite their similarities, these two books approach multiple-case research distinctly. If both present an alternative to canonical design history, Fry's main intention is rather to support the social history approach within the discipline. In this case, the cases are representative of how a methodology should be applied. How they represent design in Australia from a specific period is secondary. In Yagou's book, the cases seek to exemplify specific periods and are not advocating for a specific methodology. Her interest, equally legitimate, is rather in how to insert emergent design histories in the canon than to rethink how the canon has been shaped.

Challenges: From iterative to deductive research

As Nygaard Folkmann mentions, Fritz-kola was not an exceptional case of design culture. Writing a chapter on this, would not result in a piece of scholarship worth publishing. The missing ingredient would be a strong argumentative line – what he finds in the relevance of aesthetics – for the evidence to work as either a critical, unusual, common, revelatory or longitudinal case-study research. Nevertheless, research does not always develop in those ideal terms and sometimes there is just an abundance of evidence on a specific example that might not be worth publishing in itself. In that case, researchers might need to work reversely on that method: starting from the evidence and ending with the formulation of an argumentative line. In other words, transforming an iterative research into a deductive paper.

This was the case with my own article "Industrial design in the museum: the case of the FN milking machine, c.1947" (2010), published as an article in *The Burlington Magazine*, which argues for museum display strategies that meet the specificities of industrial design. The evidence was the life cycle of the milking machine that the Belgian manufacturer Fabrique Nationale d'Armes de Guerre (FN) produced in the late 1940s (Figure 5.2). The concept behind machine milking involves using vacuum pressure to draw milk from cows. Specially

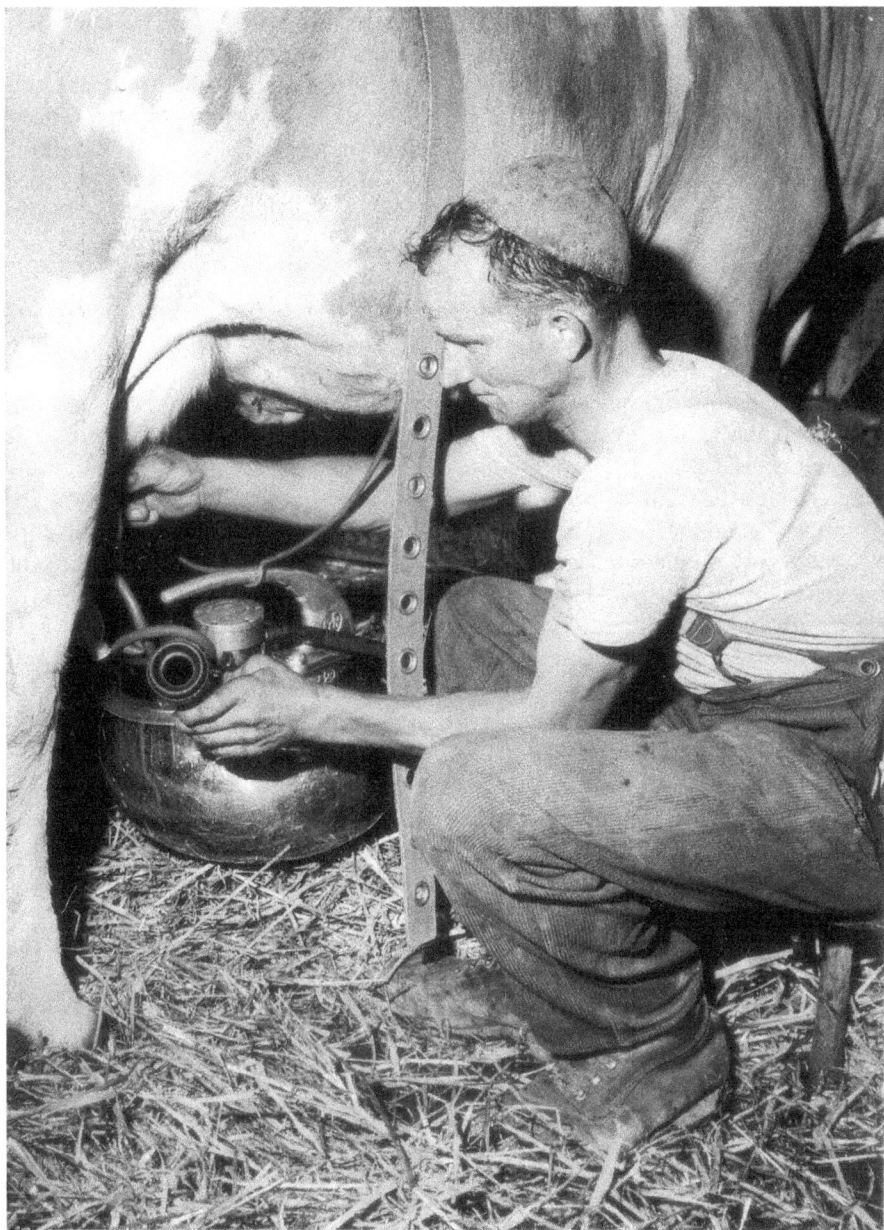

Figure 5.2 Farmer milking with FN milking machine. Photo by RDB/ullstein bild via Getty Images

designed machines maintain a consistent vacuum at the udders, effectively drawing out the milk and transferring it into a suitable container.

At the beginning of this research, I still had not defined the argumentative line. The inquiry started in the framework of a post-doctoral research fellowship investigating the Benelux-wide Signe d'Or award scheme. This milking machine received such an award in 1957 and, contrary to other awarded objects that did not receive much coverage, the milking machine was displayed in most catalogues, magazines and exhibitions. Therefore, out of curiosity I started researching this object in depth.

This research evolved through the consultation of different primary sources, starting with *Revue FN* [FN Magazine]. The in-house magazine of FN encompasses a range of topics, including updates on ongoing projects and news related to employees, such as internal sports activities as well as birth announcements, for example. Two articles were especially relevant. The November issue of 1953 offered a three-page spread about the milking machine, its different components and its use. This article showed how the machine was connected to a standard vacuum installation that made the cups attached to the udders pulsate and extract the milk that went directly into the bucket (Kets 1953: n.p.). The March issue of 1957 included an extended article on advanced lathing and yielding procedures at the factory, that shed light on the manufacturing process of this milking machine. There, it became clear that the yielding of the two parts of the bucket was electronic, offering a seamless interior that avoided the creation of protuberances in which old milk could accumulate (M.H. 1957: 2).

Regarding antecedents and market competitors, an Internet survey on patents connected this milking machine to other models that were developed in the United States in the 1920s. Those were very similar except for the yielding process. Traditional yielding techniques do not achieve a seamless bucket but one in which the upper and lower part are clearly separated by a seam (Lee Mickle 1924; New York State Agricultural Experiment Station 1925). Through an advertisement for the Surge-Melotte milking machine on the back cover of the publication for the dairy sector in Belgium, *Het Belgisch Zuivelbedrijf* [The Belgian Dairy Company], of January 1949, I could see that the FN milking machine had other competitors. The FN model was not innovative and not exclusive – why then did it get a design award? And who was the designer?

Due to the absence of an archive for the Signe d'Or Award during the 1950s, this inquiry had to rely on additional sources and archival materials. The original Signe d'Or diploma was published in the *Revue FN*. It mentioned that the award went to the stainless-steel bucket but there was no mention of the designer (Revue FN 1957). For that, the archive of Emile Langui (1903–1980), one of the members of the advisory board of the Signe d'Or, was helpful. His archive is located at the State Archives of Belgium and kept all the minutes of each Signe d'Or meeting and some additional documents. There, I got to know indirectly more about the authorship of this milking machine.

The Belgian Ministry of Work and Social Security intended to confer a prestigious medal upon remarkable Belgian employees, and they reached out to Signe d'Or to provide the names of individuals engaged in designing and producing the recognized award-worthy items up to that point. The Signe d'Or, on its part, lacked this information and needed to approach the manufacturers to uncover the fact that even major corporations like FN and ACEC (Ateliers de Constructions Electriques de Charleroi) were also unable to provide individual names. Instead, they argued that design activities grew from collaboration and suggested giving the award to the "work community" ("communauté de travail") of both firms instead (Beveren, State Archives: 168r–170r). The investigation appeared to reach a dead end, prompting the need for a shift in the research approach.

What seemed worth questioning is how the FN milking machine had been on display after passing from being a farmer's object to an awarded design. I could see that this machine was on display in the Agriculture Section of the 1958 Brussels World Fair and at the Industrial Design Section at the same event (Revue FN 1958). In the first case, the machine was on display with all the functional components including the pulsator, lid, udder cups and rubber tubes, everything but the standard vacuum installation, which was not a FN product. In the Industrial Design Section, only the bucket was displayed on a pedestal, creating a nice view but difficult to identify. This had consequences in further displays, such as in the 11th Milan Triennale in which the machine was on display in both the Belgian and international section (Revue FN 1958). The article in *Revue FN* mentioned that one of the visitors misidentified the milking machine as a samovar. Later, an article by design critic Jerzy Olkiewicz in the Polish magazine *Projekt*, similarly mistook this machine for kitchenware (Olkiewicz 1958: 9).

This investigation could have served many possible argumentative lines, regarding the intersection between the mechanisms of display and recognition of industrial design. Of the many possibilities, the article reflected finally on the necessity of displaying design properly and about offering the necessary information to identify the exhibit. To achieve this aim, the adequate secondary literature had to be sought, one that would connect the collected evidence to an ongoing debate. In this context, Guy Julier presented a critique of the exhibition strategies employed by the Vitra Museum. He highlighted the museum's reliance on distinctive, designer-created chairs and posited that design museums sometimes fail to tailor their exhibition and acquisition policies to the essence of industrial design (Julier 2000: 39). My research served as a common single-case study in this debate. I wrote this article accordingly. The collected evidence was able to expand on this idea and, like Nygaard Folkmann stated in his own case study research, to become a good example of how these phenomena articulate in real life, opening possibilities for discussion and offering specific examples on "how" some processes occur and "why" they are important to take into account.

6   Designers' monographs
Fluid authorship

The life and work of individual designers provide an effective framework for design analysis and remain a solid foundation for constructing design historiographies. However, they have been criticized for promoting a heroic approach, accused of perpetuating the establishment of a canon, and criticized for biasing towards the notion of genius, rendering it subjective and celebratory. Notably, postcolonial and feminist perspectives argue that while monographs have contributed to the exclusivity of Western design, they can also be instrumental in dismantling this canon and highlighting other identities. Yet, when the creative process is not centred on an individual but on co-creation, the role of a monograph becomes uncertain. What is its significance then? Individual lives and subjectivities are crucial, but even more so when viewed through the prism of dialogue. Considering individual subjectivity as multivocal brings collective and individual authorship closer together.

Origins: Genius-based monographs

A designer's monograph explores the body of work created by specific designers and establishes connections between their creative output and their personal life. When we seek to understand how the personality, education, personal experiences, interests, background and character of a designer have influenced their work, we turn to the principles underlying designers' monographs. These monographs construct narratives that span from the development of the designer's personal creations to the impact of historical context on their creative output.

A method championed and shaped by the discipline of art history, artists' monographs undergo constant redefinitions. These monographs often establish artists within an accepted canon and employ the evaluative skills of the monograph's author to clarify the artistic merit of the individuals discussed. The historian Pliny the Elder (23–79 AD) played a pivotal role in establishing the canon of illusionist painting, using it as a basis for assessing artists (Bod 2013: 44). Similarly, around the year 500, the painter and critic Xie He formulated his *Classification of Painters*, which outlined a canon based on six

DOI: 10.4324/9781003147282-8

principles. Xie compiled a list of 27 painters, providing concise descriptions of their works and evaluating their ability – or lack thereof – to integrate these Six Principles. Notably, Xie He utilized a point system to rank painters (Bod 2013: 49–50). This framework, consisting of the Six Principles and the point system, served as a template for subsequent art histories, including Zhang Yanyuan's *Record of Famous Painters of Successive Dynasties*, offering a comprehensive overview of renowned painters up to 847. This tradition persisted until 1365 with the work of Xia Wenyan, who created an encyclopaedic compilation detailing all known artists, their biographies and his own assessments, which he compared with those of earlier art historians (Bod 2013: 121–122).

The author that epitomizes the artist's monograph in the Western art historical tradition might be the artist and writer Giorgio Vasari (1511–1574), who published his *The Lives of the Most Excellent Painters, Sculptors, and Architects* in 1550 – with an expanded edition released in 1568. This book collects the lives and works of several painters, sculptors and architects, connecting their life and context to their work. Vasari evaluates the skills and abilities of each artist, which are a product of their genius. He determines the worthiness of each artist to be included in the canon, basing his judgements on his own experience as an artist (Fernie 1995: 11). For example, in the analysis of the artistic contributions of Giotto (ca 1267–1337), Vasari identifies Giotto as the proponent of a novel painting style deeply grounded in the observation of nature. According to him, this approach to painting, rooted in keen observation, had been absent from artistic practice in the previous two centuries (Vasari 1991[1568]: 16). Vasari sees flaws in Giotto's work, since he fails to execute vivid eyes, delicate weeping figures, hair and beards with softness, hands with their natural joints and muscles and nudes like real bodies (Vasari 1991[1568]: 53). This example shows well how Vasari combined documentary evidence, that placed Giotto within a broader context, with normative judgements, based on his own ideas of good art. Vasari employed a method that encompassed the examination of historical documents, the inclusion of anecdotes regarding the artists, and a meticulous analysis of the artworks themselves (Fernie 1995: 12). The *Lives* stresses the achievements of individual artists and their place in history, assessed by the study of the documentary evidence and the techniques of connoisseurship.

One of Vasari's main contributions to the study of artists, and its most polemic, is the idea of the genius. Aligned with the prevailing usage of the term during his time, Vasari's concept of genius asserts that certain individuals are blessed with an "extraordinary liveliness and quickness of intellect" that enables them to excel in specific endeavours and achieve notable success in the world (Vasari 1991[1568]: 15; Biow 2018: 51). According to Vasari, the genius cannot be acquired. In the case of Giotto, he was already good at drawing from nature before being discovered accidentally by his master Cimabue when drawing a sheep on a flat stone "without having learned how to draw it from anyone other than Nature" (Vasari 1991[1568]: 16). This is a key premise for Vasari. One cannot possibly develop into a remarkable artist without genius, that innate quality. It is genius and not training that makes a good artist (Biow 2018: 53). This inborn quality implies that geniuses do not necessarily come from high classes but might belong to any social class, and once again, Giotto was a perfect example. In Vasari's biography, he worked at his father's farm (Vasari 1991[1568]: 15).

Although Vasari published two of his biographical texts in separate books, that is, on Michelangelo (1475–1564) and on Jacopo Sansovino (1486–1570), it was the type of the collective history of artists that had a following among writers. This is evident in the 1604 book by Karel van Mander (1548–1606) on Netherlandish painters and later in Giovanni Bellori (1613–1696), who applied Vasarian ideas to the development of Baroque painters, Filippo Baldinucci (1624–1697), who specifically described his work as an attempt to bring Vasari up to date, Joachim von Sandrart (1606–1688), who in the late seventeenth century wrote a history of German painting and Horace Walpole (1717–1797), who produced a series of biographies of English painters in the late eighteenth century (Fernie 1995: 11–12).

Books devoted to an individual artist became current in Europe at the turn of the nineteenth century (Guercio 2006: 34). By then also the idea of genius had changed. No longer viewed as a blessing coming from the outside, the genius became during the eighteenth century – and especially with the philosopher Immanuel Kant (1724–1804) – an intellectual quality belonging to the individual. In *Critique of Judgement* (1790), Kant considers genius an innate productive faculty of the artist, arguing that genius is "the innate mental aptitude (ingenium) through which nature gives the rule to art" (Kant 2007 [1790]: 136). The distinguishing feature of an artist's genius was the ability to express "aesthetic ideas" that originated from the imagination and were accessible through intuition, without being bound by rational concepts. The artist's development in both life and art, was perceived as an inherent and interconnected process. Writing a monograph became a way to intertwine the artworks with the artist's life. Each element, whether related to the artist's life or their work, could transition between the two realms, interact with other elements and transform in the reconstruction of the artist's history (Guercio 2006: 42–43).

The nineteenth-century artists' monographs used the term "genius" to describe an individual who brings forth remarkably innovative and completely unexpected breakthroughs, consequently initiating a transformative shift in the understanding of the world. These monographs described artists in terms of their genius or interpret the artworks in relation to their human-centred and inspirational aspects, taking certain elements of Kantian aesthetics to an extreme. While Kant compartmentalized aesthetics and art, further emphasizing the division between artistic practice and other human endeavours, the romantics sought all-encompassing principles to define the genius (Biow 2018: 52). These monographs also revealed that an artist's genius was a foundational concept for understanding how and why a vital force manifests itself in an artwork.

A good example is the monograph on Albrecht Dürer (1471–1528) that the artist and art historian Adam Weise (1776–1835) published in 1819, which depicted the German artist as an authentic, original individual. Since Vasari and Van Mander, the literature on Dürer had increased little but in the early nineteenth century, Dürer was rediscovered as the personification of a visual tradition coexisting with the Italian and classical modes, but with roots in northern and Gothic imagery. Dürer was then compared to Raphael. They both were considered representatives of different but equally valid art historical ideals. Weise considered Dürer as the original interpreter of a northern artistic tradition, an artist true to himself and a symbol of national identity (Guercio 2006: 58–59).

In conclusion, the concept of genius emerged with Vasari as a way to bridge the gap between nature and art and this union fuelled the life-and-work model, which, through its combination of action and existence, demonstrated that the creative work of genius does not exist as separate from nature. The definition of the genius shifted from a blessing to an innate quality, particular to the artist in question. In both cases, artists were depicted as subjects with particular talents above the average worth being studied because of their peculiar qualities.

Development: Exploring the supraindividual

After a period in which the artist was located at the centre of the production of art, critiques came to unbalance this situation. Formalists, Marxist, and social historians and structuralists questioned both authorship and monographs in favour of the independent development of forms in history, the importance of reception processes and non-anthropocentric visions of the artistic process.

Formalism, concerned with the nature of representation, challenged the meanings and finalities of the artist's monograph in the early twentieth century. A decisive step towards regarding art as a supraindividual category was taken in *Principles of Art History* of 1915, where the art historian Heinrich Wölfflin isolates visual forms and styles: their intrinsic causation, recurring problems and evolutionary rules. He aims to understand the history of art as ultimately ruled by a system of impersonal laws of formal development. Wölfflin's plan is to offer a generative grammar of artistic vision and stylistic mutations, arguing – at least in the first edition of this book – for an "art history without names" (Guercio 2006: 255). His study transcends the conventional life-and-work model advocated since Vasari and delves into the exploration of forms. The dynamics and purpose of these forms are detached from the individual existence, encompassing a broader universe of creative expression.

In this formalist lineage, the art historian George Kubler (1912–1996) provides a pointed critique of the limitations of monographs in his *The Shape of Time* (1962). This book questions art studies moulded upon discussions of meaning, symbolism and expression. Like Wölfflin, Kubler argues for an art history focused on the progression of forms, beyond the influence of individual artists. In this sense, Kubler speaks of formal sequences linking objects of various periods, claiming the span of an artist's life cannot offer a reliable criterion of investigation. While biography is a "provisional way of scanning artistic substance," the historian of things must try to reconstruct durations that extend beyond individual experience (1962: 4).

Kubler wonders what elements would be pivotal in an investigation about the railroads of a country. It would not be enough to analyse the experiences of a single traveller on several of them – that is, the artists – but for an accurate description of railroads, it is necessary to overlook individuals and states. For him, the true essence lies in the railroads themselves, which serve as the consistent elements of continuity, rather than the passengers or the officials involved in their operation (1962: 5). Alongside, the artist is not a free agent: prior events matter more than temperament or genius. The differences between artists, Kubler states, are not so much those of talent as of their entrance in history and their position in the sequence with respect to other artists (1962: 6).

To study these impersonal forces, he proposes to follow scientific models, in particular those from biology. He suggests reconstructing the specific need that originated a form, drawing a parallel with how species adapt to their respective environments. Human creations arise as intentional solutions, transforming needs into objects that become part of formal traditions. Thus, he highlights the relationship between art and nature, but departs from the traditional Vasarian view centred around genius. Instead, Kubler presents history as analogous to biology when he says that "style is the species, and historical styles are its taxonomic varieties" (1962: 7). He claims that the historian's special contribution is the discovery of the manifold "shapes" of time (1962: 11).

During the second half of the twentieth century, Marxist and social historians equally investigated art from a supraindividual perspective, but their methods differed from the formalists. They valued the interaction between the production of art and its reception as the true study field of historians, but also recognized that the artist's monograph could also contribute to this task. One of the books that best clarifies the relationship between artists and artwork on the basis of principles of Marxism is *Art History and Class Struggle* (1973) by the art historian Nicos Hadjinicolaou (b. 1938). Since the motor of history for Marxists is class struggle, the individuals are for Hadjinicolaou of limited importance – therefore, he calls the monograph the "thorny" problem of art history (1973: 19). By aligning art history with the history of artists, Hadjinicolaou states, the model perpetuates the ideology of bourgeois individualism and precludes any approach based on historical materialism (1973: 20, 30).

Hadjinicolaou does not deny the validity of monographs but sees them rather as a means than as a goal in themselves. He attacks the psychological approaches towards artists' monographs since they limit their analysis to individual artists. Conversely, studying the social function of art and the emergence of what he calls "visual ideologies" is, according to him, the subject-matter of art history. He claims that it is wrong "to explain a painting by means of its producer's personality, but it is also wrong to refuse to make use of information about the artist if it can throw light on the conditions in which he was working" (1973: 38). The artist's monograph can function as long as it contributes to elucidate the political and ideological class struggle during their period, by studying the artist's cultural and sociohistorical conditions and how artists mediated and transformed those conditions (1973: 23, 36).

A good example of a social historical take on monographs is the monograph on the French artist Gustave Courbet (1819–1877) by the art historian T.J. Clark (b. 1943). Even when he does not mention Hadjinicolaou in his book, it follows the same rationale. According to Clark, works of art should not be studied in isolation but their historical significance must be understood in relation to their production and reception. The artist must be seen as the medium of internal and external forces that intersect personality, visual culture and the social realm (1973: 12). When discussing the political significance of Courbet's painting *Burial at Ornans*, which was exhibited in the Paris Salon of 1851, Clark stresses how this painting irritated the Parisian bourgeoisie because it challenged their mythical past in the countryside. This work depicts workers alongside the bourgeoisie of provincial towns, including a political reflection through its chosen theme – class inequality – and its visual qualities – a large format typical of historical painting to portray popular themes (1973: 10, 80–85). Similar to monographs within the Vasarian tradition, this monograph delves into the interaction between individual and historical circumstances, and between the works and the world at large. The main differences are that Clark's interpretation reveals the complex dynamics of the creation, mediation and reception of some of Courbet's paintings and focuses on a short period of time, the Second French Republic (1848–1851). His analysis scrutinizes both the artist and the historical context, deemed on a par.

Structuralism continued questioning art history's anthropocentrism in favour of a supraindividual vision. If social history looked at the reception of art as a necessary complement for production, Roland Barthes totally focused on reception as the only important question, denying the relevance of authorship and its attributes, that is, intentions, expression, experience and biography (Fernie 1995: 19). Barthes emphasized that language is a system – or structure – that pre-exists the individual speaker: communication, therefore, always employs pre-existing concepts, patterns and conventions. Barthes argued that "it is language which speaks, not the author; to write is ... to reach the point where only language acts, 'performs,' and not 'me'" (1967: 143). This idea is in stark contrast to the emphasis on the artistic genius as the centre of cultural production and is part of a larger structuralist rejection of the humanist autonomous, thinking, coherent, integrated, human subject – that had already been questioned by psychoanalysis.

For structuralists then, the scholar's primary goal becomes the unveiling of possible meanings rather than uncovering the artist's intentions (Guercio 2006: 259). In this spirit, Barthes dramatically declared that "the birth of the reader must be at the cost of the death of the Author" (Barthes 1967: 148). According to him, the author does not endow the text. Instead, the work of art is an artefact that brings together any number of codes available in the artist's culture. As articulated by Barthes, Julia Kristeva (b. 1941) and others, the concept of intertextuality reminds us that each text exists in relation to other texts, to other cultural expressions and that texts owe more to other texts than to their own makers.

In questioning the same anthropocentric perspective on authorship, the philosopher Michel Foucault (1926–1984) provided a reinterpretation of the structuralist paradigm, challenging the very notion of authorship. His essay titled "What Is an Author?" (1969) argues that the "author-function"

> is not formed spontaneously through the simple attribution of a discourse to an individual. He explores the conditions that enable authorship and approaches this concept not as a matter of "who" but rather as a "what" that refers to the objective forces that give rise to the concept of an author. Authorship results from a complex operation whose purpose is to construct the rational entity we call an author.
>
> (Foucault 1969: 326)

According to Foucault, it is not the revelation of an individual's personality, but rather a cultural construct that originated in the Renaissance and reached its zenith during the early nineteenth century. Foucault argues for a culture where discourses emerge and become public anonymously without relying on the function of an author (Guercio 2006: 355).

The artists' monographs have been nonetheless defended by postcolonial and feminist authors, who both participated and differed from the structuralist deconstruction of the subject. The literary theorist Gayatri Chakravorty Spivak (b. 1942) wrote the essay "Can the Subaltern Speak?" in 1988 (Figure 6.1). The term "subalterns" refers to groups of people who in society are marginalized and oppressed, such as women, the poor, ethnic minorities and colonial subjects. These groups have no political power and are often ignored or oppressed by the dominant power structures and prevailing ideologies of society. Chakravorty Spivak emphasizes that not only are these groups physically oppressed, but also their voices and experiences are often ignored or distorted by those who have the power to speak and tell what the truth is. Therefore, the concept of subalternity revolves around how these groups can articulate their own experiences and make their own voices be heard rather than reduced to silence. She further argues that this means that we must be aware of the constraints placed on the subaltern and strive to create space for their voices to be heard and recognized (1988: 271–315).

Agreeing with Chakravorty Spivak in the necessity to create spaces to recover "hidden stories," the feminist art historians Norma Broude and Mary D. Garrard questioned if Barthes' and Foucault's deconstruction of authorship benefitted female artists. This disempowerment of artists to the advantage of the audiences took away the possibility of granting

Figure 6.1 Literary theorist and critic Gayatri Chakravorty Spivak during her talk with author Lakshmi Subramanian, titled as "Spivak Moving," on the first day of Tata Steel Kolkata Literary Meet 2023, at Victoria Memorial Hall in Kolkata on January 21, 2023. Photo by Sankhadeep Banerjee/NurPhoto via Getty Images

recognition to women artists. They argued for a new paradigm that would allow women artists to be assessed in their own right and not within a patriarchal discourse that had been created with male artists in mind and in which female artists had difficulties fitting in (Broude and Garrard 2018 [1992]: 17).

Implementation: Is the heroic approach so heroic?

There are countless examples of designers' monographs within design scholarship. Monographs have investigated the work of one single designer such as Brooks Stevens (1911–1995; Adamson 2005) or structured publications on a whole industry such as *Great Fashion Designers* (Polan and Tredre 2009). This approach has also been used to illuminate the work of designers that were not included in the canon such as Clara Porset (1895–1981) (Salinas and Mallet 2006) or to illuminate less-known periods of consecrated designers such as in the article *Dior before Dior* (Font 2011; Figures 6.2 and 6.3). Despite this proliferation of examples, monographs have been a contested methodology within design scholarship.

Figure 6.2 Portrait of Clara Porset. Archivo Clara Porset Dumas – Archivo Clara Porset
Dumas, Centro de Investigaciones de Diseño Industrial (FA-UNAM)

In 1987, Hazel Conway criticized the "heroic approach," which she
identifies as a focus on the "rare and expensive and the major works of
major designers in any period: Adam, Wedgwood, Aalto, Dior" (1987: 7).
She argues that even when these designers are important, there are other
ways to study design more in syntony with historical studies which do not
necessarily deal with "kings and queens and battles and conquests" (1987:
7). Conway's alternative is to concentrate on how design operates in daily
life and far from museums and design auctions. In terms of methodology,
she proposes the use of oral history to keep the memories of users and
other "hidden from history" participants, such as factory operators and
women designers (1987: 7–8).

Strongly influenced by Marxist history in general and by Hadjinicolaou in
particular, John A. Walker (1989) noted that the methods that had been
implemented to date for the analysis of design came from the disciplines of
art and architecture history wherein the study of famous artists and masterpieces was common. Like Conway, he observes that both designers and
designed objects of high aesthetic quality became the central research topic
for design scholars (1989: 45). Walker objects to these kinds of monographs

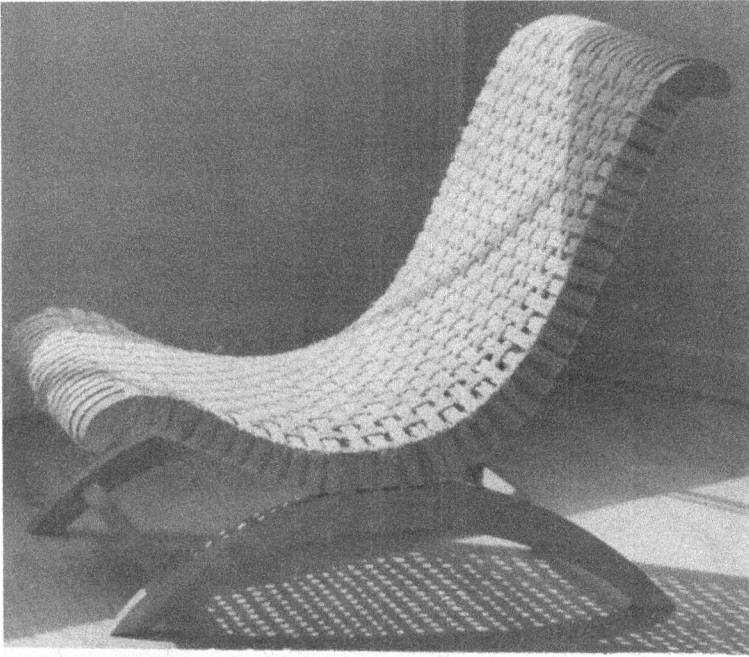

Figure 6.3 Clara Porset, *Butaque* (1957). Laminated wood and woven wicker. 73 × 65.6 × 84.9 cm. Archivo Clara Porset Dumas – Archivo Clara Porset Dumas, Centro de Investigaciones de Diseño Industrial (FA-UNAM)

arguing that they tend to be uncritical and that they do not provide a history of design, because they are mostly too narrow-focused on the designer to give attention to the numerous cross-linked relations taking place over time (1989: 46–47). Similarly to T.J. Clark, Walker therefore proposes to focus on production and consumption processes, incorporating thereby external factors that condition the creative freedom of designers (Walker 1989: 59).

Two decades after Walker's publication, Grace Lees-Maffei shared Conway's and Walker's critique on the heroic approach, again identifying this bias with an art historical tradition. She states that the book *Pioneers of Modern Design* (1936) by the art historian Nikolaus Pevsner set the tendency to study the work of great individual designers, producers or products, an art historical method that Lees-Maffei perceived as outdated (2009: 354). She argues for Walker's production–consumption model, albeit adding more emphasis on the mediation stage of the model that was underdeveloped in Walker's version (2009: 360). This mediation stage includes, for example, how design has been presented, visually and in text by all kinds of media like magazines, books, newspapers, essays, but also shops, the Internet, galleries and museums (2009: 365). Lees-Maffei concludes her argument by noting that a successful future of design history should integrate object-based analysis with an analysis of socio-historical contexts (2009: 373).

Kjetil Fallan took his critique on the existing and previous methods of design research yet a step further in his book *Design History: Understanding Theory and Method* (2010). He claims that since the first surveys of design history appeared in the late 1980s the discipline grew remarkably, but theory and methodology still need development. Despite criticism of the art historical approach within the field of design history, Fallan claims that the influence of traditional research methods from art history still remains. He emphasized design is not art and should therefore not be considered part of or equivalent to art history. Within the realm of high design – elitist, exclusive design – art and design touch, but still the economic frameworks from the two disciplines differ (2010: 15).

These accounts identify designers' monographs as part of an art historical approach to design identified as biased and outdated. As discussed earlier, art history has developed different angles to creating artists' monographs, which may not necessarily centre around the concept of genius but rather emphasize contextual factors. While some artists' monographs may exhibit a celebratory bias towards the genius artist, this is not an inherent characteristic of all monographs. When reformulated from a social history perspective, for example, they offer the possibility to link the designer to their context. Additionally, as defended in postcolonial and feminist accounts, monographs offer the possibility to reconfigure and criticise the existing canon.

The critique directed towards designers' monographs becomes increasingly debatable when considering emerging design historiographies. Dina Comisarenco expresses her frustration when teaching design history at the Campus Mexico City of the Monterrey Institute of Technology and Higher Education. She argues that the curriculum dictated by the educational institution was too dependent on foreign names and did not include a single Mexican designer, let alone a single Mexican woman designer – not even Clara Porset (2020: 75). Remarkably, this happened after Oscar Salinas' book *Historia del Diseño Industrial* [History of Industrial Design] was published in 1992 and included a chapter on Mexican design in which Porset was mentioned.

Comisarenco decided to write her own version of the history of industrial design in Mexico, far from established narratives about the influence of European design schools and the modern movement as the origin of the profession. For that, she uses the tools of art history, which, according to her, "does not involve a traditional approach that hierarchises works according to their authors and their aesthetic and temporal value, but rather an interdisciplinary approach that takes into account the complexities of cultural work" and allowed her to cover the economic, political and creative contexts of different times and places "without neglecting the material, formal and functional characteristics of industrial design" (2020: 76). The product of this endeavour was Comisarenco's book *Diseño industrial mexicano e internacional. Memoria y futuro* [Mexican and International Industrial Design. Memory and Future] (2006). In this book the author rescues the work of women designers but also works of an anonymous nature, in her words "not considered by more conservative historiographical approaches" (2020: 76).

This vision coincides with the words of Marina Garone when analysing the historiography of design in Mexico. She recognizes that numerous monographic studies have been conducted, which carry the inherent danger of establishing a canon that overlooks failures and challenges. Nevertheless, the criticisms towards monographs have encouraged the gradual appearance of texts that take reception into account. Garone claims that if the goal is to construct a social history of design, many monographs are needed that allow "to move from an individual narrative to a more collective and synchronic one" (2010: 434). Monographs can present biases as limitations, but as Garone says, can also form a solid basis to construct historiographies that otherwise lack strong foundations.

Challenges: Design for social innovation

Within the field of design, the question of authorship is intricate. Generally speaking, design is the product of a dialogue between the commissioner, the manufacturer and the designer. Moreover, designers have worked less as isolated individuals and more frequently as organized teams, even as members of larger design consultancies. In recent times, the advent of digitalization has posed challenges to conventional understandings of authorship in design. Examples include open-source design and the utilization of artificial intelligence. Additionally, co-creation processes, such as social design and design for social innovation, serve as notable illustrations in this context. Do they make the designer's monograph obsolete?

Take for example, design for social innovation, a design practice that focuses on people's needs and issues in the world and that has been referred to in multifarious ways: design for good, design for needs, humanitarian design, socially responsible design, public-interest design, social impact design and transformation design. This practice reacts against a conception of design as a product of neoliberalism that defines the individual subject primarily as a consumer with the power to make choices. It argues on the contrary for reconsidering the agency and participation of designers in communal modes of resistance and power, to even counter corporations and governments (Forlano 2017: 17–18).

Since 2015, the term design for social innovation has expanded as a result of the publication of Ezio Manzini's book *Design, When Everybody Designs: An Introduction to Design for Social Innovation*. Manzini believes that in order to solve social issues or manage social change, individuals should start with their everyday lives (re)discovering the power of collaboration. This (re) discovery will give rise to new forms of organization, that include collaborative organization, and new artefacts on which they base enabling solutions. In this sense, design for social innovation denotes a way to create social change from the perspective of design (Manzini 2015: 2). The influence of cross-disciplinarity on design for social innovation is significant. Design frequently engages with various other disciplines, including policy and planning, community development, sociology, anthropology, human geography and development studies. In these instances, design's material practices play a crucial role in translating and showcasing the knowledge and contributions from these diverse fields (Armstrong et al. 2014: 20).

An example of a social design office is T+HUIS, based in the Netherlands, founded in 2006 by three designers: Dennis Meulenbroeks, Heather Daam and Aike Heuvelink. One of their projects is the development of the Oud Woensel neighbourhood in Eindhoven. This T+HUIS project applies design thinking for community and education, aiming at improving the social cohesion in this neighbourhood by co-creating systems, with a focus on children and students reaching their potential. The project began in 2006 and has been developed in collaboration with local people, volunteers, organizations and children as the core of their social design process (T+HUIS Website 2023)

The main goal of T+HUIS is to redesign the neighbourhood system to serve the needs of the community. Apart from the three design professionals, the team of T+HUIS involves students, children and volunteers providing a multidisciplinary approach. Along with the team, the project is backed up by a board of people from different backgrounds. They provide knowledge in different areas, such as taxes, coaching, finances, communication and the social sector. The T+HUIS team uses design to produce solutions from a user point of view, in co-creation with their target group (T+HUIS Website 2023).

The authorship of this project resides in collaboration rather than in the mind of only one individual. The participation of the designers is as important as the contribution from the other stakeholders resulting in specific authorship as a product of co-design. To better understand this process, the concept of "dialogue" elaborated by the philosopher Mikhail Bakhtin (1895–1975) can be helpful. It goes beyond the traditional understanding of a conversation between two or more individuals and encompasses a broader sense of communication in verbal communication, written texts and cultural practices (1981[1934–41]: 271). In this framework, language exists both as "unitary language," a standardized language norm, and at the same time as heteroglossia – a diverse and dynamic collection of different meanings and usages, shaped by the social, cultural and historical factors (1981[1934–41]: 425).

Bakhtin's dialogue has been used not only to understand intersubjective communication but also the self. The theory of the "dialogical self" understands one's self as not a fixed or stable entity, but rather a complex, multifaceted and dynamic system of different "selves" that interact with each other in a continuous process of dialogue. It was developed by the psychologist Hubert Hermans in the 1990s and builds on two premises; the self-narratives are spatially structured, and the self is multivoiced (Hermans and Dimaggio 2004).

In essence, when applied to design for social innovation, the concept of the "dialogical self" suggests that the mechanisms behind co-design closely resemble those of subjectivity. Consequently, design for social innovation is not inherently more conceptually complex than individual authorship; both entail similar challenges. For instance, when an individual recounts a story, various "voices" contribute from specific positions in time and space, engaging in a dialogue that involves interchange, restructuring and development of the narrative (Hermans and Dimaggio 2004: 1). In this regard, others impact one's multivoicedness. The others' voices do not only exist as external, rather, in the engagement process, the self internalizes others' voices, through quoting, paraphrasing or concerning themselves with what others think or say (Aveling et al. 2015: 671).

The theory and concept of multivoicedness has been adapted by a range of academic disciplines to identify multiple identities of subjects in layered social contexts, such as refugees, immigrants and teachers (Badia and Liesa 2022; Bergset and Ulvik 2021; Kay et al. 2021). The qualitative approach of analysing multivoicedness offers a three-step method for analysing the "multi-voiced self": Identifying the voices of "I-Positions" within the Self's talk (or text), identifying the voices of "inner-Others," and examining the dialogue and relationships between the different voices (Aveling et al. 2015: 670). An "I-Position" is the position from where the self speaks, which is cultivated in a particular set of social relations and contexts in a person's life. "Inner-Others" are those in opposition to which the self defines itself, but those that nevertheless impact its identification by appearing in the self's dialogue through direct and indirect quotes, or in the form of "echoes," that is, borrowed ideas (Aveling et al. 2015: 673).

To summarize, authorship within co-design involves recognizing the contributions of various voices that shape the process of co-creation. Interestingly, this parallels the workings of individual authorship in similar ways. The only difference is that in design for social innovation, multivoicedness is distributed among different individuals. Looking through the prism of multivoicedness avoids the hierarchy between the designer and the rest. Conversely, it takes a horizontal perspective that integrates the different participants.

Multivoicedness paradoxically engages thereby with both structuralist positions – that question the very idea of authorship – and with postcolonial and feminist positions – that defend this idea, arguing for creating an inclusive context in which "subaltern" voices can be recorded and heard. Genius is not the only way of characterizing authors. Acknowledging authorship in sophisticated ways does not necessarily silence the agency of individuals and groups but evidences their complexity. Substituting the monolithic subject by a multiplicity of agencies contributes to understand both individual and collective authorship.

7   Oral history
Memories of the past and the present

Oral history is based on interviewing people. Gaining momentum in the second half of the twentieth century, it has evolved from a method that fills the gaps left by written sources to a method that problematizes how people remember. Therefore, scholarship from psychology, the social sciences and linguistics came to enrich the insights of oral historians. Within design scholarship, oral history has been used to generate new sources regarding understudied aspects, ranging from design and production to consumption and use. The visual and material character of design has benefitted from video oral history, demonstrating the importance of non-verbal communication. How to integrate environments, objects and actions in their recordings is a challenge for oral history that already had included the notation of gestures, silence and facial expressions that accompany the verbal discourse.

Origin: Documenting life

In 1996, historian Ronald J. Grele defined oral history as "the interviewing of eye-witness participants in the events of the past for the purposes of historical reconstruction," firmly situating it within the discipline of history (Perks and Thomson 2016[1998]: ix). However, oral history has undergone a broadening of its scope and integration into various disciplines. This transformation is reflected in the 2021 definition provided by social scientists Thalia M. Mulvihill and Raji Swaminathan, who characterized oral history as drawing from "educational studies, history, indigenous studies, sociology, anthropology, ethnic studies, women's studies, and youth studies." It has evolved into an "umbrella term that integrates history, life history methods, and testimony accounts" (Mulvihill and Swaminathan 2021: 4). Consequently, the incorporation of theoretical tools from diverse disciplines has enriched the approach beyond a purely historical perspective, and the methods of gathering information are now based on, but not confined to, traditional interview techniques.

An interview is quite a well-known format. Nevertheless, every interview is unique as is its purpose. Interviews for oral history research must adhere to specific characteristics that render them suitable for academic research. In this

DOI: 10.4324/9781003147282-9

context, the interview serves as the central method for collecting information, necessitating the involvement of both an interviewer and an interviewee. The interaction between the two occurs at a specific location over a limited number of sessions, focusing on a firsthand account of a particular event experienced by the interviewee. Subsequently, the interview is recorded and later transcribed by the interviewer. The quality of the research often depends on the interview, which serves as a means to generate firsthand sources. Failing to establish a sense of trust with interviewees can potentially result in the loss of crucial testimonies, compromising the integrity of the research (Abrams 2010: 9).

Traditionally, oral history has been occupied with gathering content that cannot be found in written sources. In that sense, oral history is both a way of generating own sources and a way of interpreting those sources. As a method to generate information, oral history makes use of interviews which can be stored in oral history archives whereby they not only allow for current research but also for future research (Ritchie 2015[2002]: 34). Hereby, interviews need to be interpreted as any other data by being tested against other evidence and by considering how narratives are constructed and how memory works (Ritchie 2015[2002]: 9). The strict scheme of an interview as a dialogue between researcher and respondent has remained basically the same even in times of digital technologies but has unquestionably become more sophisticated. Technical developments have made that the interview might incorporate other ways of recording, such as filming, and other ways of being disseminated, such as podcasts (Boyd and Larson 2014: 6).

There is no agreement about when exactly the use of interviews in historical studies became oral history. Many historians consider oral history an ancient practice, since historians have studied and documented important events through the use of eye-witness accounts since antiquity. Alongside, the interview has been used as a method by journalists since the middle of the nineteenth century, and by social researchers since at least the 1900s (Perks and Thomson 2016[1998]: 101). The oral source lost its significance for historians, however, under the influence of Leopold von Ranke (1795–1886), when archival research and documents were preferred for the study and writing of history (Ritchie 2015[2002]: 2–3).

Contrary to Rankean textual source criticism, African historiography has been largely based on oral transmission. One example is *The History of the Gold Coast and Ashanti* (finished in 1889 and published in 1895), by the Ghanaian historian Carl Christian Reindorf (1834–1917), who interviewed more than 200 men and women, describing the evolution and fall of the Ashanti Empire in the nineteenth century. Similarly, *The History of the Yorubas* that was finished in 1897 by the historian from Sierra Leone, Samuel Johnson (1846–1901) and re-compiled and published by his brother in 1921. Based mainly on oral tradition, Johnson wrote a history of the Oyo Empire up to and including the British Protectorate on the basis of the orally transmitted history of the Yoruba that encompassed complete genealogies and chronicles. The preference for oral history principles does not correspond to a lack of written sources in Africa but to the prestige of oral transmission in preserving knowledge about the past (Bod 2013: 269–270).

The significance attributed to oral history in Africa captured the attention of the first Western anthropologists who visited the continent. This triggered a scholarly discourse in Europe and the United States regarding the value of "oral history" and "life histories," occurring during a period when the dominant Rankean paradigm favoured textual sources. The historian Rens Bod suggests that the discovery of oral history, particularly in Africa, may have been the catalyst for the interest in oral history, as seen, for instance, among the Chicago school of sociologists in the 1930s (Bod 2022: 212).

It was only with the widespread, availability and affordability of tape recording after the Second World War that interviews could be preserved in their original form. This technological shift eliminated the dependence on transcriptions and led to a resurgence in the popularity of oral sources within the discipline of history (Perks and Thomson 2016[1998]: 1; Boyd and Larson 2014: 2). The rise of oral history took on different forms in different places. In the United States, the historian Allan Nevins (1890–1971) organized an oral history project at Columbia University in New York in 1948. The emphasis was on stories from white male elites, which represented the general interest of oral historians in the United States at the time. Meanwhile, in the first oral history projects in Britain during the 1950s and 1960s, there was much more interest in the stories of the working classes. This direction coincided with the goal of social historians in the 1960s to get to a "history from below" (Perks and Thomson 2016[1998]: 1).

By the late 1970s, oral history had become a widely adopted method among historians globally. Historian Paul Thompson (b. 1935), one of the founders of the British Oral History Society in the 1970s, played a pivotal role in establishing an international oral history movement. He articulated the primary reasons for using and valuing oral history that continue to be embraced today: it brings to light stories and experiences that might otherwise be overlooked and actively involves ordinary individuals in crafting their own histories (Perks and Thomson 2016[1998]: 2). In 1979, oral historian Alessandro Portelli (b. 1942) developed methodological tools for oral history, aiming to interpret interviews effectively and striving to position oral history as a distinct category within the discipline of history – both as a practice and a source – distinguished in content from other methods of historical inquiry (Abrams 2010: 18).

Development: Compromise and memory

Digging into what has been untold, motivates oral historians to reveal both the missing information and the power relations below these omissions (Ritchie 2015[2002]: 3, 10). Especially in the period from the 1960s to the late 1980s, oral history challenged conventional scholarship by showing its potential to empower political and social movements and marginalized groups. Oral historians focused on working-class communities, the women's movement and indigenous peoples, aiming to have an effect on social and political change with their research (Abrams 2010: 153; Perks and Thomson 2016[1998]: 183; Ritchie 2015[2002]: 19, 127). Thereby, they were prompted to reconsider the influence of their own presence during the data collection process and to reflect on their own motivations. While early oral historians viewed themselves as impartial collectors of data, a later perspective emerged wherein the interview was seen as a collaborative effort – a content-creation process where the interviewer plays an active role alongside the interviewee (Perks and Thomson 2016[1998]: 3, 360–361).

Accordingly, historians reached out to other disciplines – such as psychology, sociology, anthropology and linguistics – to learn about preparing, conducting and interpreting interviews. Essentially, interviews involve memory, whose mechanisms are studied in **psychology**. Furthermore, interviews are based on the construction of individual identities in relation to collective identities and culture at large, which is the study object of **social scientists** and **anthropologists**. Finally, interviews are discourse and require the expertise of **linguists** to conceptualize them as such (Perks and Thomson 2016[1998]: 184; Ritchie 2015[2002]: 19). The subsequent paragraphs explore the influences of these disciplines on oral history.

To comprehend the mechanisms of memory, historians turned to insights from **psychology**, revealing that individuals recall only those things they have consciously recorded or encoded at the moment of the experience. In autobiographical narratives, such as life histories, individuals employ memories in various ways: to elucidate an event for others, to demonstrate their role in an event, as a guide for subsequent behavior and as a source of reassurance. Essentially, people remember what holds importance for them. Hence, the excellence, liveliness and profoundness of memories rely on the encoding that occurred at the time and the conditions in which the remembering occurs (Abrams 2010: 83). Moreover, what holds significance for an individual may evolve over time, leading to changes in both what is remembered and how it is remembered (Abrams 2010: 103).

Generally, recent memories tend to be more detailed, emphasizing the intricacies of the "how" and "what," making these narratives richer in detail than usual (Ritchie 2015[2002]: 126–127). There is little evidence to suggest that individuals typically misremember events or experiences, and certainly not intentionally or consciously. Even age does not seem to impact the accuracy of long-term memory significantly. Memories from the past are influenced by present circumstances, and their reconstruction relies on the evolution of one's self. According to the oral historian Lynn Abrams, testimonies on sensitive topics like abortion or voting behaviour indicated that inaccuracies in recollection could be attributed to an individual's present beliefs. People often interpret the past through the lens of their current attitudes (Abrams 2010: 85–86).

Despite drawing from psychology, oral history shares similarities with, yet differs from, psychology-related fields such as memory studies or psychother- apy. Memory studies primarily focus on understanding how memory func- tions, delving into the social and cultural processes influencing recollection. Oral historians, on the other hand, are more concerned with how memory impacts the communication of factual information in order to complement interview data with other forms of evidence (Perks and Thomson 2016[1998]: 269). Additionally, memory studies encompass both oral and written forms of self-representation, ranging from autobiographies to blogging, whereas oral historians exclusively focus on oral testimonies (Ritchie 2015[2002]: 126). In their turn, psychotherapists aim to identify impediments to an individual's memory and, through analysis, seek a remedy. Oral historians seek to detect how individuals may suppress specific memories, but their objective is to construct a historical narrative rather than provide a solution to a psycholo- gical condition (Abrams 2010: 105).

Memories are conditioned by current dominant visions of the past and in the connection between individual and collective identity. Memory is not just about the individual; it is also about the community, the collective and the nation. For this, scholarship from **sociology and anthropology** is relevant for oral historians.

Dominant narratives of the past are understood under the terms of collec- tive and public memory. The term "collective memory" was coined by the sociologist Maurice Halbwachs (1877–1945) in his book *On Collective Memory* published in 1950 and became an all-encompassing category that covered "folk history," "popular history" and even "myth." It refers to the shared stories remembered by individuals within the same group. According to Halbwachs, the purpose of memory is to unify social groups, implying that commonly agreed-upon memories are likely to dominate, while alternative ones receive little recognition and consequently diminish (Abrams 2010: 95– 96; Ritchie 2015[2002]: 22).

Collective memory frequently transforms into what is termed official or public memory, denoting how events or experiences are publicly commemo- rated or memorialized, thereby endorsing a specific version of the past. Offi- cial memory often presents a simplified rendition of history, often aligning with a patriotic stance. It is endorsed by the State and sometimes conveyed through media presentations, manifesting in commemorations such as par- ades, reunions, reenactments, celebrations or through landmarks, monuments, museum exhibits, or popular histories like school textbooks and television series. As this occurs, the tension between individual and collective memory can intensify (Abrams 2010: 98, 101).

Oral historians regularly encounter cases in which individual memories diverge from collective patterns (Abrams 2010: 99; Ritchie 2015[2002]: 22). They must be aware of a community's collective beliefs but strive to move beyond public memory to explore the personal experiences of those they interview (Ritchie 2015[2002]: 21). Regarding this, the historian Anna Green warns that the cultural context should not be disproportionally emphasized over individual remembering. She objects to the rigid deployment of cultural, social and psychoanalytic theories in a "culturally determinist" way, thereby reinforcing the notion that individuals' memories conform "to dominant cultural scripts or unconscious psychic templates" (Green in Abrams 2010: 100). Abrams highlights an example from her oral history project, focusing on women's experiences from the 1950s to the 1970s. Many female interviewees identified the miniskirt as a significant symbol of change. While these women indeed wore this garment, the oral historian should bear in mind that the miniskirt is a recurring symbol in public representations of that era. The personal memories of these women were influenced by a collective memory of the period (Abrams 2010: 79).

The main differences between sociologists and oral historians is that social scientists conduct interviews to link individual experiences with larger cultural and structural issues. They often use quantitative research, mostly standard questionnaires from which they could generalize. Social scientists may also take a series of shorter interviews with members of a group in a particular community or environment, such as workers on a shop floor. Oral historians call these "episodic" interviews. Oral historians are more interested in life histories, which usually means selecting fewer interviewees and devoting more time, and multiple interview sessions, to each one (Ritchie 2015[2002]: 23, 27).

Regarding anthropologists, they use interviewing to understand different cultures from the perspectives of those within the culture. They use rather qualitative, "field-oriented" techniques, mostly participant observation. Researchers may not even take notes in the presence of those they are studying, waiting to write their notes later from memory. Unlike historians, who seek concrete evidence of what actually happened and document it as fully as possible (Ritchie 2015[2002]: 24, 123). Anthropologists are more concerned with recognizing identifiable patterns in the way people shape their narrative and are often less interested in the verification of facts, seeing folktales and folklore as no less legitimate than other stories. Oral historians concentrate on recording the personal experiences of the interviewee (Ritchie 2015[2002]: 23). Despite their differences, the combination of the methods from history, sociology and anthropology led to the creation of cooperative, interdisciplinary oral history initiatives focused on community, racial, ethnic and migration themes (Ritchie 2015[2002]: 24).

The third significant influence on oral history has originated from **linguistics**. As deconstructionists asserted that nothing exists outside the text, historians conceived texts essentially as constructions of reality. From this perspective, oral sources are equally reliable as printed sources (Ritchie 2015 [2002]: 13). Similar to historians working with archival evidence, oral historians acknowledge that interviews represent interpretations of past events, influenced by the memories of interviewees and their attempts to respond to the historians' inquiries. An interview reflects what individuals assert happened, and their recollections and statements are subject to scrutiny and analysis. Narrative theory delves into the interplay between language and thought, conceptualizing an interview as a complex document shaped through the negotiation and collaboration between the interviewer and interviewee, resulting in the creation of a textual representation (Ritchie 2015[2002]: 124).

Regarding the debate sketched above on the interdependence of individual and collective memory, linguists offer their own perspectives. Linguists will often be more concerned with the manner of telling a story than its substance. Historians keep a transcript that reproduced the words said and how they were said, but they focus on the content (Ritchie 2015[2002]: 24). The oral historian Graham Smith advocates the analysis of individual memory as the product of an active engagement with social processes, in particular the process of talking, reconstructing experiences with others and sharing a language to recollect past experiences (Abrams 2010: 102).

Although oral historians strive for objectivity by verifying information when possible, there has been an increasing recognition of the subjective nature of memory, prompting a shift towards studying this subjectivity (Ritchie 2015[2002]: 124). The fragility of memory is seen more as an opportunity than a problem for oral historians, who are now interested in whether interviewees can recall events and experiences significant to them rather than focusing solely on the quality of their memory (Abrams 2010: 79, 103; Mulvihill and Swaminathan 2021: 9–10).

Implementation: The relevance of the visual

One of the main uses of oral history for design historians has been the creation of alternative sources in absence of printed sources. There is an abundance of archives in creative disciplines like architecture, urbanism or the visual arts since they are part of bureaucratic processes that need to be recorded or because they are socially valued and their archives are considered worth being preserved. Conversely, design has less of a tradition of generating archival material because its activities are less regulated by the State and its practice less renowned. Two key publications edited by Linda Sandino reflect on the implementation of oral history within design scholarship: a special issue of the *Journal of Design History* (2006) and the reader *Oral History in the Visual Arts,* edited by Sandino and Matthew Partington in 2013 (2013: 2).

Sandino notes that artists, designers, art- and design historians use the interview in three main ways in their practice: as creative material, as a historical source on art or design or as a means to investigate the way identities are produced in the art world (Sandino and Partington 2013: 1). The last two are the most widely used within design scholarship and coincide with the general uses of oral history mentioned above (Ritchie 2015[2002]: 3). Sandino notices that interviews started to increasingly be used as a result of a paradigm shift in design history, that moved from the study of production to the study of the mediation and consumption of designed products. She warns that even when interviews are indeed increasingly being used in the study of artefacts, oral history is a study of people and their positions in the contexts of the past or present (2006: 275).

Generating own sources has been pivotal when approaching specific topics within design scholarship. Brian Donnely's exploration of graphic design in Canada (2006) provides an example of this. Donnely argues that his project can be seen as an "elite" oral history, as design is a well-established profession, and the individuals he studied are not part of a marginalized or oppressed group. Paradoxically, the lack of sources poses a significant challenge to conducting a thorough study on this subject. The history of this field has not been thoroughly archived or extensively researched, leading to a situation where the majority of knowledge and materials are in the possession of individual practitioners (Donnely 2006: 288).

For the same reasons but due to a different situation, John Clarke conducted (2013) oral history research from 1986 to 1991 into Tibetan metalwork (Figure 7.1). There was limited (indigenous) written knowledge available on the subject due to both a lack of tradition of recording these practices in print and with a conflictive context. Clarke, at the time curator of the Himalayan collection of the Victoria and Albert Museum, wanted to better understand the museum's collection of Tibetan metalwork before the Tibetan uprising of 1959. From that moment on, the Chinese government

Figure 7.1 A Tibetan student works with copper during a workshop at the Norbu-lingka Institute in the city of Dharamshala, India, which serves as the seat of the Tibetan government-in-exile. Chemo Pemba Dorje, one of Clarke's interviewees, served as the head of the metalworking workshops at this institute during the 1990s. Photo by Rebecca Conway/Getty Images

took over political power and the former social and political structures disappeared. With the help of interpreters, Clarke interviewed 35 craftsmen from different locations in and around Tibet about their work experience and the local metalwork traditions in general (2013: 105–107).

To complement the textual nature of the interview, visual materials were necessary, serving not only to evoke memories but also to gain a deeper understanding of these traditions. Clarke's primary interest in stylistic variations benefitted from presenting photographs of objects and inquiring about the style and origins of each piece during the interviews. This approach not only overcame language barriers but also prompted responses that a verbal explanation might not have elicited. Over the course of six years, Clarke revisited the region annually, engaging in multiple conversations with the craftsmen. He attributes his grounded stylistic analysis to the diverse range of interviewees scattered across a vast geographical area (2013: 111).

In both the Canadian and the Tibetan cases, oral history was used to uncover stories and knowledge that might otherwise be lost. Both cases were focused on issues of design and production. Studying consumption poses a major problem in finding written sources and has often been the focus of design historians using oral history. An example is Jo Turney's research (2004) on how amateur makers in Britain define design, craft and art. The emphasis in Turney's oral history research is on the relationship between the home-makers and the objects they create; focussing on needlecrafts, especially those made from kits and patterns. Turney interviews the makers in their homes. Importantly, she does not only report on what the interviewees say but also on how the environment looks and what role the home-crafted objects play in this living environment, adding an anthropological component necessary for her research. The home crafters clearly do not agree with the academic classification of home craft objects as marginalized, uncreative or as examples of bad taste, Turney writes (2004: 267). This also illustrates how, like various other oral history initiatives, oral history in design serves the purpose of empowering voices that have been overlooked.

With a similar focus on consumers, Liz Linthicum examines dress and disability groups (2006). If Turney's example deals with practices marginalized from an artistic canon, this case deals with groups affected by social exclusion. Linthicum deliberately employed oral history, recognizing the importance of sourcing information directly from individuals with personal experience of the subject (2006: 309). For example, through analysing the interviews, she realized that the most important element for the interviewees was the process of dressing rather than the "stylistic result" which is most often the topic when discussing clothing (2006: 312). As with Clarke's research into Tibetan metalwork, Linthicum also used non-verbal props in her interviews, more specifically a series of self-help books along with dressing tips for disabled and/or elderly people. Interestingly, these books did not only allow the interviewees to talk about new topics such as their political position in debates on disability rights, but they also illustrated how these books discriminated against their own target audience. Linthicum had to help with opening, holding or reading the book in five of the nine interviews (2006: 314). Linthicum acknowledges that her interpretation stems from a non-disabled perspective. Nevertheless, she argues that restricting oral history researchers to topics within their personal experience undermines any effort to explore another person's lifeworld and neglects the researcher's dedication to their work (2006: 315).

Jesse Adams Stein's use of oral history is present in her books *Hot Metal: Material Culture and Tangible Labour* (2016) and *Industrial Craft in Australia: Oral Histories of Creativity and Survival* (2021) that explore the relationship between design, industrial trades and working life. The first focuses on the labour and technology transitions experienced in the printing industry in the second half of the twentieth century. She researched the reactions that institutional photographs taken in a Governmental Printing Office between the 1950s and the 1980s unlocked among her repondents, discussing thereby the aestheticization of labour (2016: 25–48).

Adams Stein's second book explores further how digitization has impacted labour and skill in design and production of industrial patternmakers, who operate in the pre-production phase of the manufacturing supply chain, using engineering or design drawings to construct a three-dimensional form (a pattern), so that it can effectively produce a mould (2021: 7). In so doing, she examines the social and cultural impacts of late twentieth-century and early twenty-first-century technologies, such as computer numerically controlled (CNC) milling machines, additive manufacturing (3D printing) and CAD/CAM software (computer aided design/computer aided manufacturing). Adams Stein moves beyond a narrative of labour replaced by technology, highlighting the creative capacities of industrial craftspeople (2021: 5). Conducting interviews in the interviewees' homes allowed access to their workshops, introducing objects like tools and machinery into the conversation. Adams Stein notes the challenges of discussing objects during interviews, emphasizing the importance of documenting them through photographs when words alone fall short (2021: 22).

The digital humanities have significantly impacted the collection and dissemination of oral histories, with the Internet enabling unprecedented access to sound and video content. According to oral historians Douglas A. Boyd and Mary A. Larson, archives that once had hundreds of annual users now regularly reach thousands worldwide (2014: 4). Platforms like YouTube and SoundCloud offer rapid and free distribution of audio and video oral histories. Digital repository and content management systems provide robust infrastructure for housing oral histories in digital archives or libraries. Tools like OHMS (Oral History Metadata Synchronizer) enhance online access, linking text searches to corresponding moments in audio or video interviews. Mobile applications like Curatescape even offer a framework for users to experience oral histories not only in a particular moment but in specific locations as well (Boyd and Larson 2014: 4–5).

One example of the use of the Internet within design scholarship is the "Oral History: Design" project that Katarina Serulus and Eva Van Regenmortel developed for the Flanders Architecture Institute (Flanders Architecture Institute Website, 2023). It consists of seven video interviews with designers, specialists, a museum director and the director of a state-led institution for the promotion of design, taken between 2014 and 2015. The interviews are summarized in a 350-word description available on their website, which is useful to identify to what extent this interview can be relevant for the researcher. The interviews need to be requested via a form, since there are copyright and privacy issues involved. Once the request has been granted, the interview is accessible through Vimeo.

Another example is Zara Arshad's interviews with graphic designers from South Korea in her project "The Unheard Archive" (The Unheard Archive Website, 2023). This body of research, conducted between May and November 2019, focused particular attention on LGBTQ+ and women designers, those engaged or working with physically disabled groups, emerging designers and other underrepresented voices in design history (Figures 7.2 and 7.3). Every interview is briefly introduced with a description and transcripts have been deposited at the Asia Culture Center (ACC) in Gwangju, South Korea. Arshad states that she aimed to reconcile the imbalance of non-Western voices in design with this project on emerging female designers after conducting previous investigations on established male designers, many of whom were based in Seoul (Arshad 2021:123–130).

The advent of digital technologies presents extensive possibilities for gathering, organizing, and sharing interviews and projects. Although these technologies have addressed certain challenges related to access, preservation, contextualization and presentation, they also bring potential risks, such as heightened vulnerability for narrators, the risk of infrastructure becoming obsolete and various ethical concerns, particularly in the context of heritage collections (Boyd and Larson 2014: 4–5).

Challenges: Beyond orality

Sandino's assertion that oral history aims to comprehend individuals within the socio-historical context of the past or present underscores the crucial role of spoken language in defining humanity (2006: 275). However, oral history research within design scholarship frequently explores the interplay between individuals and visual elements, objects and environments. Numerous practices involved in creating meaning extend beyond verbal language, encompassing attitudes, gestures and actions. In the transcription of interviews, elements such as tone, pauses, moments of silence and facial expressions have been integral to the practice of oral history. Interviewees not only express themselves orally but accompany their testimonies continuously with non-verbal input.

Figure 7.2 Sunny Studio consists of Park Ji-sung and Park Chulhee. They were the designers behind the poster for the feminist candidate Shin Ji-ye, representing the Korean Green Party during the 2018 Seoul city government elections. The poster can be identified as the third one in the upper row, starting from the right. Photo by Ki Young/Shutterstock

Figure 7.3 Sunny Studio hosted a drag workshop as part of the 2017 Korea Queer Culture Festival in Seoul. They brought together individuals interested in learning about costume design and makeup, and subsequently, the participants joined the queer parade dressed in the outfits they had created during the workshop. Photo by Chung Sung-Jun/Getty Images

Oral historians recognize the constraints of relying solely on spoken communication and employ various strategies to address them. One common practice involves introducing visual materials or objects during interviews to stimulate memories. This methodological approach provides perspectives on how objects hold diverse meanings for different individuals, transcending the intentions of the designer or marketing narratives and challenging one-sided interpretations. Artefacts, in this context, serve as memory repositories that become activated through interaction with interviewees. While oral historians may be primarily concerned with the memories evoked, design scholars might be more intrigued by how these objects encapsulate meaning (see Moran and O'Brien 2014).

Furthermore, artefacts can reveal non-verbal information that is otherwise difficult to express, like in Adams Stein's research on patternmakers. The oral historian Brien R. Williams gives the example of inventors showing and handling objects they have created, pointing to and identifying their parts and explaining their functions (2011: 268). How to go beyond orality and to capture, store and disseminate non-verbal communication passes through the implementation of video oral history, which expanded in the mid-1990s when video cameras appeared that did not need special lighting and bulky equipment. Therefore, they were not as intrusive as their predecessors (Ritchie 2011: 10; Williams 2011: 273).

Matthew Partington (2006) uses video in the project "Ceramic Points of View" to study the way ceramic artists talk about and handle ceramic studio pots. Six ceramic artists were shown the same pots, which they were allowed to handle and touch. They were asked for an immediate response, so that the conversation was more about their knowledge and impressions of the pots rather than about personal memories – as is often the case in traditional oral history projects (2006: 336). For Partington, the use of video was important since it allowed analysis and experience of the connection between speech and body language, which he considers to be intertwined when makers are speaking of material objects (2006: 339). The importance of the visual to interpret the relation between words and movement is especially visible in the video recordings of potters Colin Pearson and Julian Stair. They both handle a specific pot in the same way, picking it up, and weighing it in their hands while talking about the heaviness of the pot. However, they are making opposite statements. Where Pearson dislikes the heaviness, considering it a flaw of craftsmanship, for Stair the weight positively adds to the experience of the pot (2006: 339). The combination of video and audio material allows for specific understandings and analysis of how speech and movement complement each other.

On her part, Catherine Jo Ishino's (2006) oral history project uses video differently. She takes video interviews with Chinese graphic designers and does not focus on the handling of objects, as Partington did, but analyses the interviewees' dress, body language and manner of talking which adds to her interpretation of the attitudes and positions of these Chinese designers in the global graphic design field (2006: 322–328). For example, she mentions how often the interviewees smiled, what type of clothing they were wearing, whether their talk was fast or slow, what language they spoke and their posture. She then connects these observations to the interviewees' status in the local graphic design community, their attitude towards global graphic design, and the generational differences between the interviewees.

There are some other possibilities in which oral history has gone beyond the oral, such as re-creations and enactments. Williams gives the example of an astronomer who was asked to demonstrate his observational techniques in daylight, when they normally take place in darkness. These re-creations can offer a large amount of information that otherwise might get lost but entail the risk of collecting historically inaccurate information. Anyway, as the video recording itself makes clear within what conditions the re-enactment took place, this will help to interpret the recording properly (2011: 274–275).

Furthermore, visual re-creations through drawings can help researchers to situate the memories spatially. Adams Stein notes that her interviewees recalled spatial memories about the interiors of the printing factory in which they worked. Without being asked, some interviewees felt compelled to draw, from memory, details of the factory. Memories of working at this factory are articulated in a manner that is thoroughly, and almost systematically, spatial. Within this spatial system, the former workers remember and reconstruct their own work zone in immense detail. She stresses that memories are not lofty, airy things that take place outside of space and three-dimensionality; their recollections are grounded, deeply connected to the embodied experience of the interior. The notion of a mnemonic spatial projection explores how the experience of memory is imbued in spatial information. The interiors of the factory worked both as a signifier and as a physical vessel, containing and symbolizing the institution to its employees' clients (2016: 54–55).

In her turn, Adams Stein started forming her own fragmented mental images of the factory building, which included details like hanging fluorescent lights, expansive glass windows and a regular pattern of load-bearing pillars. She observed a commonality in the spatial memories expressed by many oral history participants about their workplace. She explores how individuals can visually reconstruct their lifeworld in what the sociologist Radosław Poczy-kowski terms "graphic equivalents to oral history" (2016: 64). Adams Stein created her own drawings as a synthesis of oral histories and archival photographs, illustrating a method of consolidating stories into a spatial system – a visual representation of oral histories. In doing so, she compiles various anecdotal and historical details obtained from interviews and photographs. While her drawing represents a subjective interpretation of oral history narratives, it visually conveys the spatial context of many of the stories uncovered during her interviews. Additionally, it provides a more nuanced understanding of the history of the building and its interiors. Thus, the factory interiors serve as both a contextual aspect and a central focus of research (2016: 67).

As shown in the previous examples, oral history transcends mere reliance on spoken words, acknowledging that certain information might be lost in a purely textual transcription. Actions convey messages. Drawings add non-verbal information. Spaces place testimonials in relation to each other. Scholars have accepted correspondence, diaries and autobiographies as valid documentation, recognizing that their authors may exhibit biases or inaccuracies. Public figures may craft diaries with an eye towards eventual publication, shaping them to present themselves in the most favourable light. As any researcher can confirm, those who write letters or maintain diaries may not always address all the issues of interest to scholars. Moving beyond the textual realm does not imply a decrease in objectivity; rather, it involves a holistic approach to communication and memory.

8 Ethnography

Groups and individuals

In a contemporary landscape where design places greater emphasis on ideas and communication, ethnography becomes increasingly pertinent for design scholars. Ethnography, rooted in anthropology but widely utilized in disciplines such as sociology and psychology, is a qualitative research method. It involves a thorough exploration of specific cultural groups or communities through immersive research, shedding light on the nuances of human behaviour, beliefs and social interactions within their context. Consequently, it has proven valuable for comprehending the present and the recent. Moreover, ethnography has been used to challenge established assumptions by providing grounded insights into how users interact with objects. A notable manifestation of ethnography is auto-ethnography, wherein researchers turn the lens inward to examine their own experiences. Auto-ethnography incorporates the researcher's perspective into the analytical framework, facilitating an understanding of the narrative and narrator from a first-person viewpoint. This approach proves beneficial in establishing a connection between the reader and the research that cannot be achieved through an outsider's or third-person perspective.

Origins: Understanding culture

An investigation can be informed by different techniques such as close readings of artefacts or by studying written sources generated by others such as critical accounts published in periodicals or documents preserved in archives. Yet, there are investigations that require sources other than detailed observation and/or written sources. Take, for example, a research question that explores the conduct of users engaging with a particular artefact. This involves understanding their motivations, their interests, how they give meaning to that specific artefact and in which ways. In this case, oral history might also be insufficient, since researchers cannot rely just on testimonies. The only possibility left for researchers is to engage in a more immersive research experience to understand why people behave the way they do.

DOI: 10.4324/9781003147282-10

Often researchers need to observe what people do and talk to them. This is called ethnographic research which seeks to study the wide concept of culture on the basis of direct observation. Mostly implementing participant observation and interviews, ethnography offers in-depth analysis of a cultural reality. This method allows to glean understanding about people's lives or specific aspects thereof, guided by their own perspectives and within the framework of their actual circumstances. It goes beyond simple conversations and inquiries commonly employed in surveys and interviews, but involves an immersive learning process by observing participants, actively engaging in their daily activities, and posing questions that resonate with the nuances of their everyday encounters (O'Reilly 2012[2005]: 86).

Culture is the broadest ethnographic concept and it has been defined according to two main perspectives. From a materialist perspective, culture is the amalgamation of discernible behavioural patterns, customs and lifestyle of a social collective. Within this framework, culture emerges as a consequence of the group's interaction with its surroundings, spotlighting the interplay between human activities, societal dynamics and the tangible realm. Conversely, the ideational perspective, grounded in cognition, posits that culture entails the notions, convictions and understanding that distinguish a specific group. In essence, it embodies the intellectual output of that particular community (Fetterman 1998: 16). Both material and ideational perspectives are useful at different times in exploring fully how groups of people think and behave in their natural environment. The former focuses on lifestyle, or culture with a lowercase "c," and the latter on knowledge, or culture with a capital "C."

Routines and daily life might appear of little significance for scholarly exploration. Nevertheless, they possess pivotal value in understanding design and moreover prove complex to investigate. The philosopher Henri Lefebvre (1901–1991) defined the everyday as "the most universal and the most unique condition, the most social and the most individuated, the most obvious and the best hidden" (Lefebvre 1987: 9). This characterization is rooted in seemingly opposing terms and aligns with Ben Highmore's views, who sees "everyday life" as both quantitative and qualitative, containing commonplace actions, the very essence of routine. The everyday represents our immediate surroundings, the world we intimately encounter. Yet, within its quantifiable aspect lies the qualitative facet of everydayness. Everydayness can evoke confusion, pleasure and melancholy. Its distinct quality might even be its absence of distinct qualities, subtly unnoticeable, inconspicuous and unobtrusive (Highmore 2002: 1). In essence, everyday life is the broader category that encompasses the practical actions and routines, while everydayness focuses on the subjective and qualitative aspects that shape our perceptions and experiences of those routines. Because of its daily occurrence, the ordinary may appear devoid of significance; however, ethnography serves to unravel the complexity inherent within it.

To discern this complexity, ethnographers engage with participant observation and in-depth interviews. But how is the ethnographer's task different from just being there and asking questions? In participant observation, researchers engage in firsthand experience by immersing themselves within the community under study. This method entails living among the community members and actively participating in their daily activities. The sociologist Karen O'Reilly defines it as "not really a method on its own: it involves making notes, asking questions, doing interviews, collecting data, drawing up lists, constructing databases, being active in research." She concludes by noting that it "is never simply a matter of participating and observing" (O'Reilly 2012[2005]: 105). Through participant observation, researchers can gain a comprehensive and nuanced understanding of cultural practices, norms and values. By becoming a part of the community, researchers can better understand its traditions and social dynamics.

Along with participant observation, the other major technique is the in-depth interview, which provides an opportunity to gain deeper insights into individual experiences and perspectives. Participants share their stories, providing context for observed behaviours. What makes it academic is the systematic way of gathering information and that the action of interviewing is put at the service of a research question. O'Reilly notes that ethnographers make sense of the world as we do normally in our daily lives "and yet in a more directed, reflexive way," and that they are writing about and thinking about what they see and hear. She concludes that this reflexivity "is what makes ethnography different from simply being there" (O'Reilly 2012[2005]: 132).

Ethnography adopts a holistic perspective. Researchers aim to understand the totality of a culture rather than focusing solely on isolated aspects. This holistic approach recognizes the interconnectedness of various cultural elements, enabling the exploration of how they influence and shape each other. Therefore, the principle of long-term engagement is vital in ethnographic research, which involves extended periods of observation and interaction, often spanning months or even years. It allows researchers to witness seasonal changes, fluctuations in behaviour and the dynamics of social relationships, providing a comprehensive understanding of the culture's intricacies. Detailed field notes are maintained throughout the research. These notes capture observations, conversations, experiences and reflections. The aim is to create a comprehensive record of the researcher's experiences and interactions.

The anthropologist Bronislaw Malinowski is recognized for instigating a transformative change in the field of ethnography during the early twentieth century. In his investigations, he aimed to incorporate the perspective of the subjects under study and emphasize the cultural import of the actions he depicted. Before him, ethnographers made little attempt to represent the point of view of the people being observed; ethnography was conducted by outsiders providing a view of the actions of the people under study. The functional significance of an action was ignored and the observations simply described "objectively." To the extent of suggesting that researchers should deeply immerse themselves in the culture, Malinowski advocated for a shift from "they" to "we," blurring the lines between the observer and the observed (Naidoo 2012: 2). In other words, ethnography before Malinowski was etic, rather than emic.

An outsider's perspective is known as an etic viewpoint, while an insider's perspective is termed an emic viewpoint – representing the viewpoints of the individuals belonging to the culture under study. Holding a dual emic and etic perspective enables researchers to juxtapose their observations with the interpretations provided by the individuals being examined (Fetterman 1998: 18). To achieve this aim, ethnographers adopt a nonjudgemental stance towards reality, facilitating a more accurate understanding of cultural customs. Ethnography actively promotes cultural relativity, entailing the suspension of judgement and a pursuit to comprehend a culture from its internal dynamics, devoid of external norms or values (Fetterman 1998: 18). Throughout the research process, ethical considerations, including informed consent and confidentiality, are carefully managed. Sensitivity to participants' identities and cultural norms is of utmost importance.

In deductive research, the researcher forms a hypothesis based on existing knowledge or theory, which is then validated through real-world investigation and data collection. In contrast, O'Reilly contends that ethnography frequently embraces both iterative and inductive strategies. Rather than starting with specific testable hypotheses, the common practice involves beginning with open-ended questions, allowing for adaptability. However, careful initial planning and continuous adjustments remain crucial for the success of ethnographic research (2012[2005]: 48). While reviewing literature typically precedes research, within iterative–inductive research, this process necessitates continual revision as ethnography and analyses develop in parallel.

In conclusion, ethnography aims for a profound understanding of cultures and communities through immersive research. The researcher's active participation in the process led the anthropologists George Marcus and Michael Fischer to propose that ethnography can serve as a lens through which we can introspect about ourselves. They contend that through the study of others, researchers gain an opportunity to gain insight into their own identities, revealing that our ways are not fixed but rather shaped by circumstances and capable of change (1999[1986]: 138). According to them, a thorough analysis of other cultures constitutes a form of cultural critique that often reveals more about the researcher than the studied participants. They advocate that the real challenge in genuine cultural criticism is to bring the insights garnered from the periphery back to the centre, thereby disrupting our established patterns of thought (1999[1986]: 138).

Development: "What are the things in your home which are special to you?"

Ethnography has been used in a good number of disciplines, of which the most influential for design scholarship have been psychological approaches to consumer behaviour and consumption studies. Design history developed an interest in the role of the users and their capacity to inject design with meaning. In its interest towards aspects related to consumption and the

everyday, design history scrutinized the home as a place of meaningful practices. Ethnographic studies of psychologists and anthropologists provided
examples of how to explore this behaviour from an academic perspective.

Undertaking influential research into the personal significance of possessions, the psychologist Mihaly Csikszentmihalyi and the sociologist Eugene
Rochberg-Halton employed ethnography. Their work, conducted in 1977 and
published in 1981 under the title *The Meaning of Things: Domestic Symbols
and the Self,* included interviews with over 300 individuals from 82 families
situated in the Chicago metropolitan region (1981: 55). The selection criteria
for this sample were to gather a socioeconomically stratified sample of three-
generation families all living within the general Chicago area. The usual
course was to interview both parents, one child and one grandparent.

The primary objective of their study was to empirically unravel the
dynamics between individuals and the objects they keep in their households.
The interviews took place within the participants' homes, commencing with
inquiries about the interviewee's relationship with the neighbourhood, community and city. Subsequently, the interviewees were asked to elaborate on the
physical characteristics, atmosphere and mood of their homes. Finally, participants were prompted to discuss the items within their homes that held personal significance, with the researchers asking, "What are the things in your
home which are special to you?" (1981: 56). This research aimed to probe into
how these objects assumed symbolic roles for the individual. However, the
term "symbolic" was purposely avoided to prevent potential confusion and
constraints on participants' responses. The term "special" was preferred to
signify that these objects bore specific meanings, worth, memories, importance or emotions that were deeply tied to the individual. Thereby, the
researchers granted participants the autonomy to define the significance of the
objects, creating an open-ended framework that facilitated a wide spectrum of
interpretations (1981: 254).

Csikszentmihalyi and Rochberg-Halton reflected on the negative and positive effects of the dependence of humans on objects. They argue that this
dependence needs scrutiny in a period of energy scarcity in which humans
and material objects depend on the same resources. They consider materialism and overproduction as an issue to be combatted in times of an energy
crisis (1981: 229, 247). A rather negative view of objects is counterbalanced
by an awareness of their beneficial impact on humans. This book argues that
it is difficult to understand the psychological dependence of humans on
objects if we assume that human beings are naturally in control of what
happens in their minds. Consciousness is precarious and our bodies are
insufficient to objectify our sense of the self. Possessions can fulfil this role
(1981: 28).

Possessions can be used to convey, externalize and reinforce identities and
interpersonal connections, but users should avoid complete reliance on the
artefacts in question, according to Csikszentmihalyi and Rochberg-Halton
(1981: 164–165). Our dependence on possessions needs to be disciplined as

items become necessities and the self suffers in the absence of possessions. At that point, individuals reach a point of overly relying on the symbolic significance of objects.

The coding of the data took place in two steps; the first grouped the household artefacts that people mentioned as special into a limited number of categories, such as "furniture" or "plants." The second was more context-bound and developed meaning categories, such as "souvenir" or "gift," in an attempt to classify and statistically compare the meanings embodied in the various kinds of possessions. Both the types of artefacts and their meanings were drawn out of what seemed to be the most common descriptions given by respondents (1981: 268, 270).

The empirical data demonstrated that artefacts help objectify the self in at least three major ways: as objects of power, as a continuation of the self and as representing relationships. These objects of power are objects that others prize and that provide a solid and positive sense of one's identity. For men, these were either kinetic, objects with a great mass or things that are tasteful, ancient or innovative. For women, they had rather to do with seductiveness, fertility and nurturance (Csikszentmihalyi 1993: 25). Needless to say, this research was evidently a product of its time. The contemporary understanding of a family might significantly differ from today's perspective, and although a clear gender-based division might have been suitable in 1977, a more nuanced approach is essential in the present times.

Regarding the objects and the continuity of the self, there was a difference between young people who valued stereo sets, TV sets and musical instruments – since they produce ordered stimulation, either auditory or visual, and hence help the mind stay on track –, adults who valued furniture, paintings, sculpture and books – since these objects embody the values and tastes as well as the accomplishments of the owner – and older people who highly valued photographs as icons of the past, concrete reminders of their life. As for objects and relationship, objects were valued that stand for the links between a person to others such as family or friends (Csikszentmihalyi 1993: 27).

The codes and classifications employed in this research hold more relevance for psychologists and perhaps less so for design scholars, who might be more intrigued by the processes involved in attributing significance to objects rather than the demographics involved. Coding is undoubtedly influenced by numerous factors and could have yielded an alternate categorization. In this regard, the exploration of how artefacts externalize one's identity has been further expanded by the psychologist Marsha Richins. Her examination of both public and private meanings attributed to possessions incorporates additional categories not included in Csikszentmihalyi and Rochberg-Halton's study, such as utilitarian, appearance-related, or spiritual value, as explanations for why objects hold special significance for their owners (Richins 1994: 504–521).

Consumption studies, with special attention given to anthropologist Daniel Miller's contributions, have played a pivotal role in highlighting how consumers ascribe significance to products. Miller places a significant emphasis on the semiotic and cultural processes that occur during and after the acquisition of commodities (Woodward 2007: 98–102). What holds particular importance to Miller is the interaction between individuals and mass-consumption items. A case in point is his article "Appropriating the State on the Council Estate" (1988), which delved into the renovation of kitchens within a London council estate. This research offers a compelling contrast to the observation that working-class residents tend to view their homes through non-aesthetic frameworks. Miller's goal was to shed light on the aesthetic modifications of the original, standard kitchens that occurred over the span of approximately 15 years after the residents moved in. He characterizes this process as the transformation of an alienating environment into an appropriated form, where consumption evolves into a transformative journey by imbuing estranged elements of material culture with meaning. In particular, these spaces held value as centres of social and familial bonds (1988: 368).

He engaged in interviews with a variety of residents in council-owned flats, encompassing lower-middle and working-class backgrounds. Despite lacking substantial economic capital and belonging to a social group not conventionally associated with home renovation and decoration, these respondents exhibited a keen enthusiasm for employing diverse strategies to personalize and redecorate their kitchens. Faced with a sense of detachment from the standard kitchen layout and design, the residents employed distinct approaches. One group opted for no changes, while another sought to embellish and effectively mask their kitchen's appearance by utilizing an array of decorative items to establish a new façade and surface, essentially transforming the kitchen's aesthetic. The final group embarked on either complete or near-complete kitchen replacements. In doing so, they converted the once impersonal kitchen area into something laden with meaning and individuality, thereby reconciling the inherent "contradictions" of a larger industrial, mass-oriented society (1988: 361–364).

Based on his interviews, Miller asserts that the adoption of renovation strategies was significantly influenced by various factors, encompassing gender, race, and the sense of belonging within the estate. His findings suggest that mostly women embarked on kitchen renovation, contesting a presumed passive character of "housewifery." White males refrained from making any modifications to the original kitchen layout and decor. These men did partake in expressive activities, but these predominantly occurred in other areas of the house. In contrast, unmarried black men exhibited a positive inclination towards their kitchens, involving themselves in intricate decoration and tiling work independently – as well as conversations about cooking –, without relying on female guidance. Beyond the relevance or not of this gender divide, one of the most pronounced patterns to emerge from this research was the correlation between individuals experiencing feelings of loneliness, depression and isolation and their limited involvement in embellishing their living spaces. Substantial renovations emerged as a strong indicator of active social engagement (1988: 368).

Csikszentmihalyi and Rochberg-Halton's and Miller's studies serve as compelling instances of the nuanced complexity inherent in everyday life, as Lefebvre and Highmore have underscored. In the research by Csikszentmihalyi and Rochberg-Halton, the exploration revolves around the intricate ways in which objects amass multifaceted meanings for various individuals. Even an identical object, such as a music stereo, can hold connotations of kinship for one person, having been received as a gift from a family member, while symbolizing power for another person, due to its high cost as an acquisition. On the other hand, Miller's investigation exemplifies the diverse techniques users develop to adapt standard environments, revealing a range of responses to standardized settings. The concept of the everyday, often misperceived as a static and foreseeable reality, necessitates diverse qualitative interpretations to unveil its true nature.

Implementation: Design anthropology

Design practice is largely a generative activity, while anthropology is fundamentally analytical. Nevertheless, design anthropology encourages the alliance between the two (Garvey and Drazin 2016: 1–3). As Tim Ingold holds, both design and anthropology have parallels since they are inherently speculative and grounded in a profound understanding of human lived worlds (2014: 1). Wendy Gunn and Jared Donovan define design anthropology as an evolving area that centres on the creation of technologies aiming to harness and enhance individuals' innate physical capabilities (2012: 11). Design anthropology encompasses thereby an extensive examination of the interaction between dynamics, performance, and the fusion of action and perception (2012: 10).

Ingold considers ethnography as a speculative intervention that is done in the name of retrospective inquiry into the particularities of life (2014: 6). Neither the discipline of anthropology nor design anthropology are limited to the method of ethnography, according to Ingold. Nevertheless, as a way of scrutinizing recent history, ethnography's retrospective character has connected well with design scholarship in the analysis of present practices. The hands-on, immersive approach inherent in ethnography places certain restrictions, although not insurmountable ones, on its application within historical research (Garvey and Drazin 2016: 1). For design historians, a notable limitation was recognized by John A. Walker, who pointed out that the concept of the "ethnographic present" is not applicable to the study of historical periods (1989: 127).

Nonetheless, ethnography has found its place within design scholarship, particularly when intersecting with material culture studies. Judy Attfield's *Wild Things: The Material Culture of Everyday Life* (2000) was informed by involvement in the Oral History and Ethnography Workshop Project, which she directed at the University of Southampton starting in 1994. The project delved into the history of textiles, dress and design, drawing from recorded interviews and collaborative group projects. Attfield's book culminated a career dedicated to examining seemingly insignificant or undervalued objects within design culture, ultimately unveiling their dynamic presence in the world. Attfield characterized these objects as belonging to "design in the lower case," encompassing items like tufted carpets and reproduction-style furniture (2000: 45, 117). Her approach employed the lens of everyday life to democratize aesthetic consideration, emerging as a perspective shaped by feminism and a curiosity for how people construct their material environments.

Moreover, ethnography can be used as a way of questioning established assumptions. As an example, Csikszentmihalyi and Rochberg-Halton were interested in discussing materialism in a society embedded in an energy crisis. Miller in the creative possibilities of consumption, contradicting its assumed alienating character. As Jeffrey L. Meikle points out, the only way to discover how the mainstream consumer deals with design is to go out into the streets and question them. Ethnography solves the discrepancy between the real and the ideal inherent to design history, offering different insights than published materials being texts and images. Thereby, this method complements and might contradict the opinions of the designers and the producers about the meaning of their products (Meikle 1998: 194).

Alison J. Clarke, herself trained as a social anthropologist at University College London, stressed the importance of understanding the home as a process rather than a place in her book chapter "The Aesthetics of Social Aspiration" (2001). Whether changes are made physically or mentally, she emphasizes the social aspirations inherent to homemaking, noting that past and future trajectories are inseparable from external abstractions such as "class" and are negotiated through "fantasy and action, projection and interiorization" (2001: 25). Clarke looks into the role of refurbishing and redecorating the home within the trajectory of realizing one's dreams, revealing more underlying motivations than mere style-related. As Clarke explains: decorating the dream home is not about copying a specific style from a magazine, but rather the underlying "conceptual and value-laden configurations informing or undermining everyday household decisions (2001: 26). Continuing this research line, her edited volume *Design Anthropology: Object Culture in the 21st Century* (2011) brought insights from mostly anthropologists and design practitioners about both practice-driven and analysis-driven possibilities of design anthropology.

Similarly, Irene Maldini (2016) explores the assumption that digital DIY would lead to a "new industrial revolution," replacing the traditional model of mass production with a system in which users create their own designs, share the blueprints online and can manufacture objects on the domestic scale. Consequently, consumer participation in the design and manufacturing stages might enhance their connection to the result of their work. In reality, Maldini demonstrates that the model of digital DIY certainly enhances the agency of users and gives them autonomy from manufacturers but does not replace mass-produced objects with more durable ones, reducing the resources needed and waste produced (2016: 142). To understand the extent to which these expectations are met in digital DIY practice, Maldini's study used ethnography, studying individuals who used digital fabrication tools to make objects for their own use in the previous five years. The investigation was carried out in the Netherlands, within the community of the Amsterdam FabLab. FabLabs are laboratories where individuals can walk in and use digital fabrication tools free of charge, with the only condition being that their projects are shared online, so that the entire community can benefit from each member's experiments (2016: 146). Interviews were carried out by the author, at the location where participants actually used or kept their objects if possible. Maldini's findings suggest three key points. First, digital DIY objects do not act as substitutes for mass-produced ones; rather, they give rise to a new category of product. Second, participants place significant value on their projects and exhibit a strong attachment to them. Finally, this strong attachment, however, does not imply that the material outcomes are irreplaceable or inherently more durable. On the contrary, the technology used possesses its own agency, and makers view their objects as easily replaceable, diminishing the likelihood of an extended lifespan (2016: 143).

Digitalization has not only modified how users relate to objects but has facilitated other modalities of doing ethnography. For example, Alice Twemlow used digital ethnography– also known as netnography, a research method rooted in ethnography applied to the digital world – to explore the recent history of design criticism in her book *Sifting the Trash: A History of Design Criticism* (2017). Moving into the digital era, her final chapter brings together criticism and audiences and delves into the emergence of the "amateur" blogging culture, elaborating on how open-source technology in the 2000s led to a reconsideration of editorial values. Since the mid-2000s, shopping platforms such as Amazon.com has extended its customer reviewing options to products as well as books. Focusing on customer feedback for a self-flushing cat toilet, Twemlow identifies in these reviews a genre of product criticism in which critical consumers act as design critics (2017: 235; Figure 8.1). Twemlow deftly chronicles the newer forms of design discourse that the Internet encouraged, how bloggers argued for their "emotional connection" with readers and the Internet's ability to allow "short, conversational bursts of commentary and opinion built around links" (2017: 247). Twemlow reflects on the apparently innovative and fresh modes of communication that emerged during that era. She recognizes the concurrent resistance against the perceived elitist inclinations of patronizing and needless professional critics, practitioners, and scholars.

Just as these blogs challenged the notions of specialized training, meticulous writing and rigorous editorial oversight, contemporary political shifts can cast such stances in a naïve light. In today's landscape, where we are increasingly conscious of the more shadowy aspects of intrusive algorithms, the commercialization of websites, and manipulations within the seemingly populist realms of "digital media democracy," such assertions provoke new inquiries.

Figure 8.1 CatGenie self-washing, self-flushing cat box. Photo by Ugrashak/CC BY-
SA 4.0

Challenges: The benefits of subjectivity

Even when ethnography aims towards objectivity and even when academic research needs to be replicable, the subjectivity of the researcher is always there. Acknowledging and exploiting the possibilities of subjectivity for design scholarship deserves careful reflection. As Marcus and Fisher mentioned above, ethnographic research is partly self-exploration. Likewise, the anthropologists Paloma Gay y Blasco and Huon Wardle declare that the starting point of any ethnographic writing constitutes a valuable and distinctive way of asking and answering a recurrent question – "what does it mean to be human?" (Gay y Blasco and Wardle 2019[2007]: 1).

In auto-ethnographies, the object of study and the researcher are one and the same. Ethnographers Tony E. Adams, Stacy Holman Jones and Carolyn Ellis delineate auto-ethnography through three integral aspects or activities: the "auto," referring to the self; the "ethno," relating to culture; and the "graphy," encapsulating representation, writing and storytelling. Endeavours labelled as "auto-ethnography" encompass all three of these components. They affirm that if a project solely emphasizes one or two of these facets—for instance, a work presenting a narrative of the author's personal experience without accounting for culture, or a narrative work that extensively delves into cultural intricacies without addressing the author's role in shaping and constructing the narrative – the work might be more aptly categorized as a memoir or an anthropological narrative, rather than auto-ethnography proper (Adams et al. 2022[2013]: 3).

Within design practice, the emergence of auto-ethnography as a creative method has been conceptualized in the book *The Auto-Ethnographic Turn in Design* (2021), edited by Louise Schouwenberg and Michael Kaethler. Mostly showcasing designs from the MA Contextual Design at Design Academy Eindhoven that Schouwenberg ran until 2021, this book presents a framework within contextual design in which designers explore themselves and their particular context through their works. According to the editors, this is an observable pattern that has circulated during the decade preceding the publication of the book. This trend differs both from the idea of the "star" designer, which had a focus on ego and grand or fashionable projects, and from the designer as an agent to solve needs fulfilling a more technical role and therefore all too absent. Auto-ethnographic design recognizes that design research is deeply personal and that design needs not only to be for others but also for the self (2021: 61).

One example of this auto-ethnographic design is Hsin Min Chan's design *To-be-looked-at-ness* (2021), which reflects the designer's experience after being detained by Taiwanese authorities and placed under constant surveillance. At the start of the pandemic, the Design Academy Eindhoven was forced to close and Chan decided to leave the Netherlands to be with her family back in Taiwan. On arrival, the designer was put into isolation due to Covid protocols. She initially protested, which led to her being arrested and placed in a hospital isolation ward with a 24-hour camera above her bed. After five days, Chan decided to stage a protest against the "dehumanising" way she was being treated, by putting on a performance of hysterics. This act had an instant response as she was told that her process of testing would speed up. She was released later the same day. This made Chan realize her power to change the way she is treated, by altering the way she is perceived. Chan decided to employ the same strategy to change the way she is perceived day-to-day, particularly by men. This experience led to the design of a giant dress, accessible only with a stair, which forces those around to both take notice and give way. The structure is formed around a large metal mesh in the form of a skirt, over which Chan has added various materials including papier-mâché, fabric, resin and expanding foam. The design incorporates images of Chan's face and body and also pieces of furniture, which reference her experience in the isolation ward (Schouwenberg and Kaethler 2021: 217–218). She wore this dress during performances.

Design scholarship has also made use of auto-ethnography, for example in the study of how objects work as triggers of memories. Juliet Ash's study of the ties collection of her deceased husband (1996) refers to the power of objects to create meaning beyond "the 'objective' arena of design history" and argues for the incorporation of feeling within design history, since clothes relate to our feelings more than perhaps any other designed artefacts, and thus require "subjective" as well as "objective" analysis (1996: 219). Ash reflects on how memory interacts with artefacts bringing reassurance and disquiet together. Ash connects her personal experience with theoretical positions on memory by Julia Kristeva and on the sublime by Immanuel Kant. A mere item of clothing such as a tie can connect the present with the past by way of the imagination. Thereby, the griever can proceed from regret to a more positive comprehension of absence. The memory becomes, through imagined moments, a recognition of a shared past, at the same time connecting, through the reality of the tie, with the present moment (1996: 222). In that sense, the ties reveal how the deceased is partially present in the items which remain, meanwhile the griever is partially absent in the history they had together.

The second example is Kjetil Fallan's study of the DBS-Kombi bicycle. His article studied the production, consumption and mediation of this bicycle through all kinds of written sources. Nevertheless, he claims that subjectivity is part of the mediation of objects and that it can only be studied through the researcher's personal experience. He argues that memories do not necessarily emerge from the original object, as in Ash's account, but also from the same typology. It is actually a second-hand bike, not the original bike that he had as a child, that he writes about and that brings memories from his childhood (2012: 77). Moreover, it is the interaction with that bike that brings on other kinds of memories. When repairing the bike, memories of his father's garage, who taught Fallan the basics of bicycle mechanics, come to mind. Objects can release different kinds of memory not as static objects but depending on how users interact with them (2012: 78).

The experiences of minorities have been of particular interest for auto-ethnography, aiming to challenge the norms of methodological practices, making clear where power, privilege and biases lie (Naidoo 2012: 5). In the field of disability studies, Georgina Kleege's auto-ethnography tells how the use of a white cane alters how the subject is perceived by others (2009: 510–513; Figure 8.2). Diagnosed as legally blind, with macular degeneration, at age 11, Kleege only started carrying a cane some thirty years later. Discussing how the cane alters relationships with others, she perceives how others become afraid of the cane, what she compares to carrying a gun. People freeze and seem disoriented when noticing the cane. Others tend to ignore the cane as a signifier of blindness. When arranging her escort to bring Kleege to the gate or to the baggage claim area, airline employees struggle to verbalize that she needs an escort but not a wheelchair. Kleege asks them to be explicit about her condition with their colleagues, often without success (2009: 512). In this account, Kleege narrates how the cane, even when being one and the same signifier, awakens different reactions, ranging from marking her presence extraordinary to forcing some ordinariness in how people accommodate her presence, omitting her state.

Figure 8.2 Cane for users with visual impairments. Photo by Peter Eriksson/Getty Images

The reasons to use auto-ethnography as a research methodology are numerous. According to Adams, Holman Jones and Ellis, auto-ethnographies help us (1) foreground particular and subjective knowledge; (2) illustrate sensemaking processes; (3) make contributions to existing research; (4) challenge norms of research practice and representation; and (5) engage and compel responses from audiences (2022[2013]: 4). Auto-ethnographers openly recount intimate and vulnerable experiences that can occasionally evoke feelings of shame or sadness. These encounters encompass experiences and circumstances that have moulded their identities, along with the incidents that have influenced their emotions, ranging from happiness and bewilderment to tension, sorrow, ardour and even potential trauma. By sharing these narratives, auto-ethnographers aim to illustrate how they and those they engage with can derive meaning from their lives. In doing so, they make uncomfortable topics discussable, shedding light on narratives that have remained untold or underrepresented (Adams et al. 2022[2013]: 3).

While the results of an auto-ethnography may not possess a universally objective value, they can yield valuable insights for researching the complexities of everyday life. These personal narratives, whether aligning with or challenging prevailing norms, provide intricate and detailed accounts of individual experiences, presenting both ordinary firsthand perspectives and extraordinary tales of dissent. These narratives, whether familiar or unexpected, vividly recount the everyday.

9 Discourse analysis
Constructing reality

With an origin in linguistics, discourse analysis explores the connection of the verbal, the visual, the material, the spatial and the performative to generate coherent discourses that are presented as "truth." When achieving authority, these discursive formations condition the behaviour of humans. When becoming dominant, they exclude other discourses as non-valid. Exposing the mechanisms behind the constructions of these discourses is the goal of discourse analysis, which has been implemented within design scholarship for the study of domestic advice or the generation of specific labels. With the Internet, individuals have access to the generation of alternative discourses. These are not presented so much as "truth" but as personal interpretations of reality. Blogs not only expose the individual behind the construction but also connect to other discourses through hyperlinks. Do we need to rethink the mechanisms that generate authority?

Origins: What is social constructionism?

One might argue that discourse analysis centres on language and meaning. However, it extends beyond language in the written or spoken form, also encompassing the examination of the visual, the material and the performative (Van den Berg 2004: 30). We communicate with much more than just language, for example through the clothes we wear and our body gestures. According to the communication scholars Marianne Jørgensen and Louisa Phillips, how people talk about a particular topic in a certain context is indicative of their subjective understanding of the world and their social relations and identities. These discourses not only reflect how someone thinks but play an active role in creating and changing subjective understandings of the world, social relations and identities (Jørgensen and Phillips 2002: 1). For example, fashion bloggers and journalists might discuss a specific garment, for example a leather jacket, using language that depicts it according to the writer's motivations. This same garment can gain different connotations when inserted in different contexts, ranging from subversive to chic. These connotations reach out beyond the blogosphere or print media to condition choices and behaviours. Thereby, textual discourse conditions reality.

DOI: 10.4324/9781003147282-11

The ways our homes are structured, how our bathrooms look and how we expect our kitchens to function, are all part of certain discourses of living. Discourse analysis considers language as a social phenomenon that constructs reality, rather than representing a pre-existing reality outside of language (Gee 2014: 24). This understanding then leads to a central question to discourse analysis research: *how* exactly does language construct certain social realities and identities, and how are these realities made to seem self-evident or true? The cultural geographer Gillian Rose affirms that discourse analysis "refers to a group of statements which structure the way a thing is thought, and the way we act on the basis of that thinking" (Rose 2016: 187). As a method for analysis, it does not just examine what is said or written down, but also how it is portrayed and how it shapes reality. The basis of discourse analysis is social constructionism, which is a theory that looks at how humans understand the world and themselves and construct realities and identities according to these understandings. Discourse analysis first emerged in linguistics, but since the beginning of the 1980s has been adopted by many other disciplines – in what was known as the linguistic turn – chiefly adapting the formulations of the philosopher Michel Foucault. Foucauldian discourse analysis generates a vision of the world that is shaped socially but conditions individual psychologies. Humans learn to be and behave a certain way by the discourses they exist within (1970: 64).

Although there are many different discourses, some of them become dominant due to the claim and belief that their knowledge is true. Foucault named the grounds on which these discourses base their truth-claims as the "regime of truth" (1970: 55). Discourses are therefore divisive since they privilege one notion of truth above another, generating thereby power relations. The implementation of these discourses involves the exercise of power. Indeed, one of the broader conclusions that can be drawn is that Foucault's conception of discourse is situated far more closely to knowledge, materiality and power than it is to language. Discourse needs to be seen as an active "occurring," as something that implements power and action, and that also is power and action (1970: 59).

Discourse may therefore take textual, performative, visual and material forms, and be embodied in various kinds of practices. Therefore, discourse is intertextual. Foucault proposes an opposition between "series" versus "unity." Rather than assuming a shared likeness or supposing that each component of the analysis will be of the same type, the discourse analyst must be prepared to search for similar functions across a variety – a "series" – of different forms, such as language, practices, material reality, institutions and subjectivity. Foucault's "series" is a pivotal methodological concept in demonstrating that discourse works in discontinuous and often contradictory ways (1970: 67).

Similarly, rather than following linear successions of development, that is, vertical patterns of analyses, the discourse analyst must trace laterally, mapping parallels of regularity, that is, horizontal, "sideways" patterns of analysis, resulting in a "unity." For example, a leather jacket might have acquired the connotation of being subversive. This is possible through a unity of discourse that is coherent about the rebelliousness of that leather jacket. That unity can be achieved by a series of different discourses. One of them can be visual, through the appearance in a film in which the main character is a rebel and wears that jacket. Nevertheless, an isolated discourse might not create a regime of truth. That discursive series needs to be expanded with other discourse that might be textual, for example, a novel depicting similar circumstances. On top of that, there might be another case in which members of a music band singing on disobedience might wear that leather jacket. That would be a performative discourse that adds to that series. Hence, Foucault asserts that "discursive events must be treated along the lines of homogenous series which, however, are discontinuous in relation to each other" (1970: 69). The film, the novel and the gig do not happen at the same time but contribute to creating a homogeneous discourse about a leather jacket.

Foucault argues for an analysis of discourse not to be reduced merely to the "markings of a textuality," but to include the physicality of its effects, in the materiality of its practices (1970: 66). Rather than a mere vocabulary or language, discourse is the thing that is done, "the violence," as Foucault puts it, "with which we do things" (1970: 67). Along with the representations of the leather jacket, mentioned above, we can think of other consequences of that discourse that occur in daily life experiences. Take, for example, a hypothetical situation in which police agents in a chaotic situation after a demonstration need to decide who to follow and arrest. There are two groups, one with men wearing three-piece suits and the other wearing leather jackets. If the police agents opt to follow the latter group, this would have consequences beyond representation for those wearing leather jackets.

The question is, who produces those discourses? For example, what we consider to be private and public spaces and the rights to have access to both these spaces are very specific and culturally defined. Who decides about objects in public space? Or objects in the home? Do they bring their own discourses into our private spaces? Discourses do not need to be created top-down but generate in different locations. Foucault notes that power is not something imposed from the top of society down onto its oppressed bottom layers, "power is everywhere" (1978[1976]: 93). This is important, as it proposes that a dominant discourse does not necessarily have to be produced by powerful institutions. Once produced and appropriated by others, the same discourse can be appropriated, reproduced and generated elsewhere. Once a discourse has been generated, it leads its own life and becomes "common sense." Therefore, it is maintained and reproduced outside its source (1978[1976]: 94–95).

Doing discourse analysis involves contextualization. First, Foucault's conceptualization of discourse indispensably requires historical contextualization; discourse analysis only finds its real usefulness within the agenda of a "history of systems of thought" (1978[1976]: 24, 39). Second, for Foucault, a study of discourse must necessarily entail a focus on discourse-as-knowledge, that is to say, on discourse as a matter of the social, historical and political conditions under which statements come to count as true or false (McHoul and Grace 1997: 27). Furthermore, when proceeding with discourse analysis, one of the first steps would be to identify the origins of the discourse. As a result, discourse analysis reveals the dynamics of hegemony and oppression involved in those commonsensical discourses. In that way, discourse analysis is an exercise of resistance or at least of evidencing the power relations behind that "common sense."

Discourse analysis is qualitative rather than quantitative, which becomes manifest when comparing this method to content analysis, for example. While content analysis shares many similarities with discourse analysis – its examination of the latent content of a message, texts and images – it focuses heavily on quantitative methods, is much more systematic and claims to be "objective" and "repeatable" (Walker 1989: 109). Content analysis does not, however, exhaust all the possibilities that discourse analysis has the potential to address and, as Walker himself points out, "high frequency is not always a sign of significance – something that is pointed out once can be of most significance" (Walker 1989: 108).

The resulting discourse analysis will account for the formation of a specific discourse but not for its efficacy. Discourse analysis is therefore explanatory rather than exploratory since it aims to provide specific answers about why we might understand things in a specific way, but not if people actually understand things that way. It is about how discourse has been shaped and how it is maintained, not how it is received. Moreover, discourse analysis should not be constructed as an alternative power discourse but as a critique. It is intended to be used to deconstruct structures of power, hegemony and oppression. This deconstruction reveals the contingency of these discourses that might be considered, before their deconstruction, as neutral because of being accepted as such (McHoul and Grace 1997: 14).

Development: Intertextuality

While we are used to decoding verbal language, visual materials entail perhaps a more difficult task. Rose discusses Foucault's approach to discourse analysis in her book *Visual Methodologies* (2016[2001]), which is of special interest in the context of design. Rose emphasizes the importance of intertextuality for discourse analysis, which acknowledges that meanings of communications do not only depend on the particular communications, but also on the way they relate to other communications, which Foucault coined as "series" (Rose 2016[2001]: 188). Attached to this is the notion of "discursive formation" which refers to the existing connections of meaning within a specific discourse, which Foucault coined as "unity."

Based on Foucault's discussion of discourse, Rose defines two types of discourse analysis (2016[2001]: 188). **Discourse analysis I** studies visual images and verbal texts, interrogating how language, both visual and verbal, is used to construct a certain social reality. The main focus is on discursive formations and what they produce. This form of discourse analysis could prove valuable in examining, for example, domestic advice literature as it deals with images and text and their positioning in a more social context. **Discourse analysis II** mostly neglects particular statements and their details and instead looks at institutions. Discourse analysts of this type will look at the way institutional discourses materialize, the effects of institutional technologies and what exactly these technologies produce (2016[2001]: 223). While Rose states that both methods are linked, and source material can overlap, she argues that each method "puts Foucault's arguments to work in rather different ways, with rather different effects" (2016[2001]: 192).

Even though discourse analysis is not an easy follow-the-rulebook method, Rose attempts to pin down what exactly is being done. Starting with **discourse analysis I**, she mentions that discourse analysts often look for recurring themes within their range of sources – as Foucault argued to "examine 'the relationship between statements'" – which entails looking into associations or at certain combinations of words and images. For example, how women's magazines construct a specific stereotype of women and how this is reflected both in textual and visual elements, such as the articles included, the accompanying pictures and the ads displayed. It is equally important to attend to the things that are not being shown or said, Rose adds, and to think about the origin – which place – and the destination – which public – of the communication under study. For example, if the above-mentioned specific women's magazine excludes reference to other women's stereotypes both in its text and its visuals (2016[2001]: 205, 206, 227).

While Rose's first category of discourse analysis looks at the construction of communications, **discourse analysis II** focuses more on the practices and effects of discourse through its institutional embeddedness (2016[2001]: 215). The chosen sources can be newspaper articles, photographs, novels, artworks, museum displays, annual reports, written statements, photographs of institution buildings and actual visits, whatever seems relevant and interesting for the discourse formation. Rose advises starting with the sources that the analyst expects to be most insightful and then broadening the search from there. It is also very important, she stresses, to read and re-read and to make time for browsing to stumble upon things by accident, as time-consuming as this may be. The material should guide the analyst, since in a good discourse analysis eventually the quality of the sources is more important than the quantity (2016[2001]: 205–206).

In Rose's explanation of discourse analysis II, she uses case studies that focus on institutions such as the museum and the gallery, while referencing Foucault's seminal studies of institutions such as the prison. In her examination of institutions, Rose uses the distinction, originally put forth by Foucault, that institutions work in two ways: "through their apparatus and through their technologies" (2016[2001]: 223). His "institutional apparatus" refers to "the forms of power/knowledge which constitute the institution," such as the building an institution is housed in or more abstract forms such as the institution's philosophies, rules and regulations. For example, and to continue with the example above, the headquarters in which the publisher of the women's magazine is hosted and how it is decorated. On the other hand, "institutional technologies" are "the practical techniques used to practice that power/knowledge," such as the ways the philosophies and regulations are communicated, how journalists are briefed and according to which criteria the visuals and ads included in each magazine issue are selected. In her examination, she focuses on those analyses that have concentrated on the public display areas of museums and galleries, pinpointing various areas for examination such as the technology of a display, both textual and visual – which includes captions, wall panels and catalogues – and technologies of layout (2016[2001]: 223).

An example of discourse analysis II is the analysis of the display of the Museum of Natural History in New York City, written by art historian, literary critic and artist Mieke Bal. She aims to uncover the "text," or, what exactly is being said with the museum's displays, stressing that in a museum there is always an "I" – that refers to the museum as an institution with its own history, not necessarily the individual museum professionals – speaking to a "you" – the visitor – about a "them" – the theme of the exhibition, the collection, and so on. Bal starts by analysing the placement of the museum within the city at large (1996: 13–14). She notes that two museums are positioned across from one another, with Central Park in the middle: the Metropolitan Museum of Art on the East side, and the American Museum of Natural History on the West side of the park. This already conveys a meaning, states Bal. There is a museum for culture, the Metropolitan Museum of Art, and a separate one for nature, the Museum of Natural History, with in between a cultured natural landscape: the park. Thereby, a large part of the world population is reduced to "a static state of being" by exhibiting their cultures in the natural museum, with the cultural museum being reserved for Western art (1996: 15).

Bal moves on to discuss the architecture and the entrance of the Museum of Natural History, what Foucault would call the institutional apparatus. She points to the texts in the main hall, originating from the early nineteenth century (1996: 18). These texts should have been the first display in the museum, Bal argues, immediately making clear that the museum itself has a history of its own. Then, Bal enters a darkened room with dioramas of mammals in their natural habitats. The dioramas are dimly lit from the inside. Bal mentions that the darkness is probably necessary for conservation, but that also creates another effect: the object is highlighted, while the visitor remains in the dark and is obscured (1996: 20).

Continuing her tour through the museum, Bal pays special attention to the way the transition is made from this room with mammals to the next room, where several Asian cultures are presented. This move from nature to people is problematic, Bal states, since it obviously juxtaposes certain foreign human cultures with animals (1996: 22). The transition is marked by a bronze

Nepalese Buddha statue. The textual information for the statue retells the story of Buddha's birth, the event that the statue illustrates. Among other things, Bal stresses that this object is presented as an "anthropological evidence of a timeless culture" and not as an object of art, discussing its style or artistic expression, for example (1996: 24).

In the next room, Bal focuses on the organization of the objects, geographically around different cultures and placed in a specific timeline. By using a timeline, Bal argues, the cultures are placed in a hierarchy, communicating a "rise of civilization" that ends with the Greek, "our" culture. She continues to analyse in-depth the textual information, quoting entire texts from the museum walls and panels, with attention to the words that are used. Her aim is to uncover the meaning of the texts, how they affect the interpretation of the objects shown, and what story they tell. She looks at where text panels are placed in relation to the room and to the content of the text (1996: 29).

Rose presents a useful list of technologies of display – in Foucauldian sense – to be considered when doing this type of discourse analysis in an institution like a museum (2016[2001]: 226). How things are shown conveys meaning and no aspect can be taken for granted. Dioramas, for example, communicate differently than when an object is presented in a glass showcase. These are two different types of "truth" stories, with the diorama implying a truth about the artefact in its original setting, and the glass showcase referring to the truth of the museum with its own value system (2016[2001]: 230). There are many types of displays possible, and there are many different types of text used in exhibitions. Considering these as intentional rather than obvious choices are things to consider in discourse analysis.

Implementation: Exhibitions as discourse

In spite of the method being utilized extensively within design scholarship, discourse analysis has seldom been thoroughly explored as a method. In contrast to Gregory Votolato and John A. Walker, D.J. Huppatz recognizes discourse analysis as a method for scrutinizing design (Walker 1989; Votolato 1998; Huppatz 2018: e34). Similarly, *The Design History Reader* introduces discourse analysis in its preface but allocates limited attention to it thereafter (Lees-Maffei and Houze 2010: 385). As in Huppatz's work, this publication includes research utilizing discourse analysis, yet its significance is seldom explicitly emphasized.

Kjetil Fallan (2010) mentioned discourse analysis as a method for analysing design history. He, however, only briefly addresses the possibilities of employing discourse analysis and, for the most part, derides its usage. Fallan suggests that its main shortcoming is that discourse analysis is "ill-equipped to encounter a core concern of most design history: the materiality of objects" (2010:33). He considers that it is only appropriate "if one approaches design history as a history of textual design discourse," even when as noted above "texts" do not need to be verbal but can be also visual and material (2010: 33). It is rather the way that a sign is decoded that makes it textual, not its nature. As mentioned above, Foucauldian discourse analysis is full of visuality and materiality.

In order to understand the value of discourse analysis in the field of design scholarship, it is necessary to examine how this method has been employed. The two publications that will be analysed here are Grace Lees-Maffei's book *Design at Home: Domestic Advice Books in Britain and the USA since 1945* (2014) and Jørn Guldberg's article "'Scandinavian Design' as Discourse: The Exhibition *Design in Scandinavia, 1954–57*" (2011), both representative of Rose's discourse analysis I and II respectively. Lees-Maffei's book surveys nearly 70 years of domestic advice in the US and the UK to demonstrate the historical value of this genre of literature. In analysing the concept of "Scandinavian Design" as discourse, Jørn Guldberg focused on the *Design in Scandinavia* exhibition as his point of reference (Figure 9.1). The sources these authors chose are diverse, according to their study. Lees-Maffei limits her study to domestic advice literature. Guldberg's article employs literature, exhibition layouts and interviews with the representatives of professional associations. While both texts are indeed different, they do share

Figure 9.1 Installation view from the *Design in Scandinavia* exhibition at the Brooklyn Museum, New York, that ran from April 20 to May 16, 1954/Brooklyn Museum

commonalities, addressing central themes such as truth claims, persuasion, exclusions, omissions and power.

Lees-Maffei is primarily seeking to demonstrate "the historical value of domestic advice literature as a genre of word and image" and somewhat secondary to that, revealing the construction of a "discourse of dominance" (2014: back cover). The publication addresses themes such as etiquette, homemaking and home decoration advice in an attempt to demonstrate the historical importance of the genre to historians. In order to do this, Lees-Maffei examines areas such as the connections between advice, housing and the middle class as well as the relationship between advice and gender. She employs Foucauldian discourse analysis, as well as the tripartite model of legitimization coined by the sociologist Max Weber (1864–1920; 2014: 11). Invoking Weber's theories on authority being based on traditional, rational and charismatic processes of legitimization, Lees-Maffei examines the various ways that the authors of domestic advice literature invoked authority in their writing (2014: 79).

Lees-Maffei's use of discourse analysis correlates most strongly with Rose's discourse analysis I which "tends to focus on the production and rhetorical organisation of visual and textual materials" (Rose 2016: 220). As a result of the content she is examining, Lees-Maffei focuses largely on textual analysis but also considers accompanying images, as well as the design of the books themselves. For example, when discussing *Lady Elizabeth Anson's Party Planners Book*, Lees-Maffei juxtaposes an analysis of the symbolic imagery on the book's cover, motifs such as ribbons, roses and swords, with the aesthetics of Anson's party interiors as described by Anson in the book (2014: 20, footnote 63).

In order to gain an understanding of the discourse of dominance present in domestic advice literature, she compares and contrasts images and texts from different sources. A good example of this is where she compares two similar images, one published in the *Woman's Own Book of Modern Homemaking* (1967) and the other from the Council of Industrial Design's (CoID) book *Storage* (1970) by Geoffrey Salmon (2014: 106). In her analysis of these two images, she deduces the marginal differences between the way a storage unit is presented and written about. Although both "exemplify gender stereotypes," the CoID publication emphasizes production and status, while the other focuses on personal consumption (2014: 107).

The implied reality of domestic advice literature is also addressed. Lees-Maffei acknowledges that domestic advice literature lies between fact and fiction and can therefore be seen as a "narrative of ideology." Regarding this, she adds that advice literature "can help historians to understand what people may have *thought*, but it cannot tell us what they *did*; advice literature exists between prescription and practice" (2014: 71). Her emphasis on mediation is underscored as she describes domestic advice literature as a "mediating discourse" (2014: 51, note 68). Therefore, how advice was received or understood by consumers is logically ignored in her analysis. Discourse analysis can

be employed to describe the formation of a discourse and its possible implications. To know exactly how a discourse has been interpreted or ignored, a
reception study, for example through oral history, needs to be undertaken.

A good example of discourse analysis II, Jørn Guldberg's article analyses
how the exhibition *Design in Scandinavia* produced a certain "Scandinavian
Design" discourse. This exhibition was organized by the Virginia Museum of
Fine Arts and travelled through the United States from 1954 to 1957. His
sources are the main text of the exhibition catalogue, an article from the *New
York Times Sunday Magazine*, a review in *Interiors* magazine and the exhibition itself (2011: 41).

Guldberg also uses primary sources to study the context of the exhibition
to support his argument, such as correspondence between the organizers. He
focuses on the agents behind the organization of the exhibition such as
American editor-in-chief of *House Beautiful*, Elizabeth Gordon as well as
Leslie Cheek, the director of Virginia Museum of Fine Arts, and the national
associations of craft, applied art and design in Denmark, Finland, Norway
and Sweden and the American Federation of Arts. Guldberg is concerned
with matters outside the texts, for example, the way in which the exhibition
was constructed. Regarding this, Guldberg notes how Cheek "favoured 'settings' for the presentation of art works and who liked to engage audiences
both intellectually and physically – the latter by means of an almost choreo-
graphic staging of the visitor's passage through the galleries" (2011: 47). His
discussion of Cheek's curatorial "settings" alludes to Gillian Rose's discourse
analysis II and her description of "technologies of layout" in a museum,
which focuses on the power relations at work in institutions of visual display
(Rose 2016: 238).

This investigation goes behind the scenes and scrutinizes the very construction of the texts by considering various versions of one article and noting
changes that were made and by whom. It exemplifies the complexities of
assigning authorship to one individual, by explaining the different people
involved from the conception of the text to its publication. Guldberg elaborates
on the persuasive element of the texts and visuals (2011: 47). Not only does he
examine their placement and content, he also brings into question their construction by providing contextual information: "Liljegreen even suggested that
Huldt engaged a particular Swedish photographer, Sune Sundahl, who he said
knew how to make 'Americanesque' pictures" (2011: 49, footnote 73). By
highlighting this, Guldberg allows the reader to see how both texts and images
are injected with ideology in line with Foucault's "institutional technologies."

In leaving out all the aspects that make Scandinavian countries different
from each other, the authors of the texts – and organizers of the exhibition –
could present Scandinavia as a homogenized state. Like Lees-Maffei, Guldberg addresses what is not included in the text: "absence of polarities, dramatic changes, demographic and cultural differences, and segregation within
the product cultures and so on" (Guldberg 2011:49). As Rose suggests, what
is absent is just as important as what is included in discourse analysis.

Both Lees-Maffei and Guldberg are aware of the ideological mindset of their study objects. Lees-Maffei acknowledges the limitations of her approach, namely that the literature she examines cannot be taken as direct evidence of past experience and how the advice was received or understood by consumers is largely ignored. Guldberg describes the fabrication of a narrative, examining rhetorical devices and continuity and takes steps to examine feedback of some form. While he does not acknowledge the reactions of visitors to the exhibition, he does highlight the response from the representatives of the four Scandinavian professional societies involved.

Challenges: Truth in times of Web 2.0 technology

Critics of discourse analysis argue that it tends to overlook individual choice. While various discourses can be articulated and presented as truth, they are not necessarily influential in shaping people's perspectives (McHoul and Grace 1997: 14). The coexistence of multiple discourses allows consumers to exercise their own choices, viewing conflicting truths more as alternatives than absolute truths. A notable illustration is the generation of content by non-specialists on the Internet, where alternative discourses can be easily formulated. In this context, individuals may express their positions overtly, framing their advice as opinions rather than indisputable truths.

Digital technology has altered long-held norms of, for example, fashion mediation, creating new spaces for the production of fashion content and discourse. In the mid-1990s, digital media and Web 2.0 technology led to the creation of blogs – a type of digital media platform where Internet users can freely upload, publish and share their thoughts and ideas on a specific topic (Rocamora 2011: 408). Since their emergence in the early 2000s, fashion blogs, which are "often the creation of fashion outsiders," have carved out a place among "the mainstream fashion media, bringing to light the shifting nature of fashion journalism" (Rocamora 2012: 92).

Magazine writers and bloggers employ different rhetorical techniques to convey their opinions and position themselves as authoritative voices on the topic of fashion. Agnès Rocamora focuses on the textual analysis of discourse in fashion media. She specifically looks at how fashion blogs mediate fashion and position themselves as fashion communicators in comparison to traditional print fashion journalism and conventional modes of fashion media. Rocamora states that the rise of fashion blogging has shifted the control of power in the fashion media industry to individuals who resided on the fringes, with no "institutional affiliation to the field of fashion" before the creation of their blog (2012: 100).

Rosie Findlay explains how bloggers were positioned as "outsiders" not just for their alternative modes of dressing and perspectives on fashion, but also for the "very activity of blogging itself" (2015: 169). The content produced by fashion bloggers has been met with criticism from established fashion media such as *GQ* and *Women's Wear Daily*. According to the editors of these magazines, who identify themselves as fashion insiders, bloggers do not possess the same historical understandings and "critical faculties" (Rocamora 2012: 100). This situation evidences the defence of a "regime of truth" in which established media position themselves as authorities excluding new platforms.

Hypertextuality is a distinguishing feature of blogs that differentiates them from print fashion media. Rocamora defines hypertextuality as the use of hyperlinks in online content that enables the user to move through a network to access other written sources and images in the blogosphere and digital landscape. Hypertextuality is then intertextual, like Foucauldian discourse, and makes visible a vast network of interrelated producers. Magazines conversely do not refer to other publications to "[imply] their independence from the rest of print publications and a status as the one authoritative fashion source," according to Rocamora (2012: 96). The hypertexuality of blogs has contributed to the de-centring of the dominant voice of fashion magazines by blurring the boundaries separating professionals from amateurs. In this constellation, a regime of truth generates not as a monolithic, obvious discourse but as a sum of parts. Blogs thereby weaken the regime of truth generated by established media and evidence the creation of a Foucaldian "series" around a specific "unit," making the creation of a discourse visible.

Rocamora identifies Susie Lau's *Style Bubble* as one of the initial fashion blogs to emerge (2012: 99). Similarly, Findlay classifies personal style blogs into two waves, and uses *Style Bubble* as an illustration of a first-wave fashion blog that played a significant role in shaping the subgenre (2015: 167). Lau dedicated herself full-time to her blog from 2006 until she shifted her focus to Instagram in 2018. Her blog features Lau's reflections, personal experiences and observations on fashion, with a particular emphasis on showcasing young and lesser-known talent.

Similarly to online magazines such as *Vogue.com* and *Elle.com*, Lau's rhetoric aims to persuade readers of the validity of her point of view and authority as a fashion mediator. Is she then constructing an alternative "truth"? As pointed out by Rachel Matthews, authenticity is a defining feature of the rhetoric on fashion blogs (2015: 62). On her "FAQ" page, Lau emphasizes the importance of being authentic online. The values of genuineness, individuality and high-quality content aim to confer credibility and honesty to her posts (Style Bubble 2013). On the other hand, the "Press" page on her blog features numerous fashion publications that recognize her wide influence, including *Teen Vogue, W Magazine, The New York Times, Elle US* and *Vogue UK* (Style Bubble 2009). Lau's authenticity is thereby reinforced by the network of fashion media to which she belongs.

As Matthews contends, Lau's authority stems from a subjective perspective and an expressive writing style (2015: 62). For instance, in her assessment of the fashion house Gucci, Lau evaluates the designer's creations in a post dated March 29th 2016, titled "Gucci IRL," where "IRL" signifies "in real life." In this entry, Lau commemorates the surge in Gucci's sales following the appointment of Alessandro Michele as creative director, aiming to refute any prior scepticism. She endeavours to share her firsthand experience of donning these garments, seeking to unravel the distinctive characteristics that define the Gucci label. Among the items discussed is a green lace dress, showcased in a picture where Lau is seen wearing it on the street. The photograph captures her in profile, with her face turned towards the camera. This positioning enables her to present a Gucci handbag hanging from her shoulder directly to the camera. This photo shoot is set against the backdrop of a street featuring a brick building adorned with a "Library" sign. Notably, this presentation markedly differs from the frontal display of the same dress on the catwalk photographs, and the street setting serves as a stark contrast to the interior venue of the fashion show. Both images are carefully stylized, but in different ways.

Along with the image, Lau states that seeing the dress physically bought and worn in real life

> is the all-important component to the 180-degree transformation of the house. For all the ornamentation on the runway – the romantic prints, the lavish embroidery and the abundance of frou in the form of marabou, sequins and cats, there is something beneath all that surface that is anchored to a reality and also to the recognisable codes of Gucci.
>
> (Lau 2016)

Lau's review derives from her personal, firsthand account of these coveted pieces. She stresses the need for wearing the clothes to actually develop a judgement. In addition, her rhetoric is solely dependent on her experience and knowledge. These features of Lau's discourse insinuate an authority based on personal perception. To what extent can we talk of a "regime of truth" in a Foucauldian sense, when the mechanisms behind the discourse are so individualized?

Online fashion media such as *Vogue.com* and *Elle.com* tend to be less personal in their opinions. The discourse on *Vogue.com*, for example, draws on other rhetorical devices. These linguistic persuasive techniques are evident in the website's mission statement and in Steph Yotka's article about predicting the fashion trends of 2017. *Vogue.com* describes its team of writers, editors and photographers as "internationally recognized" professionals who produce the "strongest editorial coverage." This rhetoric employs ethos in emphasizing *Vogue.com*'s credibility, which persuades its readers of the website's expertise in ensuring accurate and reliable information. Yotka presents a logical basis for her arguments. For instance, she substantiates her claim that "pink is the new camel" by referencing multiple designers that featured the bright hue in their runway collections. In her description of "Raf Simons is the new Calvin Klein," Yotka attempts to rationalize Raf Simons' appointment as the new head at Calvin Klein by explaining how "Simons' own aesthetics line up well with those of Calvin Klein – always on the hunt for the throbbing heartbeat of youth culture" (Yotka 2016: §2).

Digital fashion media platforms articulate authority in different ways through the use of various discursive and rhetorical devices. A fundamental difference between the discourses of fashion blogs and online magazines is a subjective versus objective point of view. Jørgensen and Phillips explain that different discourses employ certain "modalities," or modes of address, to construct a particular identity and social position. They state that the mass media "often present interpretations as if they were facts" through the use of objective modalities, which "both reflects and reinforces their authority" (2002: 84). *Vogue.com* is a large media platform that uses an objective modality for a large proportion of its content. Online magazines present their interpretations as facts to detach writers' personal opinions from statements and conceal biases. In contrast, the author of *Style Bubble* uses a subjective modality, writing in the first person, to convey a personal connection to the subject matter.

Lau's discourse formation might share similarities with other constructions of a regime of truth since she still wants to validate her point of view for her readership. However, their connection with other discourse formations through hypertextuality and their presence as an individual weaken the regime of truth of bloggers' discourse. In the case of Lau's blog, it is her exposure as an individual that refrains her opinions to become "common sense." So, how should discourse analysis be adapted to times of an increasing personalization of discourses? Their constructions of "regimes of truth" might share similarities with other discourses but there are also differences that need to be taken into consideration.

Part II
Approaches

10 Industry

Economic and legal frameworks

Manufacturers, museums, educational institutions, professional associations and governmental bodies have played significant roles in shaping the field of design on regional, national and global scales. The study of these entities shifts the focus away from individual designers and specific products. International connections between design associations can be traced through organizations like the International Council of Societies of Industrial Design (ICSID). The realm of economics has generated a diverse body of literature that relates to the domain of design, originating in different disciplines such as economic history, business history, cultural political economy and discussions surrounding intellectual property rights. It delves into the intricate connections between culture and economics, as well as between the public and private sectors. This literature has not only explored the role of design in society but also how societal factors in their turn have influenced the field of design. Concepts of authorship and property rights have been challenged by recent advancements in artificial intelligence, inviting a posthumanist perspective into the discourse.

Origins: Economy and business history

In the realm of economics, design is an inherent and inseparable component of entrepreneurial endeavours, whether they involve global corporations, medium-sized companies or small-scale ventures. Furthermore, governmental regulations and economic strategies significantly shape the landscape of design, with their effects being observable through various means such as patents, design awards and the establishment of institutes for design promotion. Additionally, international organizations play a crucial and transformative role in fostering connections and relationships across diverse national contexts.

When examining these multifaceted elements, economic and business history provides valuable insights. These insights encompass the historical development of marketing tactics, the roles assumed by businesses and entrepreneurs as influential political entities, the positioning of corporations as

DOI: 10.4324/9781003147282-13

essential cultural institutions, the adaptability of businesses in driving inno-vation and adopting emerging technologies as well as the internal workings and dynamics within firms, ranging from large multinational conglomerates to closely-knit family-run enterprises (Berghoff 2015: 22–25).

In the nineteenth century, the field of economic history emerged in Ger-many and Great Britain as a response to the theories of, on the one hand, Georg Wilhelm Friedrich Hegel (1770–1831) and, on the other, Karl Marx. Economic history criticized these ideologies for relying too heavily on abstract theoretical concepts when explaining economic processes. A new generation of historical economists believed that a more promising approach to under-standing economic phenomena could be found through the study of history and human agency. Prominent figures from this generation included Gustav von Schmoller (1838–1917) in Germany and William Cunningham (1849–1919) in the UK, as well as their successors Max Weber and Werner Sombart (1863–1941). These German and British schools, in addition to the institu-tional economics linked to Thorstein Veblen (1857–1929), laid the foundation for economic history to become a subject of academic inquiry and formal instruction, solidifying its place by the early twentieth century. While some of these studies incorporated quantitative analysis, there was limited emphasis on employing explicit economic theories to analyse past economic events or processes (Kipping et al. 2017: 21).

In contrast to Marx's historical materialism, Weber did not simplify social relations by reducing them to economic determinism, nor did he view them as inevitably evolutionary. Acknowledging the existence of historical diversity, he utilized what he referred to as "ideal types," aiming to develop "multicausal" explanations that combined both material and ideational elements. One of his most significant works, *The Protestant Ethic and the Spirit of Capitalism* (1905), proposed that capitalism was a contingent result of a specific ascetic Calvinist–Protestant ethic and the regulating influence of Puritan dedication to labour. This focus on religious devotion as the driving force behind a par-ticular economic organization challenged Marx's assertion of the causal dominance of the mode of production, what he called the "economic base" (Biebuyck and Meltzer 2017).

By the mid-twentieth century, economic history had evolved into a dis-cipline largely distinct from economics (Godden 2015: 51). Within economic history, entrepreneurial history primarily emerged in response to the desires of corporations and entrepreneurs to cultivate their public image. The early twentieth century also witnessed the establishment of the first systematically organized company archives. This led to the creation of numerous commis-sioned biographies, company histories and autobiographical accounts. For instance, in 1912, Richard Ehrenberg (1857–1921), known for his early com-pany history of Siemens Brothers (1906), co-authored a study examining the Krupp workforce and their families. This research explored the policies of the heavy-industry sector in the Ruhr region. In the United States, economic and entrepreneurial history had an immediate and significant influence through the international flow of scholars and ideas. Edwin F. Gay (1867–1946), who had received his doctoral education with Schmoller in Germany, obtained a position in economic history at Harvard University and, more importantly, became the first dean of Harvard Business School (HBS) in 1908, where a chair in business history was created (Berghoff 2015: 21).

Distinct from entrepreneurial history, business history developed further under the business historian Henrietta M. Larson (1894–1983), who had joined HBS as a research associate in 1926. She was instrumental in establishing business history and drove forward its development as a separate academic discipline, distinct from economic history (Wilson et al. 2022: 7; Kipping et al. 2017: 22). Entrepreneurial history delves into the lives and activities of individuals engaged in entrepreneurial endeavours, with a specific focus on their distinctive social identities, behaviours and the impacts they made, not only within the business context but also in the broader social, cultural or political arena. Conversely, business history predominantly revolves around the progression of organizations, with a primary focus on economic achievements. Similar to economic historians, business historians are interested in unravelling the evolution of organizational structures and the dynamics of authority that facilitated various forms of organization and control mechanisms, a dimension closely associated with Weber's contributions (Kipping et al. 2017: 21). Nevertheless, in practice, there are often intersections between institutional and biographical approaches within these fields (Berghoff 2015: 21).

In Japan, scholars who had previously studied historical economics in Germany returned to establish economics departments at the universities of Tokyo and Kyoto in 1919. The study of business and economic history provided a wealth of material that served as a foundation for developing classifications or categorizations of the evolution of businesses. After the Second World War, a predominant school of economic history coalesced around the ideas of Otsuka Hisao (1907–1996), a professor at the University of Tokyo, that blended Marxist economics with a Weberian perspective on society and ethics to elucidate the origins of "modernity" in the Western world and what they perceived as the "backwardness" of the Japanese economy (Kipping et al. 2017: 23, 26). Economic historians with an antipathy to orthodox Marxism and ones dissatisfied with the approach of the "Otsuka School" were attracted to business and entrepreneurial history. The emerging sub-discipline was free from the highly negative views on Japanese tradition and the role of merchants held by Otsuka, and it attracted scholars with more optimistic assessments of postwar Japanese business and society (Kipping et al. 2017: 27).

In contrast to the US, where university-based business schools saw widespread development, Britain saw limited growth in separate higher education institutions dedicated to business education. Business history in Britain emerged as a subfield of economic history in the 1950s, following the publication of several company histories. One of the most influential was Charles Wilson's *History of Unilever*, the first volume of which was published in 1954. These studies were conducted by economic historians who were interested in the pivotal role played by leading firms in the broader industry's development, going beyond mere corporate histories (Toms and Wilson 2017: 9).

From the moment it entered academia, business history borrowed methodologies from neighbouring disciplines, particularly economics and management studies but also from history, sociology, political science and anthropology (Berghoff 2015: 22). The interest in entrepreneurial history went into decline in the 1960s and 1970s, just as popular interest in entrepreneurship was on the rise. The reasons for this decline were at least partly attributable to the increasing methodological sophistication of business history and economic history (Kipping et al. 2017: 26).

Development: Cultural political economy

One of the key focal points within the field of business history is the exploration of an ideal organizational framework concerning strategy, technology and market dynamics. Significant contributions to this inquiry were made by Alfred D. Chandler Jr. (1918–2007), a prominent business historian who joined Harvard Business School in 1970. His goal was to furnish social scientists with concrete empirical evidence that could be used to formulate broad generalizations and theories – thereby transcending the realm of isolated case studies and advancing a comprehensive framework for examining industrial capitalism (Berghoff 2015: 23; Kipping et al. 2017: 25).

In *Strategy and Structure* (1962) Chandler examined the organizational transformations within the largest American corporations. He combined a large-scale survey, that was relatively straightforward in terms of statistics, with in-depth case studies of four companies: General Motors, DuPont, Standard Oil and Sears Roebuck. His analysis illustrated how these pioneering firms, independently of one another, had implemented decentralized structures to accommodate their growth and diversification. Chandler's subsequent work, *The Visible Hand* (1977), emphasized the superior performance of managers – referred to as salaried entrepreneurs – when compared to owner–entrepreneurs. These studies have come to be regarded as classic examples of comparative research that contributes to theory-building in the field of management (Berghoff 2015: 23; Kipping et al. 2017: 25).

Chandler's third significant work, *Scale and Scope* (1990) expanded his research to include Great Britain and Germany. He concluded that variations in national competitiveness were the result of different approaches to leveraging economies of scale. In adopting this perspective, Chandler elevated the American model of managerial capitalism, characterized by major investments in production, management and marketing infrastructure, as a universal formula for achieving success (Berghoff 2015: 23). This assertion sparked strong opposition. The ensuing debate ultimately challenged Chandler's idealization of the American model of large-scale industry. Critics argued that Chandler had overlooked factors such as labour relations, culture, regulation, politics and smaller companies outside of the top 200 (Berghoff 2015: 23).

Chandler's work in the field of business historiography has been so influential that many discussions about its development now categorize it into two distinct phases: the Chandlerian phase and the post-Chandlerian phase. During the Chandlerian phase, the primary focus was on studying the emergence of large industrial firms and the managerial hierarchies that governed them. In the post-Chandlerian phase the attention shifted towards a wider array of organizational forms, including small and medium-sized enterprises, family businesses, business groups and networked organizations. Additionally, this phase represents a broader interest in business history that goes beyond examining organizational structures to encompass institutions, entrepreneurship and the cultural, social and political factors that underlie business enterprise (Kipping et al. 2017: 19).

Paradoxically, business history maintained its significance even during times when the subjects it studied were undergoing crisis. Following the student movements of the 1960s, entrepreneurs and corporations faced severe criticism. Then, in the 1970s, the pioneering nations of the industrial era entered into a structural crisis that, within a short span of time, resulted in the decline of previously dominant sectors such as mining, iron, steel and textiles. These disruptions led to the establishment of numerous museums and business archives, which have since become centres for research (Berghoff 2015: 22).

Starting from the 1980s, the "linguistic or cultural turn," which emphasized literary and linguistic analysis over quantitative methods, had a transformative impact not only within the humanities but also in the social sciences (Ray and Sayer 1999: 1). Consequently, while economic history continued to explore trade, commerce, industrialization and growth, the research priorities of social and cultural historians from the 1980s onward increasingly focused on themes such as race, gender, identity, consciousness and collective memory. Within the realm of social sciences, this "cultural turn" challenged positivist approaches to social research, which had traditionally assumed that social phenomena could be objectively understood through scientific methods. Culture was often treated as a dependent variable in these traditional approaches. However, the growing recognition of its constitutive role put culture at the centre of political economy (Bonnell and Hunt 1999).

This led to the emergence of a transdisciplinary approach known as cultural political economy, which focuses on the semiotic and structural dimensions of social life and their interconnections. It draws on concepts from critical and historically informed semiotic analyses, as well as from critical evolutionary and institutional political economy (Sum and Jessop 2013: 1). Cultural political economy posits that ideas can have a performative and constitutive influence on economic structures and relationships. Therefore, it emphasizes the need to differentiate between the "real economy," representing the totality of economic activities, and "economic imaginaries," which imbue the economic realm with meaning. The formulation and evolution of an economic imaginary should be understood within the broader context of a complex interplay between semiotic and non-semiotic processes. This involves considering not only discursive elements but also structural, agential and technological factors (Gerosa 2022: 132).

In this changing balance between culture and economy, it is possible to understand the direction of the change in quite opposed ways: the economization of culture and the culturalization of economy (Ray and Sayer 1999: 16). Regarding the economization of culture, one of the topics studied within cultural political economy is global development, not limited to cultural homogenization, nor to more nuanced analyses of hybrid forms or "glocalization." More centrally, global economic transformations themselves have been conceived of in cultural terms, including ideas about a shift from an industrial to an informational economy (Castells 2003) and the significance of the symbolic content of commodities (Lash and Urry 1994).

The sociologists Scott Lash and John Urry conclude that postmodernity involves de-differentiation. The modern period was one of vertical and horizontal differentiation, the development of many separate institutional, normative and aesthetic spheres, each with its specific conventions and modes of high and low cultures, science and life, art and popular entertainment. Nevertheless, in postmodernism, this differentiation dissolves. Lash and Urry recognize a breakdown of each sphere's distinctiveness as a result of the pervasive effect of the media and the aestheticization of everyday life. Some differences between the cultural object and the audience dissolve as legislation is replaced by interpretation and, finally, the relationship between representations and reality. This has led to a breakdown of the system of the modern period in which a horizontal and vertical differentiation, the development of many separate institutional, normative and aesthetic spheres, each with their specific conventions and modes of evaluation and with multiple separations of high and low culture, science and life, were the standard (1994: 272).

The development of this de-differentiation in the fields of museum curating and design retailing is explained through a specific case of the art funding system in America by the sociologist Sharon Zukin. In her book *The Cultures of Cities* (1995), she explains how and why the New York museums became dependent on private-sector financing, including both donations and stock market-based endowments, which produced a creative tension between high culture and speculative commerce. This occurred because of the belt-tightening of governmental financial support for arts and culture institutions in the aftermath of the fiscal crisis of 1975. The resulting peculiar system of funding the arts is more market-driven as cultural institutions have become more dependent on admission fees, gift shop sales and image differentiation. Art has therefore become more like for-profit culture industries in many ways since museums connect art, capital and the public space (1995: 118–120).

Regarding the culturalization of the economy, this shift involves a focus on the expansion of cultural industries and the various ways in which culture has become a normalized element in discussions of global and corporate development (Thrift 2001). Around the early 2000s, sociologists such as Richard Florida (2019[2002]), David Hesmondhalgh (2019[2002]) and John Howkins

(2013[2001]) gained recognition for popularizing the concept of creative industries and creative economies, ideas which had been circulating in academic circles, through articles in magazines and books aimed at a broader audience. These publications shared a common theme: the idea that actively nurturing the creative sector could lead to economic growth for cities. Richard Florida, in particular, played a prominent role in this movement with his Creative Class Theory, presented in his book *The Rise of the Creative Class* (2019[2002]), which was considered essential reading for aspiring city planners at the time. Unlike more moderate proponents of creative industries, Florida envisioned a significant reorganization of post-industrial city society.

How public–private coalitions fit into the discussion of strategic urban representations has been further developed by the political scientist Clarence Stone, who criticizes the privatization of local governments in his article "Urban Regimes and Problems of Local Democracy" (2002). He argues that in partnerships between governments and the private sector, the shared interests of the public can often become entangled with the distinct interests of private entities. Stone asserts that politics is about people coming together to collectively address the challenges they face. Private actors will inevitably shape a system in which they thrive, and their services become indispensable, whether or not this is beneficial for the larger community. Moreover, Stone highlights that individual isolated initiatives to solve systemic issues typically do not address long-standing failures, resulting in governmental structures and the creative sector being largely ineffective in the long term (2002: 3).

Implementation: The de-differentiation between the private and the public

Before the "cultural turn" that gained momentum in the 1980s, Marxism held significant sway in the 1970s and early 1980s. In the field of art history, Marxist perspectives focused on aspects related to production, mediation and consumption, ideology and the artefacts themselves. A notable example of such an approach applied to a design organization is seen in Ellinoor Bergvelt's study of the Good Living Foundation (Stichting Goed Wonen; 1979), which existed in the Netherlands from 1946 to 1968. Originally, this foundation was a collaborative effort involving consumers, distributors, designers and manufacturers. However, by 1954, it had transformed into a consumer association The foundation advocated for the ideals of socially and politically motivated modernism and it even marketed its own collection of furniture and household items. Furthermore, it granted its seal of approval to products that were functional, reliable and affordable.

Along similar lines, John A. Walker presented entrepreneurial and company histories as well as design institutions as pivotal to delineate the object of study of design history (1989: 55, 65). He mentions some existing company histories around Marks & Spencer, Habitat or the Sony Corporation. He values the contextual information that they provided but alerts of a lack of critical evaluation and objectivity if these are not well-researched and/or commissioned by the firm itself (1989: 56). Nevertheless, examples of critical histories of companies, sometimes affecting a whole sector, existed by then. Perhaps the best-known is Ralph Nader's *Unsafe at Any Speed: The Designed-In Dangers of the American Automobile* (1965), in which the author criticizes the resistance of car manufacturers to introduce safety features (such as seat belts), due to monetary considerations.

The burgeoning interest in consumption studies during the 1980s facilitated a closer connection between design and **business historians**. Regina Lee Blaszczyk, who had a background in business history, recognized that very few historians were exploring the strategic intersection of design practice, consumer preferences and evolving demand (2000: ix). Her doctoral research, later published as *Imagining Consumers: Design and Innovation from Wedgwood to Corning* (2000), aimed to investigate the role played by manufacturers and retailers in shaping consumerism in the United States during the late nineteenth and early twentieth centuries. She approached this subject not by portraying them as manipulative entities using coercion but rather as contributors to a consumer revolution designed to cater to diverse tastes.

Instead of employing ethnographic methods like anthropology-based consumption studies, such as those by Daniel Miller, Blaszczyk conducted her research using corporate archives, manufacturing records, trade journals, oral histories of managers and industry publications. Her objective was to delve into the supply side of the intricate relationship between businesses, designers, consumers and their preferences. She argued that while large corporations indeed aimed to boost sales of standardized products through direct consumer advertising, peripheral firms concentrated on studying consumers and responding to their desires rather than attempting to create new needs in the market (2000: 2).

There has been a growing emphasis on studying companies and institutions, leading to investigations into various subjects such as the Bauhaus school (Oswalt ct al. 2009), corporations like Ikea (Kristoffersson 2014) or Olivetti (Brennan 2015), and publicly funded entities like the design centres in New Zealand and Belgium (Thompson 2011; Serulus 2018). The public sector has also been extensively examined, particularly in the context of nation-building processes where the state plays a pivotal role, both as a promoter of design and as a client of designers for initiatives related to institutional graphic identity (Gimeno Martínez 2016: 93–146).

The realm of fashion has seen further exploration in Regina Lee Blaszczyk's subsequent works (2008; Blaszczyk and Wubs 2018), as well as in the research of another business historian who has delved into design history, Véronique Pouillard. Initially centred around fashion history (2021), Pouillard's work has expanded to encompass luxury industries (Donzé et al. 2022), adding to the existing body of scholarship on this subject by Peter McNeil and Giorgio Riello (2016). Moreover, international organizations have been the subject of in-depth studies, revealing their transnational reach and global impact (Aynsley et al. 2022).

As a method to study design dynamics, **cultural political economy** is notably evident in Guy Julier's book *The Culture of Design* (2014[2000]) but even more in his *Economies of Design* (2017: 3). In this work, he contends that the increasing blurring of lines between the private and public sectors necessitates hybrid approaches where companies and institutions collaborate on shared objectives and strategies. These changes should be seen within the broader historical context of neoliberalism, which transformed capitalism into the dominant framework influencing the direction of design and its organizational structure (2017: 7–14). Julier argues that since the 1980s, the public sector has shifted from a model of "public administration" to what is known as the "New Public," which prioritizes marketization and competition. This transition has also reduced the influence of local governments on their creative industries, resulting in the rapid growth of specialized commercial consulting firms (2017: 144). Julier warns about the limitations of this structured approach, particularly in terms of its ambiguous stance on commercial interests within the realm of public affairs. He argues that these structures may not prioritize human-centred design because they primarily focus on managing systems and achieving politically determined targets and goals, such as sustainability, circular economies and inclusion (2017: 151).

This tension between the private and the public interest and between economy and culture has been often addressed by design scholars when discussing the museum as an institution. To different extents, displaying strategies reproduce the de-differentiation between the public and the private and inject the exhibits with social meaning, beyond their use-value or aesthetics. The following three examples illustrate the strategies of a design museum, a state-funded organization for the promotion of design and a corporate museum, exploring the interactions between the private and the public.

A first example is how Julier delves into the role of museums in mediating products and observes different hierarchies within the realm of design, characterized by two extremes (2014[2000]: 91–96). At one end of this spectrum is what he terms "anonymous design," referring to objects, spaces and images conceived without prominently featuring the designer's name. At the opposite end, Julier places "high design," where conscious designer input, authorship and pricing play a substantial role in establishing an artefact's cultural and aesthetic significance (2014[2000]: 89–90). The classification of a particular product into one of these categories is not solely determined by its inherent qualities but is heavily influenced by the strategies used for its display. Julier contends that creating an impression of uniqueness and value, typical of "high design" is accomplished by showcasing a single exemplar of each product, much like how traditional museum objects have been curated (2014[2000]: 91). Similarly, retail spaces such as Alessi stores address these display strategies in their stores and catalogues. When photographing their products for commercial catalogues, the products are presented in isolation, devoid of any everyday context, and set against abstract backgrounds, thus emphasizing their distinctiveness (2014[2000]: 110).

Whereas Julier particularly speaks of exhibiting high design, not all design on display is considered "high design" or aims to gain that status. A second example is Ness Wood's study on the exhibition strategies of the London Design Centre, a state-funded organization for the promotion of design (2016: 27). The Design Centre positioned itself midway between a not-for-profit organization and a commercial one to: "encourage people to buy better goods, not to buy more goods" (2016: 29). The Centre had an exhibition space displaying mass-produced domestic products in a way that combined retail store display and museum practice (2016: 28). For its "Designs of the Year" exhibition, the exhibits were positioned on glass and plastic reflective shelving; overhead lighting enhanced their appearance. Only single examples of each item were on display with a relevant caption, showing the designer's name, which appeared first, before the manufacturer. However, unlike most museum exhibitions, the visitors were able to touch and handle the exhibits (2016: 31). Wood concludes that in this case designed objects were displayed depending on who selected the objects and the involvement of manufacturers, who financially backed this exhibition (Wood 2016: 35).

Along with the design museum and design centres, there are the corporate museums, which maintain museum status but manifestly serve commercial goals. They are thematic, commercial buildings, owned by a particular firm, where the history of the company brand and products' development are presented on the background of the local social environment. The architectural researcher Ksenia Katarzyna Piatkowska studies the corporate museums of three German car manufacturers: Porsche, Mercedes and BMW. For example, the exhibition at the corporate museum BMW (*BMW Welt* [BMW World]) illustrates the history of the company and the history of its products, from the first specimen up to the latest models (Figure 10.1). Another section includes the cars and motorcycles currently being produced, which can be purchased at any time (2014: 31). After studying all three cases, Piatkowska concludes that the purpose of a corporate museum appears to be integral to the corporate identity programme, exposing the company's values and philosophy. Corporate museums are usually located next to the factories where the brand products are manufactured, extending the exhibition route to sectors of the production line (2014: 33). This brings corporate museums into a complicated and often misunderstood position, straddling both the cultural and traditional world of the public museum and the profit-motivated and ever-changing business world.

These three cases of exhibition venues – including design museums, design centres and corporate museums – reflect the construction of the status of design with mechanisms that intertwine the cultural, the political and the social and that generate economic imaginaries regarding uniqueness, accessibility, anonymity and authorship. According to Julier, the design museum will create the impression of uniqueness. State-funded organizations to educate the public taste will create accessibility, partly because they serve the goals of manufacturers, according to Wood. The corporate museum creates a corporate prestige and builds up the popularity of products among visitors, connecting

Figure 10.1 The BMW corporate museum, BMW Welt (BMW World), is featured in the foreground, while the BMW headquarters can be seen in the background, both situated in Munich, Germany. Photo by Bjoern Goettlicher/Construction Photography/Avalon/Getty Images

the prestige of a museum to commercial ends, adds Piatkowska. The distance of proximity between design and users will be created through exhibition display, shaping cultural perceptions and influencing economic value.

Economic and cultural imaginaries do not only condition perception but also result in law, as legal frameworks regulate questions of originality in design. In this sense, Anne Massey uses the fast-growing market of imitations to elaborate on authorship in her book *Chair* (2011). She argues that the fetishization of designer chairs is closely linked with the celebrity designer (Massey 2011: 55). Massey attributes the emphasis on originality to the relevance of authorship in design and the growing interest of museums in designed objects. Whereas, at first, the chairs were seen as a metaphor for the potential user, the existence of chairs in the museum altered this conception, and the chair came to be interpreted as standing for the presence of the designer (Massey 2011: 56).

Carma Gorman argues in her essay to make a "greater use of the law as a lens for understanding design" (2014: 269). She highlights that national borders greatly influence what designers and manufacturers can or cannot do and therefore play an essential role in the final design's appearance. A chair which has been widely studied regarding its originality and its relatedness to law and patent is the typology of the cantilever chair. The art and economic historian Tobias Vogelgsang is one of the many scholars who has conducted in-depth research into the development of this chair regarding authenticity and originality. In his article "Law, Design, and Market Value: Lessons from the Cantilever Chair, 1929–1936" (2017), he explores the design development of the cantilever chair and traces the many lawsuits and patent matters. By doing so, he examines how questions surrounding intellectual property rights influence market values. Authenticity or originality can, according to Vogelgsang, allow the manufacturer to add a financial markup on the product (2017: 561).

Challenges: Posthumanism and artificial intelligence

A subject that generates notable attention among a multitude of disciplines is the emergence and development of artificial intelligence (AI), which has recently entered the realm of content creation, affecting the design industry. Since the 1990s, machine learning (ML) has been utilized for a variety of functions (Figure 10.2). It was, however, restricted in processing significant data because of hardware limitations of the time. Due to technological advancements since the 2010s, those limitations have been lifted, enabling the circumstances under which ML and AI could develop (Kim et al. 2019: 141). Nevertheless, the implementation of AI has not been free of criticism. Graphic design created "by" intelligent machines, for example, has been criticised as flat. By always operating on historic data, AI design essentially produces more of the same (Mattern 2020: 576).

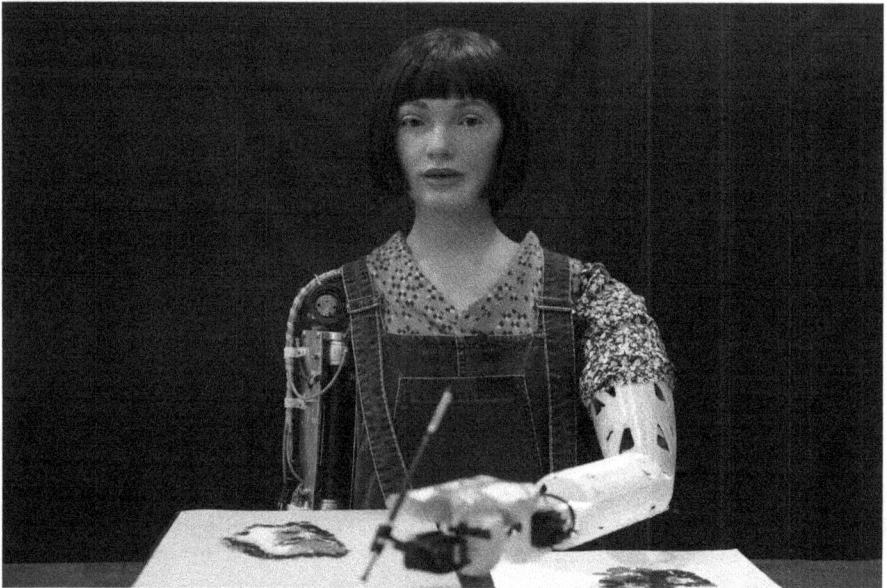

Figure 10.2 Ai-Da Robot, an ultra-realistic humanoid robot artist, paints during a press call at The British Library on April 4, 2022 in London, Great Britain. Photo by Hollie Adams/Getty Images

There is a sense of threat present in AI literature along with a concern expressing that AI needs to be under control of humans. The social scientist Shannon Mattern (2020) raises questions about the uses of AI in the future while giving examples of current practices. She examines the ethical opportunities and risks people might face when AI-driven design practice is programmed to serve the needs and desires of consumers and clients (Mattern 2020: 571). Furthermore, Mattern opposes two common predictions of the ethical implications of AI. Employing AI could reduce the workload for designers and eliminate entry-level positions. However, this implies designers losing their jobs in favour of more efficient and less mistake-prone AI (Mattern 2020: 577). Within graphic design, Mattern foresees the possible disappearance of the web designer profession. There are numerous examples of AI web designers where the human gives the parameters and content of the website and AI does the rest (Mattern 2020: 575).

Concerning the matter of originality, neither the Berne Convention nor the World Intellectual Property Organization Copyright Treaty (WCT) have established a definitive standard at this point. Whether or not AI-generated works are copyright-protectable depends on national legal frameworks. For example, the Chinese legal framework demands that the specific work "can be reproduced in a tangible form." As legal scholar Han Wang has demonstrated (2023), there is still some ambiguity in establishing the attribute of works generated by computers. How is AI prompting new understandings of law frameworks? The existence and potential agency of this "intelligent" nonhuman questions the traditional human/non-human or natural/artificial dichotomy. If both copyright law and ideas of authorship are human-centric, how can we interpret the role of AI beyond these models?

In Chinese academia, there are different attitudes on this issue. For example, some scholars believe that regardless of the use, value and social evaluation, the works generated by machines should be protected by copyright if it is done independently by machines. Other legal scholars, on the other hand, believe that AI-generated works are the result of the application of algorithmic rules and highly homogenous templates. They leave no room for creativity and reflect no individual characteristics of the creator; thus, they cannot satisfy the work's originality requirement (Wang 2023: 903)

Theoretically, there is no unified answer to the question if machines are creative; it will depend on the theoretical perspective adopted. What is apparent is that AI creativity demands a posthumanist approach. Posthumanism, a condition in which the human becomes decentralized, is one that has roots in the late 1970s in the work of literary theorist Ihab Hassan, "Prometheus as Performer: Towards a Posthumanist Culture?" (1977). In the mid-1980s, social scientist Donna Haraway's "A Cyborg Manifesto" (1985) explored the boundaries between human, machine and animal through the metaphor of a cyborg, anticipating transhumanism and posthumanism. In essence, posthumanism is the rejection of traditional Western anthropocentric humanism. As a term, it is defined by its confrontation with humanism, an ethical philosophical attitude originating from the Enlightenment. Humanism places the human at the centre of its philosophy, an autonomous agent that is separate but still engaged with nature. As posthumanism became more defined in critical theory, it became entangled with theories such as actor–network theory, object-oriented ontology and new materialism. As the demand for a posthuman condition is becoming more apparent in the thinking around the Anthropocene, the subject has gained relevance and attention (Bolter 2016: 1; Forlano 2017: 16–17).

Discussions on posthumanism within the field of design tend to decentralize the designer, and by extension the human in general (Slavin 2016: 12). The article *Design as Participation* (2016) by the artist and media specialist Kevin Slavin discusses the topic of the designer in a posthuman world, examining different roles and levels of participation of a designer in a design process and in society (Slavin 2016: 3). He argues for an approach in which designers engage with the complex adaptive system that surrounds them, which motivates the perspective that humans are nothing more than participants in systems that have no centre (Slavin 2016: 17). Likewise, the book *Politics of Things* (2020) by design researchers Michelle Christensen and Florian Conradi, opposes the idea that human designers are the creators of things and that designing involves "negotiating power with things," prompting shared agency between humans and non-humans (2020: 11–14).

The sociolinguist Feifei Zhou (2020: 197–209) explores posthuman implications of creativity in intelligent machines. She compares the linguistic notions of the humanist, integrationist view to a posthuman, distributed view in their perspective of creativity and AI. The framework of distributed cognition considers creativity not necessarily as the product of an individual, but rather a distributed effort involving both human and non-human contributors, thus challenging our interpretation of creativity. This, according to Zhou, aligns with the posthumanist view as it sees both human and machine cognition as "the same," operating in a distributed system (2020: 206). Zhou concludes that distributed creativity can thus be creative. However, Zhou also suggests that according to a humanist view if machines do not "understand" these contributions in an "embodied, historical, contextualized manner," AI cannot be said to be truly creative by itself (2020: 209).

Regarding the issue of agency and legal responsibility, Zhou questions how much control is needed from the human side and how much responsibility humans can give to machines. These are issues of agency, responsibility and morality, that according to Zhou stem from a human-centred view (2020: 207). The posthuman perspective makes no distinction in cognition between humans and machines. It therefore would not constitute questions about responsibility as both entities would be completely equal (2020: 207).

Similarly, the philosopher of technology Judith Simon (2015) addresses the subject of responsibility and agency within complex interconnected socio-technological systems. Invoking actor–network theory and some posthuman authors, Simon asks the question who is to blame when something goes wrong in these interconnected networks: "[...] who is to blame: designers, users, the technologies or rather the distributed and entangled socio-technical systems?" (2015: 145). Her chapter concludes with a warning that accountability should not be completely taken out of the hands of humans (2015: 154–158).

If AI is allowed to perform in a manner of equal agency to human designers, would there still be a need for human designers? In investigating the views of authors in posthuman design literature for the possible role of human designers in an AI-dominated world, a notable resistance against posthuman sentiment emerges. While theoretical posthuman literature might provide a possible framework for the Anthropocene where humanity enters a harmonious contract with AI, that framework might not be comprehensively applicable or desirable to finding solutions to contemporary issues.

The attitude of most literature discussed revolves around what humans ought to do with this new, potentially radically influential technology, that prompts humans to lose agency to machines. Throughout this body of literature, the first notion places the role of AI as "supporting" the human designer. The literature advocating for this stance often comes from AI-oriented research exploring the practical implications of AI on design. The other view, mainly purported by Slavin, Christensen and Conradi, argues for decidedly decentralizing the human, striving for a true posthuman condition, in which there is an equal playing field for humans and non-humans. Posing the question of what role will human designers fulfil in an AI-dominated world, is to ask what that world will look like.

11 Geopolitics

National interactions

Categorizing creative works based on their country of origin has long been a practice within art history. This approach often seeks to find justification for artistic styles in factors like landscape, climate, geography and even the perceived national character of a place. Consequently, it led to the development of national identities, their comparison and even their contestation within an increasingly global art community. This practice also gave rise to stereotypical views that, in turn, perpetuated political inequalities. Some cultural identities were adopted strategically for political or state-related purposes. The emergence of postcolonial thinking prompted a re-evaluation of the geopolitical dynamics of colonization concerning artistic expression. In the realm of design scholarship, there has been a concerted effort to challenge the field's modernist biases, including a reconsideration of previously overlooked geographical areas and a reconsideration of research methodologies. The central focus of recent design scholarship has been on the process of decolonizing the discipline.

Origins: A national character

The division of art depending on geography has a long history. In antiquity, two significant themes emerged to explain the differences in art production by different ethnic groups. The first revolves around the concept of the environment, particularly climate, that would exert an influence on the visual arts. The second is the cultural explanation, which involves linking specific types of artistic objects to particular cultures or regions (DaCosta Kaufman 2004: 26)

At the core of an environmentalist explanation lies the practice of dividing the Earth and its inhabitants based on climate zones. The physician Hippocrates (460–370 BCE) laid the foundation for understanding how the environment affects humans, offering climatic explanations for practices like gymnastics and medicine, which could potentially be applied to explain various other cultural phenomena. Consequently, more authors, including Nikolaus Pevsner, have

DOI: 10.4324/9781003147282-14

referred to Hippocrates as one of the pioneers who linked climate to national character (Pevsner 1956: 13; DaCosta Kaufmann 2004: 24–25).

Regarding the cultural division of the arts, the natural philosopher Pliny (23/24–79 CE) distinguished three genera (or "kinds") in art: the Ionic, the Sicyonian and the Attic, creating thereby a key tool for the historiography of art – since this concept would later be used by seventeenth-century authors, who translated Pliny's genera as "schools" in the sense of "schools of art." It is noteworthy that the categories used for this distinction were geographical ones, so named after peoples associated with particular places. Additionally, Pliny introduced the concept of the enduring continuity of these peoples throughout history, suggesting that they never vanished and retained their consistent physical and moral characteristics over time (Michaud 2019[2015]: 3; DaCosta Kaufman 2004: 25). During the Middle Ages, this mindset endured and concepts that are currently related to style or manner were likewise tied to nations, like the expression "in the French manner" (ad modum franciae; DaCosta Kaufman 2004: 26).

In the seventeenth century, the concept of school was extended to denote the artistic production of cities, regions and countries. The first testimony in which art is defined by schools, according to their distinct manner ("maniera"), is the *Treatise on Painting* by Giovanni Battista Agucchi (1570–1632), written in 1615, but published posthumously in 1646. His defence of Italian art according to schools of art must be seen as a reaction to Vasari's preference for Tuscan artists. In the sixteenth century, Giorgio Vasari's *The Lives of the Most Excellent Painters, Sculptors, and Architects* only used the term "maniera" to denote that of an artist, like Masaccio or Raphael. Even then, Vasari was keen on discerning local and regional differences in art, preferring Florentine art over that produced in either Siena or Venice, and the drawing skills of Tuscan painters above the Venetian colourists (Vasari 1991[1568]: xv, 501). Cultural identities were forged in response to transnational competition. They foreshadowed the instrumentalization of art for political aims typical of later nation-states.

The idea of schools of art began to spread beyond Italy with the release of art literature in the northern and southern Netherlands, including works by Karel van Mander (in 1604) and Cornelis de Bie (1661–1662). Germany also contributed to this development with the three-part publication *Teutsche Academie* by Joachim von Sandrart, that appeared in 1675, 1679 and 1680. France joined in with the writings of André Félibien (1619–1695) in 1666 and of the diplomat and art theorist Roger de Piles (1635–1709) in 1699, who elaborated a clear idea of the concept of a nation. De Piles's overview of European art was theoretically supported by an important chapter on "Of the Taste of Several Nations." He argued that artworks on view in countries shape the national tastes of their inhabitants, namely the Roman, the Venetian, the Lombard, the German, the Flemish and the French. He attributed to each school a distinct taste. Whereas manner had to do with the body, and in particular, the hand, taste was first of all a matter of judgement, something intellectual (Michaud 2019[2015]: 16).

In the eighteenth century, the two themes of environmental and cultural explanations of art merged, resulting in essentialist, stereotypical visions of national characters. The philosopher Montesquieu (1689–1755) explored in his work *The Spirit of the Laws* from 1748 the connection between government and climate, focusing on national and racial distinctions. According to his perspective, northern climates promote freedom, while harsh or warm climates encourage indolence and despotism. Some of the emerging cultural and even racial ideas that would later trouble the field of historiography were already evident in Montesquieu's work. These include his division of Europe into East and West, as well as his argument for the subjugation of Africans into slavery based on racial considerations (DaCosta Kaufmann 2004: 36).

Much like Montesquieu, the art historian Johann Joachim Winckelmann, in his work *The History of Art of Antiquity* published in 1764, continued to explore how climate influences the customs, physical form, complexion and the art of different peoples. According to Winckelmann, various factors, including education, government, as well as the inherent and cultivated characteristics of the people, contributed to the development of the visual arts. He explicitly stated that climate shaped "national character," and this "national character" in turn influenced art. He observed that the warm climate of Greece allowed its inhabitants, particularly Greek men, to wear minimal or no clothing, which in turn provided ancient Greek artists with the opportunity to freely study the human body (DaCosta Kaufmann 2004: 36). Like Pliny, Winckelmann appeared to regard the influence of climate as not only causal but also persistent. Both climate and national characters remained constant across the centuries contributing to a stereotyping of different ethnic groups across time (Michaud 2019[2015]: 34; DaCosta Kaufmann 2004: 37).

By the late eighteenth century, some writers still adhered to the concept of environmental determinism. However, others, notably the philosopher Johann Gottfried Herder (1744–1803), presented a different viewpoint. He broke away from Enlightenment thinking by emphasizing the diversity rather than the unity of the concept of culture. This distinction laid the groundwork for cultural theories that persisted for over a century and can be seen as a precursor to contemporary discussions on "multiculturalism." Herder argued that while a people's character is influenced by their geographical location and can vary due to climate, it is also shaped by tradition. He introduced the idea that culture is moulded by the *Volksgeist*, which can be understood as the spirit of a people, a concept that Montesquieu had previously touched upon. Because culture involves numerous unquantifiable variables such as geography, language and climate, each culture is inherently unique and deserving of respect.

Herder was not an advocate of nationalism or racialism. However, his concept of the *Volksgeist*, which is deeply rooted in a people's history and manifested through their cultural creations, contributed to the enduring argument that the spirit or essence of ethnic groups plays a significant role in shaping the character or quality of their art. This idea also laid the groundwork for the persistent notion of ethnic or racial essentialism, becoming one of the fundamental concepts in the field of art geography (Gimeno Martínez 2016; 38–42; DaCosta Kaufmann 2004: 47). The emergence of public art museums and the rise of nationalist art history intimately linked art to the realm of politics, and instrumentalized the idea of the spirit of the people in processes of nation-building.

Whereas the history of collecting describes a human activity that has occurred at all times and places, that of museums is distinctly modern. As a national enterprise, the museum is largely understood as a state-funded institution that is rooted in the late eighteenth, but even more so in the nineteenth, century. Several distinctive characteristics are the introduction in museums of collection systematization and specialization, education, public access and conservation, which is broadly dated ca. 1750. Museums are in close relationship to the shaping of nation-states as agents that promote and spread images of national identity. The Napoleonic Wars had a profound impact on European museums. In 1794, the first campaign of Napoleon (1769–1821) marked the beginning of a series of art confiscations from conquered territories, transported to Paris. The pivotal moment in these turbulent developments was the establishment of the Louvre Museum around 1800, showcasing the spoils of war, later known as the Musée Napoléon. This national museum set a remarkable precedent, amassing an extensive international art collection, influencing Europe, and prompting nations to establish their own museums after their art and scientific treasures were reclaimed following Napoleon's defeats in 1813 and 1815 (Berger 2015: 21; Bergvelt et al. 2009).

National values and notions of Western civilization are expressed in the national museum culture in Europe, including the values of the Enlightenment, which results in a variety of interpretations of universal, national and transnational phenomena. In numerous countries, national interests found expression in the interpretation of the visual aspects of artworks. Compositions were viewed as reflections of distinct styles originating from a specific land, people, and ultimately, a nation. The earlier concept of the "spirit of the people" had evolved into that of the "spirit of the nation," which found its expression in art (DaCosta Kaufmann 2004: 54–55). The foundation of national galleries and other forms of national art institutions in various European countries, the decoration of public buildings and the placement of monuments aimed to determine the national character of art or to demonstrate how cultural artefacts demonstrate national characteristics. National museums need therefore to be analysed as manifestations of cultural and political desires, rather than straightforward representations of historical or national "facts" (Berger 2015: 13–32).

Given that race could also be interchanged with the ideas of the people or the nation or be assumed to be at the core of a people's formation, racialist notions were often present in much of this discourse. For instance, the ideas of the art historian Alois Riegl (1858–1905) about national distinctions and historical development were rooted in the racial characteristics of European nations, forming the basis for arguments that advocated the existence of enduring national and racial traits in art. Another art historian, Wilhelm Worringer (1881–1965), explicitly adopted Riegl's concepts and applied them to explore the "Nordic" characteristics of pre-Renaissance art, ultimately attributing the Gothic style to a fundamentally racial phenomenon (Michaud 2019[2015]: 37; DaCosta Kaufmann 2004: 57–58). What unites these discussions is an essentialist vision of ethnic groups and their creative output.

Development: Postcolonialism and cultural appropriation

In the 1960s, essentialist nationalism encountered criticism. The idea that nationalism was a product of modernity, originating in early nineteenth-century Europe, gained wider acceptance. If the concept of the nation was constructed, then the spirit of the people was also a construction. Numerous authors, including political theorists like Frantz Fanon (1925–1961) and Kwame Nkrumah (1909–1972), as well as writer Albert Memmi (1920–2020), produced works examining the impacts of colonization in countries like Algeria, Tunisia and Ghana (Fanon 1961; Memmi 1957; Nkrumah 1964).

Postcolonial literature began to scrutinize the formation of nations in formerly colonized regions, where nations had not previously existed. Ironically, instead of reverting to pre-colonial territorial and political divisions, post-colonial nations embraced the political frameworks left behind by their colonizers, including the structures of nation-states. This imposition of political organization, in the form of a state, offered a rich field of study for examining the concept of the nation as a "cultural" construct, as opposed to an inherent or "natural" reality. Constructivist approaches showed that nationalism was something externally – socially – created, assumed by the citizenry and exported through colonization (Özkirimli 2000: 64–74). Despite that, the colonized negotiated imposition in several ways, adding complexity to the straightforward portrayal of the colonialists as having agency while presenting the colonized as lacking it.

To scrutinize postcolonialism, theorists employ various binary oppositions to analyse power dynamics between the dominator and the dominated, such as Self/Other, centre/margin, Occident/Orient and, most commonly, colonizer/colonized. Nevertheless, these identities are not mutually exclusive but intertwined with each other. This means that every identity category within the binary is inherently influenced by the other, forming an integral part of its own constitution. For instance, the colonizer comes to recognize its superior status in contrast to the constructed "inferiority" of the colonized, while the colonized is situated, through coercion, within the oppressive frameworks established by the colonizer. The critical theorist Homi K. Bhabha introduced the term "hybridity" to describe this relational process, which highlights the pitfalls of essentializing or romanticizing either category as the fundamental basis for ethical engagement (1994: 110–115).

In his influential anti-colonial book *The Wretched of the Earth* (1961), Fanon described how the colonizers, by subjecting the colonized to their racist colonial system, fabricated and perpetuated a perception of the colonized as the "other," the "savage" or the "animalistic." This classification served to reinforce the dominance of the white/modern colonizer and justified violence and oppression by the colonizers against what they considered primitive bodies (Fanon 1961: 2–7; Vázquez 2020: 69). Regarding this, the literary theorist Gayatri Chakravorty Spivak articulates how colonization is embedded in the discursive nature of power. In her seminal essay "Can the Subaltern Speak?", Chakravorty Spivak (1988) states that both the colonizer and the colonized are embedded in power relations. What is recognized as worthy of being said and heard are both governed by "rules of recognition." These rules pre-exist the speaking subject and reflect the worldview of the dominant culture (Chakravorty Spivak 1988: 292, 294).

Expanding on Fanon's ideas, Bhabha delves deeper into the concept of ambivalence. He posits that the colonizer maintains a complex relationship with the colonized, shaped by colonial ideologies that position the colonized as subordinate individuals in need of "rescue" or "guidance" through imitation of the colonizer's values and behaviours. However, this process is marked by ambivalence because the colonizer also harbours apprehensions about the mimetic practices of the colonized. Such imitation can approach the behaviours of the colonizer, blurring the lines between dominance and subordination. In response, the colonizer distinguishes the colonized as different from and, consequently, inferior to themselves by categorizing the colonized as entirely comprehensible, unalterable and predictable. In simpler terms, the colonizer seeks to simultaneously eliminate the Otherness of the colonized by encouraging assimilation into the dominant culture while also reclaiming certain aspects of the colonized identity as a way to highlight the differences (and perceived inferiority) of the colonized (Bhabha 1994: 60–61, 80–82).

Among postcolonial theorists, the literary critic Edward Said is notable for deconstructing the Eurocentric framework of intellectual and cultural history. In *Orientalism* (1978), Said examined colonization as a cultural phenomenon and delved into the emerging geo-cultural dynamics between former colonizers and colonized regions. More recently, other postcolonial theorists, including semiotician Walter D. Mignolo and sociologist Rolando Vázquez, concur that modern aesthetics and knowledge are shaped by geopolitical forces that assert their dominance in representing the world's reality under the guise of universality. This, in turn, marginalizes and suppresses other realms of sensory experiences and meanings that are deeply rooted in the body and local histories (Vázquez 2020: 38–39; Mignolo 2011: 132–133). The colonized populations are denied the authority of representation and the validation that it entails. Colonial art is often denigrated as "primitive" and objectified for the consumption of the white/modern observer (Vázquez 2020: 96).

As the validator of a dominant aesthetic, the museum has been questioned as a colonial institution since the 1980s. The anthropologist Christina Kreps states that professional Western museology has rested almost exclusively on one knowledge system: the modern Western one. This knowledge system has dictated why and how non-Western cultural materials have been collected as well as the ways in which they have been perceived, curated and represented. Within this particular knowledge system, non-Western objects have been systemically organized and reconfigured to fit into Western structures and ideas of art, culture, history and heritage. Because of the hegemony of Western museology, most people have difficulties thinking, talking and writing about museums, curation and heritage in terms other than those provided by the Western museological discourse (Kreps 2010: 962–963). To counteract this imbalance, art events surfaced that questioned the Western art discourse from a postcolonial point of view, which resulted in exhibitions built around the concept of multiculturalism. According to cultural theorist Madina Tlostanova, these exhibitions may have displayed different cultures and nationalities, but their perspective remained Western (Tlostanova 2017: 75).

Unequal relations stemming from coloniality have resulted in debates on cultural appropriation, regarding the cultural exchange between the colonizers and the colonized. Cultural appropriation is primarily associated with the reuse of already existing elements from another context and the act of adapting and integrating them into one's own culture. In *Borrowed Power* (1997), the legal scholars Bruce Ziff and Pratima V. Rao stress that appropriation revolves around relations of power. They consider appropriation to be one form of cultural transmission that can be either an assimilative or an appropriative practice depending on whether a group is identified as dominant or subordinate (Ziff and Rao 1997: 5–6). The assimilative practice describes the process in which cultural minorities are stimulated to adapt or assimilate the dominant's group cultural forms and norms. Appropriative practices, on the other hand, are described as going in the opposite direction and encompass processes in which dominant groups appropriate cultural forms of subordinate groups (Ziff and Rao 1997: 7).

Cultural appropriation has not always been considered in negative terms but also positively as a cross-fertilization between cultures, rather multi-directional than uni-directional. The media theorist Richard A. Rogers discusses appropriation as a cultural phenomenon – potentially but not necessarily abusive – when two different cultures come into contact with each other (Rogers 2006: 474). He defines cultural appropriation as "the use of one culture's symbols, artefacts, genres, rituals, or technologies by members of another culture – regardless of intent, ethics, function, or outcome" (Rogers 2006: 476). Like Ziff and Rao, Rogers considers that when two cultures meet, their differences can have the effect of being dominated and altered or dominating and altering the other. Rogers acknowledges the relevance of concepts such as cultural exchange, cultural dominance and cultural exploitation, especially for safeguarding the cultural heritage of marginalized communities (Rogers 2006: 478–480).

While some facets of cultural appropriation involve enforcement, others pertain to adaptation and mutual learning. Following the concept of "transculturation," as defined by James Lull and originally coined by anthropologist

Fernando Ortiz in 1947, Rogers defines transculturation as a multifaceted process characterized by the multidirectional exchange of cultural elements, ultimately giving rise to entirely new cultural components (Roger 2006: 291; Lull 2000: 241–249). Rogers contends that when different cultures encounter one another, cultural appropriation becomes an inevitable outcome, and he challenges certain conceptualizations of cultural appropriation that tend to essentialize the notion of culture (Rogers 2006: 474, 475). He rejects the Western concept of culture as an organism and, instead, perceives culture as a communal entity capable of adapting and surviving even when crucial elements such as "religion, language, land, blood, leadership, etc." are lost (Rogers 2006: 492). He refutes the idea that cultures possess a fixed essence, a single origin, authenticity, purity or an intrinsic nature within their cultural expressions. Rather, he argues that cultural forms do not evolve from "pure" antecedents, emphasizing that cultural hybridity precedes any notion of cultural development (Rogers 2006: 491).

To illustrate his ideas, Rogers brings attention to the example of Hopi katsina dolls, which are crafted by Native American communities in the Southwestern United States (Figure 11.1). A discussion about these dolls' authenticity or their lack thereof entails essentialist perspectives on culture. These dolls represent a version tailored for tourists and collectors, distinct from the traditional Hopi katsina dolls originally used in religious ceremonies. The katsina-like dolls diverge from the originals chiefly as they no longer have a religious purpose. Moreover, they incorporate unusual decorative elements, utilize different materials and are created by individuals from various tribes, including Hopis and Zunis – tribes for whom katsina dolls had held religious significance – and Navajos – for whom they had not –, as well as non-Native dollmakers. Disregarding them as inauthentic conceals the intricate cultural dynamics of a living practice and community (Rogers 2006: 493–494; see also Pearlstone 2001: 16–21, 38–48).

Implementation: The global and the indigenous

The Eurocentric bias of early design historiography has been counteracted by efforts to internationalize the field. Initially, historical narratives focused primarily on the Industrial Revolution and limited their scope to a select few nations. The global expansion of design history has since embraced previously overlooked geographical areas. Initiatives like the International Committee on Design History and Studies (ICDHS, 1999–) and projects like Globalising Art, Architecture and Design History (GLAADH, 2001–3) have played pivotal roles in this endeavour. Anna Calvera (2005) argued that design historians must consider the local, national, regional and global contexts since design, both past and present, originates within these diverse settings. As stated by D.J. Huppatz, it is evident that this conception of globalization entails viewing it as a dynamic and multidirectional series of movements – of people, material goods and information – across geopolitical boundaries, rather than a single, deterministic process culminating in a standardized world modelled after Europe or the United States of America (Huppatz 2015: 2).

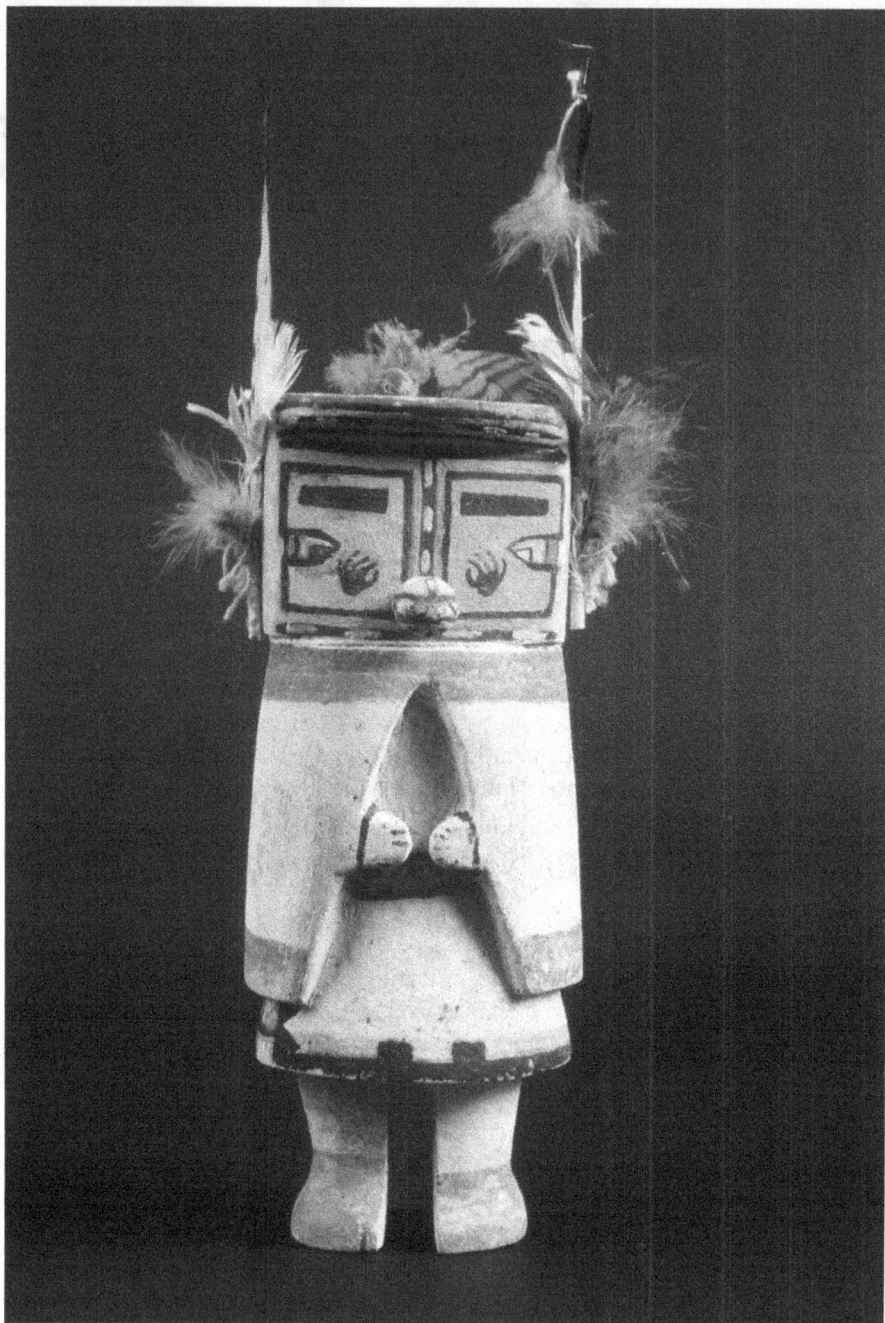

Figure 11.1 Hopi katchina doll, E3843, Museum of Northern Arizona, Flagstaff, Arizona. Photo by: Universal Images Group via Getty Images

In this discussion, the legitimacy of the "national histories of design" format came under scrutiny as it exemplified how design history perpetuates methodological nationalism. A number of studies problematized the phenomenon to a greater extent, reflecting on how designed artefacts convey national identity. They reflect on how national identity is expressed through design, what agents participate in this and what the perception is from the consumers. These accounts connect design history with theoretical frameworks stemming from the studies of nationalism that allow reflection on how designed artefacts contribute to creating nationality (Fallan and Lees-Maffei 2016; Gimeno-Martínez 2016; Goodrum 2005; Smelik 2017; Sparke 2013).

The issue with "national histories of design" revolves around methodology rather than geographical scope. Determining which artefacts to include or exclude has been mostly connected to the nationality of the designers. This criterion inevitably results in the exclusion of many objects that circulate and are used within a country. In essence, the chosen objects only represent specific values and practices associated with the country but do not provide a realistic portrayal of its visual and material reality. Globalizing design history entails not only researching and documenting the histories of nations and regions that have been historically underrepresented, such as New Zealand (Smythe 2011), Greece (Yagou 2011), Portugal (Souto 2011), Asia (Fujita and Guth 2019; Huppatz 2020) and Latin America (Devalle and Garone Gravrier 2020), but also re-evaluating methodological nationalism in favour of more sophisticated approaches such as transnational accounts (Teunissen 2011; Kikuchi and Lee 2014).

World design histories like those authored by Kirkham and Weber (2013) and Margolin (2015) expanded upon the earlier narrow chronological framework found in early scholarship. In these comprehensive works, the authors aim to give equal consideration to all major geographical regions and time periods. Furthermore, they emphasize the interconnectedness of these regions in terms of global trade, power dynamics and the mutual influence of aesthetics. These publications not only prompted a re-evaluation of design's chronology and geography but also represented a shift in the very definition of the concept itself, now encompassing pre-industrial objects. Design was no longer exclusively the process of conceiving and creating items for mechanized mass production, as in its purest form of "industrial design," but rather the conception and creation of useful artefacts in a broader sense, thereby expanding the scope of inquiry (Huppatz 2015: 7).

In terms of research methods, the effort to transcend the Western bias led to the emergence of new approaches like global design history, as discussed in the book by Glenn Adamson, Giorgio Riello and Sarah Teasley (2011). This book posits that global design history is not merely a subject, but a distinct method set apart from "transnational" and "world" design histories (2011: 3). It focuses on examining the globally interconnected and diverse ways in which design is practised. The book's introduction outlines a methodology for global design history and presents two fundamental models: the "connections" model, which investigates network relationships and the flow of goods and information across geographical boundaries, and the "comparative" model, which aims to reveal national and regional distinctions and discontinuities. These methodologies provide a platform for addressing key issues related to globalization, including a historical perspective on globalization, power imbalances stemming from colonization, orientalism, cultural appropriation and the indigenization of practices.

Each chapter sheds light on a specific case that is subsequently analysed by another author in a response. For instance, Gökhan Karakuş explores the emergence of a local furniture design practice in Turkey from the 1940s to the 1970s, which produced modern furniture using non-industrial manufacturing techniques. Karakuş argues that the conventional canon of Western design history, largely centred around industrialization, has overlooked non-industrial tools and craft techniques. A notable example of what he terms "handmade modernism" is the metal furniture manufacturer Kare Metal in the 1950s, which produced furniture inspired by the work of Charles and Ray Eames, Harry Bertoia, Isamu Noguchi and others (Figure 11.2). While the manufacturer employed industrial materials, the production process was

Figure 11.2 This armchair, designed and produced by İlhan Koman (1921–1986) and Sadi Öziş (1923–2012) in 1957, was produced by Kare Metal (Istanbul, Turkey) using chicken frame for the back and the seat. SALT Research, Sadi Öziş Archive

rather artisanal (Adamson et al. 2011: 123). Edward S. Cooke, Jr., in his critical response, questions the uniqueness of the Turkish experience and compares Karakuş' account with the history of similar practices in the USA. He argues that a close analysis of modern furniture production, spanning from Marcel Breuer to Alvar Aalto, reveals that all modern furniture, until the advent of injection-moulded plastic furniture or metal contract furniture, relied on some elements of artisanal skill and non-industrial tools. This production method could be categorized as jigged batch production rather than mass production. Such a revised perspective situates the Turkish narrative firmly within a global context, rather than singling it out as an exceptional or unique case (2011: 136).

Other methods to facilitate the emergence of these interconnections have been proposed by Jonathan Woodham and D.J. Huppatz. Woodham (2005: 263) suggests analysing the roles played by design organizations like the International Council of Societies of Industrial Design (ICSID), the International Council of Graphic Design Associations (ICOGRADA) and the International Federation of Interior Architects/Designers (IFI). On the other hand, Huppatz recommends examining the biographies of objects, companies, consultancies or designers as potential avenues for constructing global design histories through manageable case studies (2015: 13).

Huppatz further argues that a critical aspect of global design history is recognizing that design cultures outside the West are on an equal footing with Western design cultures (Huppatz 2015: 14). The recognition of indigenous contributions by design historians dates back to the late 1990s. Gregory Votolato challenged the conventional, uniform narratives of American design by highlighting the significance of Adirondack and Pueblo traditions, which might not neatly align with mainstream American design narratives but are integral to them. Votolato emphasized that a comprehensive analysis of national design must consider a spectrum of attitudes, including minority perspectives (Votolato 1998: 268). Inevitably, the integration of these perspectives into design history raises issues of cultural appropriation. For example, Kirkham and Weber observed how indigenous regalia, designs and objects were appropriated for nationalist or commercial purposes within settler societies (2013: 567). While they did not explicitly delve into the concept of cultural appropriation, their work illustrates that these dynamics have always been part of design practices. They also noted that the desire for handmade, culturally distinctive objects emerged as a response to the flood of cheap industrial goods in modernity (2013: 580).

In alignment with critical perspectives on exoticism, Alison J. Clarke argued that indigenous objects have been used as a consistent counterpoint to contemporary design (2018: 11). Designers and critics like Italian Superstudio (1966–1978) and Victor Papanek (1923–1998) often leverage so-called "ethnic" objects to critique the inauthenticity of modern capitalist consumerism. Papanek, for instance, extensively drew from "anthropological objects" in his research, ranging from Japanese combs to Inuit shelters. After exploring these alternative design paradigms, Papanek advocated for a "holistic design model" in which objects are inseparable from their social relationships, customs, rituals and histories (Clarke 2018: 11). In his book *Design for the Real World*, Papanek argued for applying this model to Western capitalist-driven design industries. However, despite Papanek's well-intentioned efforts, Clarke points out that the appropriation of such objects as a source for critical reflection on Western culture often oversimplifies the true diversity and complexity of "other" cultures (2018: 41). Indigenous objects tend to become symbols of a romanticized vision of the Other as uncomplicated, untainted and inherently authentic (2018: 79).

Although the validation of indigenous design aimed to subvert capitalist homogeneity, there are mechanisms at stake that correspond to cultural appropriation. What is notable in Papanek's case is his ability to apply his analytical principles for the material culture of the Other to Western industrial objects (Clarke 2018: 79). This illustrates, as Rogers suggests, that cultural appropriation is not inherently exploitative or morally questionable and can effectively raise awareness of design practices beyond the Western tradition.

Challenges: Decolonizing design scholarship

In a broader context, decolonization refers to the process involving the withdrawal of European imperial powers from their colonies and the subsequent efforts to restore political and economic autonomy to regions once colonized by Western nations. The term commonly comes up in discussions concerning the restoration of former colonized regions, particularly in the post-Second World War era. To counter colonial perspectives, authors advocate for decolonial strategies that shed light on the negative impact of modernity, chart alternative ways of perception and promote the exploration of alternative viewpoints to facilitate a reassertion of cultural existence.

Within this framework, globalization is often seen as a predominantly negative and homogenizing influence, in stark contrast to the positive and inclusive attempts to globalize design scholarship mentioned earlier in this chapter. According to Eleni Kalantidou and Tony Fry, globalization encompasses more than just economic aspects; it extends to the broader system of modernity that seeks to universalize various facets of life. Within this paradigm, design becomes subject to the desires propagated by and for global consumer culture (2014: 3). Kalantidou and Fry frame globalization as a form of epistemological colonialism, indicating that it inadvertently perpetuates Western-centric frameworks as the dominant lens through which the world is understood. This situation fosters the development of design practices influenced by a particular Eurocentric worldview (2014: 5).

Mignolo and Vázquez have outlined a three-step decolonial approach. The first step involves tracing the lineage of a particular concept within Western modernity. Consider design historiography as an example. Examining its development reveals a historical inclination towards modernism in the past, but it has since expanded beyond that singular perspective. The second step entails revealing the colonial nature of this concept, illustrating how it has been used to marginalize, silence or devalue other ways of perceiving and engaging with the world. Back to the example of design historiography, this requires demonstrating that prevailing narratives have overlooked certain geographical regions, practices and social groups. Finally, the third step involves establishing the decolonial option, which represents a non-normative space open to diverse alternatives. In this phase, the goal is to incorporate these neglected geographies, practices and groups within the existing design historiography, rather than replacing it (Mignolo and Vázquez 2013). It is important to note that decoloniality does not introduce an entirely new paradigm or mode of critical thought; instead, it highlights the presence of alternatives to the dominant paradigm of coloniality (Mignolo and Walsh 2018: 4–5).

In terms of design practice, Elizabeth Tunstall (2023) has outlined a decolonizing agenda consisting of five action points: prioritizing indigenous perspectives, dismantling the technological bias inherent in European modernism, addressing the racial bias within European modernism, going beyond mere diversity, equity and inclusion efforts, and re-evaluating existing resource allocation. Her perspective aligns with the views of Mignolo and Vázquez, who argue that modernity and coloniality have shaped a system that appears to be the natural order of things. According to Tunstall, the decolonization process should not only involve incorporating indigenous, racially diverse and non-technical viewpoints but also include making amends through measures like restitution payments and cluster hire quotas in design education (2023: 12–13).

To actively break free from the colonial order, Mignolo and Vázquez introduce the concept of "delinking," a term originally coined by sociologist Aníbal Quijano (1928–2018). Mignolo explains that decolonial delinking follows two paths: de-westernization and decoloniality (Mignolo and Walsh 2018: 126). De-westernization challenges those who oversee and control the system, while decoloniality actively seeks to disengage from it (Mignolo 2021: 321). Delinking serves as a means to cultivate new ways of perceiving and signifying that acknowledge the modern-colonial order (de-westernization) but actively aspire to establish and recognize alternative relationships beyond this binary framework (decoloniality). This approach paves the way for "a horizon beyond resistance and beyond modernity" (Vázquez 2020: 127).

Understanding de-westernization necessitates first grasping the very concept of Westernization. Colonization and Westernization denote distinct aspects of European expansion since 1500: colonization pertains to control and management, while Westernization relates to education (Mignolo 2021: 315). De-westernization, as articulated by Mignolo, is not so much about resisting the West as it is about exploring different possibilities (2021: 339). Economic de-westernization does not imply disengaging from a capitalist economic model. Cultural de-westernization entails proposing alternative cultural possibilities that possess equal validity but differ from the dominant colonial paradigm (2021: 325).

Decoloniality involves reclaiming what has been silenced and asserting a "re-existence." Practices of re-existence strive to recover the "presence of voices, bodies, and forms of existence that have been subjugated or erased within the modern-colonial order" (Vázquez 2020: 174). To achieve this, Mignolo and Vázquez emphasize a pluriversal mode of being, which entails creating a form of hybridity that does not merge identities into a single entity but rather encourages the coming together of equals while preserving their distinct characteristics. If the decolonial approach embraces pluriversality, it envisions a space where various equal identities and perspectives can coexist.

In the realm of aesthetics, the concept of pluriversality represents a reconfiguration that extends beyond the prevailing framework imposed by the Western perspective. Decolonial aesthetics, in contrast, empowers the "emergence of alternative aesthetic narratives and overlooked historical trajectories. It signifies a newfound voice" (Vázquez 2020: 176). Modernism constitutes just one sphere where discussions on aesthetics originate, implying that it is not the sole source of value. Mignolo and Vázquez propose replacing the notion of the aesthetic, which is tied to Enlightenment-based notions of beauty, with "aesthesis" as a plural concept that encompasses diverse definitions of beauty unrelated to modernity (2013: n.p.). Vázquez further expounds that decolonial aesthetics marks a transition from an era defined by the control of representation and global ownership by the colonial order to an era characterized by listening (2020: 176).

Many aspects related to decolonial initiatives have been addressed within the field of design scholarship. These include challenging the Western-centric canon through de-westernization, recognizing silenced historical episodes and reviving forgotten narratives. However, one aspect that remains to be addressed is the notion of "academic aesthetics," which pertains to how scholars communicate knowledge through academic conventions. Scholars may need to scrutinize academic writing to determine whether it aligns with the logics of coloniality as related to modernity. Should academia incorporate hybridity and embrace alternative means of knowledge transmission that can stand alongside traditional academic writing? This question has been explored by Sarah Cheang, Katie Irani, Livia Rezende and Shehnaz Suterwalla in their article "In Between Breaths" (2023). In this piece, they advocate for alternative modes of historical writing that encompass translation, opacity, embodiment, positionality and nonlinearity as means of transforming design history. The article presents a transcript of their conversation, where they discuss their reflections, previously visualized in collages, using experimental methodologies to create a collective "eco-system of ideas." Their discussion encompasses a wide range of subjects, from a Billy Holiday cassette to the works of the artists Kehinde Wiley and Kara Walker, probing questions about the role of history for historians and the value of transparency in academic writing.

The concept of positionality, as discussed by Chakravorty Spivak, emphasizes the need for "ethical relations with the Other" (2004: 526). She argues that researchers, regardless of their well-intentioned motives, must continually and attentively examine the complexities and entanglements of their own positions. She has shifted from her earlier idea of "unlearning one's privilege" (Danius et al. 1993: 25) to a new approach focused on "learning to learn from below" (2004: 551). This advancement goes beyond simply shedding privilege; it involves gaining insight into the process of learning itself, including the historical, cultural and social conditions that validate certain forms of knowledge as learnable while dismissing others as primitive, outdated or rooted in superstition. This transformation requires challenging the sense of superiority and certainty that universal reason instils in the consciousness of the Enlightenment subject. Chakravorty Spivak contends that we should cultivate research environments that lack fixed assurances. Instead, the ethical research encounter should embrace complexity and uncertainty, welcoming ambiguous and provisional certainties without insisting on consensus, a shared language, identity or cause.

12 Society and culture
Manners, morals and customs

Social history looks at the intersection of methods from history and the social sciences. If originally historians were interested in validating their research through the quantitative methods of sociology, the focus moved in the 1960s to more anthropological approaches that favoured the qualitative above the quantitative. Subsequently, the linguistic turn originated a greater interest in the cultural aspects of social history and feminist scholarship put the attention on minorities. The implementation of social history in design scholarship offered an alternative to scholarly traditions based primarily on aesthetics and validated the role of consumers and mediators. These accounts favoured the analysis of the social context above object analysis. The relevance of the aesthetic value of objects needs therefore reconsideration when the analysis of design is at stake.

Origins: History from below

Examining the historiography of graphic design in Chicago, Victor Margolin observed the conspicuous absence of Black designers. The tension between their active participation and their practical invisibility was attributed, in part, to the methods employed in design history. Margolin advocated for a shift, asserting that "to make the contributions and struggles of black graphic designers in Chicago more visible, we need to tell the story of graphic design in the city as a social history and not an aesthetic one" (Margolin 2001: 15; Figure 12.1).

Social history holds notable significance within design scholarship, particularly as it provides alternative perspectives to narratives centred on authorship and aesthetics. Traditionally, social history encompasses three primary domains: histories related to economic matters, the history of working classes and minorities, and cultural history. In the context of the latter, it is often referred to as cultural history (Walker 1989: 129). In essence, cultural history is inherently a subset of social history, but social history is not always cultural history.

The historian Ibn Khaldun (1332–1406) implemented the principle of sociologically analysed sources, emphasizing the critical comparison of each source with respect to its social context and the governing laws of society.

DOI: 10.4324/9781003147282-15

Wayne Boyer John Siena Tom Freese Fred Ota David Blumenthal Tom Mitier

Morton Goidsholl Millie Goidsholl John Weber Susan Keig James Logan William Langdon

Figure 12.1 The staff of Morton Goldsholl Associates in 1963, including Thomas Miller (1920–2012), who worked there as a graphic designer for thirty-five years on projects including the 1970 redesign of the 7-UP packaging and identity

This approach led to his historical and sociological exploration of the cyclical pattern involving rise, peak and decline. According to Ibn Khaldun, if a society attains the status of a leading civilization or dominant culture in a region, its peak is inevitably succeeded by a period of decline. This implies that the subsequent cohesive group conquering the civilization is perceived as barbarians in comparison. Once these conquerors establish control, they are drawn to the more refined aspects of the civilization, such as literature, art and science, which they assimilate or appropriate. Consequently, the succeeding group of conquerors repeats this process, resulting in an accumulation of knowledge and culture (Bod 2013: 97).

While the pattern identified by Ibn Khaldun was previously observed in the works of Herodotus, Thucydides and the historian Sima Qian (c. 145–86 BCE), Khaldun's analysis and explanations for this pattern surpass Thucydides's simple analogy of human ascent and decline or the mandates bestowed and withdrawn by heaven as discussed in Sima Qian's work. Ibn Khaldun formulated a historical–sociological mechanism that provides a more profound insight into the workings of the cyclical pattern. This mechanism elucidates how a new group is drawn to the knowledge of a preceding dominant group, leading to the accumulation of knowledge over time (Bod 2013: 97).

Discontent with the evolutionist, linear pattern that had dominated nineteenth-century historiography in the West, some historians questioned if it could be supported empirically. For example, Oswald Spengler (1880–1936) proposed a history of civilizations in which cultures develop, mature and die. In his *The Decline of the West*, published in 1918, he underpinned his views on the grounds of eight major world civilizations – Indian, Babylonian, Chinese, Egyptian, Arabic, Mexican, Graeco-Roman and Western. Similarly, Arnold Toynbee (1889–1975) also used a model of the rise and fall of cultures. He based his analysis on an even bigger synthesis of world history. According to Toynbee, civilizations began to flourish when they tried to face up to a series of serious challenges. If a culture was no longer able to do this, it began to decline. Civilizations died because of suicide, not murder. Toynbee expressed his great admiration for Ibn Khaldun's systematic exposition of the trends of history. Yet Toynbee's work was fiercely criticized because of his frequent use of myths and metaphors. In this regard, he ignored Ibn Khaldun's criticism of myths (Bod 2013: 262).

A group of prolific French historians named after the academic journal founded in 1929 by Marc Bloch (1886–1944) and Lucien Febvre (1878–1956) *Annales d'histoire économique et sociale*, the Annales School further developed the social history approach by equally including and emphasizing the importance of all social and economic classes in society. The sociological history of Ibn Khaldun influenced the Annales historians and Bloch discussed his method (Bod 2013: 260). The authors of the French school sought to gain a fuller sense of how a given society came together in all its interrelated elements, as well as an entity in which all historical moments partake and influence. Their vision was a massive inductive project incorporating numerous local histories that would allow for a "history of society." The Annales school carried divided interests: on one side, an interest in social transformation, specifically the transition from feudalism to capitalism, and on the other, an interest in the "manners, morals and customs" of the less wealthy concerning those transformations (Boyd 1999: 1110).

Social history could be identified in its distinctive features and scattered data. It resulted, for example, in the 1942 study of city life in eighteenth-century Philadelphia by Carl and Jessica Bridenbaugh (1903–1992, 1910–1943); a series of impressions, statistics and considerable descriptions of building aesthetics was made with attention to the merchant elite (Stearns 1994: 684). As a result of their growing popularity, several other schools in social history emerged, such as the Bielefeld School in Germany, which, with its leading scholars being Hans-Ulrich Wehler (1931–2014) and Jürgen Kocka (b. 1941), "stressed the need for a synthetic history that used social science – quantitative and comparative – methods and theories" (Boyd 1999: 1289).

In the 1960s, the "new social history" emerged and grew exponentially across Europe and North America. Febvre had already advocated for a "history from below" in 1932 but it became especially popular simultaneously with the emergence of this "new social history" when Edward Palmer Thompson (1924–1993) published his essay "History from Below" in 1966. Thompson was a Marxist historian, who published a biography on William Morris in 1955 and along with other leading historians such as Raphael Samuel (1934–1996) and Eric Hobsbawm (1917–2012) organized the History Workshop starting in the late 1960s and later also set up the eponymous *History Workshop Journal* in 1974. The English school maintained an interest in social and cultural aspects and sought to examine the "manners, morals and customs" of the English people. To achieve this aim, Thompson and other social historians saw the need for new ethnographic, qualitative sources in studying human experiences to the detriment of demographic, quantitative ones (Stearns 1994: 686).

The History Workshop historians tended towards studies of class and culture in historical processes. A decisive turn from class towards culture is evident in the topics of their workshops, which gradually included cultural theory. The topics from 1967 to 1979 surveyed mainly social groups such as workers, women or children, including very few but some cultural aspects such as a paper on "Toys" by Peter Wollen in 1972 or "Women and Home in the Chinese Revolution" by Delia Davin in 1973. From 1979 onwards, the interest in methodology and culture was more evident, starting in 1979 with a full workshop entitled "People's History and Socialist Theory" including a plenary session with Thompson, Stuart Hall and Richard Johnson. The following year the workshop focused on "Language and Society" and in 1985 on the "Uses of History" (History Workshop 2012).

By the early 1980s, "linguistic or cultural turn" inaugurated new modes of analysis, which had an impact on cultural and social history. An increasing interest in literary theory replaced the original Marxist perspective on historical inquiry when searching for different explanations of how societies work. A close examination of texts, visuals and actions resulted in pluralist interpretations instead of the elaboration of new master narratives or social theories (Hunt 1989: 22; Bonnell and Hunt 1999: 2). Cultural analysts supplanted the social and economic with the cultural and linguistic. Regarding this, Victoria E. Bonnell and Lynn Hunt state that "sign" replaced "class" as the key concept of analysis but actually served the same function, reminding cultural analysts that these concepts remain conceptual terms serving heuristic purposes rather than ultimate constituents of reality (1999: 13). In this process, the deconstruction of power structures by Michel Foucault played a pivotal role in showing the importance of other groups apart from the white male elite. Accordingly, recent work in social history was revised. For example, Thompson's work was criticized for analysing the expressions of interest of the working class without taking into consideration the discursive structures of political language that condition these expressions. His identification between "social being" and "social consciousness" was seen as unsophisticated and problematic, leaving little space for the constitution of a particular language of class outside the individual (Hunt 1989: 6).

Feminist scholarship questioned social history for assuming that male-gendered experiences were considered universal class experiences. The addition of a gender perspective problematized these studies and called into question the primacy of class in historical analysis without considering other minority groups (Boyd 1999: 1112). Thereby, some of the main contributions of social history were produced, with attention to racial minorities, immigrants, women, LGBTQ+ people and the elderly. These arguments helped to critically engage social history, which significantly enriched contemporary understandings of past societies. The scholars Deborah Valenze (b. 1953) and Barbara Taylor (b. 1950) revisited topics such as religion which showed realities for women that were overlooked by Thompson. Accordingly, Christine Stansell (b. 1949) discussed gender and working-class formation in New York City in her work *City of Women* (1987). Social history was adapting a more egalitarian approach with authors dealing with the social history of Victorian prostitution by Judith Walkowitz (b. 1945), deep intersections of class and gender in the formation of the English middle class by Catherine Hall (b. 1946), as well as the manner in which class, gender and race influenced each other and every aspect of social life in the nineteenth century by Mary Poovey (b. 1950; Boyd 1999: 1111).

Development: Social histories of art and technology

Gregory Votolato maps the impact of cultural and social history on design scholarship back to its roots in art history (1998: 269). This shift played a decisive role in shaping the early stages of design history. Subsequently, the integration of social history by scholars in science and technology will also wield significant influence on the field of design scholarship.

Votolato refers to *Social History of Art* (1951) by Arnold Hauser, whose book was representative of a social history of art that emerged in the mid-twentieth century and that was shared by other authors such as anthro-pological art historian Meyer Schapiro (1904–1996) and social art historian Frederick Antal (1887–1954; Fernie 1995: 18). Hauser set out a framework for the analysis of art through its connections to social forces, giving socio-economic explanation to stylistic changes in the history of art. For example, he would locate the stylistic differences between Peter Paul Rubens (1577–1640) and Rembrandt (1606–1669) in the specificities of the Flemish and Dutch contexts: Flanders being Catholic, courtly-aristocratic in which flam-boyance and display were of central importance, and the Netherlands bour-geois and commercial, with a less ostentatious public life. He would state that

> [t]he fate of art in Holland is, therefore, decided not by the Church, not by a monarch, not by a court society, but by a middle class which attains importance more by reason of the great number of its well-to-do mem-bers, than by the outstanding wealth of individuals.
>
> (Hauser 1999[1951]: 197–198)

This would explain that two painters with similar backgrounds being con-temporary, geographically contiguous and based on common cultural tradi-tions developed different styles. Existing art historical methods based on visual analysis, such as Panofsky's iconographical approaches and the recon-struction of the artist's intentions would fall short in explaining art (Harris 1999: xxi). Similarly, Hauser would minimize individual circumstances by declaring, for example, that the fact that Rubens, unlike Rembrandt, went to Italy would not be decisive for their different styles since Mannerism was known in the early seventeenth century both in the northern and in the southern provinces (Hauser 2018[1959]: 16).

The main explanatory principle for Hauser would be Marxism, that is, the centrality of class and class struggle, the predominant influence of the base on the superstructure, and the determining influence of modes of economic production on art (Harris 1999: xiii). The understanding of styles might not be separated from the influence of these factors or "systems of production and consumption," which, for Hauser, are the result of capitalism's general rise in Europe. Tracing the circulation of creative work from production to consumption has been precisely the most influential aspect for other art historians and design scholars. The conditions in which a commission was made – what the function of the work was, how it was made, what the available techniques were and how the audience reacted – have been later incorporated into models within the cultural studies and cultural approaches to consumption. As also happened with cultural and social historians, the Marxist perspective has been gradually replaced by other forms of understanding social dynamics (Harris 1999: xl).

In the early 1970s, art historiography was criticized for focusing on artists and depicting them as geniuses, for a set of methods based chiefly on connoisseurship, for the uniformity of degree curricula offered by art history departments and for ignoring the social context of art and structures of power (Fernie 1995: 18). At first sight, the New Art History emerging from this critical position might consider Hauser one of its main forerunners, but this is only partially so. If previously attacked by traditional art historians for the lack of analytical engagement with specific artworks, the New Art History judged Hauser's text as reactionary, sexist, racist and elitist. Hauser's concerns on social issues did not allow him to look into gender imbalance in the history of art or the representation of ethnic and racial minorities. His vision of the history of art coincided with a canonical history of art in terms of works and artists. Moreover, his periodization, albeit corresponding to social motivation, reproduced the well-known stylistic divisions that had been created by the same authors that he criticized (Harris 1999: xxii).

The New Art History investigated the influence of social context on art and artists, surpassing Hauser's analysis with more sophisticated economic models and detailed historical evidence. The art historian T.J. Clark, a key proponent of this paradigm shift, further developed the social history of art by examining how ideologies operate within art history. In his 1973 study on Gustave Courbet (1819–1877), Clark delved into the contextual implications of Courbet's work, akin to Hauser, but with a more nuanced approach independent of an ideological Marxist perspective, in contrast to Hauser (Fernie 1995: 19). Clark and the New Art History maintained the Marxist correlation between base and superstructure, background and foreground and the determining influence of modes of economic production. However, they departed from the centrality of class and class struggle as the driving forces of history.

The multidisciplinary field of Science and Technology Studies (STS) notably embraced social history through the influential work of the historian Ruth Schwartz Cowan. While all of STS incorporates a socio-historical aspect, Cowan stands out for her explicit acknowledgement and consideration of the significance of social history in her contributions. In her book *More Work for Mother: The Ironies of Household Technology* (1983), she suggests that new household technologies did not eliminate but added work for women, thereby accentuating gender inequality. Innovations such as the iron stove had the effect of reducing men's labour – less fuel meant less chopping – while increasing that of women – stoves required more cleaning than a hearth and they made more complex meal preparation possible (Cowan 1997: 173–200). Similarly, her book chapter "The Consumption Junction" (1987) spawned a research programme on consumerism and technology exploring the role of mediators of technology such as telephone operators, sales agents and home economists.

In her book *A Social History of American Technology* (1997), Cowan defines the history of technology as the evolution of artefacts throughout time, asserting that these artefacts are integral to humanity, comparable to the importance of ideas and governance. Cowan makes a clear distinction between the history of technology and the social history of technology, with the latter encompassing a broader integration of technological history into the entirety of human history. She emphasizes the interconnectedness of society and technology, positing that changes in one realm can and have influenced changes in the other (1997: 3).

In Chapter 7, for example, she explores how industrialization implies the existence of technological systems having both physical and social components, implying that innovation, is more than the invention of devices. Her discussion on the electricity telegraph and telephones includes their inventors, Samuel Morse (1791–1872) and Alexander Graham Bell (1847–1922) respectively, but also the construction of elaborate physical networks, and the consequent development of extensive social links for finance and marketing. The result is a focus both on the individual – for example, inventors, entrepreneurs, system builders, farmers, printers and factory workers –, and on newer topics in the history of technology, such as the interconnection of material forces – for example, inventions, supply networks – and social forces – for example, economic circumstances, institutions, personal connections (Cowan 1997: 149–172).

Cowan's ideas are developed in three sections: (1) native and European-style agriculture, along with household and mechanic arts during the colonial period; (2) industrialization, daily life and the ideology of technology in the nineteenth century; and (3) an examination of significant technologies that emerged in the twentieth century, such as the automobile, aviation, communication and biotechnology. In this last section, Cowan presents the impact of these technological systems on society and culture, both through their achievements and through their problematic consequences, such as pollution, the rise of the military industry, the control on communications and the social implications of technoscience in agriculture and medicine (1997: 221–327). Cowan's narrative delves into the reciprocal influence between technology and society, departing from a Marxist approach. Conversely, she views society as more than a mere backdrop for understanding the work of creative individuals, a perspective similar to T.J. Clark's work.

Kjetil Fallan argues for a cultural history of design that would allow design history to distance itself from its art–historical roots; he considers that design scholarship today can no longer constitute a mere "history of objects and their designers, but it is becoming more a history of the translations, transcriptions, transactions, transpositions and transformations that constitute the relationships among things, peoples and ideas" (2010: 10). He sees STS and the social construction of technology (SCOT) theory as an alternative influence, adding that: "both people and objects become more eloquent when considered parts of collectives and systems" (Fallan 2010: 61). However, cultural history has been incorporated both in art history, STS and SCOT. Art history has expanded its focus on integrating social history and STS does not obviate the influence of individuals. As mentioned above with T.J. Clark's example and discussed further below, cultural and social history do not necessarily involve neglecting artists and designers but contextualizing their work within society. Moreover, distancing from art history does not guarantee less interest in designers, as Cowan's work demonstrates. The opposition between the two fields is not as stark as it might seem.

Implementation: Individuals, products and society

A prime illustration of the impact of social history on the field of design studies can be found in Adrian Forty's work, *Objects of Desire: Design and Society since 1750* (2010[1986]). In this book, Forty undertakes an examination of various themes spanning the years 1750 to 1980, encompassing topics such as design and mechanization, differentiation in design, the home, the office, electricity and corporate identity. He delves into the way social dynamics manifest in tangible objects. Employing a Marxist perspective, Forty identifies capitalist society as a driving force behind diversification. According to his argument, the proliferation of products cannot be attributed solely to one societal agent – whether consumer, designer or manufacturer – but rather results from the interplay among these three entities within the framework of a capitalist society. Consumers seek class distinction while manufacturers pursue enrichment.

Three alternative explanations are presented by Forty. First, diversification facilitates individuality, departing from a needs-based explanation to emphasize the importance of personal distinction. Second, manufacturers aim to boost sales by creating slight variations on existing products, thereby increasing consumption. The third explanation involves the manufacturers' efforts to tailor products to the preferences of their target consumers, who may belong to specific social classes, genders or age groups (Forty 2010[1986]: 87–89).

Forty has been praised by Walker for displacing the attention from individual designers to the objects themselves and the social context. Walker considers it a challenge for design historians "to demonstrate how the design process is embedded within particular social relations whom it helps to reproduce or to alter" (Walker 1989: 136). He questions whether the analysis of designed objects can give access to the ideas and emotions of a social group. For that, a mediation and reception study are necessary, which is absent in Forty's account because of its Marxist bias, Walker observes (Walker 1989: 132–133).

The importance of mediation was included in Alison J. Clarke's *Tupperware: The Promise of Plastic in 1950s America* (1999), which offers a cultural history of the manufacturer of plastic home products Tupperware, combining methodological tools typical of history and anthropology. She starts with biographies of both the businessman Earl Tupper (1907–1983) and Brownie Wise (1913–1992), who was responsible for marketing. The focus is on exploring the origins of Tupper's ideals, discussing social reform and utopianism, and linking his conception of everyday domesticity to his personal life (Clarke 1999: 8). Clarke utilizes sources such as Tupper's journals to offer an intimate perspective on the designer's thoughts, visions, daily routines and personal growth, although the design process is explored to a lesser extent (Clarke 1999: 12). Wise's biography is based on her public writings and speeches, articles in corporate publications and her autobiography. The historian Ellen M. Litwicki regrets nonetheless the lack of depth in the analysis of Wise and misses more research on Wise's personal sources (Litwicki 2000: 247–249).

Clarke argues that a range of manufacturers faced a similar challenge to Tupperware in the late 1940s and 1950s, that is, how to secure large consumer markets for products derived from wartime experiments in plastics technology. She explores processes of mass consumption and object appropriation in everyday life, connecting with historians' discussions of a wide range of issues, from the origins of later twentieth-century feminism to the interplay between suburbanization and material culture (Clarke 1999: 14). Clarke gives examples of designers' projects as reactions to social change, so she describes the utopian theme park Cosmopolita World [sic], which Tupper envisioned as an educational and friendly central information bureau that would help broaden the minds of the average American (Clarke 1999: 16). Clarke's analysis of the Tupperware's sales force is based on newspapers and magazines, supplemented by interviews. She elaborates on society's changes, discussing the situation in the advertising sector and the economic situation. In doing so, she challenges the academic stereotype of the post-war suburban housewife, demonstrating that the sales force included blue-collar and lower-middle-class women, divorcees, single mothers, and ethnic and racial minorities (Clarke 1999: 13).

Additionally, Clarke investigates the Tupperware object in terms of the ideologies it represented, elucidating the social relations and cultural beliefs during its design period. Her attention is directed towards understanding Tupperware's popularity, technological innovation and marketing success, particularly attributed to Wise (Clarke 1999: 10). The design object is placed in this context only briefly. There is little concrete information present on how the project worked and how it looked (Clarke 1999: 17). Litwicki notes that there is limited insight into what Tupperware products signified for end customers, as opposed to the sales force. Clarke's examination of the meaning attributed to Tupperware products relies on Wise's gifts to her sales force rather than on feedback from Tupperware consumers. As a result, the perspective of the consumers is missing, and the significance of the products is more assumed than validated. Conducting interviews with Tupperware consumers could address these gaps (Litwicki 2000: 247–249).

The interest in social history relegates the object itself mostly to a background process, a by-product and a side effect of the changes occurring in the everyday life of the people and the designer. While much is explained on the position of the designer in society and the relations of product, designer and consumer; design fades into the background in Clarke's explanations (Clarke 1999: 35). Analysing design within society without losing the artefact from sight seems a challenging task.

One potential strategy to integrate the product into social history involves combining it with object-centred methods, such as close readings and typological analysis. One example is David Raizman's "Chapter 14: Dimensions of Mass Culture" in his *History of Modern Design* (2010), in which he examines design in the 1960s. A social–historical approach makes it possible to analyse the mass consumer culture and its counter-culture in the period and to connect it to new formal vocabulary and home interiors, such as the kitchen (Raizman 2010: 349). Raizman discusses social activism among designers, their understanding of experimentation and rebelliousness, and their political and social activism. He uses the examples of anti-design in Italy and the manifesto "First Things First" (1964) of graphic designer Ken Garland (1929–2021), to note a growing consciousness among designers to distance themselves from mass production and direct their creative activity in ways meaningful to society and its needs. In this chapter, Raizman questions the relationship between design and consumer culture, which allows him to explain the conflicts between designers' social concerns and their professional practices as well as to discuss the reasons behind their rhetoric (Raizman 2010: 356, 359).

Design scholarship influenced by actor–network theory has further integrated the roles of objects, social context and environmental conditions. Joana Meroz's analysis of the *Dutch Design for the Public Sector I* (1973–1977) and *Dutch Design for the Public Sector II* (1978) exhibitions goes beyond object and social aspects to consider how environmental conditions shaped their design (Meroz 2022: 245–161).

The *Dutch Design for the Public Sector I* exhibition showcased a comprehensive array of public design, including examples from service companies and citizen interventions. The exhibition, designed for nearly four years of European touring, maximized its adaptability and comprehensiveness. Accordingly, it included several examples of design implemented by public service companies, such as a clock commissioned by the Dutch Railways, and examples of citizen interventions that attempted to redress inadequate public spaces and services, such as a full-size White Car: a pioneering, free, car-sharing project that aimed to reduce urban traffic congestion caused by private automobiles (Meroz 2022: 250).

Expanding to an international exhibition circuit, *Dutch Design for the Public Sector II* exemplifies "plastic diplomacy," according to Meroz, by creating a flexible and robust exhibition that accommodates various constraints to maximize the mobility of Dutch culture. The designers enhanced plasticity through features such as folding screens that served dual purposes as displays and crates. To address climatic challenges, materials like clear Perspex and a new plastic–aluminium composite were used to ensure adaptability to different environments, such as sweltering tropical conditions in Indonesia (Meroz 2022: 252). Regarding its content, the shift to *Dutch Design for the Public Sector II*, due to long-distance travel constraints, led to a more condensed exhibition focused predominantly on graphic design. The narrative had to be adjusted to align with the smaller scale and specific artefact type suitable for international travel (Meroz 2022: 254).

Challenges: The social vs. the aesthetic?

The social has proven compatible with the individual and the objectual, as Raizman's and Meroz's accounts demonstrate, but is it also compatible with the aesthetic? As mentioned above, cultural and social history have been seen as alternatives for a design scholarship based on aesthetics, seen as an inconvenient heritage from art history (Fallan 2010: 1–15). According to Mads Nygaard Folkmann, however, this has led to aesthetics becoming a neglected area of research in the contemporary field of design. He refers to how the work of design is constituted by a specific form that either reveals its meaning or resists its understanding. Along these lines, he contends that the aesthetic experience is as much part of the construction of the meaning of design. Design establishes a sensuous relation with the perceiving subject, that is conveyed by means such as colour, form, materials and texture (Nygaard Folkmann 2023: 58–68). The use of certain styles and motifs, colours and textures is an essential part of the communication of certain ideas that design entails.

The following example of the website of *Low-tech Magazine* (2018) illustrates how social, ethical, technological and aesthetic aspects are intimately connected to each other and that obviating one of them would result in misunderstanding the whole. *Low-tech Magazine* was founded in 2007 by Kris De Decker to question "the belief in technological progress and highlights the potential of past knowledge and technologies for designing a sustainable society" (*Low-tech Magazine*. "About this Website" 2018: §1). Before De Decker started *Low-tech Magazine*, he had been a science and technology journalist for ten years but decided to move to Spain in 2007 and establish this publication. Since 2018, when the magazine launched a solar-powered website, the online website has been supplied with energy by a solar PV system on the founder's balcony in Barcelona (Vansintjan 2019: §4).

Low-tech Magazine's philosophy is based on the idea that new technologies will not solve the climate crisis. De Decker argues that economical technologies like electric cars, windmills and energy-saving lamps are often unjustly considered to be beneficial for our economy, energy and CO_2 emissions (De Decker 2009: §1). Taking a small city windmill as an example, De Decker describes that these types of technological "gadgets" frequently generate less energy than was used to produce them (De Decker 2009: §3). Moreover, he highlights the misconception that energy-efficient technology is automatically energy-saving, that is, energy-efficient engines did not result in energy-saving cars, but rather in bigger, heavier and faster cars, which use more energy (De Decker 2009: §6). He gives the example of the bicycle dynamo to illustrate the benefit of traditional technologies. De Decker considers this invention, which is powered by only a small amount of physical effort, to be way more efficient and energy-saving than the batteries that are predominantly used for bicycling lights today (Figure 12.2). As he states, we need to "take distance from our technology-fetishism" to allow for a movement towards less, but better 'stuff'" (De Decker 2009: §11).

The online articles of *Low-tech Magazine* revolve around the above-described philosophy. From "The Revenge of the Circulating Fan" (2014) to "Urban Farming in the 1600s" (2015) and "Ditch the Batteries" (2018), each article either informs about the misunderstandings regarding new technologies or about the idea that past knowledge is crucial for a sustainable future.

Figure 12.2 Lalbhai Dalpatbhai Engineering College Professor N.H. Pancholi (C) looks on as students Mehul Baldaniya (2R), Khushagara Makwana (R), Abhishek Pandey (3R) and Parth Pankhaniya (L) display the "Pedal Operated Laundry" washing machine at their college workshop in Ahmedabad on April 22, 2017. The inner drum of "Pedal Operated Laundry/washing machine" is made of stainless steel and the outer is made from fibre material. It requires some 25 litres of water compared to the 40 litres which is commonly used by electric operated washing machines. Photo by SAM PANTHAKY/AFP via Getty Images

The new website was created through a collaboration between De Decker, the developer and artist Roel Roscam Abbing, who worked on the website's hardware and plug-in development, and the designers Marie Otsuka, who designed the website, and Lauren Traugott-Campbell, who designed the printed-format publication. The site addresses two issues that are considered to be major causes for the growing energy use of the World Wide Web. The first is "heavier" and "larger" websites with resource-intensive content. The second is people spending more and more time on the web (*Low-tech Magazine.* "About this Website" 2018: §11–12). With its solar-based platform, *Low-tech Magazine* aims to show that with certain design decisions, these issues can be largely bypassed.

Before De Decker started working with Otsuka, his articles were published on a so-called "Typepad blog," which is one of the oldest blogging platform services. Little to no attention was spent on the website's design. Otsuka showed De Decker that the communicative power of design could reinforce his low-tech principles and messaging. Otsuka's interest as a designer revolves around tools and methods of making in graphic design, web development, type design and type engineering (Otsuka 2019, 2020). One of Otsuka's most important objectives was to make the design of the website part of its content (Campbell-Dollaghan 2018: §10). De Decker's written content predominantly revolves around using low-tech inventions from the past as a solution for environmental issues of the future. For this reason, Otsuka decided to look back at the past too and be inspired by the very first website ever published on the World Wide Web.

She noticed that the simplistic aesthetic of this "age-old" website was entirely determined by the default settings of the browser (Otsuka 2019). Nowadays, websites predominantly use custom typefaces and imagery, which require lots of storage space and energy use. Default settings, on the other hand, radically reduce energy consumption. Therefore, Otsuka made the informed decision to use a default typeface, that is, Arial, Times New Roman, Georgia and Verdana, for the magazine's text. Further reducing energy use, the designer chose to utilize only one weight of the font. This way, she wanted to demonstrate that "content hierarchy can be communicated without loading multiple typefaces and weights" (*Low-tech Magazine.* "About this Website" 2018: §24). For similar reasons, Otsuka created a typographic logo in the same default typeface. To give the logo a visual element, the hyphen between the word "Low" and "Tech" was replaced by a left-facing arrow.

The historical website of *Low-tech Magazine* did not contain any images, since they are very resource-intensive, especially the higher the resolution becomes, and the more colours are used. To reduce the website's energy use, eliminating images would have been the most obvious option. However, since De Decker considered imagery to be crucial to convey the magazine's message, Otsuka came up with another low-tech design solution: dithered images (Campbell-Dollaghan 2018). This type of image is achieved through a long-outdated image compression method called "dithering," which converts multi-coloured images to black and white with four levels of grey. Hereafter, these black and white images were coloured through the browser's image manipulation capacities (*Low-tech Magazine*. "About this Website" 2018: §22). As a result, the images on the solar-powered website are ten times less resource-intensive than the images on De Decker's previous "Typepad" blog (Otsuka 2019). However, if size reduction had been Otsuka's only intention, she could have chosen a newer type of image compression that does not affect the aesthetic of the images as much. However, Otsuka considered the grainy aesthetic of dithered images to be of importance as the particular look shows that the images are compressed, which is a powerful message since it empha-sizes that they consume less energy (Otsuka 2019). In other words, the dith-ered images embody the reality of energy usage.

Like the dithered images, the infrastructure of the website reflects energy usage too. The background colour of the website changes with the voltage in the battery of the solar panel. If the panel receives full sun, the entire back-ground of the website is yellow. In cloudy weather, the background of the website becomes partially blue. If the website runs out of solar energy, it is offline. De Decker explains that this makes the reader aware of "what they're doing now consumes energy; depending on how many articles you read, it's going down" (Campbell-Dollaghan 2018: §13). In this sense, one could state that the website's design actively nudges the reader to consume less energy. As described by Otsuka, "what we wanted to do with the design was to show the materiality of the website to make clear that there is some hardware behind it" (Stefanski 2018: §4). This is also reflected in the website's so-called "sta-tistics dashboard," where the viewer can access information regarding the server's power demand, power supply and energy storage.

This example would have been only partially understood with a social his-tory of design. There, the ethical position of both De Decker and Otsuka might be considered less important. Their position indeed participates in a social concern regarding sustainability and technological criticism. Never-theless, they have a particular approach to this issue that partially explains the design of the website. Technological and ideological issues are indeed behind the design of this website but there are also aesthetic considerations. Including the dithered images is an option that reinforces the message of the content. Other options for compressing images are available but they would commu-nicate the magazine's core ideas less efficiently. If the cultural and social dimension of design is important, the aesthetic contributes to understanding design as a product of communication and creativity.

13 Gender studies

Questioning heteronormativity

Feminism questions heteronormativity to defend the place of women in patriarchal societies. With origins in psychoanalysis and evolving towards structuralism, feminist positions explored how individuals were socialized in a specific gender. The debate shifted thereby from anatomical differences to social processes encapsulated in the use of language. Increasingly, the struggle against patriarchy has been seen as independent of women. Visions on gender have relativized the centrality of the concepts of man and woman, allowing different combinations and alternatives. Design has participated in these debates, first in as much as design scholarship reproduced patriarchal ideas, marginalizing a feminine discourse. This has prompted the recovery of female designers who were not included in a male-dominated canon. Subsequently, queer studies has allowed questioning heteronormativity from a different perspective and has posed challenges in issues of intersectionality and non-binary identities.

Origins: Institutionalizing feminism

Gender studies trace their roots to the emergence and propagation of feminism, characterized by the advocacy for women's equal rights as a social and political movement. This movement unfolds through distinct waves: the first wave (1850–1920), the second wave (1960–1980) and the ongoing third wave (1980–today). However, even before the formalization of feminism, traces of it can be identified as soon as women were recognized as an oppressed societal group. Earlier instances can be found in patriarchal societies, notably since the seventeenth century, gaining more prominence in the eighteenth century during movements such as the fight for individual rights in the American Revolution (1775–1783) and the French Revolution (1789–1799), which were perceived as advancements in women's rights as well (Easton 2012: 99).

It was after 1850 that feminism began to organize, with groups predominantly comprising women – but also men – advocating for enhancements in the social, cultural and political status of women. Various feminist movements shared a common objective of increasing women's influence in both

DOI: 10.4324/9781003147282-16

society and family life. However, their specific goals diverged, encompassing equal opportunities in education, access to all professions, establishing independence for married women, addressing low wages and securing a more substantial presence in politics.

In Europe during the First World War (1914–1918), women became more actively involved in society due to a significant portion of the male population being deployed to the front lines. Assuming non-traditional roles brought women's societal standing closer to that of men. The war's aftermath saw the realization of several feminist objectives in some countries, including women's suffrage and access to university education in many Western nations. However, gaining voting rights and university education did not result in full participation of women in public life, as cultural norms dictated women's primary role as housewives. Consequently, their involvement in the labour market was limited and upon marriage their paths were often predetermined (Paletschek and Pietrow-Ennker 2004: 3–6).

The second wave of feminism emerged in the 1960s, driven by dissatisfaction with these constraints and aimed at women's emancipation from patriarchal dominance. Key issues in this movement included advocating for equal pay, autonomy over one's body, and dismantling stereotypical gender roles (Paletschek and Pietrow-Ennker 2004: 6). The resistance to certain gender norms also manifested in rejecting uncomfortable items such as bras, high heels and eyelash curlers. Second-wave feminism embraced characteristics like armpit hair and the adoption of trousers as symbolic of challenging traditional gender roles (LeGates 2001: 364).

A progressively leftist and more radical character imbued this second-wave feminism, drawing heavily on the theories of the psychoanalyst and psychiatrist Jacques Lacan (1901–1981) in psychoanalysis and Julia Kristeva in semiotics. These theorists played pivotal roles in establishing the theoretical distinction between sex and gender as independent concepts. Examining the historical trajectory of feminism and its objectives also traces the evolution of gender studies. Lacan championed the separation of biological sex from gender identity, providing valuable insights into gender biases and societal roles. His reinterpretation of Sigmund Freud (1856–1939), particularly transforming the concept of the "penis" into the "phallus," exemplifies this approach. While Freud considered the sexual organ crucial in shaping sexual identity, both masculine and feminine, Lacan introduced a psychosocial interpretation. He depicted the phallus as a mere signifier of authority, detached from its direct connection with the sexual organ. According to Lacan, language operates as a symbolic order that precedes and enables human subjectivity, imposing normativity and moral laws that mould perceptions of masculinity and femininity. In essence, Lacan's perspective aligns with a structuralist approach to psychoanalysis overall, with a specific focus on defining gender (Ragland-Sullivan 1982: 6).

Both Freud and later Simone de Beauvoir (1908–1986) rejected the idea of a disembodied, non-sexed human being and concurred that one does not inherently possess a gender but rather becomes a man or a woman through a social or psychological process, as opposed to a biological or natural given. They shared an interest in understanding the mechanisms of this sexualization process. The point of departure with Lacan lies in his integration of psychoanalysis into structural linguistics, particularly drawing from Ferdinand de Saussure and Roman Jakobson (1896–1952), and structural anthropology, primarily influenced by Claude Lévi-Strauss. Lacan argues that the intrusion of language and law marks a departure from nature, transforming the world by investing it with meaning. As individuals come into contact with language and law, they are separated from the immediate experiences of their bodies. Their interactions with the world, themselves and others are mediated through words and representations (Lacan 2006[1970], 575–585; McKey Carusi 2020: 12).

Kristeva drew on Lacan and expanded on his notions, considering language and representation as the ways of configuring identity in general and gender in particular. She agreed with Lacan that in patriarchal societies, the normative conveyed in language is connected to masculine values. She coined that level as the Symbolic. The preceding level, not conditioned by language, was coined as the Semiotic and related to the feminine. In as much as the Semiotic challenges the authority of the Symbolic, it has revolutionary qualities since it breaks with conceptions of sexual difference (Oliver 1993: 10, 165).

The realms where the Symbolic intersects with the Semiotic, as seen in areas like poetry, aiming to subvert patriarchal norms, were Kristeva's focus of attention. Through these explorations, she brings to light and celebrates the suppressed aspects of the Symbolic, challenging univocal interpretations in favour of multiple meanings (Butler 1999[1990]: 108–109). In this context, Kristeva introduces the concept of "women's writing" as dissenting, active research influenced by contemporary art that seeks to break codes and discover a distinct discourse closer to emotions and the ineffable aspects repressed by the social contract (Kristeva et al. 1981: 24–25).

It is important to note that "women's writing" in Kristeva's view is not confined to works produced by women; rather, it represents a syntax embodying social marginality that can be adopted by anyone. According to Kristeva, feminism should therefore reject the notion of a fixed "Woman" and actively oppose it, aiming instead to safeguard the "feminine." Kristeva warns against feminist ideologies and others that categorize individuals into groups, as they risk becoming dogmatic by overlooking differences in individual character, gender and sexuality. In her perspective, the primary objective of feminism should not merely be placing women in leadership roles, as this approach has shown to be ineffective in altering the system. Instead, the true aim is to establish an alternative system that challenges the existing one (Kristeva et al. 1981: 27–28).

Some authors saw the disruptive potential of "women's writing" to challenge patriarchy but argued that it was unclear what the goal of this subversion was (Butler 1999[1990]: 114). From the 1980s, this lack of a constructive alternative plagued feminism, which became a critique of hegemonic power but without its own political programme.

Development: Femininities and masculinities

The 1980s are considered to be the beginning of post-feminism or the third wave of feminism, characterized as a reaction to 1970s feminism towards the mainstreaming of previous feminist theories (Gillis et al. 2004: 1–2). Inserted in post-modernism, third-wave feminism questioned hegemonic discourses but did not present any alternative. Design historian Penny Sparke summarizes the scholarship on feminism and post-modernism as follows:

> Most agree that while the challenge to cultural authority opened up a space, the lack of a political agenda in post-modernism meant that it could not ultimately be harnessed by feminists seeking to overthrow hegemonic culture and to inject their own culture into the gap.
>
> (1995: 224)

Feminism and other peripheral discourses attacked hegemony but did not present an alternative. Consequently, they gained visibility but had to adapt themselves to political correctness.

The gender theorist Imelda Whelehan has portrayed this generation of feminists as those who "feel obliged to construct their own identities in opposition to what they see as the worst sins of Second Wave feminism – stridency, man-hating, joylessness and bad clothes" (Whelehan 2004: 4). Similar to typical stereotypes, this perception oversimplifies the intricacies of second-wave feminism, relying on exaggerated perspectives. However, it characterizes third-wave feminism more as a celebration than a form of protest. It doesn't position itself in opposition to men but rather challenges patriarchy. Moreover, it embraces attributes traditionally associated with women, such as body decoration, rather than condemning them.

Third-wave feminism has been portrayed as the mainstreaming of the originally political feminist. For example, Janice Winship has defined post-feminism as a popularized, de-politicized, common-sense version of feminism (1985: 25–26; 1987) and Tania Modleski as the appropriation of feminist ideas for non-feminist ends (1991: 8). This mainstreaming of feminism can be interpreted as either a failure of the "real" 1970s feminism or a natural evolution of feminist principles. The anthropologist Summer Wood considers third-wave feminism as a swift removal of political significance from the term and a frequently misguided alignment of feminist ideology with consumer demands. She argues that this alignment is often invoked to justify the right to purchase a wide range of products targeted at women, spanning "from cigarettes to antidepressants to diet frozen pizzas" (Wood 2004: 423–424). Conversely, media theorist Charlotte Brunsdon, considers post-feminism simply to be post-1970s feminism rather than non-feminism (Brunsdon 1997). Both positions convey the controversy surrounding post-feminism; on the one hand, as a failure of feminism's original ideals and, on the other, as the logical consequence of a mature stage of feminism.

Building further on Kristeva, the philosopher Judith Butler added in the early 1990s that gender is primarily a social construction, a performance of an identity that meets the norms of society. Contrary to the previous authors, Butler would not consider that individuals first get socialized in one or other gender and then express gender differences. It is by "doing" that individuals amalgamate gender characteristics. Butler proposes that gendered behaviour never precedes culture but follows culture. Individuals create an identity according to the norms of society and then perform it for the rest of the world (Butler 1999[1990]: xiv–xv).

Butler argues that gender identity is created through classifying "masculine" or "feminine" behaviour in a man or a woman and reproducing it. Because of this, gender has no real core, merely consisting of the regular performance of certain aspects and functions of gender. A major consequence of this statement is the negation of any form of gender realism, that is, the concept of viewing women as a collective with shared characteristics, experiences or common conditions that define and shape them, in contrast to, for example, men. The gendered body is performative since it has no ontological status apart from the acts, gestures and desires produced on the surface of the body, fabrications manufactured and sustained through corporeal signs and other discursive means (Butler 1999[1990]: 173). Along these lines, modern-day feminism embraces socially constructed femininity as opposed to biologically determined.

Similar to Kristeva, Butler argues for the individual, intersectional analysis in which concrete "women" are constructed (Butler 1999[1990]: 19–20). For Butler, the fault lies in defining the term "woman" at all, since it prescribes normative and thereby exclusionary properties, and can therefore never be used in an unideological way. Individuals not exhibiting typically female traits are not really a member of the socially constructed category of "women," and according to second-wave feminist theories neither do they qualify for feminist political representation (Francis 2002: 40).

Regarding these ideas, Butler has been considered along with Michel Foucault and gender theorist Eve Kosofsky Sedgwick as pioneering queer studies (Somerville 2020: 7). Butler challenges the notion that for the categories of man and woman to exist, women must adhere to being females with feminine behavioural traits and to being heterosexuals whose desire is directed at men. Similarly, men are expected to be males with masculine behavioural traits, and to be heterosexuals whose desire is directed at women. This conventional gender sequence is considered normative, and individuals who deviate from it are often socially criticized for "doing it wrong." According to Butler, these normative foundations of gender are arbitrarily constructed by culture and society, representing a series of stylized performances (Butler 1999[1990]: 23–24).

Queer studies emerged in the late 1980s and early 1990s in academia and its theoretical premises have been psychoanalysis, feminist theories and the deconstruction of power structures by Michel Foucault. It deals basically with sexual and gender identities that are non-normative but expands its scope also to interlocking categories of difference and power, including race, caste, indigeneity, gender, class, nation and religion. These identities describe a historically specific relation to power, rather than an identity per se. In that sense, queer studies incorporates but is not limited to gay and lesbian studies. For example, queer studies would distinguish heterosexuality from heteronormative. Since at specific moments, heterosexuality has been criminalized in cases of interracial heterosexuality or the stigmatization of unmarried women, these cases also challenge heteronormativity and therefore are the object of study of queer studies (Somerville 2020: 2–5).

Implementation: Gendered objects, women designers and queer stories

The influence of feminism and gender studies in design scholarship goes back to the 1980s. Pioneering studies have been Cheryl Buckley's article "Made in Patriarchy: Towards a Feminist Analysis of Women and Design" (1986), Judith Attfield's chapter "FORM/female FOLLOWS FUNCTION/male: Feminist Critiques of Design" (2009[1989]) and Judith Attfield and Pat Kirkham's *A View from the Interior: Feminism, Women and Design* (1989). These three publications evidence the patriarchal, gendered language within the preceding design scholarship. The authors analysed design historiography to demonstrate that it had been divided into two semantic fields. The first would relate to men, creativity, seriousness and functionality and the second to women, consumption, frivolity and decoration. This ideology was the cause and the consequence of a focus on modernist design and male designers, leaving non-modernist practices, such as crafts or fashion, and women designers in the margins. These accounts were moreover influenced by second-wave feminist scholarship, arguing that a lack of documentation on female designers creates an incomplete representation of the contribution of women to the field of the applied arts and design (Lees-Maffei and Houze 2010: 347–348, 381–382).

Debunking the social construction of femininity is the goal of Buckley's essay in which she argues that femininity is socially constructed, with sexuality and gender identity being acquired at conscious and unconscious levels in the family and through language acquisition (Buckley 1986: 3). Buckley argues for a more inclusive design history that considers not only the production side of the design process but also its mediation and consumption aspects (Buckley 1986: 7). She furthermore argues that patriarchal structures should be considered in relation to the work of female designers and the construction of design history (Buckley 1986: 4). Attfield, on her part, argues that the modernist-dominated design historiography prevents female designers from being included in the canon, relegating women designers and women's taste to invisibility. She stated, for example, that "a hierarchy has built up around types of objects which gives importance to industrial design and 'the machine aesthetic' i.e. the more obviously masculine – while considering areas such as fashion as trivial and synonymous with 'feminine'" (Attfield 2009

[1989]: 51). Attfield and Kirkham's book (1989) illustrates these issues through specific examples.

This line of literature claiming for greater visibility of female designers gained momentum as Marjan Groot's publications on the Dutch case demonstrate (2007, 2011). Groot discusses gender as a culturally and socially constructed concept and analyses the different contexts that influence the meaning of design in relation to gender (Groot 2007: 18). She includes the work of not only female designers but also curators of applied arts and design who were active in the Netherlands between 1880 and 1940. A small number of women were often highly dedicated to their jobs in galleries, magazines and social networks, supporting their own work and that of other women (Groot 2007: 30).

Due to the push for increased visibility of women designers, there has been a proliferation of exhibitions and publications that highlight and support the work of women designers or delve into traditional areas of women's production that were previously overlooked (see, for example, Holsapel 2001; Salinas and Mallent 2006; Rossi 2009). Rebecca Houze argues that this approach has prompted insightful examinations of the institutional structures shaping design and has revealed gender imbalances in design partnerships. In addition to focusing on women producers, design scholarship has turned its attention to the objects themselves through approaches like embroidery, textiles or cosmetics (Lees-Maffei and Houze 2010: 381).

The decreasing popularity of second-wave feminism in the 1990s is epitomized by the fact that Attfield and Kirkham were asked by their publisher The Women's Press to delete the word "feminism" from the title of the second edition of their book *A view from the interior: Feminism, Women and Design* in 1995. This fits in with a general trend that Attfield described as the debilitation of the political aim of feminism in its encounter with post-modernism (Attfield 2003: 77). At the same time, feminist approaches were substituted by gender studies in the 1990s, encompassing men and masculinity, which attracted criticism from feminists for removing women from the focus of analysis (Lees-Maffei and Houze 2010: 348). If femininity was a construct, masculinity was that too, and deserved to be studied (Breward 1999; Mort 1996).

Simultaneously, the intersection with studies on consumption promoted the acknowledgement of women as active participants in modernism, rather than being excluded from it. An illustrative example is found in Penny Sparke's work, *As Long as It's Pink* (1995), which delves into women's unique experience of modernity by examining their role as consumers – whether in the realm of fashion, clothing, domestic decorations or implements. The focus on consumption allows Sparke to develop arguments that attribute a certain level of agency to women in terms of appropriation, negotiation and even subversion. Despite modernism's emphasis on innovation, reform and revered designers, Sparke's recognition of female consumption does not imply an acceptance of the idea that consumption is inherently feminine. This perspective avoids perpetuating the essentialist notion that associates consumption with "feminine" and production with "masculine." Instead, Sparke explores the implications of feminizing the consumer and sheds light on aspects of the modernist era that have been obscured by the prevailing narrative.

Since 2000, the interest in queer culture has expanded mostly in the field of fashion and the interior. Shaun Cole's *"Don We Now Our Gay Apparel:" Gay Men's Dress in the Twentieth Century* (2000) narrates the development of sartorial codes for gay men since the early eighteenth-century industrializing Europe, with a focus on the post-1960s period. Cole integrates primary sources and oral history, including the findings of 24 interviews with gay men whose ages ranged from 30 to 89. The centrality of their testimony is indicated in the preface to the text, which provides a discussion of the interview process. The book commences with an exploration of homosexual dress codes. Green carnations, suede shoes, tight trousers, mauve shirts, Vince posing pouches, green and pink cigarette packets, Liberty silk ties. The contention of this book is that "clothing, along with adornment and demeanour, has been a primary method of identification for and of gay men" (Cole 2000: 1). Perhaps Cole's bigger contribution is the analysis of the relationship between gay men and their dress to post-war music and club cultures. Cole contends that most subcultural studies have been heterosexist with an uncomplicated understanding of masculinity. Although disco and punk are often placed on the binary gay and straight, Cole argues that there was a complex overlapping with a group such as the gay punks (Cole 2000: 146–151).

With the same British focus as Cole's book, two publications on interiors appeared in 2014: Matt Cook's *Queer Domesticities: Homosexuality and Home Life in Twentieth-Century London* (2014) and John Potvin's *Bachelors of a Different Sort: Queer Aesthetics, Material Culture and the Modern Interior in Britain* (2014). Arguing that the home has traditionally represented the heteronormative family, they explore queer alternatives within similar timeframes. Potvin starts in the 1880s and works up to the 1950s, whilst Cook starts at the same point but goes right up to the 1990s. This tendency for broad overviews is to the detriment of historic specificity, which is one of the main problems of these two studies.

Both authors agree that a queer home is not a total rejection of family, but a renegotiation of its boundaries. In establishing these points, Cook produces a series of instructive domestic biographies of some queer men based in London. Beginning with the artists and collectors Charles Shannon and Charles Ricketts and concluding with a discussion of the visual artist Derek Jarman, Cook explores personal diaries, memoirs and oral histories to reconstruct a variety of queer domesticities in modern Britain. In both books, there is a dominant semiotic methodology basing their findings on close readings of images. This results in abstract conceptualizations of domesticity, obscuring the materiality of the home, as conceived and realized by gay men, which both authors clearly set out as their central concern.

In places, it feels as though the sources would not quite allow Potvin and Cook to answer the questions they were trying to address. Potvin's work begs the question of just how much one can ever theorize or categorize either the queer/normative, or the public/private in design history and beyond; the very fluidity of the ideas and identities explored may mean that the queer interior and its queer inhabitants can only ever be defined as such on a case-by-case basis (2014: 8). Similarly, Cook suggests that there are multiple dimensions to identities and identifications, and understandings of desire intertwine with individual material, economic, cultural and social circumstances in complicated ways. At times, this meant that Cook's conclusions were more speculative than substantiated, as the source material offered no straightforward or unproblematic unravelling of interior lives and domestic arrangements. Considering the artistic backgrounds of so many of the case studies, this identification might have interacted with queerness, colouring the conclusions of this research. That said, Cook acknowledges that the book is experimental in nature and that after his analysis he could not find a model of queer domesticity (2014: 5–6). Claiming a queer identity made a difference to the domestic lives of the men he describes, who negotiated their homes and families in ways that enabled them both to fit in and to express difference. The question is whether this would ever be traced in the way they arranged their homes.

In the field of fashion, Valerie Steele's edited volume *A Queer History of Fashion: From the Closet to the Catwalk* (2013) provides an overview of the eponymous exhibition of which this publication became the catalogue, examining the intersections of gayness or queerness and fashion since the eighteenth century. The essays in this book centre around three related themes: the presence of LGBTQ+ individuals in the fashion industry and their influence on fashion; the influence of LGBTQ+ subcultural styles on fashion; and "how dissident ways of relating to fashion as a cultural form have resulted in a gay or queer sensibility that embraces both idealizing and transgressive aesthetic styles" (Steele 2013: 11). Steele expressed that the main goal is "to put gay people back into history," which resulted in some dubious results, when discussing the work of fashion designers Christian Dior (1905–1957), Yves Saint-Laurent (1936–2008) and Rudi Gernreich (1922–1985), who actually have been always part of the canon (Brumfitt 2013: §3).

The same year, the book *Queer Style* was published, authored by Adam Geczy and Vicki Karaminas, and offered a more substantial and coherent reflection on queerness. The connection between queerness and gay or lesbians is more nuanced than in the previous example, since "being queer does not necessarily entail being gay or lesbian, although it generally does" (2013: 2). It is going against heteronormative styles which originates queer styles. It raises the question of whether the disconnection observed between queer identity and that of gay or lesbian individuals is reciprocal. Does the identification as gay or lesbian inherently imply queerness and the sharing of subversive sartorial codes? If this were the case, queer style might not be exclusively confined to gay and lesbian communities. Historical instances of cross-dressing beyond these categories, like the robe redingote worn by women in late eighteenth-century France or shawl lapels in early nineteenth-century men's jackets, suggest a broader context. Nevertheless, the authors establish a normative code based on heterosexuality – suits for males and dresses for females – against which queer style asserts resistance. They attribute a consistent set of characteristics, such as nonfunctionality and exaggeration, as the basis for this resistance (2013: 4).

Moreover, this book offers a most welcomed global perspective, including male transsexual or transvestite ladyboys of Thailand, masculine Thai lesbians known as tomboys, feminine-identified Thai women known as "Dees" who have relations with other women, women-identified males known as the Kathoeys, transgender women of Samoa called "fa'afafine" and the Albanian sworn virgins who elect to become men (Geczy and Karaminas 2013: 123–140; Figure 13.1). This scholarship is necessary to recognize the Euro-American construction of queerness and understand other constructions similarly related to a prevailing social order but in very different ways. It is again most striking that the authors acknowledge specific strategies to resist heteronormative and at the same time recognize localized interpretations.

From the above, it can be deduced that studies on gender and queerness need to go beyond the woman/man and straight/queer individuals and concentrate on discrediting patriarchy, as Kristeva and Butler have demonstrated. Furthermore, gender identities do not define heterogeneous groups and this diversity needs to be acknowledged, as Butler would put it. How to orchestrate these two requires acknowledging the challenges they entail.

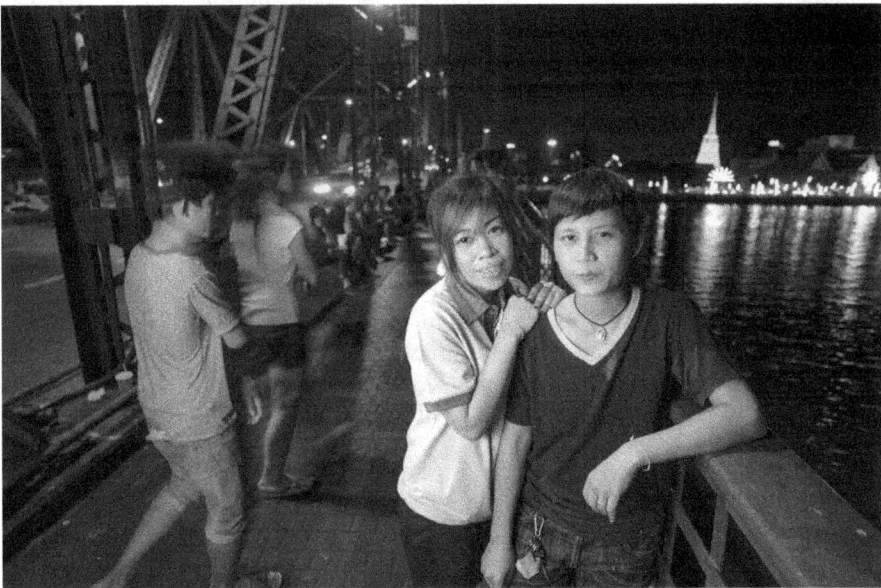

Figure 13.1 A woman and her tomboy partner pose on a bridge together over a river in Bangkok city. Photo by Jonas Gratzer/LightRocket via Getty Images

Challenges: Just binary oppositions?

Gender and queer studies can be questioned when it comes to delineating collective identities, as there is a risk of cultural homogenization. Recognizing these intricacies involves acknowledging that individual identities are shaped not solely by gender but also by other factors, such as race, nationality or religion. It is crucial to understand that these parameters are interconnected, influencing one another. Moreover, there is a growing interest in acknowledging gender identities that extend beyond the heteronormative/queer dichotomy, embracing notions such as gender neutrality.

The intimate interconnection of partial identities is an aspect to take into consideration. Generalizing about what it means to be a man, a woman or queer involves complex interactions with class, gender, race and likely other yet-to-be-identified forms of identity and designation. A post-structural approach to gender recognizes that there is no singular authentic queer history, but rather numerous histories. Similarly, there is not a singular authentic queer identity; instead, there are many identities that remain fluid and dynamic.

The historian Evelynn Hammonds discusses how the definition of queer has been mostly identified with white queerness (1994). For her, the term lesbian, for example, without the racial qualifier can be simply read as a white lesbian. She stated: "When I am asked if I am queer I usually say yes even though the ways in which I am queer have never been articulated in the body of work that is now called queer theory" (1994: 1). Similarly, the artist Kaushalya Bannerji comments on her disconnection from the white queer androgynous aesthetic as she adorns herself in traditional South Asian attire, which has multiple readings for her as a South Asian Canadian lesbian but read as a "femme" or hyperfeminine identity in a white lesbian context. She challenges the roles and behaviours attributed to that hyperfeminine identity, which complicates how to negotiate ethnicity and sexual identity in a Western context (1993: 59).

In these circumstances, there arises a necessity for a distinct approach to understanding sexuality that goes beyond prevailing patterns of visibility, same-sex desire and identity both within and in opposition to various cultures. The idea of a universal category like "queer" that encompasses all individuals with diverse gender, race and ethnicity seems no longer tenable. On the contrary, gender, race and ethnicity play pivotal roles in shaping the substance of a queer theoretical framework (Massaquoi 2015: 768).

But how to articulate this complexity? In 1991, the feminist lawyer and legal scholar Kimberlé Crenshaw developed the concept of intersectionality to detect the motives behind discrimination (1991: 1241). Each individual is advantaged or disadvantaged because of their gender, race, ethnicity, class, sexual orientation, religion, disability, citizenship, and so on. For instance, a woman can experience some disadvantages in a patriarchal, racist, homophobic society. However, this same woman would enjoy privileges associated with being straight and white. While this woman and a Black lesbian are both subject to some discrimination because of their gender, the latter is subject to further discrimination due to her race and sexual orientation. Put simply, there is no common "women's experience," "Black person experience" or "lesbian experience." This would assume that the situation could be tackled from a single-axis approach, while the construction of identity and the reasons behind discrimination respond to a multiple-axis approach. As the philosophy scholar Shannon Dea emphasizes, individuals are not exclusively defined as just a woman, solely Black or only lesbian (Dea 2016: 17).

Heteronormative codes reveal themselves to be even more arbitrary when considered from a global perspective. Artist and fashion designer Alok Vaid-Menon, whose parents are Punjabi from India and Malayali from Malaysia, said: "I grew up with men who wore so many different vibrant colours, who had different accessories, even men who wore skirts" (Weikle 2022: §6; Figure 13.2). Dominant notions of heteronormativity entail Westernized versions, and de-gendering implies also decolonizing gender stereotypes.

Oversimplifications become even more apparent when the opposition heteronormative–queer is put at stake by gender identities that question binary divisions. One of these identities is the non-binary – individuals that identify as neither men nor women. In the case of Vaid-Menon – who identifies as a gender non-conforming person – their designs are not just subversive of normative heterosexual styles. Vaid-Menon relates in their book *Beyond the*

Figure 13.2 Alok Vaid-Menon speaks during #BoFVOICES on November 22, 2019 in Oxfordshire, UK and comments on their gender-neutral fashion collection from 2017 designed along with Adrianne Keishing. Photo by Samir Hussein/Samir Hussein/Getty Images for The Business of Fashion

Gender Binary that they wear a teal dress, purple lipstick and a full beard (2020: 11). The definition of a non-binary gender identity passes through the appropriation of heteronormativity but mixed with references to both genders, not just subverting the existing codes. Moreover, it is not just the clothes that alter the codes but the interaction between the clothes and the wearer that deviate them from heteronormativity.

In Vaid-Menon's 2019 fashion collections in collaboration with Adrianne Keishing, the garments are not more or less functional or exaggerated than in any other fashion collection (Alok 2019). Allusions to nightgowns, underwear, folk dress, print combinations, volume contrast and evening dress are present. In other men's or women's collections, these references have been assigned specific gender connotations. What sets this collection apart is that these elements are degendered – they are appropriated and interpreted without undergoing explicit subversion. What Vaid-Menon wears and designs does not fit in with Geczy and Karaminas' categorization but also not with Cole's list. Instead of looking for gay-specific or unisex styles, Vaid-Menon argues for de-gendering fashion.

Narrow definitions of queerness can be reductive since they still validate binary gender division. Applying a sartorial code for queer style implies monolithic definitions of both heteronormativity and queerness. The characterization of queer style as "non-functional and exaggerated" by Geczy and Karaminas might therefore appear too dogmatic – and as dogmatic as identifying heteronormative codes with suits for men and dresses for women. There might be other more complex negotiations, since presenting alternatives to heteronormativity does not mean subverting its codes but appropriating, negotiating and individualizing those codes.

14 Style

Period, group and individual

Style, considered as the outward manifestation of the inner being of a place, a period, a social group or an individual, has been one of the most important critical concepts deployed by art historians. Stylistic analysis begins with description and classification, depending on the features replicated in some work or repertory of works, and results in the segmentation of historical periods or social groups, which needs to be coherently explained. It basically makes inferences from observable data – the replicated patterns – to general principles – a theory. Generated in art history and developed in the framework of nineteenth-century idealism, stylistic analysis first looked at how forms were symptomatic of changes in conceptual frameworks. This mono-causal interpretation of style change was substituted in the twentieth century by other accounts supported by empirical data, reaffirming the fact that the delineation of any style is a construct. Some trends have negated their belonging to any style, claiming timeless aesthetic qualities. This chapter argues that timelessness does not escape from stylistic analysis but rather plays with its conventions.

Origins: A product of idealism

The etymology of the word "style" derives from the Latin "stilus," a writing implement that facilitates personal expression. Comparative stylistic analysis developed in the nineteenth century, and was stimulated by the very lively trade in the art of previous periods. Giovanni Morelli's approach was grounded in the notion that each artist possesses a distinctive style, beyond the artist's conscious control. Even when attempting to adopt a different style, an artist's characteristic "hand" becomes discernible through the examination and categorization of elements such as the portrayal of ears, noses, hands, various body parts, as well as depictions of clouds, leaves, folds and individual brushstrokes (Bod 2013: 312–313). The origin of the term "style" refers to the individual, and when we speak of, for example, the "style of the 1960s," personal style is being expanded metaphorically (Summers 2003: 145).

DOI: 10.4324/9781003147282-17

The defining factors of a style are always formal but identify divisions based on chronology, such as the art-nouveau style which characterizes the period between 1890 and 1914; geography, such as the Hungarian and Scottish variants of art nouveau as being distinctly different; group identity, such as the group of designers working under the name of the Nancy School in France; and the individual, such as the influence of the dancer Loie Fuller (1862–1928). In this sense, style searches for meaning in form, connecting it to a specific characterization of collective or individual identities.

Style has been both a defining factor and a ferociously contested concept. The art historian George Kubler, for example, compared the concept of style to a rainbow, since we can see it only briefly and it vanishes when we try to revisit it. Kubler was genuinely interested in the changes of form over long periods of time, but he questioned nonetheless the fixed, invariant qualities of styles. As a tool to characterize periods in a set of characteristics, style was useful but full of exceptions (Kubler 1962: 118). Similarly, the poet Walt Whitmann (1819–1892) compared style to a curtain, defending that the best poets do not recur to stylistic tricks, "not the richest curtains." Defending his straightforward writing, he stated that what he tells is precisely what it is. One century later, the art critic Susan Sontag (1933–2004) discussed Whitmann's metaphor arguing that style is not decoration (1965: 16). Style is not a curtain in the sense that once parted, the matter will be revealed. She questions why metaphors on style place matter on the inside and style on the outside and if how we appear to others is just a question of style and not our true being (1965: 17–18).

These discussions about style being illusionist as a rainbow or superficial as a curtain correspond with the theoretical foundations of style in nineteenth-century idealism, which asserted that style (form) was a way to get into the essence (idea). The origins of this mode of thinking can be traced back to the philosopher Georg Wilhelm Friedrich Hegel who questioned late eighteenth-century formalism represented by Immanuel Kant and its interest in art for art's sake.

Hegel's main contribution was his search for an explanation for the succession of styles (1835–38: 80–88). The connection between style and a specific group had already been explored by Johann Joachim Winckelmann and Johann Gottfried Herder. Winckelmann believed that the art of antiquity could be explained by considering social circumstances, climate, forms of government, ways of thinking and perceiving, and society's understanding of the role of the artist. Similarly, Herder argued that artworks were products of particular societies with distinct cultural values (Hatt and Klonk 2017[2006]: 22). Hegel went beyond these positions and introduced a diachronic explanation of the evolution of art, acknowledging the unique individuality of past art forms. In other words, Winckelmann and Herder grouped cultural manifestations of a specific moment in a coherent manner, encompassing areas such as art, philosophy, religion, economy and class system, which shape and are influenced by one another. Hegel sought to explain the transition from these all-encompassing styles to others.

The principle of idealism, positing that ideas constitute the fundamental foundation of all existence, informed Hegel's metaphysical system. For Hegel, the shape of history is the result of the workings of the Absolute Idea, or a world spirit, which realizes itself more fully with each successive age. The Idea manifests itself in the products of the human mind. Consequently, the forms assumed by works of art were considered expressions of the Idea of a particular age, rather than the result of individual actions or even the social forces surrounding their creation (Fernie 1995: 16). In this manner, the sensory nature of art becomes imbued with idealism, as the Idea becomes manifested in a tangible form. What is apprehended by the senses serves not as an ultimate goal in itself but as a means to grasp the ideal, which holds true significance (Podro 1984: 19).

Hegel proposed a solution to reconcile two apparently contradictory claims: (a) the assertion that art objects possessed timeless intrinsic worth, and (b) the recognition that they were fleeting and deceptive phenomena. According to Hegel, art served a dual purpose as both a means to express the Idea and an index of its progressive development (Preziosi 2009[1998]: 116). Hegel identified three fundamental steps in the historical development of art: the Symbolic, the Classical and the Romantic (1835–38: 84–87). Each phase makes its appearance in a specific culture. The Symbolic originated in ancient India and Persia and reached its peak in Ancient Egypt. In this stage, there is no sense of the difference between a spiritual idea and a material body. His examples are the abstract manifestations of the Hindu god Brahma or the pyramids in Egypt. The Classical characterizes ancient Greece and reached its peak in the second half of the fourth century. Here, there is an increasing awareness of the spiritual, in which the spirit permeates matter completely. Hegel's example is the harmonic depiction of the human figure In Greek sculpture. The Romantic stage corresponds with the rise of Christianity and reached its peak in the art of Leonardo da Vinci (1452–1519) and Raphael (1483–1520) in the sixteenth century. In this stage, human self-examination becomes the source to understand the Idea, following the concept that God is present in every individual (Hatt and Klonk 2017[2006]: 26–33).

Hegel's mono-causal and a priori explanation of the development of art, in which the Idea guided its material manifestations, resulted in an optimistic historicism in a state of constant creative evolution. Each stage contains the preceding ones, since they originate from them, and each stage supersedes all previous stages, approaching perfection, since they configure a development based on progress (Popper 1990[1947]: 36–37; Preziosi 2009[1998]: 116).

What entails stylistic analysis then? According to Hegel, the historian's task is not to find out what connections there may be between the different aspects defining a specific society, for this connection is assumed on metaphysical grounds. One assumes without question that the Gothic style of architecture expresses the same essential attitude as the scholastic philosophy that resulted in medieval feudalism. What is expected of the historian is to demonstrate this unitary principle and to identify its visible traces. The practice of art history, according to Hegel, involved systematically and empirically tracing the development of the spirit of a specific era (*Zeitgeist*) or a particular community (*Volksgeist*) through the genealogy of their artistic production (Preziosi 2009[1998]: 116).

Hegel's idealism was criticized already in the nineteenth century and more evidently from materialist positions. Inverting Hegel's principle, Marxism asserted that material conditions are not a manifestation of the spirit, but rather that the spirit is a byproduct or superstructure of the material conditions of production. According to Marxists, material conditions gave rise to medieval feudalism, which subsequently originated both scholastic philosophy and Gothic architecture, rather than the reverse relationship suggested by Hegel (Gombrich 1968: 136). The Marxist thinker Leon Trotsky (1879–1940) wrote that the Gothic cathedral could not be understood apart from the medieval town, the system of guilds and the hierarchy of the Church. He interpreted the Renaissance as a period in which a new class emerged from Gothic oppression, gaining control of the means of production, the educational system and the communication media (Schneider Adams 1996: 59). Marxists questioned Hegel's idealist causality and they substituted it with a materialist, yet equally mono-causal, explanation of history.

Development: "The mask is the face"

In the twentieth century, critiques of mono-causal interpretations of style came from formalism, Marxist and cultural history. All three theoretical frameworks need to be placed against the background of Hegelianism to which they both reacted and found inspiration in various ways.

Early twentieth-century **formalists** criticized the development of great narratives and all-encompassing interpretations and disconnected styles from the history of cultural ideas, politics, economics or science. They were interested in the formal characteristics of art and how they were experienced (Preziosi 2009[1998]: 117; Schneider Adams 1996: 34). In his renowned work *Principles of Art History*, first published in 1915, the art historian Heinrich Wölfflin questioned that factors such as temperament, *Zeitgeist* or racial character were behind the styles of individuals, periods or peoples. According to him, changing modes of perception explain the succession of styles (Hatt and Klonk 2017[2006]: 74).

Wölfflin's aim was to develop a comprehensive descriptive framework capable of capturing the visual forms of an era without assuming further explanations. For this, he focussed on explaining the transition from the High Renaissance, with its classic style, to the Baroque style of the seventeenth century (Schneider Adams 1996: 24). Both periods were characterized by different formal organizations that Wölfflin characterized as linear, plane, closed form, multiplicity and absolute clarity for the High Renaissance and painterly, recession, open form, unity and relative clarity for the Baroque (Schneider Adams 1996: 25). Stylistic analysis for Wölfflin was not about how ideas manifested in forms but about putting into words what the historian could see.

In his comparative analysis of two vases – that is, a baluster-shaped tankard designed by Hans Holbein (ca. 1497–1543) and a rococo vase from the Schwarzenberg Garden in Vienna – Wölfflin argues that in the former the unity of the form is fully revealed (Figures 14.1 and 14.2). The linear arabesque decoration echoes the curvilinear baluster shape of the vase contributing to a general impression of clarity. In the rococo vase, the handles have been replaced by sea creatures. The decoration resembles natural forms in relief, adding volume and not only decorating the vase structure. The resulting volumes create shadows that add pictorial complexity and lack of clarity to the whole. In Holbein's tankard, the emphasis lies rather in the outline. In the garden vase, the emphasis lies on the modelling and filling of the surfaces. The rococo artist intentionally avoided what Holbein pursued. The form of the rococo vase can never be entirely grasped, preserving multiple angles for the viewer (Wölfflin 1950[1915]: 225).

George Kubler, like other fellow formalists, minimized the role of artists and designers by putting style at the forefront of art history. In his book *The Shape of Time* (1962), he argued that "art" should embrace the whole range of man-made things, integrating design as part of it. Art history, ethnology and archaeology need to be considered as partial studies of the bigger concept of material culture, what he prefers to call "history of things." His book was a notable synthesis of the entire formalist tradition as seen from the perspective of a mid-century reaction to growing disciplinary emphases on content, social context and symbolism (Preziosi 2009[1998]: 118).

Kubler argued, for example, that in iconology, the word was more important than the image, which was the true interest of art historians, saying that "what a thing means is not more important than what it is; that expression and form are equivalent challenges to the historian; and that to neglect either meaning or being, either essence or existence, deforms our comprehension of both" (1962: 115). He discussed Wölfflin's idea of the substitution of a style by another, arguing, for example, that seventeenth-century architects would design curviplanar shapes, which Wölfflin characterized as Baroque, but also planiform shapes, which leaned towards the classical. Therefore, coining all seventeenth-century art as Baroque was confusing. Not everything made in that century was so homogeneous and so different to the High Rennaissance (Kubler 1962: 117). For Kubler, style is a construction, following his metaphor of the rainbow. He summarized this idea by saying that style "pertains to the consideration of static groups of entities. It vanishes once these entities are restored to the flow of time" (1962: 118). The stylistic segmentation of periods presumes that styles are confined within specific chronological borders, but not how they disappear and reappear.

From the field of **cultural history**, Ernst Gombrich (1909–2001) defended the Hegelian intuition that things in life are not isolated and cultural creations are connected to contextual aspects. However, in his aim to develop a "true cultural history," he would not imply that there is only one major cause or that forms translate culture visually (Gombrich 1969: 36; Fernie 1995:

Figure 14.1 A baluster-shaped tankard designed by Hans Holbein and engraved by Wenceslaus Hollar (1607–1677). Photo by Heritage Art/Heritage Images via Getty Images

Figure 14.2 A rococo vase (right). View of the fountain of the garden of the Palais Schwarzenberg near the city of Vienna, Mesard, 1700–1799, Numbered: 1. Publisher: Mesard, (mentioned on object), print maker: anonymous, publisher: Paris, print maker: France, 1700–1799, paper, etching, brush, h 276 mm – w 386 mm. Photo by: Sepia Times/Universal Images Group via Getty Images

225). Gombrich blamed Hegel for the weak basis of cultural history and his influence on later cultural historians. He gave the example of Burckhardt, who – willing to depart from a Hegelian vision in favour of working with the facts – actually corroborated Hegel's spirit of nations or *Volksgeist*. For example, the art historian Jacob Burckhardt (1818–1897) advised art historians studying fifteenth-century painting to wonder "how does the spirit of the fifteenth century express itself in painting?" (Gombrich 1969: 16, 28). Even when Burckhardt was decidedly against Hegel's metaphysical systems, he evidently acknowledged some useful aspects of Hegelianism in the extent to which they helped understand history (Fernie 1995: 14).

So far in this chapter, style has been discussed as the product of collective agency rather than of individuals. Hegel, Winckelmann, Herder, Trotsky, Wölfflin and Burckhardt identified society with its dominant group, nurturing the idea that societies are homogeneous and that style emerges from that homogeneity. In order to contest this, Gombrich made the difference between periods and movements. A period is a Hegelian idea, a collective event in which individuals are subordinate to the whole. A movement, on the contrary, is started and maintained by individuals. Gombrich argues that Hegel saw periods erroneously as movements and that thinking of people as subsumed into a collective had been reductionist for the understanding of history dynamics (Gombrich 1969: 35). According to Gombrich, art historians should acknowledge that the success of specific artistic styles may reflect shifting attitudes, yet they should refrain from utilizing evolving styles and trends as definitive signs of deep-seated psychological transformations (Gombrich 1969: 37). His observation opened new interpretations of style as belonging to small groups and individuals – thereby bringing the discussions on style back to its original etymological meaning.

Marxist scholars refined their positions in the twentieth century, using more sophisticated economic models and more detailed historical evidence. Following Frederick Antal and Arnold Hauser, the art historian Nikos Hadjinicolaou states that style does not belong to a period, a nation, a region or an individual but to a social group. He argues that societies are heterogeneous and composed of different social groups – for him meaning social classes –, which are homogeneous enough to generate a style – which he coined "visual ideology" (1978[1973]: 98). For Hadjinicolaou, style reflects ideology and is reflected in the way "in which the formal and thematic elements of a picture are combined on each specific occasion" (1978[1973]: 95). Therefore, a specific period necessarily shows different styles, since different classes coexist (Hadjinicolaou 1978[1973]: 33). The Marxist art historian Svetlana Alpers (b. 1936) shows a similar mistrust in the characterization of periods by a homogeneous style. She stresses that styles are not the result of a specific period but of specific social conditions; if those social conditions reappear, then the style will equally re-emerge (Alpers 1979: 161–162).

Acknowledging the political power of style and the agency of the individual defies Hegelianism at its core. Hegel defends that forms are important only as long as they represent ideas, confronting the superficial character of the former with the essential character of the latter. However, if forms have agency, then this relation switches and forms acquire a more determinant role than ideas. Styles not only represent ideas but can change them. Susan Sontag's "On Style" (1965), encapsulates this paradigm shift vehemently. According to her, style and content are not separate entities and there should be no distinction made between the two since they are intertwined. An illustrative statement of this viewpoint is when she affirms that "our manner of appearing is our manner of being," adding that "[t]he mask is the face" (Sontag 1965: 18). Thereby, Sontag defines style essentially as the language through which artists express their art. Contrary to what Whitmann stated, style is not quantitative. One work cannot be more straightforward or more stylized than another work. Style is there always and it is not symptomatic of something else, it is an agent of change in itself.

Implementation: Style as resistance

Even when it is a contested concept, daily life is full of references to styles, such as "techno" subcultures or "steampunk" design. Its importance has not declined but rather increased. Within design scholarship, design has been grouped into periods, such as in the book *Design in the Fifties* (Marcus 1998) and into music-based groups such as hip-hop (Romero and Way 2023) or Goths (Hodkinson 2002). There have been studies on wide-range styles with specific formal characteristics such as post-modernism (Adamson and Pavitt 2011) and of more specific styles, such as populuxe – that was characteristic of the 1950s and 1960s in the United States and featured pastel-coloured plastic objects, such as clocks and radios, with metallized plastic trim that simulated chrome, evoking a sense of luxury (Hine 1987).

Design history incorporated stylistic analysis with caution, recognizing its close association with art history, from which design history aimed to distinguish itself. Fran Hannah and Tim Putnam (1980) complain that the vocabulary for stylistic analysis is rather tied to visual analysis, which is important but insufficient for design history for which knowing how objects are made and used is paramount. They state that "the analysis of style becomes the analysis of styles of life, of models of use of the produced environment, both directly and indirectly" (Hannah and Putnam 1980: 145). Their distinction between direct and indirect models of use is significant.

For Hannah and Putnam, *direct usage* refers to utilitarian or functional aspects, in which objects take part in daily life regardless of whether they are intimately connected to a lifestyle. For example, hip-hoppers might cook in a stainless-steel pan, without that specific pan participating in their identification as hip-hoppers. *Indirect usage*, on the contrary, deals with the symbolic usage of objects, in which their characteristics manifestly contribute towards the construction of an identity and a lifestyle. The obvious example is hip-hoppers wearing grills as teeth jewellery, an attribute that identifies them with a specific subculture unequivocally. Hannah and Putnam argue that both usages need to be studied simultaneously to understand the impact of design on history. Direct usage presents a reality that is practical but one-dimensional. Indirect usage ignores the practical rationality of objects but explores the different dimensions in which identities are shaped. The combination of both offers a better idea of how design integrates into daily life (Hannah and Putnam 1980: 143–145).

The importance of small groups and individuals not to follow but to confront dominant styles has been developed by authors such as media theorist Dick Hebdige, whose book *Subculture: The Meaning of Style* (1979) became one of the most influential works to emerge from Birmingham University's Centre for Contemporary Cultural Studies (CCCS). By combining sociology and semiotics, Hebdige explores the subversive implications of style in post-war British subcultures defining subculture as "[t]he expressive forms and rituals of subordinate groups" (Hebdige 1979: 2). He suggests that dress and value systems from the dominant culture were transformed and even subverted when interpreted by subculture. The tension between a dominant culture and a subculture is complex since subcultures subvert codes from the parent or dominant culture but cannot escape its power. Consequently, mass cultural forms attempt to tame or control subcultural styles into mainstream fashions. Thereby, subcultural expressions are transformed by the dominant culture into a mainstream material culture or into deviant behaviours (Heilbronner 2008: 586; Gelder and Thornton 1997: 87). When defining style as an instrument of rebellion and resistance, Hebdige reverses the usual attention to style and substance, with style moving beyond the surface to take centre stage.

Hebdige's book originated two major avenues for thinking about subcultures. First, about how they actually work and what their articulation is within dominant cultures. Second, about the role of style as an element of resistance. Regarding the first, the debate has been transformed into a post-subcultural discussion. Individualistic behaviour, self-expression and fluid or hybrid identities became the standard in a new globalized world. Regarding this, the sociologist Paul Hodkinson writes: "[y]oung people each develop eclectic individual portfolios of tastes, interests and social networks which cut across genres and communities" (Hodkinson 2007: 9). Since post-subcultural style is expressed by means of individual lifestyle and consumption, it seems less combative. These new perspectives led to a schism in the debate about subcultures in the 1990s that declared the subcultural theories of the CCCS obsolete because of its inefficacy to identify the diverse and plural subcultures present at that moment (Muggleton and Weinzierl 2003: 6).

Although there seems to be a plurality in defining subcultural theory, the sociologist Sophie Woodward considers subcultures, even when more or less individualistic, still as going against the mainstream. She states that "[The] innovations of subcultures (which is now alleged to have given way to the creativity of individuals) is defined in opposition to the mainstream, which is seen as sterile and conformist, frequented by unimaginative fashion victims" (Woodward 2009: 87–88). Thus, the core essence of a subculture preserves its opposition to mainstream.

Regarding the discussion on style as an element of resistance, the communication scholar Barry Brummett examines the centrality of style as part of a vast global system of culture and communication. He argues that style is the major site on which claims of identity are made and contested today and therefore style is political (Brummett 2008: 87). In a world in which images get a central function, Brummett's study locates style within late capitalism. Brummett goes beyond reversing the importance between style and surface. Similarly to Sontag, he argues that the style–substance distinction has collapsed and proclaims that style is perhaps the major way in which cultures are now formed (Brummett 2008: xii, 11).

Brummett departs from Hebdige in claiming that style is always an instrument of rebellion and resistance, arguing that style can be an instrument of domination, an instrument of control by empowered interests. He gives the example of the use of architecture, pageantry and costume to control the masses in national socialist Germany (Brummett 2008: 82). Also today, style works as the core of political discourse. Brummett considers politics less and less the sending of primarily verbal messages to targeted audiences and more and more a matter of stylistic performance. He states that

> we say who we are, what roles or offices we are fit for, with whom we align, and with whom we do not. To understand why candidates get elected, why bills are passed, and how power is struggled over, we will increasingly need to examine style as political.
>
> (Brummett 2008: 111)

In line with Judith Butler's ideas on gender construction – in which she argues that gender is an imitation for which there is no original and sees the original as "an *effect* and consequence of the imitation itself" (Butler 1991: 21, emphasis in original) – Brummett observes a similar condition to understand style when proclaiming that "[w]e replicate incessantly the gestures, movements, and expressions that we find in texts of popular culture so as to manage impressions and facilitate communication using style" (Brummett 2008: 30).

In the surface/essence divide, style has therefore evolved from being the surface to becoming the essence, from being a means to becoming the goal. The conceptualization of style is complex and difficult to escape since it encompasses geography, history, groups and individuals.

Challenges: Timelessness, revival and aesthetic sustainability

One of those attempts to escape from stylistic categorization has been timeless design, which presumes the absence of style. Similarly to the ideas of Whitmann, there have been designers that consider their work as detached from any style. As mentioned above, the question is rather if the absence of style is even possible. If that were to be the case, timeless design would be consistently defined in a specific way. On the contrary, timeless design has been defined in different terms in different periods, basically through the ahistorical and the classic. Although timeless design is commonly understood as resistant to the effects of time, Mark Mussari posits that material culture cannot be divorced from temporal considerations; even modernist design is time-bound rather than timeless (Mussari 2016: 165). The strategies to escape from style are in themselves worth studying as they validate, rather than negate, the use of stylistic analysis.

Over time, various explications of timeless design have surfaced. Modernist timelessness was interpreted as the absence of ornamentation. Historical styles have served as markers of temporal divisions; their absence detached the objects from any period styles reducing their design to a presumed fundamental essence, making them thereby age-less (Guffey 2006: 151; Massey 2008: 82–83). Most notably, Adolf Loos (1870–1933) advocated for unornamented design to achieve an "evolution of culture." His interpretation came to dominate the understanding of many modernist thinkers, among which twentieth-century designers such as Le Corbusier. Besides advocating for the adoption of highly utilitarian and mass-produced furniture, Le Corbusier intended to demonstrate that timeless products all represent the same absolute, universal aesthetic. His aim was to produce objects outside the logics of fashion, allowing them to meet the needs of users over an extended period of time (de Rijk 2010: 110). The products emerging from this historical period were thus distinguishable by their unadorned appearance and simplistic shapes, which have since become synonymous with the aesthetic concept of timeless design.

But what about objects that are considered as timeless because they exist continuously over a prolonged temporal span? They might possess longevity, despite not being de-historicized or reduced to their fundamental core. This trend interprets timelessness as design that lasts not because of its lack of ornament but because of its endurance over an extended period of time, such as the "design classics" (Oddy 2016: 498). Paradoxically, temporal disengagement manifests itself in objects that are attached to historical styles. Timeless design results from integrating the past, present and future into one all-encompassing entity (Mussari 2016: 155–156; de Rijk 2010: 208–210; Gasparin and Neyland 2018.

Elizabeth Guffey touches upon retro design as a conception of timelessness where historicity is related to a somewhat altered or idealized representation of the past (Guffey 2006: 9). Retro objects possess certain resemblances with their predecessors, but they are not exact imitations. As argued by Guffey, retro design focuses on the near past with "unsentimental nostalgia" (Guffey 2006: 10). It involves a perspective that views the future by referencing the past, typically "denoting an undefined time gone by" (Guffey 2006: 9). As a result, retro designs appear unattached to a specific moment in time. On his part, Timo de Rijk gives the example of the American motorcycle manufacturer Harley Davidson, a pioneer of retro motorcycles. After 1982, the brand solely pursued the development of Harley motorcycles influenced by historical models, with little emphasis on technological advancements. The achievement of timelessness was attained through creating a historical narrative, whereby the physical characteristics of the classical model were merged with current levels of comfort and nostalgic advertisements (de Rijk 2010: 208–210).

Likewise, Marta Gasparin and Daniel Neyland (2018) examine how furniture manufacturer Fritz Hansen showcases their new products alongside the firm's iconic chairs (2018: 366). The iconic chairs represent the past. In the context of the Fritz Hansen company, however, they are displayed alongside recent models that incorporate thereby values of "enduring iconicism," aspiring to become iconic objects in the future (2018: 367). In this regard, the chairs become detached from a specific moment in time and connect to multiple temporalities instead (2018: 369). The new chairs "express time by pointing towards a past, present and future while simultaneously stepping outside these conventional frames to allude to an enduring and non-changing state – timelessness" (2018: 356).

Timeless design has not just been a mode of de-historicization in which the lack of ornamental features disassociates the object from its historical context. On the contrary, stressing the historical origins of an object also establishes timelessness. In the case of retro motorcycles like Harley Davidson, subtle perceptible alterations distinguish each model from its predecessors, positioning these products as both separate from and connected to their origins (Gasparin and Neyland 2018: 356). Timeless design folds the past, present and future into one singular unity.

These two definitions of timelessness, the ahistorical and the classic, denote different approaches towards timeless design, both acceptable but at first sight impossible to combine. But is that really the case? A third definition of timelessness regards the durability of a specific design. In this perspective, timeless design involves a sustainable approach that does not negate or embrace the past as in the examples above but looks towards the future, to improve product longevity (Flood Heaton and McDonagh 2017; Van Nes and Cramer 2006). Since sustainability is related to conditions of production but not to a specific aesthetic, a sustainable style has incorporated the two conceptions of timelessness mentioned above, the ahistorical and the nostalgic.

The potential for product lifetime expansion through timeless design is argued by Alex Lobos (2014). Influenced by the idea that specific design aesthetics pertain to a deeper and more impactful connection with consumers, he proposes timeless ahistorical aesthetics as resistant to fashions and therefore more durable (Lobos 2014: 170). The timeless aesthetic must be so minimalistic that it becomes difficult for the consumer to determine the novelty of the products at hand. Similarly, Rachel Flood Heaton and Deana McDonagh argue for a timeless aesthetic that goes towards the "essence of the object" using "abstraction in form," objects that exhibit a form of visual simplicity that accurately represents the archetype of the original product category (Flood Heaton and McDonagh 2017: 111, 118).

On the other hand, Theresa Wallner, Lise Magnier and Ruth Mugge search to extend the lifespan of consumer products by exploring the significance of timeless design styles in refurbished objects. These authors explore refurbished products, to evaluate the extent to which nostalgic design incorporates timelessness. They do not prioritize the development of aesthetic-based design strategies; instead, they direct their research towards the potential of re-use (Wallner et al. 2020: 12).

Sustainability allows both ideas on timeless design to coexist, even when being aesthetic opposites. The mediation of two recent interiors debunks the apparent impossibility of reconciling the ahistorical and the nostalgic. The first example is the Design Forever exhibition organized by the publication *Elle Decor* and curated by the designer duo Calvi Brambilla as part of the 2022 Milan Design Week (Studiolabo 2022). Design Forever was officially announced to the public as an exhibition affiliated with the concept of time-lessness. An article in *Elle Decor* described the exhibition as a celebration of the "long-lasting spirit of design" (Benedetto and Bergamasco 2022: 95). This exhibition displayed four marked set-ups for the rooms, that is, Mobile, Bold, Pure and Hybrid, described by the magazine as "all recalling the current lifestyle that blends sustainability with the responsible choices of long-lasting design" (Benedetto and Bergamasco 2022: 95). The room called "Pure," is described as only containing neutral, rectangular furnishings. The "pure" furniture, as characterized by the article, is distinguished by its minimalistic and geometric aesthetic (Benedetto and Bergamasco 2022: 98).

The other interior appeared in the *Architectural Digest* article under the title: "Inside Architect Charles Zana's Own 18th-Century Paris Apartment" (Hemonet 2023). The article presents an in-depth description of the domestic interior design of Charles Zana, an architect, focusing on his "Louis XVI apartment" in the Par-isian neighbourhood of Saint-Germain-des-Prés (Hemonet 2023). The high ceil-ings and ornately detailed mouldings within the space evidence historicism, as do the railing located in the hallway, the oak panelling featured within the bedroom and the classical fireplace. This interior was described nonetheless as a "timeless design masterpiece" by Studio Hommés in their blog (Hommés Studio 2023). Likewise, the publication *Architectural Digest* described it as displaying a "timeless atmosphere" that seamlessly integrates past and present elements (Hemonet 2023).

These examples show how malleable the definition of timeless design is. Far from situating itself outside stylistic conventions, it engages with contextual facts of a period. The interest in sustainability has blended the two seemingly opposite defi-nitions of timeless design into one, demonstrating again the relevance of style to reveal how aesthetics conveys convictions in sophisticated and multivocal ways.

15 The typological approach
Categories and belonging

Typologies are a product of the social construction of reality. A typological approach demonstrates that objects answer to specific shared patterns. On the other hand, objects differ from others within the same type. Thereby, a typological approach is rather a tool to categorize than to analyse. The challenge is making this categorization culturally relevant. The use of the typological approach in archaeology and architectural history has contributed to reconstruct anonymous history. The categorization processes that define typologies are multifarious. They can be generated bottom-up, through the generation of needs, top-down, through the insertion of new designs in the market or a combination of both. Nevertheless, as design dematerializes, it is increasingly difficult to define strict typological boundaries.

Origins: Taxonomies

When organizing artefacts, we tend to instinctively sort them into various types. Consider a personal closet as an example; we naturally group items based on their common features, such as putting T-shirts with T-shirts, trousers with trousers, and organizing undergarments and socks separately. Typology serves to bring structure to complexity by classifying specific artefacts into predefined categories. However, the process of defining these types is not always straightforward.

The typological approach involves examining types, which are a collection of phenomena characterized by one or more shared traits. According to John A. Walker, the concept of a "type" aligns with the definition provided by sociologist Edward Tiryakian (b. 1929). Tiryakian suggests that a "type," as indicated by its etymology derived from the Greek word "typos" – meaning an impression, a cast or a model – possesses recurring, overarching distinctive features that are not specific to the individual in isolation (Tiryakian quoted in Walker 1989: 111). The typological approach revolves around the specific connection between types, such as *the* washing machine, and tokens or individual artefacts, like *a* particular washing machine (Walker 1989: 112).

DOI: 10.4324/9781003147282-18

The difference is that types are conceptual categories and tokens are artefacts. How do tokens become part of types? Do types generate tokens or is it the other way around? The linguist William Labov (b. 1927) conducted a study involving vessel profiles characterized by measured variances, such as a gradual increase in width relative to height (Labov 1972). Using graphical representations, Labov illustrated the transition from a cup to a bowl. Then, he asked individuals to draw a line between the two types. As a cup widens, its resemblance to a bowl intensifies until a distinct shift occurs. Labov demonstrates that this shift can be influenced by various factors, such as the presence of handles or if the vessel contained mashed potatoes. Labov observes that "in the world of experience, all boundaries exhibit some degree of vagueness" (1972: 342). This inherent vagueness in categories is encountered whenever we apply our concepts to investigating social phenomena.

Archaeologists have dealt with the categorization of artefacts without other evidence than the artefacts themselves. The archaeologist Kwang-chih Chang (1931–2001) argues that for establishing a culturally meaningful classification, there is a tension between establishing a taxonomy from outside the cultural system studied or doing it from within. He holds an ambivalent position about which is preferable. Chang prioritizes the structural types, formulated from within, over the comparative types, formulated cross-culturally, because they represent the categorization of the society under study. But the opposite is also true; types in archaeology can be considered structurally meaningful provided they work comparatively in terms of a general theory of classification. Archaeologists often only have their own terms to arrive at a culturally meaningful typological classification. The structural classification is often unknown. Historians might have written sources at their disposal and ethnographers might have respondents, but archaeologists only relate to physically observable differences (Chang 1967: 72, 77).

A type is delineated primarily by its discontinuity from other types, according to Chang. The method for defining a type is to locate the area of discontinuity that separates members of opposing types. Two objects under typological study are assigned to two different types as much because they are less similar to each other than because they are more similar to something else. Based on this delineation, we have at least two sets of data: (1) their intrinsic properties and (2) their interrelationship and their relations with other objects (Chang 1967: 80). There is no strong conviction on how general or how specific a type must be. Within the realm of design, we can contemplate diverse types, spanning from items like "posters" to garments like "skirts." We distinguish them because they resemble other posters or skirts and because they are different from other types such as websites or trousers. Types do not need to be such general categories but can be further refined, such as "silkscreen posters" or "red skirts."

Archaeologists employ the comparative method to categorize diverse types like spears, pots or jewellery, diverging from linguists who use it to identify common origins of words (Chang 1967: 78). Chang suggests a four-step process: initially categorizing data into provisional groups based on attributes, then organizing these categories into meaningful units within the assemblage through statistical methods. Next, expanding the analysis across multiple assemblages to compare patterns of attribute occurrence. Finally, constructing historically meaningful types, organizing them into hierarchical models within settlements (Chang 1967: 84). Archaeologists focus on the characteristics of artefacts in their analysis and linguists on the components of the words. They both scrutinize their objects of analysis. The difference is that the observable attributes of artefacts are superimposed on each other. The components of words follow each other sequentially.

The shift from provisional categories to significant units is bound to a disciplinary background. Types that might be culturally relevant for archaeologists might not be so for other disciplines. Within architectural history, for example, the criteria to define types in architecture are either based on use/function – such as churches, city halls or schools – and types based on morphology/form – such as hall-shaped floor plans, buildings with courtyards or buildings covered with cupolas (Forty 2013[2000]: 304).

The architect Jacques-François Blondel (1705–1774) is often credited with originating the system of functional types with his list of building "genres" that he included in his book *Cours d'Architecture* first published in 1750. There have been unexpected associations to discuss functional types within history. Functional types cannot only be connected to styles but also intimately to specific historical periods. Thereby, they encapsulate the symbolic connotations of the period and convey them across the centuries. Accordingly, Koos Bosma, Aart Mekking, Koen Ottenheym and Auke Van der Woud (2007) state that specific functional building types can characterize whole historical periods. Churches and castles capture medieval architecture. The palace took centre stage from the sixteenth century until the beginning of the nineteenth century, and from the nineteenth century onward, the residential house increasingly came to the forefront. During that specific period, these types conditioned the design of other buildings, originating migrations of shapes and uses. For example, palace ballrooms served as inspiration for churches in the seventeenth century (Bosma et al. 2007: 9).

On his part, Jean-Nicholas-Louis Durand (1760–1834) formulated the morphological typology by establishing a technique of designing based on formal compositions that could later be altered to a specific function (Forty 2013[2000]: 305). Morphological typologies find frequent application in architecture as they unveil comparable yet unique technical approaches to common challenges. For instance, a typology like "buildings with a central floor plan" facilitates a comparison between Istanbul's Hagia Sophia and the Cathedral of Brasilia, despite their geographical and temporal differences. Both structures, though distant and distinct in time, share the common architectural challenge of covering a spacious central area and introducing light from the centre – a contrast to buildings with a basilica floor plan where light enters from the sides.

Within design, functional types – such as shoes, posters or chairs – are common. Morphological categories might be less common because the types that design encompasses tend to be more diverse than in architecture. Consider the creation of a morphological typology centred on "designs with a spherical form." This typology could include items like a football, disco ball, spherical hat, TV set or a lip gloss container. Their construction might be very different as are their materials and uses. In terms of manufacture techniques, this typology might not be culturally relevant. However, there might be other symbolic aspects associated with spherical forms in which all these artefacts participate. In that case, this typology would be culturally relevant.

Morphological types in design might result in display criteria for museums, even when they might seem unconventional at first sight. For example, the Berlin Werkbund Archive – Museum of Things (*Werkbundarchiv – Museum der Dinge*) groups exhibits combining highly contrasting colours such as yellow and black, which allows for comparisons between electric appliances, all-purpose adhesive, 1950s ceramics and graphics for electrical hazard warning signs. Thereby, this type reveals how the same colour combination can convey different messages such as technological excellence, a specific sense of domesticity, danger and efficiency.

The question remains whether tokens can modify types. The psychologist Jean Piaget (1896–1980) formulated his genetic epistemology by adopting an interactionist view of humans, who are seen to develop categorization processes through their active searching out and construction of their world. He distinguishes between two processes: assimilation and accommodation. Assimilation is the inward-directed tendency of a structure to draw environmental events towards itself, while accommodation is an organism's outward tendency of the inner structure to adapt itself to a particular environmental event (Piaget 1972: 22–26, 59). When adapted to design typologies, this implies that individual physical tokens may vary while still adhering to the fundamental description of their type. For example, a particular silkscreen poster can either conform to or challenge the broader category it belongs to. The use of the silkscreen technique may involve printing posters with uniform colour zones until an example emerges featuring silkscreens with colour gradients. This not only introduces new possibilities for subsequent silkscreen posters but also alters the essence of this type permanently.

Development: On anonymous history

If Walker located the origins of the typological approach in architecture, Gregory Votolato opts for art history. Genre painting, for example, allows the study of art through similar vertical categories as building typologies. He argues that a typological approach allows for a comparison of everyday, iconic design artefacts among them and that similarly blurs the relevance of the designer (Votolato 1998: 251–255, 264).

Despite their differences in where to locate the origin of the typological approach, either in architectural history or in art history, both Walker and Votolato reference the art historian Sigfried Giedion (1888–1968), whose book *Mechanization Takes Command: A Contribution to Anonymous History* (1948) became a pivotal example of an anonymous history of design. Giedion traces the various ways in which, for better and for worse, mechanization assumed control over everyday life from the late-nineteenth century – a time of full mechanization – up through the first half of the twentieth century (see Molella 2002 374–389). Giedion covers subjects ranging from hygiene systems and waste management to agricultural production, furniture and household mechanization. They are illustrated with images from sales catalogues, industrial manuals and magazines.

Giedion was a student of the art historian Heinrich Wölfflin and was influenced by his analysis of the formal elements in art and how they evolve over time (Hatt and Klonk 2017 [2006]: 65–67). Giedion's use of types is very broad, since he does not only look at specific types of artefacts, but also includes general categories such as "bathing." For Giedion, the type is defined by the social behaviour of its users, and it is the task of the historian to study the relationship between the two. Giedion examines the bath as both an object and a custom, considering both the bathtub and the Roman bath buildings equally, despite their differences. He goes beyond singular definitions of types and expands into a broader area of study (Walker 1989: 115–116).

The reason behind Giedion's book was the lack of specialized research into the anonymous history of commonplace objects, the mass-produced artefacts of contemporary life. He was unable to find any account "of such revolutionary events as the development of the production line or the introduction of mechanical comfort and its tools in the intimate environment" (Molella 2002: 43). In response to this gap, Giedion argues in his book that the study of anonymous history is crucial due to its significant impact on culture, surpassing the influence of publicly recognized pieces shaped by prevailing tastes. Thus, Giedion aims to convey to readers the importance of understanding how their work and inventions continuously influence and reshape life patterns. He emphasizes that an era lacking awareness of these influential elements will struggle to comprehend its position or, even more so, its objectives (Giedion 1948: 2).

Giedion's exploration of interiors from the nineteenth century serves as a prime illustration of his account of how artefacts shape and are shaped by societal patterns. Giedion meticulously traces the impact of upholsterers on the living spaces of an expanding bourgeoisie. By dissecting what he sees as the "theatrical and bulky" interiors crafted by upholsterers, Giedion elucidates how this unattributed historical narrative can be interpreted as a response to the harsh industrialism prevalent during that era (1948: 364–388).

During the nineteenth century, Giedion notes, upholsterers resembled decorators, recognized for employing cross drapery at windows and wall hangings. Over time, upholsterers expanded their influence to encompass furniture design. Under their guidance, chairs and sofas transformed into substantial pieces of upholstery. Giedion contends that their focus was on a theatrical form of embellishment, not on original creation. This involves arranging upholstered furniture, draped hangings and decorative articles to achieve a coherent effect. According to Giedion, the upholsterer constructed a fantastical realm to enchant the dreariness of the industrial age (1948: 364).

The upholsterers were effective in producing interiors that presented a stark contrast to the reality outside. Giedion suggests that the sterile industrialization of the period prompted the need for these dramatic interiors. He asserts that individuals were "unwilling to confine themselves within their own existence, leading inevitably to the grotesque" (1948: 370). According to Giedion, this sentiment also fuelled a penchant for all things Oriental. Mechanization sought an ambience distinct from its immediate milieu. The East became an idealized realm associated with leisure, contrasting the strained existence of the Western world (1948: 370).

By establishing connections between diverse objects and subjects, Giedion broadens both the scope of his investigation and the perspective of design historians. It is worth noting, however, that these linkages, which connect specific objects to overarching generalizations, come with inherent risks. Votolato expresses reservations about the bridges that Giedion constructs within his typologies, characterizing them as a somewhat rudimentary model for his approach. The distinctions between types developed a fresh view towards design history but its overgeneralizations could pose challenges in discerning the connections among the tokens within these types and among them and their societal explanations (Votolato 1998: 264). Additionally, Walker criticizes Giedion's observations, deeming them outdated and applicable to only a specific society within a defined timeframe. Giedion generalizes his findings without confining their relevance to particular societies (Walker 1989: 116). Despite the revolutionary nature of Giedion's use of typology, it became evident that further refinement was necessary.

Even when Giedion's theory was inspired by Wölfflin in its anonymous approach to history, he goes beyond the pattern-seeking approach of his master. Wölfflin's formalism searched for patterns without assigning a causality other than changes in perception. His goal was to develop a formal vocabulary for art historians (Schneider Adams 1996: 24). On the contrary, Giedion's approach seeks to explain these formalist patterns beyond perception, incorporating the social and cultural context. Thereby, Giedion's explanations connected rather with Jacob Burckhardt's cultural history, opposed to but still reminiscent of Hegelianism. Wölfflin's master, Burckhardt wondered how the spirit of the fifteenth century expressed itself in painting. Similarly, Giedion wondered: "How does the nineteenth century like to sit?" (Giedion 1948: 400). He acknowledges the emergence of a new way of sitting, slightly reclined, that explains the proliferation of patents for reclining chairs (Gombrich 1969: 16, 28; Fernie 1995: 14). The Hegelian reminiscences in Giedion's work are reflected in how he establishes connections between the different aspects defining a specific society, demonstrating a unitary principle, and how they are visibly reflected in their artistic production (Preziosi 2009[1998]: 116).

Giedion used the typological approach in his teaching as well. His students were asked to pick a type and study its origin and development in style and form (Vyas 2006: 31). Types conceal an internal complexity, since they implicitly propose a vision of the world, establishing links with geography and chronology. Geographically, the diversity and uniformity inherent to typologies connect globalization with regional peculiarities. Types, connected to specific regions because of their use of local materials and vernacular techniques, can become altered by foreign influences and then originate identity-related debates. Chronologically, types endure but advances can make those typologies appear, disappear and reappear in a relatively short period of time. The typological approach is mostly useful for categorizing objects but insufficient to generate a strong argumentative line that explains stylistic changes. Other methods need to be involved that connect with the logic behind the defined types.

Implementation: From failure to new materialism

The typological approach invites the researcher to reflect on the reasons behind the proliferation of artefacts. Explanatory ideas have shifted according to different authors. Giedion used basically two explanations. The first has been called "functionalist" and argues that the diversity of artefacts responds to a diversity of needs. Once a need is created, artefacts come to fulfil it (Giedion 1948: 400). The second is his "ingenious designer" theory in which the creativity of designers would propel the diversification of a typology. Designers come with new shapes, which enter the market and are consumed by the general public (Giedion 1948: 419). In both cases, Giedion explains diversification through the success of specific types in the market. This success might depend either on the artefact itself in the "functionalist" explanation or on the designer in the "ingenious designer" one.

A different perspective is taken by civil engineer Henry Petroski. He considers that the proliferation of types and tokens is not so much due to their success but to their failure, which prompts to look for alternatives. His book *The Evolution of Useful Things* (1992) poses this question to an array of objects such as forks, paper clips and the telephone (1992: 9). Petroski investigates the evolutionary patterns of what he describes as low-tech artefacts, to provide an understanding of the more complex engineering of ordinary things, such as telephones and aeroplanes (Figure 15.1). He explores the implications of failures – whether physical, functional, cultural or psychological – for the shape of objects. Thereby, he refutes the "form follows function" functionalist principle and sees inventions conversely as the identification and correction of defects in existing devices. As inventions typically address perceived shortcomings in older devices, innovations often retain numerous features from their predecessors. However, they may not

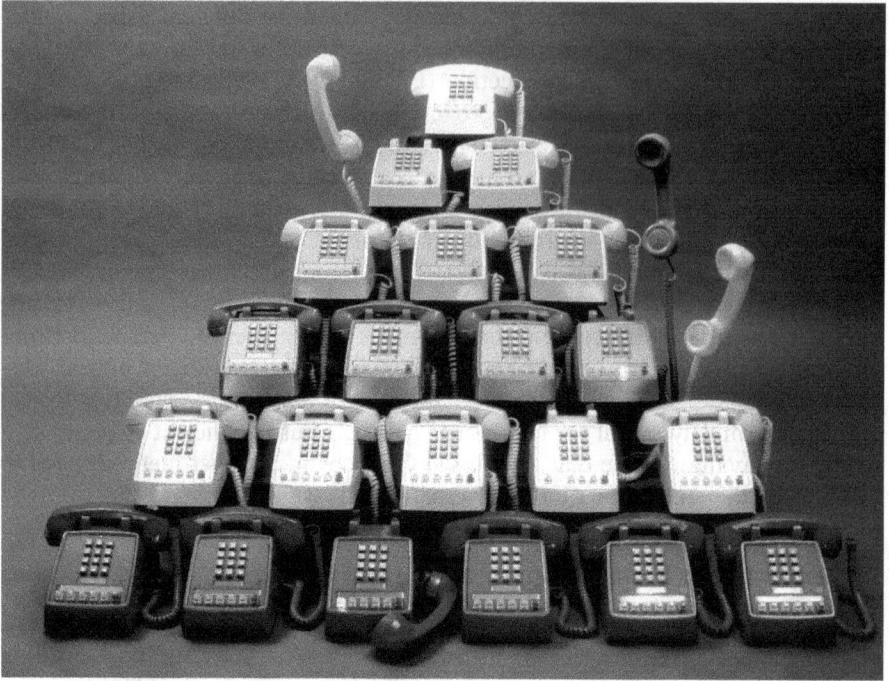

Figure 15.1 Petroski reflected in his book on his ambivalent feelings about evolving technology. When the first push-button telephones appeared, he missed the rotary dial ones. But when he got used to the new system, he found the old one annoying (1992: 239). In the picture, a commercial photo of a pyramid of push-button phones in the 1970s. Photo by David Attie/Getty Images

perform as effectively as the devices they aim to replace, as their success often relies heavily on how well they align with prevailing practices and the understanding of potential users.

Petroski states that "it is really *want* rather than need that drives the process of technological evolution [...] Luxury, rather than necessity, is the mother of invention" (1992: 22, emphasis in the original). He argues that humans need food but not per se a fork to eat it. The tradition of using such an instrument in Western societies prevents users from looking for alternatives. The typological approach gives Petroski a structure to follow and build his narrative following a pattern of substitution by failure. A history of failure is uncommon when writing design history and Petroski must be acknowledged for it.

Failure stories can be as revealing as success stories, but these are not mutually exclusive and can guide different stages of the same product. These narratives are of increasing importance in the case of digital technologies, in which new products rapidly substitute old ones. A good reflection on this dynamic is Paul Atkinson's "A Bitter Pill to Swallow: The Rise and Fall of the Tablet Computer" (2008), an article narrating the presumed design failure of tablet computers that took place in the 1980s and 1990s. Atkinson shows shifting outcomes for tablet computers that, when he wrote the article in 2008, were considered a failure. Ironically, this happened just before the iPad was massively launched by Apple in 2010 to partly substitute portable computers.

Unlike Petroski, Atkinson focuses only on one product, the tablet computers and their history. He opens his essay with a look at the production of tablets where large corporations wanted to be first in line to produce the next big item in the technological world (2008: 3). The tablet computer had every marking to be the newest hit product through the digitizing of pen and paper. Atkinson does introduce a range of theories, including the social construction of technology and actor–network theory, that define the success or failure of a technological object as embedded in techno-social imaginaries (Atkinson 2008: 6).

Atkinson discusses factors related to production and mediation. Despite tablet computers receiving substantial funding and numerous companies vying to be the first to introduce them to the market, there was minimal demand for the product. Additionally, the technology utilized in manufacturing the tablets was inadequate for mass appeal, leading to glitches and ineffective handwriting recognition in many devices (Atkinson 2008: 21). Atkinson draws correlations between the object and its social construction, suggesting that various social factors contributed to the tablet computer's decline, such as its failure to replicate the pen-and-paper experience and the public's preference for keyboards. This research illustrates how intricate concepts about societal functioning reveal the complex mechanisms influencing the creation and dissemination of design. These theoretical frameworks propose alternatives to the relationship between technology and society, moving beyond Giedion's "functionalist" theory and his concept of the "ingenious designer."

Types can undergo not only diversification through the introduction of new product ranges but also homogenization through the disappearance of variety. Irene Maldini's investigation of the portable water heater SUN (which stands for Spanish *Soy Una Novedad*, meaning "I am a Novelty") reflects the disappearance of this type (Maldini 2014). Used in Uruguay to prepare mate tea, it consisted of 40 centimetres of standard electrical wire and a moulded plastic plug connected to a simple metallic resistance; a ceramic cylinder that holds the resistance and dissipates its temperature and a moulded plastic cover that is expected to add an element of safety (2014: 115). It was commercialized from 1983 by the manufacturer Beta until 2010, when it was prohibited because it did not cover the minimum safety requirements for its user, due to its lack of proper electrical isolation (2014: 119). Maldini uses the concept of the anthropologist Robert Wilk, who states that globalization promotes difference instead of suppressing it, albeit a difference of a particular kind. He argues that global structures organize diversity, rather than replicating uniformity (2014: 113). Mate is consumed in different locations and the SUN answered the need for heating water on the road and directly inside the thermal bottle (2014: 115). Redesigning the portable heater to comply with these new regulations would result in it becoming as expensive as a teakettle, against which this product could not compete (2014: 118). Globalization might increase the production of teakettles since they align with global prerogatives, but the water heater type considerably reduced its portability with the disappearance of this sub-type.

Apart from narratives detailing the life cycle of types, the typological approach is often used to amalgamate horizontal and vertical analyses, encompassing both synchronic and diachronic perspectives. Thereby, the typological approach enables the integration of diverse methods within a single research framework and facilitates interdisciplinary investigations centred on the study of a particular type. For instance, Anne Massey's book *Chair* (2011) employs the typological approach as a framework for various lines of inquiry, ranging from the evolution of the designer chair within design history to dedicated chapters exploring the representation of chairs in photography, advertising and the visual arts – thus bridging design, art and media history. The categorization principle of typology serves as a unifying element in this context, allowing the connection of interdisciplinary narratives surrounding the construction of our understanding of a specific typology.

Similarly, Jane Tynan's *Trench Coat* (2022) explores this garment in its materiality and its symbolic value both through the history of this garment and its representation chiefly in cinema. The difference with Massey's research is that Tynan connects this combination of approaches as serving a new materialist approach (2022: 9). She argues that this garment needs to be seen in its materiality and therefore participating in the material resources of the planet, developing its own system of provision, manufacture, colonialism and exploitation since the eighteenth century (2022: 13–14). At the same time, this type has been constructed symbolically representing issues related to danger, power and hostility. It encapsulates connotations typical of stereotypical characters like the soldier, explorer, reporter and settler (2022: 139).

As Massey and Tynan demonstrate, the typological approach is rarely employed in isolation; instead, it is frequently utilized in conjunction with other methodologies. It serves as a means to classify and study artefacts, enabling subsequent analyses through methods like the life cycle of objects and facilitating the development of cultural and social stories, emphasizing the artefact itself.

Challenges: Types in an age of digitalization

Precisely because typology deals with classifying design into existing types, this approach deals well with the well-established and less so with the fluid. Yet, unclassifiable designs have a long story. Giedion mentions "patent furniture" as an example, what he describes as "[a]n armchair that changes into a couch, a couch that changes into a cradle, can justly be termed combination furniture, as can a bed that turns into a sofa, into a chair, into a table, into a railway seat" (1948: 423). A specific design can be difficult to classify even when its functions are not.

Examples of unclassifiable designs are multiple and well represented in Karl Elsener's Swiss army knife from 1891, a multi-tool pocketknife that includes a main spearpoint blade plus other blades and tools such as screwdrivers, a can opener, a saw blade and a pair of scissors. Then, is this object a knife? Scissors? Or a can opener? Other examples are Masami Takahashi's ramen spoon/fork designed in 2007 which originates from the fusion of a spoon and a fork, both necessary to eat ramen; walking canes combined with a folding chair or the recurrent combination of a CD player, radio and wake up alarm. In all the examples, complementary typologies coalesce to create hybrids that challenge typological classification.

Along these lines, digitalization poses new challenges to a traditional typological approach. For example, disparate types – such as agenda, camera, calendar, telephone, map, and so on – become one and the same inside the smartphone, that is, the app (Figure 15.2). Can we, therefore, talk of inter-medial types?

Mobile applications used on mobile phones incorporate design, media and technical aspects. In addition, mobile apps also offer a wide range of functions for their users, from gaming to social media. The media theorists Carlos Alberto Scolari, Juan Miguel Aguado and Claudio Feijóo attempt to define and neatly sort all things related to mobile devices and applications. These authors begin by acknowledging the fragmented approaches to studying mobile media and see their article as a stepping stone to a restructuring of theory related to the subject (Scolari et al. 2012: 29). Covering the progression

Figure 15.2 A smartphone unlocked on the application screen. Photo by Edward Berthelot/Getty Images

from the Web to mobile media, the article starts by showing notable advancements in technology such as the release of the iPhone and iPad. Nevertheless, after exploring various aspects of mobile devices and apps, Scolari, Aguado and Feijóo determine that the field is dynamic, requiring regular reassessment of any theoretical approach. Consequently, developing concepts, categories and taxonomies is challenging due to the constant introduction of new devices, applications and products in the mobile market, each of which has the potential to disrupt the mobile ecosystem (Scolari et al. 2012: 36). Such an "effervescent" subject as mobile devices and apps is challenging for historians. The changing market, technology and user-generated content are just some of the elements making a taxonomy or typology difficult to define.

The most relevant field outside of design in relation to the study of mobile applications is media studies. As a digital object, the mobile application is a hybrid of design and media, therefore neither study would be complete without the other in reference to a mobile app. Despite their differences, the scholarship on design and media, specifically in the case of typologies, has a common predecessor in the essay *The Work of Art in the Age of Mechanical Reproduction* from 1935 by the philosopher Walter Benjamin (1892–1940). Walker claims that Giedion's inspiration comes from Benjamin to the extent to which Giedion is interested in artefacts that affect everyday life. In media studies, the theorists Jay Bolter and Richard Grusin discuss Benjamin's essay explicitly in their book *Remediation: Understanding New Media* (1999) and push his theory further into the digital world. More specifically, they use Benjamin's work to explain digital auras as well as a transition into the power that technology holds over its users. A digital aura, as explained by Bolter and Grusin, is the translation of an aura from an artwork or other media into a digital interface, in other words, they locate the inspiration for the design of digital products such as mobile applications in the non-digital world (1999: 55).

Applications now function as notepads, cameras and calendars, all items that used to only exist in the material world. Often these remediated objects still hold their original aesthetic forms in the digital interfaces that they occupy today. However, even when artefacts retain the aura of their predecessors, this remediation adapts to a new medium adopting its characteristics. Therefore, as objects are becoming digital, their place in an established typology becomes more difficult to determine. The typical calendar app not only functions as a calendar but also as a notebook, a checklist and even a personal assistant giving reminders to the user about appointments they have scheduled. Evidence of the difficult categorization of apps is that, for example, in the Apple App Store calendars are categorized under "Productivity," a category that is vague and vast. Accordingly, a focus has been put on the search option rather than the list of categories to find apps. It is much simpler and more accessible to search for a particular app rather than sort through categories. This move away from sorting apps by type and searching tools using keywords reflects the difficulty associated with creating a typology of apps.

Even when looking at a single app, the task of creating a defined and clear study of mobile applications becomes no easier. A specific app can be studied in comparison to other similar apps – take, for example, those belonging to the category "social media" – but this comparison will be cut short when it becomes clear that they are very different. For example, the Being app allows the user to see the Instagram feed of another user. If someone follows someone else through Instagram, the Being app allows the follower to see what this someone else gets on their Instagram app. Its integration into Instagram changes the user's perspective through access to another user's feed, and the user's inability to create content makes the Being app unique and difficult to accurately categorize. Many other apps have multiple functions and serve many roles for the user. The typological approach, while excellent for the organization of objects, does not leave space for observation of many unique and changing objects such as mobile applications.

Mobile apps in general resist their exploration under the typological approach. The approach calls for comparisons between objects of the same type, however in the case of mobile applications many characteristics are not compatible across different platforms. In addition, design styles and elements vastly change from updates to applications that change apps even after the user has downloaded them. Users also play a role in the complication of the study of mobile apps. Due to the user's large amount of control over settings, they can effectively change the design of the app. This is prevalent in social media apps where the user not only changes their settings but also creates content and curates what content they view in the application. The design of applications is also made complex because of the many "layers" that can be utilized in the design, not only a flat-plane approach to graphic design (Scolari et al. 2012: 36).

Since the publication of *Remediation*, Jay Bolter has continued his study of media and recently focused on augmented reality design. In an essay co-authored with Maria Engberg and Blair MacIntyre (2013) the authors wonder if it is possible to reframe media studies to make it a productive theory, a theory that can be applied to practice, to designing artefacts. They further incorporate an examination of design aesthetics, encompassing emotional responses to design, such as empathy and enchantment. Regarding media aesthetics, the authors advocate for a focus on how the world can be perceived through new technologies (2013: 38).

Noteworthy conclusions arise from references to the philosopher Marshall McLuhan (1911–1980) and his depiction of a once linear and analytical world transformed by the introduction of media, giving rise to an "electronic man." Bolter, Engberg and MacIntyre term this evolving phenomenon, now encompassing more media than in McLuhan's era, as digital media aesthetics. It contends that McLuhan's approach was too singular, asserting that technology not only serves as an extension of humanity but also operates within a feedback loop where users play a vital role. This essay posits that our worldview influences our designs, and our utilization of new artefacts and designs, and in turn, alters our perception of the world (2013: 38).

How then would archaeologists define these fluid types? If humans classify objects into types and new artefacts alter our perception of the world, then who classifies who? As Claude Lévi-Strauss famously points out, natural species are not chosen because they are "good to eat" but because they are "good to think." Similarly, material objects extend beyond serving practical purposes; their symbolic function lies in enabling humans to construct and attribute meanings within their cultural context (Woodward 2007: 67). In this context, designers bear a significant responsibility in creating not just objects but also shaping perception. According to Clive Dilnot, humans are capable of transforming their surroundings in alignment with desired structures of organization and significance. This arrangement of materials and aspects of societal existence aligns fundamentally with the essence of the design process. Professional design channels this capacity, developing special skills and abilities (Dilnot 1984: 19).

The concept of type is elastic but how much elasticity does it allow in fields such as apps? How relevant is the study of a type whose tokens are so diverse? Does our classification of types reflect who we are? Moreover, is it relevant to use the typological approach in times when types rise, fall and rise again? Probably the answer is yes, but the redefinition of types passes through the acknowledgement of their diversity more than their cohesion.

16 Materials and techniques

Transforming nature

Materials and techniques form the basis of the relationship of the designer with the world and its transformation. This approach has been used extensively in museology, art history and art theory. If originally linked to the pedagogy of designers and craftspeople, it has been also used for questioning established hierarchies within art. Particularly, the debate on textile art has been at the core of the distinction between art and crafts. More recently, other scientific approaches have discussed the implications of materials in the framework of the environmental humanities and new materialism. Within design scholarship, discussions on materials and techniques have equally participated in the categorization between craft and design. Moreover, they have produced studies on the global traffic of materials and their impact on the environment. With the expansion of biodesign, scholars might need to re-evaluate traditional approaches towards the relationship between designers and their way of transforming the world.

Origins: Subversive crafts

Understanding design in terms of materials and techniques requires contemplating the human connection to the material world and the processes through which it undergoes transformation. Consequently, the scope of design becomes extensive, as does its potential for causing harm (Mareis et al. 2022: 11). From this perspective, designers bear a responsibility towards the environment. In alignment with this notion, Kjetil Fallan assigns design a complex role within the environmental crisis. On one hand, design contributes to the predicament by considering the detrimental impacts of discarded materials. On the other hand, it can also play a role in addressing the issue by recognizing its potential for shaping the world (Fallan 2019b: 1). This chapter discusses the multifarious integration of materials and techniques within the realm of design scholarship. The cultural significance of these elements spans a wide spectrum, encompassing discussions on craftsmanship, the delineation between art and design, sustainability dialogues and the interconnectedness of humans and nature.

DOI: 10.4324/9781003147282-19

Approaching artefacts according to their material or manufacturing techniques can be traced further back in history. What we consider nowadays as a distinction between art and craft, might not have been so clear. For example, the study of art was put under mineralogy and the application of materials in Pliny's *Natural History* (ca. 77 CE). Pliny himself defines his scope as the natural world, or life (Bod 2013: 8, 44). Similarly, encyclopaedic handbooks appeared in the eleventh century, such as the *Samarangana Sutradhara* [Architect of Human Dwellings] by king Bhoja (ca. 1010–1055 CE), and in the twelfth century the *Manasollasa* [The Joy, Delighter or Entertainer of the Mind] by king Someshvara III (r. 1127–1138 CE). Visual art is only one of the forms of art that were discussed in these works, in which the close ties to all types of art were emphasized, from architecture, literature, music and drama to rhetorical art and poetry. These manuals gave a detailed description of painting practice and techniques, from paintings on walls and wood to canvas (Bod 2013: 122).

Many of these handbooks are not necessarily historical in nature, they simply served as explanations for artists, helping them in their practice. For example, the book *On Various Arts* by Theophilus Presbyter (ca. 1070–1125), written in the early twelfth century, describes the production of painting and drawing materials, stained-glass window techniques and the working of precious metals. It also makes one of the earliest references to oil paint and even includes an introduction to organ building (Bod 2013: 118). Another example is the *Treatise on Ceramics* by Abu'l Qasim, a technical handbook on the manufacture of tiles and other ceramic objects dated 1301 (Bod 2013: 123). In the sixteenth century, Giorgio Vasari's *Lives of the Most Excellent Painters, Sculptors, and Architects* included, a discussion of techniques from architecture, sculpture and painting. Vasari discusses, for instance, types of stones, techniques of sculpting in marble and wood, methods of drawing, fresco painting, oil painting and tempera painting (Vasari 1991[1568]: xvi).

The materials and techniques approach was implemented primarily in European museums dedicated to applied and decorative arts, that replaced the traditional workshop-based educational model associated with guilds. Initially established for educational purposes, museums dedicated to applied arts were frequently integrated into larger educational institutions. These museums aimed to enhance the quality and production of applied arts to improve the international economic standing of the country. To realize this objective, there was a recognized need to educate practitioners about the advancements and available knowledge related to materials and techniques, as well as matters of taste and design (Tibbe 2013: 252).

The display of objects in museums of applied arts adopted the scientific classification system developed by taxonomist Carl Linnaeus (1707–1778). Exhibits were structured along 30 classes ranked according to the amount of treatment the materials received, starting with raw materials (class 1–4), followed by machines and instruments for processing these materials (class 5–10), then moving to the treated materials, such as fabrics, leather, paper, metals, glass, ceramics and furniture (class 11–25), to finally arrive at the last stage with decorative and fine art objects (class 26–30). The *Conservatoire national des arts et métiers* [National Conservatory of Arts and Crafts], founded in 1794 in France, stands as one of the earliest examples of such an educational institution. This establishment combined a school with a public depot that housed machinery, tools, models, drawings and instructional manuals, providing explanations and classifications of fabrication methods based on materials (Tibbe 2013: 255–256).

This system was adopted by world exhibitions from the mid-nineteenth century onwards and gradually abandoned by the museums of decorative arts. From the 1870s onwards, a new organizational system started to take over in which the emphasis shifted from materials and techniques to aesthetic qualities based on chronology (Tibbe 2013: 262). This shift was prompted partly because of increasing industrialization. Schooled craftsmen were less needed in a mechanizing society, which diminished the educational role of the museum towards the applied artists and manufacturers. The museum shifted its role towards the education of the general public on taste (Tibbe 2013: 169, 266–267).

Concurrently with this process, there was the emergence of new art theories, such as the one put forth by the art historian Alois Riegl, which separated the realm of forms from that of materials (Tibbe 2013: 270). In his book *Problems of Style* of 1893, Riegl introduced the concept of *kunstwollen*, challenging to translate precisely, though "will to art" is one possible interpretation. Initially defined as the human drive to establish an artistic order in the world, Riegl believed that the formal development of art occurred autonomously, independent of material and technical constraints (Hatt and Klonk 2017[2006]: 82–83). Subsequently, art theory began to prioritize the autonomous over the functional, culminating in the twentieth century with the work of the art critic Clement Greenberg (1909–1994). Greenberg associated the "decorative" with amateurism, domesticity and forms of art considered of lower regard. This perspective emerged despite Riegl's original ideas. In his book *Altorientalische Teppiche* [Antique Oriental Carpets] of 1891, Riegl had praised textiles, asserting that their materiality and visuality, along with their circulation, promoted various art forms. Therefore, textiles formed the foundation of arts and culture, where "style" and the social were intricately intertwined (Frank and Buchmann 2015: 13).

Theories of autonomous art were questioned particularly from the field of textile art in the post-war period, discussing the hierarchical division between different media typical of modernist art theories. Greenberg had emphasized "flatness" as medium-specific and beneficial to painting and constituted abstract expressionism as the culmination of modern art. Modern painting as male-coded, on the one hand, and textiles as a female-specific practice, on the other, have institutionalized gendered specifications and divisions of labour (Frank and Buchmann 2015: 12–13). Hierarchies such as these between "high" and "low" creative labour have perpetuated hierarchical classifications of practice and materials (Corso Esquivel 2019: 4).

Taken under the wings of renowned art professionals Jack Lenor Larsen (1927–2020) and Mildred Constantine (1913–2008), textile art took off in Europe and America in the early 1960s and navigated a modernist art world dominated by prevailing hierarchies between craft and art, becoming intertwined with feminist positions (Wells 2019: 158, 235). Modernist art theory, as encapsulated in Greenberg's disdain of the "decorative," was interpreted as qualitative prejudices rooted in cultural conceptualizations of gender and sex and based on misogyny, classism and power preservation (Fowler 2014: 46; Corso Esquivel 2019: 3). The art historian Rozsika Parker captured the debate about feminism and textiles in her book *The Subversive Stitch: Embroidery and the Making of the Feminine* (1984), serving as a cornerstone for this discourse. It links second-wave feminism to the historical intertwinements of "femininity" and textiles. Parker demonstrates how feminist art history correlates to fibre and textile because their historical marginalization directly connects to the oblivion of women's creative practices from dominant art circuits (Corso Esquivel 2019: 4).

Since the 1990s, discussions around textiles have evolved into a flexible framework for discourse and research. The concept of "craftivism" embodies the politics and social practices associated with manual craftsmanship, highlighting textiles' pivotal role in discussions on politics, processes, materiality, gender and race. Art historian Julia Bryan-Wilson argues that textiles disrupt the traditional hierarchical distinction between high and low categories in art and craft, considering their political significance. Examining the thread-based sculptures of the artist Cecilia Vicuña (b. 1948), Bryan-Wilson asserts that textiles occupy a vast space between artistic and political spectrums – between high and low, untrained and highly skilled, conformist and disobedient, craft and art. Consequently, they reveal the contradictions and gaps within the established art system. By examining textiles in this manner, Bryan-Wilson aims to deconstruct the rigid categorizations of "high" and "low," treating them as fluid and constantly evolving terms (Bryan-Wilson 2017: 5).

More recently, artist and researcher Catherine Dormor has conceptualized textiles around the idea of a "matrix," which serves as a connecting and unifying force between humans and materials. In her interpretation, the term "matrix" draws from its Latin roots, signifying a "womb" or "source," representing naturally enclosed entities from which things can originate or take shape. This concept diverges from notions of the genius and intellectual individual, the autonomous artist, and other abstract and self-centred ideas about valuable art creation. Dormor's foundation in mathematics and linguistics underlines the matrix as a non-hierarchical, non-binary structure that emphasizes relational connections and the interweaving of multiplicity. This challenges symbols and concepts of value marked by individuality and singularity, particularly those rooted in a "phallocentric" perspective (Dormor 2020: 3, 41).

Textile theory and practice have expanded into a comprehensive domain of knowledge and activity, providing critical analyses of established art and cultural historiography. This field encapsulates various aspects and roles of textiles as both theory and practice, ranging from their function as symbols of marginalized practices and tools for critical reflection on hierarchical distinctions between craft and art, to their role in preserving tactility, fostering subversive practices and embodying personal connections. The materiality and technique of textiles serve as the common denominator for these perspectives.

Development: The Anthropocene and the environmental humanities

The interaction with materials has served to define civilizations since the nineteenth century. One of the most influential of these is the system of three prehistoric ages – the Stone Age, the Bronze Age and the Iron Age – which was introduced in 1848 by the archaeologist Christian Jürgensen Thomsen (1788–1865). Thomsen based these categories on the materials used to make the artefacts that were found (Bod 2013: 324). Materials and techniques have been explored in their historical and sociological aspects from a wide range of disciplines, that is, the humanities, the arts, the social sciences and the biological sciences, resulting in what has been denominated the environmental humanities, that reflect on the relationship between nature and culture as well as on the urgencies of the ecological problems that face the planet (Hubbell and Ryan 2022: 1).

According to Gregory Votolato, the book *Technics and Civilization* published in 1934 by sociologist Lewis Mumford represents a significant milestone in the exploration of materials and techniques. Mumford contends that humans are inherently technical beings, and the development of various technologies is aimed at safeguarding and enhancing our well-being, providing us with control over our environment. In contrast to Thomsen's emphasis on materials, Mumford categorizes the historical progression into three phases based on the dominant technologies of each era: Eotechnic – involving wood, wind and water –, Paleotechnic – centred around iron and steam –, and Neotechnic – involving steel, plastics and electricity (Votolato 1998: 261).

In more recent times, the categorization of geological time based on technical criteria has centred on the Anthropocene, a term coined by chemist Paul Crutzen in 2000 and informally used in scientific discussions (Steffen et al. 2007: 614–620). The onset of this geological epoch is typically associated with the commencement of the Industrial Revolution in 1700, marking the point at which humans transformed into an industrial species. Subsequently, the human population has experienced rapid growth, and the terrestrial biosphere has undergone a crucial shift from primarily wild to predominantly anthropogenic, surpassing the 50% threshold in the early twentieth century (Ellis et al. 2010: 589). The Anthropocene is characterized as an era of accelerated environmental degradation, which has widened the gap between human and non-human species. The impact of human activity has not only been detrimental to the planet and non-human entities but also poses risks to humanity itself. Environmental phenomena such as prolonged droughts, recurrent wildfires, heatwaves and floods endanger agriculture, destroy homes and displace people. Consequently, there is a heightened and persistent concern for the future, further intensified by political inaction in addressing global warming (Fitzgerald 2019: 271–272).

The Anthropocene has been the product of a human-centred vision of the world that rejects all organisms and systems that do not benefit the interests of humans; a vision that has been seen as extremely excluding and limiting. The current discourse around the Anthropocene, about its definition, its name, its starting date and its impact, has been developed in many fields of study, from geology (Lewis and Maslin 2015: 171–178), anthropology, philosophy, extending to art (Davis and Turpin 2014: 3–31) and design (Weller et al. 2019: 1–3). Counteracting a human-centred vision, increasing attention towards materials within the humanities and the social sciences has resulted in new materialism, which examines the significance of materials within society more closely (Gamble et al. 2019: 111).

New materialism posits that environmentally destructive actions stem from viewing matter as passive. However, the conceptualization of matter as active can be traced back to the atomist tradition in antiquity. A notable figure in this tradition is Lucretius (99–55 BCE), who conceptualized life as consisting of tiny particles that continually combine and separate to form structures, influencing the cycle of life. An essential aspect for new materialists is the idea that humans, composed of the same atoms as everything else, are inherently interconnected with the world around them. This perspective suggests that humans are not in opposition to their natural environment or separate from it; instead, they are an integral component of it (Hoppe and Lemke 2021: 9).

Despite the presence of these foundational theories, Western philosophy has predominantly adopted an anthropocentric point of view. This perspective is rooted in the notion that human intellect, encompassing the ability for abstract thought and intentional action, distinguishes humans and establishes their superiority. In philosophical terms, this is referred to as the subject–object dichotomy, an ontological dualism attributed to philosopher René Descartes (1596–1650; Hoppe and Lemke 2021: 10–11; Bennett 2010: 7). This dichotomy shapes a worldview wherein the non-human is viewed as passive, relegated to be manipulated by humans. Consequently, humans are granted the authority to cultivate and dominate nature (Hoppe and Lemke 2021: 10).

Some contemporary theorists increasingly question the notion of subject–object separation, including actor–network theory (ANT; Hoppe and Lemke 2021: 11). Other theorists have followed ANT to undermine the vertical understanding of the relationship between humans and the material world, arguing the profound entanglement between the two. The new materialists, like ANT, also question the common ranking of placing humans as superior to the material world. These authors agree that progress in the future can only work in union with nature and that humans must start to consider their actions in the context of the complex system of nature. This is certainly something that can only be achieved with the cooperation of many different disciplines and interventions and that requires a shift in our understanding of matter itself (Gamble et al. 2019: 130).

Alongside ANT's horizontalization, the political scientist Jane Bennett further develops the notion that all matter is itself active and acts without human intervention. She ascribes to all matter the quality of being "active" and also engages with Lucretius that everything is interwoven (Bennett 2010: 9).

Thinking of the basic principle of materialism, she adds that today we would call it "atoms, quarks, particle currents or matter-energy" that everything is made up of (2010: 12). Similarly to ANT, Bennett acknowledges that the sources of agency could be both human and non-human, ascribing political agency to the material/natural world. An essential distinction with ANT is that Bennett not only describes a heterogeneous network of equal actors but marks everything as living matter. She not only allows the material world to interact with humans but also ascribes a liveliness to it, which she also calls "vital" or "vibrant" (2010: 8).

Redefining notions of both matter and techniques are intrinsically connected to how humans interact with nature. The anthropologist Tim Ingold challenges accepted notions of what it means to design and make an object such as a basket in opposition to natural constructions such as beehives and a spiral gastropod shell. Ingold states that the properties of the material actually condition the form-generating process (2000: 345). The understanding of design as something that starts in the designer's mind to later being imposed on the material prevents alternative interpretations of the same process. He proposes thinking about how materials condition the design and how designing is more about working *with* the material than *on* the material. To illustrate his thought, he gives the example of weaving a basket in which the maker follows the possibilities of the material to generate the form (Ingold 2000: 341). An apparently novel take on techniques, this concept was already advanced by textile designer Anni Albers (1899–1994) when she prompted craftspeople to listen to the material before starting working, because the material "does not err" (Albers 1943: 3; Figure 16.1). Material properties are not attributes, but stories, according to Ingold. By this, he means that the properties of materials are not fixed but are constantly changing in interaction and relationship with their entire environment, including the interventions of the designer (2007: 12–15).

Focusing on material properties in the design process as it is proposed by Bennett and Ingold implicates a shift in the depiction of matter as a passive entity towards an active understanding of matter in which, as Albers anticipated, the material co-designs.

Implementation: Pottery, cotton and steel

The environmental responsibility of designers has been present within design scholarship at different stages. The designer and theorist Victor Papanek discussed design in relation to technology in his book *Design for the Real World*

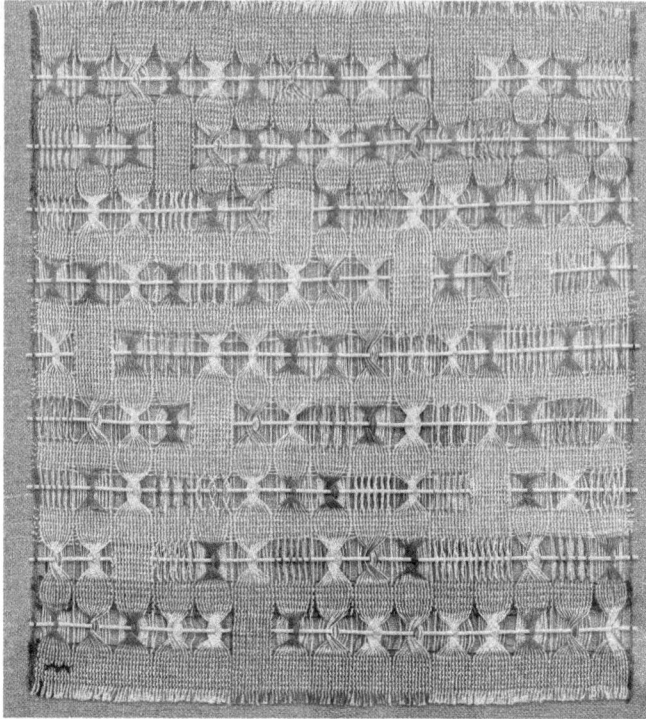

Figure 16.1 Anni Albers, "Variations on a Theme," 1958, rayon, linen, cotton, plastic. Photo by Tolo Balaguer

(1971), advocating for alternative technologies. He saw the Industrial Revolution as a point of change where humanity changed itself and its surroundings, similarly to the above-mentioned accounts on the Anthropocene (2019 [1971]: 28). Furthermore, he commented on the unique relationship that humans have with the environment. Animals adapt *autoplastically* to changes in the environment, that is, by growing thicker fur in the winter or evolving into a new species; however, only humanity transforms the environment itself to suit their needs determined *alloplastically* (2019[1971]: 220). Therefore, design has become the most powerful tool humans use to shape environments, societies and themselves (2019[1971]: 1).

Papanek urged designers to be ecologically responsible and socially responsive and urged users to consume less, use things longer and recycle materials (2019[1971]: 347). His vision of who is a designer is quite broad; since he considers design a fundamental human activity and deems all humans as designers (2019[1971]: 4). He contends that industrial production results in the depletion of natural resources, often of an irreplaceable nature. The environmental impact extends beyond this initial stage, progressing through two subsequent phases. The pollution persists in the design and manufacturing processes, involving packaging. Additionally, according to Papanek, the product's usage contributes to further pollution, and the disposal of products adds to this environmental burden (2019[1971]: 250–251).

Similar to Papanek in the 1970s, in *Defuturing: A New Design Philosophy* (2020[1999]) Fry urges designers to create sustainable ways to deal with the problems that humans have created. It is inherent that pollution causes environmental issues, having a significant impact on the earth's climate. Fry argues that human beings have reached a critical point in their existence and that it is no longer guaranteed that we will have a future. This is what Fry calls "defuturing," which is the essence of unsustainable practices that take the future of humans and other living species away (2020[1999]: 1).

Taking a different perspective, the materials and techniques approach has been employed not solely to address the environmental impact of designers' work but has found application in various contexts. Scholars in design have explored how materials and techniques carry gendered connotations (Smith 2014; Vincentelli 2000), shape global connections (Riello 2013), and reshape approaches to cultural history by considering how materials contribute to forms of extraction, lifestyles and recycling (Fry and Willis 2015).

In terms of a gendered construction of materials, T'ai Lin Smith studies how women were assumed to enrol for some workshops such as textiles and less so for others such as furniture at the Bauhaus school (1919–1933; Smith 2014: 128–135). Along with textiles, another example has been pottery. Through her analysis of this craft technique, Moira Vincentelli points towards the existence of a masculinist tone within design scholarship. She argues in *Women and Ceramic: Gendered Vessels* (2000) that even when design history had moved towards a socio-historical approach, its focus on industrial production and Western culture had prevented handcraft production to acquire a central place. She acknowledges some exceptions such as the Arts and Crafts Movement and key figures such as William Morris (1834–1896). Nevertheless, those modernist meta-narratives of design have not allowed ceramic designers to be considered innovators (2000: 2).

Vincentelli's geographical and chronological scope is vast, from the ancient Japanese ceramics of the Jomon period (10,500–300 BCE) to the late twentieth century, including Wok and Ife figures from Nigeria, and indigenous U.S. Southwest Mimbres pottery (2000: 5). She offers an overview of the association of women and ceramics as both makers and users, considering first the important roles of women as writers, teachers and promoters of ceramics. The marginalization of women had to do with ceramic production moving into larger-scale manufactories during the seventeenth century. Bringing increased specialization, women began to be associated with certain types of work, and in the main became cheap, unskilled labourers. They were often employed as assistants to men who were likely to be family members and were also increasingly employed in decoration, a field usually perceived as feminine, superficial and "lacking in intellectual rigour." Furthermore, Vincentelli addresses consumption, exploring the role of ceramics as objects functioning in communications between people, conveying messages, representing particular values about gender relationships, personal space within the household and relationships of power and group identity (2000: 77).

His specialization in global history moved Giorgio Riello to look at it through a material lens. His book *Cotton: The Fabric that Made the Modern World* (2013) elaborates a world history of cotton and thereby develops a model of global economic history. He positions his book within the material turn in global history, which he defines as how material culture can help global history to revaluate its conception of space, with a particular emphasis on the connectivity that defined the premodern world, and to consider the ways in which the agency of individuals can have meaningful value in global narratives. He argues that "small things" might be used to challenge established narratives and to provide different scales of analysis that range from micro to macro (2022: 232).

Riello narrates the story of cotton production, trade, Asian manufacturing, European industrialization, triangular trade and slavery, presenting a global history of cotton spanning about a thousand years, from 1000 AD to the present. He challenges simplistic accounts of economic development, emphasizing the prolonged and multifaceted nature of change, in contrast to analysis centred on the triumph of capitalism. Riello divides his book into three parts: the first focuses on South Asia's dominance in cotton production (1000–1500), the second explores the shift from Asia to Europe, and the third delineates the characteristics of the subsequent cotton system dominated by Europe and North America (1750–2000).

If previous accounts on cotton overly emphasized individual explanatory factors such as technology or institutions, Riello specifically avoids technical determinism. He illustrates how cotton served as a link between India and the UK, with cotton cloth being re-exported not only to Europe and America but also to various other regions. Between 1699 and 1800, approximately 40% of cloth exported to Africa originated from India (2013: 138). The demand from Atlantic markets played a role in stimulating industrialization from 1750 to 1800. Additionally, plantation production of raw materials in the American South facilitated mechanization in Manchester and led to the specialization of labour on a truly global scale, redirecting resources and capital from emerging peripheries to a new European core (2013: 197). As a consequence, Riello reinterprets industrialization as a consequence, rather than the instigator, of new world trade systems.

A different use of materials has been to reformulate cultural history. Materials allow for mapping global connections, have an impact on the environment and modify cultural connections. An example of this take is the study *Steel: A Design, Cultural and Ecological History* (2015) by Tony Fry and Anne-Marie Willis. The authors argue against the general impression that economies dematerialize and that experience becomes increasingly virtual. They argue that an immaterial economy might have decentred materials but the truth is that material production has migrated to "newly industrializing" regions (2015: 1). They see different ecologies of steel in different regions since the material relates to the environment in particular ways.

Fry and Willis' neo-materialist framework fosters an approach based on relationality. They look at how the natural, the material and the human interconnect, acknowledging the difficulty of keeping the three separated. By doing this, Fry and Willis negate that the concept of ecology is only composed of nature (2015: 5). Therefore, they develop a "design, cultural and ecological history" of steel. The question remains as to how their approach differs from a pure "design historical" account such as, for example, Giorgio Riello's overview (2013). Fry and Willis stress the impact on nature of the extraction, transportation and consumption of steel. Riello focusses rather on global trade and consumption. A focus on technology and ecology provides the backbone to Fry and Willis' book while Riello directly considers the ecological impact of cotton, mostly in his three last chapters that concentrate on the most recent period (2013: 211–287)

Fry and Papanek repeatedly critiqued the design practice. Papanek already set the tone when he stated that industrial design is one of the most harmful professions. Fry calls for a design-led solution for the environmental problems for which design is partly responsible (2020[1999]: 10). Design might have been historically linked to the growth of capitalism and consumption, as well as a contributor to contemporary environmental and societal issues. However, some branches of design have tried to change and detach themselves from the system in which they participated, with movements such as the "cradle-to-cradle" design in the early 2000s and biodesign today.

Challenges: Biodesign, designing with nature

If design has been the problem, it can offer solutions too. Engineers, scientists and technicians are devoting their attention to the design discipline in search of solutions to the ecological crisis (Fallan 2019b: 5). One example is the field of biology where there is an increasing collaboration with designers. This intersection has been called biodesign and turns its focus to new materials, both their design and their application. Mentions of the term "biodesign" can be found from 1999 (Datschefski 1999: 42–51) but gained recognition since the publication of the book *Biodesign: Nature, Science, Creativity* by the curator William Myers (2018[2012]).

Biodesign is not necessarily a new practice as the root bridges in the northeastern state of Meghalaya in India demonstrate (Figure 16.2). These bridges are coaxed from the slow-growing Ficus elastica, trees with a strong rooting system. The growth of their many secondary roots, which would normally fan out in all directions, can be guided using a betel nut trunk. Placed across a river, these trunks ensure that the thin, tender roots grow straight and eventually reach the opposite bank, where locals direct them to take hold in the soil. These living structures adjust over time and are never fully complete. Some of these root bridges, which take approximately 15 years

Figure 16.2 Root bridges in the northeastern state of Meghalaya in India. Photo by BIJU BORO/AFP via Getty Images

to become functional, are more than 30 meters long (Myers 2018[2012]: 28–31). The very shape of these bridges is self-explanatory of their construction, evidencing the symbiotic relationship between the work of humans and the trees themselves to configure these bridges.

Biodesign promotes the idea that the designer would become an explorer, a "mediator between the artificial and the natural," carefully accompanying or guiding processes rather than dominating them (Antonelli 2020: 36). The design process includes the design of the material itself rather than using materials already produced. Very much in line with Ingold's ideas, biodesign dissolves the separation between design and materiality. Additionally, it serves as an example of a manufacturing process, that combines handcrafting techniques and conscious reflections on the impact of material properties (Antonelli 2020: 23).

Biodesign focuses chiefly on moist media, for instance, microorganisms and fungi, with the aim to propose new alternatives of processes and materials (Meyer et al. 2020: 2; Meyer and Rapp 2020: 14). The production of fungal material requires the interaction between designer and material and the activeness of matter. Fungi are usually associated with their fruiting body, that is, the mushroom. In the production of fungal-based materials, however, it is the mycelium that is used, the root of the mushroom that grows under the ground. Mycelium starts to grow out of a fungal spore in a moist and nutrient-rich environment, building hypha, the parts that make up the network (Meyer et al. 2020: 2). Mycelium can be thought of as a vast network that grows in a constantly interconnecting process. This process can be directed just so that the hypha grows in certain directions and thus yields certain shapes (Moore 2005: 80).

Thus, to produce mycelium material, a nutritive environment must be created, that is, biowaste must be collected, a fungal spore must be added and the shape into which the fungus will grow must be determined. Often fungi are not distinguished from plants, even though they do not belong in the plant category. This is because they nourish in a fundamentally different way. Plants use radiant energy while fungi absorb digestive products (Moore 2005: 79–80). This means that fungi consume dead plants while decomposing them, transforming the dead plant's molecules into their own biomass. The growth can be stopped by drying the mycelium, which results in finished composite material. This material can already be used as packaging material or insulation material and can achieve different aspects (Meyer et al. 2020: 7).

Designers and artists use and cultivate fungal material for their projects and explore its potential for commercial purposes (Meyer et al. 2020: 9). One example is Philip Ross, who already in the 1990s created works of art and designed objects with fungi-based materials (MycoWorks Official Website). His design research on fungal materials eventually led to the foundation of MycoWorks. Together with Sophia Wang, he founded this company in 2013 and today it is one of the largest producers of fungi-based leather worldwide, cooperating with fashion brands such as Hermès (Meyer et al 2020: 9; MycoWorks Official Website).

To produce MycoWorks' leather-like materials, further processing is needed. This more specific material production has become possible primarily through genetic manipulation, which means that the metabolic processes are modified (Meyer and Rapp 2020: 6). This allows not only certain shapes but also functions, such as water repellency. After the material has been grown and the growth process is stopped, the material can be hardened and finished using industrial techniques and then processed like conventional animal leather (Meyer et al 2020: 7, 9). In the case of leather, the advantages are that no animals get harmed. Furthermore, the production of fungi-based materials requires far less energy and water than conventional production and no fossil fuels at all. In addition, the material is flame-retardant and heat-insulating, durable and decomposable (Meyer et al 2020: 9; Meyer and Rapp 2020: 15).

The use and design of bio-fabricated materials in the design process shifts the focus from the form of an object to the properties that a particular material can offer for the formation of a certain object. The preconditions for the growing process and the treatments necessary to unfold the optimal results of the material determine the procedure. In this process, the designer's behaviour patterns change depending on the properties of the material. The designer needs to observe the behaviour of the material's properties in relation to its environment in order to strive for the best design outcome.

The natural properties of materials are key in the final design, indicating the presence of a living organism in the object and in the design process. To a certain extent, the designer becomes a co-creator, working together with microorganisms on their conditions. The interactive character in the design process and the agency of matter here becomes evident in the abstract formation of ideas that depend and emerge out of material properties instead of imposing an object on a material. In this context, we no longer understand the designer solely as a "form-giver," but as an initiator of processes within ecological systems (Antonelli 2020: 32).

The mutual collaboration between materials and designers is evident in the root bridges of Meghalaya, but it may be less pronounced in MycoWork's leather as it replicates existing materials. If the goal is to raise awareness among both designers and users, the question arises whether biodesign should prominently showcase a different way of working with nature or seamlessly integrate into the broader material and visual culture. Can designers not only create more sustainable products but also foster awareness? Can any form of biodesign contribute to this cause? Essentially, can design alone allow us to move beyond the Anthropocene into a symbiotic era in harmony with the planet, or is it public awareness that holds the key to achieving this transition?

Bibliography

Abrams, Lynn (2010) *Oral History Theory*, London/New York: Routledge.

Adams Stein, Jesse (2016) *Hot Metal: Material Culture and Tangible Labour*, Manchester: Manchester University Press.

Adams Stein, Jesse (2021) *Industrial Craft in Australia: Oral Histories of Creativity and Survival*, Cham: Palgrave Macmillan.

Adams, Tony E., Stacy Holman Jones and Carolyn Ellis (2022[2013]) *Handbook of Autoethnography*, London/New York: Routledge.

Adamson, Glenn (2005) *Industrial Strength Design: How Brooks Stevens Shaped Your World*, Cambridge: MIT.

Adamson, Glenn (2013) "Design History and the Decorative Arts," in Peter N. Miller (ed.) *Cultural Histories of the Material World*, Ann Arbor: University of Michigan Press.

Adamson, Glenn and Jane Pavitt (2011) *Postmodernism: Style and Subversion 1970–1990*, London: V&A Publications.

Adamson, Glenn, Giorgio Riello and Sarah Teasley (eds) (2011) *Global Design History*, Abingdon/New York: Routledge.

Akrich, Madeleine (1992) "The De-Scription of Technical Objects," in Bijker, Wiebe E. and John Law (eds) *Shaping Technology/Building Society*, Cambridge/London: MIT.

Akrich, Madeleine (1995) "User Representations: Practices, Methods and Sociology," in Rip, Arie, Thomas J. Misa and Johan Schot (eds) *Managing Technology in Society: The Approach of Constructive Technology Assessment*, London/New York: Pinter Publisher.

Akrich, Madeleine and Bruno Latour (1992) "A Summary of a Convenient Vocabulary for the Semiotics of Human and Nonhuman Assemblies," in Bijker, Wiebe E. and John Law (eds) *Shaping Technology/Building Society*, Cambridge/London: MIT.

Albers, Anni (1943) "Designing," *Craft Horizons*May: 2–3.

Alok Official Website (2019) "Design," www.alokvmenon.com/design, accessed May 2022.

Alpers, Svetlana (1979) "Style is What You Make It: The Visual Arts Once Again," in Berel Lang (ed.) *The Concept of Style*, Philadelphia: University of Pennsylvania Press.

Antonelli, Paola (ed.) (2020) *Neri Oxman: Material Ecology* [exh.cat.] New York: The Museum of Modern Art.

Armstrong, Leah, Jocelyn Bailey, Guy Julier and Lucy Kimbell (2014) *Social Design Futures: HEI Research and the AHRC*, London: University of Brighton and Victoria and Albert Museum. https://mappingsocialdesign.files.wordpress.com/2014/10/social-design-report.pdf, accessed November 2023.

Arshad, Zara (2021) "Diskurs. Oral History & Design," *Form* 291: 22–29.

Ash, Juliet (1996) "Memory and Objects," in Pat Kirkham (ed.), *The Gendered Object*, Manchester/New York: Manchester University Press.

Atkinson, Harriet, Verity Clarkson and Sarah A. Lichtman (eds) (2022) *Exhibitions Beyond Boundaries: Transnational Exchanges through Art, Architecture, and Design 1945–1985*, London/New York/Dublin: Bloomsbury.

Atkinson, Paul (2006) "Do It Yourself: Democracy and Design," *Journal of Design History* 19 (1): 1–10.

Atkinson, Paul (2008) "A Bitter Pill to Swallow: The Rise and Fall of the Tablet Computer," *Design Issues* 24 (4): 3–25.

Attfield, Judith (2003) "What does History have to do with It? Feminism and Design History," *Journal of Design History* 16 (1): 77–87.

Attfield, Judy (2000) *Wild Things: The Material Culture of Everyday Life*, Oxford/New York: Berg.

Attfield, Judy (2009[1989]) "Form/Female Follows Function/Male: Feminist Critiques of Design," in Hazel Clark (ed.), *Design Studies: A Reader*, Oxford: Berg.

Attfield, Judy and Pat Kirkham (1989) *A View from the Interior: Women and Design*, London: Women's Press.

Auslander, Leora (2005) "Beyond Words," *American Historical Review* 110 (4): 1015–1045.

Aveling, Emma-Louise, Alex Gillespie and Flora Cornish (2015) "A Qualitative Method for Analysing Multivoicedness," *Qualitative Research* 15 (6): 670–687.

Aynsley, Jeremy, Alison J. Clarke and Tania Messell (2022) *International Design Organizations: Histories, Legacies, Values*, London/New York/Dublin: Bloomsbury.

Badia, Antoni and Eva Liesa (2022) "Experienced Teachers' Identity Based on Their I-Positions: An Analysis in the Catalan Context," *European Journal of Teacher Education* 45 (1): 77–92.

Bakhtin, Mikhail Mikhailovich (1981[1934–41]), *The Dialogic Imagination: Four Essays*, Austin: University of Texas Press.

Bal, Mieke (1996) "Telling, Showing, Showing Off," in Mieke Bal, *Double Exposures: The Subject of Cultural Analysis*, London: Routledge.

Bannerji, Kaushalya (1993) "No apologies," in Rakesh Ratti (ed.), *A Lotus of Another Color: An Unfolding of the South Asian Gay and Lesbian Experience*, Toronto: Alyson.

Bardzell, Jeffrey and Shaowen Bardzell (2015) *Humanistic HCI*, California: Morgan & Claypool.

Barthes, Roland (1977[1968]) "The Death of the Author", in *Image, Music, Text*, London: Fontana.

Benedetto, Francesca and Porzia Bergamasco (2022) "Design Forever," *Elle Decor Italia*, July/August: 90–108.

Bennett, Jane (2010) *Vibrant Matter: A Political Ecology of Things*, Durham and London: Duke University Press.

Berger, Stefan (2015) "National Museums in Between Nationalism, Imperialism and Regionalism, 1750–1914," in Peter Aronsson and Gabriella Elgenius (eds) *National Museums and Nation-Building in Europe 1750–2010: Mobilization and legitimacy, continuity and change*, London/New York: Routledge.

Berghoff, Hartmut (2015) "Business History," in James D. Wright (ed.) *International Encyclopedia of the Social & Behavioral Sciences*, Amsterdam: Elsevier.

Bergset, Kari and Oddbjørg Skjær Ulvik (2021) "Parenting in exile: Refugee parents' multivoiced narratives," *International Social Work* 64 (3): 412–424.

Bergvelt, Elinoor (ed.) (1979) *Wonen TA/BK. Goed Wonen. Een Nederlandse Woon-cultuur 1946–1968* [Quality Living: A Dutch Home Culture 1946–1968] [Special Issue] 4 (5).

Bergvelt, Ellinoor, Debora J. Meijers, Lieske Tibbe and Elsa van Wezel (eds) (2009) *Napoleon's Legacy: The Rise of National Museums in Europe 1794–1830*, Berlin: G & H.

Beveren, State Archives, Archives of the Fine Art and Museums Department, Ministry of the Flemish Community/Transfer2005 (1945–2004) (FAMD), vol. 2013, "*Octroi de distinctions spéciales à certains travailleurs d'entreprises ayant remporté le Signe d'Or*," fols.168r–170r.

Bhabha, Homi K. (1994) *The Location of Culture*, London: Routledge.

Biebuyck, William and Judith Meltzer (2017) "Cultural Political Economy," in *Oxford Research Encyclopedia of International Studies*. https://oxfordre.com/internationalstudies/view/10.1093/acrefore/9780190846626.001.0001/acrefore-9780190846626-e-140, accessed November 2023.

Biow, Douglas (2018) *Vasari's Words: The "Lives of the Artists" as a History of Ideas in the Italian Rennaissance*, Cambridge: Cambridge University Press.

Blaszczyk, Regina Lee (2000) *Imagining Consumers: Design and Innovation from Wedgwood to Corning*, Baltimore/London: Johns Hopkins.

Blaszczyk, Regina Lee (ed.) (2008) *Producing Fashion: Commerce, Culture and Consumers*, Philadelphia: University of Pennsylvania Press.

Blaszczyk, Regina Lee and Ben Wubs (ed.) (2018) *The Fashion Forecasters: A Hidden History of Color and Trend Prediction*, London: Bloomsbury.

Bod, Rens (2013) *A New History of the Humanities: The Search for Principles and Patterns from Antiquity to the Present*, Oxford: Oxford University Press.

Bod, Rens (2022) *World of Patterns: A Global History of Knowledge*, Baltimore: Johns Hopkins University Press.

Boedeker, Deborah (2011) "Early Greek Poetry as/and History," in Andrew Feldherr and Grant Hardy (eds) *The Oxford History of Historical Writing. Volume 1. Beginnings to AD 600*, Oxford: Oxford University Press.

Bolter, Jay D. (2016) "Posthumanism," in Klaus Jensen, Jefferson Pooley, Eric Walter Rothenbuhler and Robert T. Craig (eds) *The International Encyclopedia for Communication Theory and Philosophy*, New Jersey: Wiley.

Bolter, Jay D. and Richard Grusin (1999) *Remediation: Understanding New Media*, Cambridge: MIT.

Bolter, Jay D., Maria Engberg, Blair MacIntyre (2013) "Media Studies, Mobile Augmented Reality, and Interaction Design," *Interactions* 20 (1): 36–45.

Bonnell, Victoria E. and Lynn Hunt (eds) (1999) *Beyond the Cultural Turn: New Directions in the Study of Society and Culture*, London/Los Angeles: University of California Press.

Bosma, Koos, Aart Mekking, Koen Ottenheym and Auke Van der Woud (eds) (2007) *Bouwen in Nederland, 600–2000*, Zwolle: Wbooks.

Bouet, Pierre (2010) *Hastings: 14 octobre 1066*, Paris: Tallandier.

Bouet, Pierre (2015) "Guillaume: de 'bâtard' à 'conquérant'," *Historia*, May/June: 68–71.

Boyd, Douglas A. and Mary A. Larson (eds) (2014) *Oral History and Digital Humanities: Voice, Access and Engagement*, New York: Palgrave Macmillan.

Boyd, Kelly (ed.) (1999) *Encyclopedia of Historians and Historical Writing*. Vol. 2. London: Fitzroy Dearborn.

Brennan, Ann Marie (2015) "Olivetti: A Work of Art in the Age of Inmaterial Labour," *Journal of Design History* 28 (3): 235–253.

Breward, Christopher (1999) *The Hidden Consumer: Masculinities, Fashion and City Life 1860–1914*, Manchester and New York: Manchester University Press.

Brodersen, Søsser, Meiken Hansen and Hanne Lindegaard (2015) "Script of Healthcare Technology: Do Designs of Robotic Beds Exclude or Include Users?" *Design Issues* 31 (2): 16–28.

Broude, Norma and Mary D. Garrard (eds) (2018 [1992]) *The Expanding Discourse: Feminism and Art History*, New York and London: Routledge.

Brumfitt, Stuart (2013) "A Queer History of Fashion: From the Closet to the Catwalk – Review", *The Guardian*. www.theguardian.com/fashion/fashion-blog/2013/sep/25/queer-history-fashion-closet-catwalk-review, accessed May 2022.

Brummett, Barry (2008) *A Rhetoric of Style*. Carbondale: Southern Illinois University Press.

Brun Petersen, Trine (2021) "Suiting Children for Institutions. The Development, Calibration and Stabilization of the One-piece Snowsuit," *Journal of Design History*, 35 (1): 1–15.

Brunsdon, Charlotte (1997) *Screen Tastes: Soap Opera to Satellite Dishes*. London: Routledge.

Bryan-Wilson, Julia (2017) *Fray: Art and Textile Politics*, Chicago: University of Chicago Press.

Buckley, Cheryl (1986) "Made in Patriarchy: Towards a Feminist Analysis of Women and Design," *Design Issues* 3 (2): 3–14.

Butler, Judith (1991) "Imitation and Gender Insubordination," in Diana Fuss, *Inside/Out: Lesbian Theories, Gay Theories*. London/New York: Routledge.

Butler, Judith (1999[1990]) *Gender Trouble: Feminism and the Subversion of Identity*, New York and London: Routledge.

Calvera, Anna (2002) "The Influence of English Design Reform in Catalonia: An Attempt at Comparative History," *Journal of Design History* 21 (3): 83–100.

Calvera, Anna (2005) "Local, Regional, National, Global and Feedback: Several Issues to be Faced with Constructing Regional Narratives," *Journal of Design History*, 18 (4): 371–383.

Campbell, Colin (2005) "The Craft Consumer: Culture, Craft and Consumption in a Postmodern Society," *Journal of Consumer Culture* 5 (1): 23–42.

Campbell-Dollaghan, Kelsey (2018) *"The Future of Web Design is Less, Not More,"* *Fast Company*, www.fastcompany.com/90246767/the-future-of-web-design-is-less-not-more, accessed April 2021.

Castells, Manuel (2003) *The Internet Galaxy: Reflections on the Internet, Business, and Society*, Oxford: Oxford University Press.

Chakravorty Spivak, Gayatri (1988) "Can the Subaltern Speak?," in Cary Nelson and Lawrence Grossberg (eds) *Marxism and the Interpretation of Culture*, Basingstoke and London: Macmillan.

Chakravorty Spivak, Gayatri (2004) "Righting Wrongs," *South Atlantic Quarterly* 103 (2/3): 523–581.

Chang, Kwang-chih (1967) "Chapter 5. Typology and the Comparative Method," in *Rethinking Archaeology*, New York: Random House.

Cheang, Sarah, Katie Irani, Livia Rezende, Shehnaz Suterwalla (2023) "In Between Breaths: Memories, Stories, and Otherwise Design Histories," *Journal of Design History* 36 (2): 175–196.

Christensen, Michelle and Florian Conradi (2020) *Politics of Things: A Critical Approach Through Design*, Basel: Birkhäuser.

Clark, T.J. (1973) *Image of the People: Gustave Courbet and the Second French Republic 1848–1851*, London: Thames and Hudson.

Clarke, Alison J. (1999) *Tupperware: The Promise of Plastic in 1950s America*, Washington/London: Smithsonian.

Clarke, Alison J. (2001) "The Aesthetics of Social Aspiration," in *Home Possessions, Material Culture behind Closed Doors*, Oxford/New York: Berg.

Clarke, Alison J. (2011) *Design Anthropology: Object Culture in the 21st Century*, Wien/New York: Springer.

Clarke, Alison J. (2018) "The Anthropological Object in Design: From Victor Papanek to Superstudio," in Alison J. Clarke (ed.) *Design Anthropology, Object Cultures in Transition*, London: Bloomsbury.

Clarke, John (2013) "Oral History Work with Tibetan and Nepalese Metalworkers (1986–91)," in Linda Sandino and Matthew Partington, *Oral History in the Visual Arts*, London and New York: Bloomsbury.

Clifford, James (1988) "Collecting Ourselves," in Susan M. Pearce (ed.) (1994) *Interpreting Objects and Collections*, London and New York: Routledge.

Cole, Shaun (2000) *"Don We Now Our Gay Apparel": Gay Men's Dress in the Twentieth Century*, Oxford and New York: Berg.

Comisarenco Mirkin, Dina (2006) *Diseño industrial mexicano e internacional. Memoria y futuro* [Mexican and International Industrial Design. Memory and Future], Mexico D.F.: Trillas.

Comisarenco Mirkin, Dina (2020) "Entre la realidad y el mito: las crónicas contemporáneas del diseño industrial mexicano," in Verónica Devalle and Marina Garone Gravier (eds) *Diseño Lationoamericano. Diez Miradas a una historia en construcción*, Bogotá: Universidad de Bogotá Jorge Tadeo Lozano/Universidad Santo Tomás/Politécnico Grancolombiano.

Conway, Hazel (ed.) (1987) *Design History: A Students' Handbook*. London/New York: Routledge.

Cook, Matt (2014) *Queer Domesticities: Homosexuality and Home Life in Twentieth-Century London*, New York: Palgrave Macmillan.

Cooper Hewit Official Website, https://collection.cooperhewitt.org/people/2318807353/objects/, accessed November 2023.

Corso Esquivel, John (2019) *Feminist Subjectivities in Fiber Art and Craft: Shadows of Affect*, London/New York: Routledge.

Cowan, Ruth Schwartz (1983) *More Work for Mother: The Ironies of Household Technology from the Open Hearth to the Microwave*, New York: Basic Books.

Cowan, Ruth Schartz (1987) "The Consumption Junction: A Proposal for Research Strategies in the Sociology of Technology," in Wiebe E. Bijker, Thomas P. Hughes and Trevor Pinch (eds) (2012[1987]) *The Social Construction of Technological Systems. New Directions in the Sociology and History of Technology*, Cambridge/London: MIT.

Cowan, Ruth Schwartz (1997) *A Social History of American Technology*, Oxford: Oxford University Press.

Crenshaw, Kimberlé (1991) "Mapping the Margins: Intersectionality, Identity Politics, and Violence against Women of Color," *Stanford Law Review* 43 (6): 1241–1299.

Creswell, John W. (2013) *Qualitative Inquiry and Research Design: Choosing Among Five Approaches*, Thousand Oaks: Sage.

Csikszentmihalyi, Mihaly (1993) "Why We Need Things," in Steven Lubar and W. David Kingery (eds) *History From Things: Essays on Material Culture*, Washington: Smithsonian.

Csikszentmihalyi, Mihaly and Eugene Rochberg-Halton (1981) *The Meaning of Things: Domestic Symbols and the Self*, Cambridge: Cambridge University Press.

DaCosta Kaufmann, Thomas (2004) *Toward a Geography of Art*, Chicago: University of Chicago Press.

Damrosch, David, Natalie Melas and Mbongiseni Buthelezi (2009) *The Princeton Sourcebook in Comparative Literature. From the European Enlightenment to the Global Present*, Princeton/Oxford: Princeton University Press.

Danius, Sara, Stefan Jonsson and Gayatri Chakravorty Spivak (1993) "An Interview with Gayatri Chakravorty Spivak," *Boundary 2* 20 (2): 24–50.

Datschefski Edwin (1999) "Cyclic, Solar, Safe – BioDesign's Solution Requirements for Sustainability," *The Journal of Sustainable Product Design* 8 (January): 42–51.

Davis, Heather and Etienne Turpin (2014) *Arts in the Anthropocene: Encounters Among Aesthetics, Politics, Environments and Epistemologies*, London: Open Humanities Press.

De Decker, Kris (2009) "Mag het een Zuinig Lampje Minder Zijn?" [Can it be one energy-efficient bulb less?], *NRC Handelsblad*, www.nrc.nl/nieuws/2009/03/03/mag-het-een-zuinig-lampje-minder-zijn-11691422-a474501, accessed April 2021.

de Rijk, Timo (2010) *Norm = Form: On Standardisation and Design*, Deventer: Thieme Art.

Dea, Shannon (2016) *Beyond the Binary. Thinking about Sex and Gender*, Peterborough: Broadview.

Devalle, Verónica and Marina Garone Gravier (eds) (2020) *Diseño Lationoamericano. Diez Miradas a una historia en construcción*, Bogotá: Universidad de Bogotá Jorge Tadeo Lozano/Universidad Santo Tomás/Politécnico Grancolombiano.

Dilnot, Clive (1984) "The State of Design History, Part II: Problems and Possibilities," *Design Issues* 1 (2): 3–20.

Donnely, Brian (2006) "Locating Graphic Design History in Canada," *Journal of Design History* 19 (4): 283–294.

Donzé, Pierre-Yves, Véronique Pouillard and Joanne Roberts (eds) (2022) *The Oxford Handbook of Luxury Business*, Oxford: Oxford University Press.

Dormor, Catherine (2020) *A Philosophy of Textile: Between Practice and Theory*, London: Bloomsbury.

Douglas, Mary (2000[1966]) *Purity and Danger: An Analysis of the Concepts of Pollution and Taboo*. New York: Routledge.

Douglas, Mary and Baron Isherwood (1996[1979]) *The World of Goods: Towards an Anthropology of Consumption*. New York: Basic Books.

Du Gay, Paul, Stuart Hall, Linda Janes, Anders Koed Madsen, Hugh Mackay and Keith Negus (2013[1997]) *Doing Cultural Studies: The Story of the Sony Walkman*, Los Angeles/London/New Delhi/Singapore: Sage.

Easton, Martha (2012) "Feminism," *Studies in Iconography* 33: 99–112.

Ellis, Erle C., Kees Klein Goldewijk, Stefan Siebert, Deborah Lightman and Navin Ramankutty (2010) "Anthropogenic Transformation of the Biomes, 1700 to 2000," *Global Ecology and Biogeography* 19 (5): 589–606.

Errington, Joseph (2008) *Linguistics in a Colonial World: A Story of Language, Meaning, and Power*, Malde/Oxford/Victoria: Blackwell.

Escobar, Arturo (2018 [2016]) *Designs for the Pluriverse: Radical Interdependence, Autonomy, and the Making of Worlds*, Durham/London: Duke University Press.

Fallan, Kjetil (2010) *Design History: Understanding Theory and Method*. Oxford/New York: Berg.

Fallan, Kjetil (2012) "Kombi-Nation: Mini Bicycles as Moving Memories," *Journal of Design History* 26 (1): 65–85.

Fallan, Kjetil (2019a) "Design Culturing: Making Design History Matter," in Guy Julier, Anders V. Munch, Mad Nygaard Folkmann, Hans-Christian Jensen and Niels Peter Skou, *Design Culture: Objects and Approaches*, London/New York: Bloomsbury.

Fallan, Kjetil (2019b) *The Culture of Nature in the History of Design*, London and New York: Routledge.

Fallan, Kjetil and Grace Lees-Maffei (eds) (2016) *Designing Worlds: National Design Histories in an Age of Globalization*, Oxford/New York: Berghahn.

Fanon, Frantz (1961) *Les damnés de la terre* [The Wretched of the Earth], Paris: Maspero.

Fernie, Eric (1995) *Art History and Its Methods: A Critical Anthology*, London: Phaidon.

Fetterman, David M. (1998) *Ethnography: Step by Step*, London: Sage.

Findlay, Rosie (2015) "The Short, Passionate and Close-Knit History of Personal Style Blogs," *Fashion Theory* 19 (2): 157–178.

Fitzgerald, Cathy (2019) "Goodbye Anthropocene – Hello Symbiocene: Eco-social Art Practices for a New World," in Magdalena Ziółkowska (ed.) *Plasticity of the Planet: On Environmental Challenge for Art and its Institutions*, Milan: Mousse Publishing.

Flanders Architecture Institute Website, www.vai.be/advies/oral-history-design#I5, accessed November 2023.

Flood Heaton, Rachel and Deana McDonagh (2017) "Can Timelessness through Prototypicality Support Sustainability? A Strategy for Product Designers," *The Design Journal* 20 (sup1): S110–S121.

Florida, Richard L. (2019[2002]) *The Rise of the Creative Class. And How It's Transforming Work, Leisure, Community and Everyday Life*, New York: Basic Books.

Font, Lourdes (2011) "Dior before Dior," *West 86th* 18 (1): 26–49.

Forlano, Laura (2017) "Posthumanism and Design," *The Journal of Design, Economics, and Innovation* 3 (1): 17–29.

Forty, Adrian(2010[1986]) *Objects of Desire: Design and Society since 1750*, London: Thames & Hudson.

Forty, Adrian (2013[2000]) *Words and Buildings. A Vocabulary of Modern Architecture*, London: Thames & Hudson.

Foucault, Michel (1969) "What Is an Author?" in Donald Preziosi (2009[1998]) *The Art of Art History: A Critical Anthology*, Oxford: Oxford University Press.

Foucault, Michel (1970) "The Order of Discourse," in Young, Robert (ed.) *Untying the Text: A Post-Structuralist Reader*, Boston, London and Henley: Routledge and Kegan Paul.

Foucault, Michel (1978[1976]) *The History of Sexuality, Volume I: An Introduction*, New York: Pantheon.

Fowler, Cynthia (2014) "A Sign of the Times: Sheila Hicks, the Fiber Arts Movement, and the Language of Liberation," *The Journal of Modern Craft* 7 (1): 33–51.

Francis, Becky (2002) "Relativism, Realism, and Feminism: An analysis of some theoretical tensions in research on gender identity", *Journal of Gender* 11 (1): 39–54.

Frank, Rike and Sabeth Buchmann (eds) (2015) *Textile Theorien der Moderne: Alois Riegl in der Kunstkritik* [Textile Theories of Modernity: Alois Riegl in Art Criticism], Berlin: B books.

Franke, Nikolaus, Martin Schreier and Ulrike Kaiser (2010) "The 'I Designed It Myself' Effect in Mass Customization," *Management Science* 56 (1): 125–140.

Fry, Tony (1988) *Design History Australia*, Sydney: Hale and Iremonger.

Fry, Tony (2020[1999]) *Defuturing: A New Design Philosophy*, London, New York, New Dehli and Sidney: Bloomsbury.

Fry, Tony and Anne-Marie Willis (2015) *Steel: A Design, Cultural and Ecological History*, New York/London: Bloomsbury.

Fujita, Haruhiko and Christine Guth (eds) (2019) *Encyclopedia of East Asian Design*, London/New York: Bloomsbury.

Gamble, Christopher N., Joshua S. Hanan and Thomas Nail (2019) "What is New Materialism?"*Angelaki: Journal of the Theoretical Humanities* 24 (6): 111–134.

Garone Gravier, Marina (2010) "Para una historia crítica del diseño," in Giovanni Troconi (ed.) *Diseño gráfico en México. Cien años. 1900–2000*, Mexico D.F.: Artes de México.

Garvey, Pauline and Adam Drazin (2016) "Design Dispersed: Design History, Design Practice and Anthropology," *Journal of Design History* 29 (1): 1–7.

Gasparin, Marta and Daniel Neyland (2018) "We Have Always Been Modern(ist): Temporality and the Organisational Management of 'Timeless' Iconic Chairs." *Organization* 25 (3): 354–373.

Gay y Blasco, Paloma and Huon Wardle (2019[2007]) *How to Read Ethnography*, London/New York: Routledge.

Geczy, Adam and Vicki Karaminas (2013) *Queer Style*, London, New Dehli, New York and Sydney: Bloomsbury.

Gee, James Paul (2014) *An Introduction to Discourse Analysis*, New York: Routledge.

Gelder, Ken and Sarah Thornton (eds) (1997) *The Subcultures Reader*, London/New York: Routledge.

Gerosa, Alessandro (2022) "The Hidden Roots of the Creative Economy: A Critical History of the Concept along the Twentieth Century," *International Journal of Cultural Policy* 28 (2): 131–144.

Gerring, John (2017[2006]) *Case Study Research. Principles and Practices*, Cambridge: Cambridge University Press.

Giberti, Bruno (1991) "Design History and the History of Design, by John A. Walker. The Meanings of Modern Design: Towards the Twenty-First Century, by Peter Dormer," *Design Book Review* 22 (Fall): 53–56.

Giedion, Sigfried (1948) *Mechanization Takes Command. A Contribution to Anonymous History*, New York/Oxford: Oxford University Press.

Gillham, Bill (2000) *Case Study Research Methods*, London/New York: Continuum.

Gillis, Stacy, Gillian Howie and Rebecca Munford (eds) (2004) *Third Wave Feminism: A Critical Exploration*, Basingstoke: Palgrave.

Gimeno Martínez, Javier (2010) "Industrial Design in the Museum: The Case of the FN Milking Machine, c. 1947," *The Burlington Magazine* 152 (1290): 603–608.

Gimeno Martínez, Javier (2016) *Design and National Identity*, London/New York, Bloomsbury.

Godden, Chris (2015) "Economic History," in James D. Wright (ed.) *International Encyclopedia of the Social & Behavioral Sciences*, Amsterdam: Elsevier.

Gombrich, Ernst Hans (1968) "Style," in Donald Preziosi (ed.) (2009[1998]) *The Art of Art History. A Critical Anthology*. Oxford: Oxford University Press.

Gombrich, Ernst Hans (1969) *In Search of Cultural History*, Oxford: Clarendon.

Goodrum, Alison (2005) *The National Fabric: Fashion, Britishness, Globalization*. Oxford/New York: Berg.

Gorman, Carma (2014) "Law as a Lens for Understanding Design," *Design and Culture* 6 (3): 269–290.

Gosden, Chris, Frances Larson and Alison Petch (2007) *Knowing Things: Exploring the Collections at the Pitt Rivers Museum, 1884–1945*, Oxford: Oxford University Press.

Grassby, Richard (2005) "Material Culture and Cultural History," *Journal of Interdisciplinary History* 35 (4): 591–603.

Griffiths, Devin (2016) *The Age of Analogy: Science and Literature Between the Darwins*, Baltimore: Johns Hopkins University Press.

Griffiths, Devin (2017) "The Comparative Method and the History of the Modern Humanities," *History of Humanities* 2 (2): 473–505.

Griffiths, Devin (2021) "The Ecology of Form," *Critical Inquiry* 48 (1): 68–93.

Groot, Marjan (2007) *Vrouwen in de vormgeving in Nederland 1880–1940* [Women in Design in the Netherlands 1880–1940], Rotterdam: 010.

Groot, Marjan (2011) *Design en gender; van object tot representatie* [Design and Gender. From Object to Representation], Amsterdam: Amsterdam University Press.

Guercio, Gabriele (2006) *Art as Existence: The Artist's Monograph and Its Project*, Cambridge: MIT.

Guffey, Elizabeth (2006) *Retro: The Culture of Revival*, London: Reaktion.

Guldberg, Jørn (2011) "'Scandinavian Design' as Discourse: The Exhibition *Design in Scandinavia*, 1954–57," *Design Issues* 27 (2): 41–58.

Gunn, Wendy and Jared Donovan (eds) (2012) *Design and Anthropology*, Farnham/Burlington: Ashgate.

Hadjinicolaou, Nikos (1978 [1973]) *Art History and Class Struggle*, London: Pluto.

Hammonds, Evelynn (1994) "Black (W)holes and the Geometry of Black Female Sexuality," *Differences* 6 (2–3):1–10.

Hancock, Dawson R. and Bob Algozzine (2006) *Doing Case Study Research: A Practical Guide for Beginning Researchers*, New York: Columbia University.

Hannah, Fran and Tim Putnam (1980) "Taking Stock in Design History," *BLOCK* 3: 25–33.

Haraway, Donna (1985) "A Manifesto for Cyborgs: Science, Technology and Socialist Feminism in the 80s," *Socialist Review* 15 (80): 65–107.

Harris, Jonathan (1999) "General Introduction" and "Introduction to Volume II", in Hauser, Arnold (1999[1951]) *Social History of Art. Volume 2: Renaissance, Mannerism, Baroque*, London/New York: Routledge.

Hassan, Ihab (1977) "Prometheus as Performer: Towards a Posthumanist Culture?" *The Georgia Review* 31 (4): 830–850.

Hatt, Michael and Charlotte Klonk (2017[2006]) *Art History: A Critical Introduction to its Methods*, Manchester: Manchester University Press.

Hauser, Arnold (1999[1951]) *Social History of Art. Volume 2: Renaissance, Mannerism, Baroque*, London/New York: Routledge.

Hauser, Arnold (2018[1959]) *The Philosophy of Art History*, London/New York: Routledge.

Hebdige, Dick (1979) *Subculture: The Meaning of Style*, London/New York: Routledge.

Hegel, Johann GottfriedHerder (1835–38) "Philosophy of Fine Art," in Donald Preziosi (ed.) (2009 [1998]) *The Art of Art History: A Critical Anthology*, Oxford: Oxford University Press.

Heidegger, Martin (1971) "The Thing," *Poetry, Language, Thought*, New York: Harper & Row.

Heilbronner, Oded (2008) "From a Culture for Youth to a Culture of Youth: Recent Trends in the Historiography of Western Youth Cultures," *Contemporary European History* 17 (4): 575–591.

Hemonet, Marina (2023) "Inside Architect Charles Zana's Own 18th Century Paris Apartment," *Architectural Digest*, May. www.architecturaldigest.com/story/inside-architect-charles-zanas-own-18th-century-parisapartment, accessed May 2023.

Hermans, Hubert J. M. and Giancarlo Dimaggio (2004) *The Dialogical Self in Psychotherapy*, New York: Brunner/Routledge.

Hesmondhalgh, David (2019[2002]) *The Cultural Industries*, London/Thousand Oaks/New Delhi: Sage.

Higham, Robert (2003) "Timber Castles – A reassessment," in Robert Liddiard (ed.) *Anglo-Norman Castles*, Woodbridge: Boydell.

Highmore, Ben (2002) *Everyday Life and Cultural Theory: An Introduction*, London/New York: Routledge.

Highmore, Ben (2008) *The Design Culture Reader*, New York and London: Routledge.

Hine, Thomas (1987) *Populuxe*, New York: Alfred A. Knopf.

History Workshop (2012) "An Introduction & Index to the Material," Available at www.historyworkshop.org.uk/the-history-workshop-archives-an-introduction/, accessed March 2022.

Hodkinson, Paul (2002) *Goth: Identity, Style and Subculture*, Oxford/New York: Berg.

Hodkinson, Paul (2007) "Youth Cultures. A Critical Outline of Key Debates," in Paul Hodkinson and Wolfgang Deicke, *Youth Cultures: Scenes, Subcultures and Tribes*. London/New York: Routledge.

Hoenigswald, H.M. 1993[1963] "On the History of the Comparative Method," *Anthropological Linguistics* 35 (1/4): 54–65.

Holsapel, Eveline (2001) *Ida Falkenberg-Liefrinck (1901). De rotan stoel als opmaat voor een betere woninginrichting*, Houten: Bonas.

Holterhoff, Kate (2017) "From Disclaimer to Critique: Race and the Digital Image Archivist," *DHQ: Digital Humanities Quarterly* 11 (3), http://digitalhumanities.org:8081/dhq/vol/11/3/000324/000324.html, accessed November 2023.

Homies website "B-Boy" www.homies.tv/homies_bboy.html, accessed November 2023.

Homies website "Gordo the Chef," www.homies.tv/homies_gordothechef.html, accessed November 2023.

Hommés Studio (2023) "A Serene Apartment by Charles Zana – Timeless Design In Paris," *Hommés Studio* (blog), April 4. https://hommes.studio/journal/charles-zana-timeless-design-in-paris/, accessed May 2023.

Hoppe, Katharina and Thomas Lemke (2021) *Neue Materialismen zur Einführung* [New Materialisms: An Introduction], Hamburg: Junius.

Howkins, John (2013[2001]) *The Creative Economy: How People Make Money from Ideas*, London: Penguin.

Hubak, Marit (1996) "The Car as a Cultural Statement," in Lie, Merete and Sørensen, Knut H. (eds) *Making Technology Our Own? Domesticating Technology into Everyday Life*, Oslo: Scandinavian University Press.

Hubbell, J. Andrew and John C. Ryan (2022) *Introduction to the Environmental Humanities*, London/New York: Routledge.

Hunt, Lynn (ed.) (1989) *The New Cultural History*, Berkeley and Los Angeles: University of California Press.

Huppatz, D.J. (2015) "Globalizing Design History and Global Design History," *Journal of Design History* 28 (2): 182–202.

Huppatz, D.J. (2018) "Introduction to Methodology: Virtual Special Issue for the Journal of Design History 2018," *Journal of Design History* 33 (1): e25–e40.

Huppatz, D.J. (2020) *Modern Asian Design*, London/New York: Bloomsbury.

Ikea Hacker Website, www.ikeahackers.net/, accessed November 2023.

Ikea Official Website, "*Ikea Ideas*," www.ikea.com/be/en/ideas, accessed November 2023.

Ikea Official Website, "*Planners-Ikea*," www.ikea.com/be/en/planners/, accessed November 2023.

Ikea Official Website, "*The Ikea Concept*," www.ikea.com/jp/en/this-is-ikea/the-ikea -concept-pube700d670, accessed November 2023.

Ingold, Tim (2000) *The Perception of the Environment: Essays on Livelihood, Dwelling and Skills*, New York and Oxon: Routledge.

Ingold, Tim (2007) *Lines: A Brief History*, New York and Oxon: Routledge.

Ingold, Tim (2014) "*Design Anthropology Is Not, and Cannot Be Ethnography.*" https:// kadk.dk/sites/default/files/08_ingold_design_anthropology_network.doc>, accessed August 2023.

Ishino, Catherine Jo (2006) "Seeing Is Believing: Reflections on Video Oral Histories with Chinese Graphic Designers," *Journal of Design History* 19 (4): 319–331.

Jones, Rodney H. (2012) *Discourse Analysis. A Resource Book for Students.* London and New York: Routledge.

Jørgensen, Marianne and Louisa Phillips (2002) *Discourse Analysis as Theory and Method*, London: Sage.

Julier, Guy (2006) "From Visual Culture to Design Culture," *Design Issues* 22 (1): 64–76.

Julier, Guy (2011) Locating Design Culture. Talk given at Premsela Design Cultures Symposium. www.designculture.info/reviews/ArticleStash/GJLocatingDesignCultures2011. pdf, accessed May 2022.

Julier, Guy (2014 [2000]) *The Culture of Design*, London: Sage.

Julier, Guy (2017) *Economies of Design*, London: Sage.

Julier, Guy, Anders V. Munch, Mads Nygaard Folkmann, Hans-Christian Jensen and Niels Peter Skou (eds) (2019) *Design Culture: Objects and Approaches*, London/New York: Bloomsbury.

Kalantidou, Eleni and Tony Fry (2014) *Design in the Borderlands*, London/New York: Routledge.

Kant, Immanuel (2007[1790]), *Critique of Judgement*, Oxford/New York: Oxford University.

Kay, Emma, Alex Gillespie and Mick Cooper (2021) "Application of the Qualitative Method of Analyzing Multivoicedness to Psychotherapy Research: The Case of 'Josh'," *Journal of Constructivist Psychology* 34 (2): 181–194.

Kets, R. (1953) "Connaissez-vous la machine à traire FN Licence Declaye?", *Revue FN* 4 (November): n.p.

Kikuchi, Yuko and Yunah Lee (2014) "Transnational Modern Design. Histories in East Asia: An Introduction," *Journal of Design History* 27 (4): 323–334.

Kim, Sang-Gook, Sang Min Yoon, Maria Yang, Jungwoo Choi, Haluk Akay, Edward Burnell et al. (2019) "AI for Design: Virtual Design Assistant," *CIRP Annals – Manufacturing Technology* 68: 141–144.

Kipping, Matthias, Takafumi Kurosawa and R. Daniel Wadhwani (2017) "A Revisionist Historiography of Business History. A Richer Past for a Richer Future," in John Wilson, Steven Toms, Abe de Jong and Emily Buchnea (eds) *The Routledge Companion to Business History*, Abingdon/New York: Routledge.

Kirkham, Pat and Susan Weber (eds) (2013) *History of Design: Decorative Arts and Material Culture, 1400–2000*, New York/New Haven: Bard Graduate Center/Yale University Press.

Kirschenbaum, Matthew G. (2009) "Hello Worlds." *The Chronicle of Higher Education*, January 23. www.chronicle.com/article/hello-worlds/, accessed November 2023.

Kleege, Georgina (2009) "My Secret Weapon," in Fiona Candlin and Raiford Guins (eds) *The Object Reader*, London/New York: Routledge: 510–513.

Knott, Stephen (2013) "Design in the Age of Prosumption: The Craft of Design after the Object," *Design and Culture* 5 (1): 45–67.

Kopytoff, Igor (1986) "The Cultural Biography of Things: Commoditization as Process," in Arjun Appadurai (ed.) *The Social Life of Things: Commodities in Cultural Perspective*, Cambridge: Cambridge University Press.

Krantz, Frederick (ed.) (2009) *History from Below: Studies in Popular Protest and Popular Ideology in Honour of George Rudé*, Cambridge: Cambridge University Press.

Kreps, Christina (2010) "Non-Western Models of Museums and Curation in Cross-cultural Perspective," in Sharon Macdonald (ed.) *A Companion to Museum Studies*, Chichester: Wiley-Blackwell.

Kristeva, Julia, Alice Jardin and Harry Blake (1981) "Women's Time," *Signs* 7 (1): 13–35.

Kristoffersson, Sara (2014) *Design by IKEA: A Cultural History*, New York/London: Bloomsbury.

Kubler, George (1962) *The Shape of Time: Remarks on the History of Things*, New Haven/London: Yale University Press.

Labov, William (1972) *Sociolinguistic Patterns*, Philadelphia: University of Pennsylvania Press.

Labrusse, Rémi (2010) "Face au chaos: grammaires de l'ornement [In the Face of Chaos: Grammars of Ornament]," *Perspective. Actualité en histoire de l'art* 2010 (1): 97–121.

Lacan, Jacques (2006) *Écrits: The First Complete Edition in English*, New York/London: W.W. Norton.

Langmead, Alison, Christopher J. Nygren, Paul Rodriguez and Alan Craig (2021) "Leonardo, Morelli, and the Computational Mirror," *DHQ: Digital Humanities Quarterly* 15 (1). https://dhq-static.digitalhumanities.org/pdf/000540.pdf>, accessed November 2023.

Lash, Scott and John Urry (1994) *Economies of Signs and Space*, London/Thousand Oaks/New Delhi: Sage.

Latour, Bruno (1987) *Science in Action – How to Follow Scientists and Engineers Through Society*, Harvard: Harvard University Press.

Latour, Bruno (1992) "Where Are the Missing Masses? The Sociology of a Few Mundane Artifacts," in Fiona Candlin and Raiford Guins (eds) (2009) *The Object Reader*, London/New York: Routledge.

Latour, Bruno (2005) *Reassembling the Social. An Introduction to Actor-Network-Theory*, Oxford/New York: Oxford University Press.

Latour, Bruno (1993[1984]) *The Pasteurization of France*, Harvard/Cambridge: Harvard University Press.

Lau, Susie (2016) "Gucci IRL," *STYLE BUBBLE*. www.stylebubble.co.uk/style_bubble/2016/03, accessed May 2017.

Law, John(1999) "After ANT: Topology, Naming and Complexity," in JohnLaw and JohnHassard (eds) *Actor Network Theory and After*, Oxford/Keele:Blackwell and the Sociological Review.

Law, John (2009) "Actor Network Theory and Material Semiotics," in Bryan S. Turner (ed.) *The New Blackwell Companion to Social Theory*, Malden/Oxford/Chichester: Blackwell.

Lee, Hermione (2009) *Biography: A Very Short Introduction*. Oxford: Oxford University Press.

Lee Mickle, F. (1924) "Milking Machines. VIII The Sanitary Efficiency of a Simplified Type of Milking Machine," *New York State Agricultural Experiment Station* 524 (November): 3–48.

Lees-Maffei, Grace (2009) "The Production-Consumption-Mediation Paradigm," *Journal of Design History* 22 (4): 351–376.

Lees-Maffei, Grace (2014) *Design at Home: Domestic Advice Books in Britain and the USA since 1945*, London: Routledge.

Lees-Maffei, Grace and Rebecca Houze (2010) *The Design History Reader*, Oxford/New York: Berg.

Lefebvre, Henri (1987) "The Everyday and Everydayness," *Yale French Studies* 73: 7–11.

LeGates, Marlene (2001) *In Their Time: A History of Feminism in Western Society*, London and New York: Routledge.

Lewis, Simon L. and Mark A. Maslin (2015) "Defining the Anthropocene," *Nature* 519: 171–180.

Linthicum, Liz (2006) "Integrative Practice: Oral History, Dress and Disability Studies," *Journal of Design History* 19 (4): 309–318.

Litwicki, Ellen M. (2000) "Tupperware: The Promise of Plastic in 1950s America. By Alison J. Clarke," *Journal of Social History* 34 (1): 247–249.

Lobos, Alex (2014) "Timelessness in Sustainable Product Design," in Juan Salamanca, Pieter Desmet, Andrés Burbano, Geke Dina Simone Ludden and Jorge Maya (eds) *The Colors of Care: Proceedings of the 9th International Conference on Design & Emotion*, Bogotá: Universidad de Los Andes.

Low-tech Magazine (2018) https://solar.lowtechmagazine.com/, accessed May 2022.

Lukács, Georg (1971) *History and Class Consciousness: Studies in Marxist Dialectics*, trans. R. Livingstone. Cambridge: MIT Press.

Lull, James (2000) *Media, Communication, Culture: A Global Approach*, New York: Columbia University Press.

M.H. (1957) "A travers le Pré madame. La tolerie à main", *Revue FN 40* (March): 2.

Maldini, Irene (2014) "Design and the Global Structures of Common Difference," *Design and Culture* 6 (1): 111–124.

Maldini, Irene (2016) "Attachment, Durability and the Environmental Impact of Digital DIY," *The Design Journal* 19 (1): 141–157.

Manzini, Ezio (2015) *Design, When Everybody Designs: An Introduction to Design for Social Innovation*, Cambridge: MIT.

Marcus, George H. (1998) *Design in the Fifties: When Everybody Went Modern*, Munich/New York: Prestel.

Marcus, George M. and Michael M.J. Fischer (1999[1986]) *Anthropology as Cultural Critique. An Experimental Moment in the Human Sciences*, Chicago/London: University of Chicago Press.

Mareis, Claudia, Moritz Greiner-Petter and Michael Renner (2022) *Critical by Design? Genealogies, Practices, Positions*, Bielefeld: Transcript.

Marez, Curtis (2009) "The Homies, or the Last Angel of History in Silicon Valley," in Fiona Candlin and Raiford Guins (eds), *The Object Reader*, London/New York: Routledge: 473–477.

Margolin, Victor (1985) "From the History of Decorative Arts to the History of Design: Some Problems of Documentation," *Art Libraries Journal*/Winter: 24–36.

Margolin, Victor (2001) "Can History Be Corrected? Needed: An Inclusive History for Chicago Graphic Design," *Inform* 13 (3): 11–15.

Margolin, Victor (2015) *World History of Design*, London/New York: Bloomsbury.

Marx, Karl (1954[1867]) *Capital: A Critical Analysis of Capitalist Production*. Moscow: Progress Publishers.

Marx, Karl (1975[1844]) *Economic and Philosophical Manuscripts of 1844*. New York: International Publishers.

Massaquoi, Notisha (2015[2001]) "Queer Theory and Intersectionality," in Neil J. Smelser and Paul B. Baltes (eds) *International Encyclopedia of the Social & Behavioral Sciences* vol. 19, Amsterdam: Elsevier.

Massey, Anne (2008) *Interior Design Since 1900*, London: Thames & Hudson.

Massey, Anne (2011) *Chair*, London: Reaktion.

Master Wace (2013 [ca. 1175]) *His Chronicle of the Norman Conquest from the Roman de Rou. The Original Classic Edition*, Brisbane: Emereo.

Mattern, Shannon (2020) "Calculative Composition: The Ethics of Automating Design," in Markus D. Dubber, Frank Pasquale and Sunit Das (eds) *The Oxford Handbook of Ethics of AI*, Oxford: Oxford Handbooks.

Matthews, Rachel (2015) "Contemporary Fashion Tastemakers: Starting Conversations that Matter," *Catwalk: The Journal of Fashion, Beauty and Style* 4 (1): 51–70.

McHoul, Alec and Wendy Grace (1997) *A Foucault Primer: Discourse, Power and the Subject*, New York: NYU Press.

McKey Carusi, Rahna (2020) *Lacan and Critical Feminism: Subjectivity, Sexuation, and Discourse*, London/New York:Routledge.

McNeil Peter and Giorgio Riello (2016) *Luxury: A Rich History*, Oxford: Oxford University Press.

Meikle, Jeffrey L. (1998) "Material Virtues: On the Ideal and the Real in Design History," *Journal of Design History* 11 (3): 191–199.

Melas, Natalie (2007) *All the Difference in the World: Postcoloniality and the Ends of Comparison*, Stanford: Stanford University Press.

Memmi, Albert (1957) *Portrait du colonisé; suivi de portrait du colonisateur* [Portrait of the Colonized; Followed by Portrait of the Colonizer], Paris: Buchet.

Meroz, Joana (2022) "A 'Tropic-Proof Container Exhibition:' The Role of Environmental Factors in Configuring Design, a Dutch Case Study," in Harriet Atkinson, Verity Clarkson and Sarah A. Lichtman (eds) *Exhibitions Beyond Boundaries: Transnational Exchanges through Art, Architecture, and Design 1945–1985*, London/New York/Dublin: Bloomsbury.

Meyer, Vera, Evelina Y. Basenko, J. Philipp Benz, Gerhard H. Braus, Mark X. Caddick, Michael Csukai, Ronald P. de Vries, Drew Endy, Jens C. Frisvad, Nina Gunde-Cimerman, Thomas Haarmann, Yitzhak Hadar, Kim Hansen, Robert I. Johnson, Nancy P. Keller, Nada Kraševec, Uffe H. Mortensen, Rolando Perez, Arthur F. J. Ram, Eric Record, Phil Ross, Volha Shapaval, Charlotte Steiniger, Hans van den Brink, Jolanda van Munster, Oded Yarden & Han A. B. Wösten (2020) "Growing a Circular Economy with Fungal Biotechnology: A White Paper," *Fungal Biology and Biotechnology*, 7 (5): 1–23. https://doi.org/10.1186/s40694-020-00095-z, accessed May 2022.

Meyer, Vera and Regine Rapp (eds) (2020) *Mind the Fungi*, Berlin: Universitätsverlag der TU Berlin. http://dx.doi.org/10.14279/depositonce-10350, accessed May 2022.

Michaud, Éric (2019) *The Barbarian Invasions: A Genealogy of the History of Art*, Cambridge: MIT.

Mida, Ingrid and Alexandra Kim (2015) *The Dress Detective: A practical Guide to Object-based Research in Fashion*, London/New York: Bloomsbury.

Mignolo, Walter D. (2011) *The Darker Side of Western Modernity: Global Futures, Decolonial Options*, Durham/London: Duke University Press.

Mignolo, Walter D. (2021) *The Politics of Decolonial Investigations*, Durham: Duke University Press.

Mignolo, Walter D. and Catherine E. Walsh (2018) *On Decoloniality: Concepts, Analytics, Praxis*, Durham: Duke University Press.

Mignolo, Walter D. and Rolando Vázquez (2013) "Decolonial AestheSis: Colonial Wounds/Decolonial Healings," *Social Text/Periscope* 11 (11). https://socialtext journal.org/periscope_article/decolonial-aesthesis-colonial-woundsdecolonial-hea lings/, accessed November 2023.

Miller, Daniel (1987) *Material Culture and Mass Consumption*, Oxford: Basil Blackwell.

Miller, Daniel (1988) "Appropriating the State on the Council Estate," *Man* 23 (2): 353–372.

Mills, Albert J., Gabriel Eurepos and Elden Wiebe (eds) (2010) *Encyclopedia of Case Study Research*, Thousand Oaks: Sage.

Modleski, Tania (1991) *Feminism Without Women: Culture and Criticism in a "Post-feminist" Age*, London: Routledge.

Molella, Arthur P. (2002) "Science Moderne: Sigfried Giedion's 'Space, Time and Architecture' and 'Mechanization Takes Command'," *Technology and Culture* 43 (2): 374–389.

Moore, David (2005) "Principles of Mushroom Developmental Biology," *International Journal of Medicinal Mushrooms* 7: 79–101.

Moran, Anna and Sorcha O'Brien (eds) (2014) *Love Objects: Emotion, Design and Material Culture*, London/New York: Bloomsbury.

Moriarty, Catherine (2016) "Monographs, Archives, and Networks: Representing Designer Relationships," *Design Issues* 32 (4): 52–63.

Mort, Frank (1996) *Cultures of Consumption: Masculinities and Social Space in Late Twentieth-Century Britain*, London and New York: Routledge.

Muggleton, David and Rupert Weinzierl (eds) (2003) *The Post-Subcultures Reader*, Oxford/New York: Berg.

Mulvihill, Thalia M. and Raji Swaminathan (eds) (2021) *Oral History and Qualitative Methodologies: Educational Research for Social Justice*, London and New York: Routledge.

Mussari, Mark (2016) *Danish Modern: Between Art and Design*, London/New York: Bloomsbury.

MycoWorks Official Website, "Heritage", www.mycoworks.com/our-heritage, accessed May 2022.

Myers, William, (2018[2012]) *Biodesign: Nature, Science, Creativity*, London: Thames and Hudson.

Nader, Ralph (1965) *Unsafe at Any Speed: The Designed-In Dangers of the American Automobile*, New York: Grossman.

Naidoo, Loshini (2012) "Ethnography: An Introduction to Definition and Method," in Loshini Naidoo (ed.) *An Ethnography of Global Landscapes and Corridors*, Rijeka: IntechOpen.

Neuhart, John, Marilyn Neuhart and Ray Eames (1989) *Eames Design: The Work of the Office of Charles and Ray Eames*, New York: Harry N. Abrams.

New York State Agricultural Experiment Station (1925) "A Simplified Type of Milking Machine," *New York State Agricultural Experiment Station. Popular Edition* 524 (February).

Nkrumah, Kwame (1964) *Le Consciencisme: philosophie et idéologie pour la Décolonisation et le Développement, avec un référence particulière à la Révolution Africaine*, Paris: Payot.

Nygaard Folkmann, Mads (2019) "The Glowing Black of Fritz-kola: Aestheticization in Design Culture," in Guy Julier, Anders V. Munch, Mads Nygaard Folkmann, Hans-Christian Jensen and Niels Peter Skou (eds) *Design Culture: Objects and Approaches*, London and New York: Bloomsbury.

Nygaard Folkmann, Mads (2023) *Design Aesthetics: Theoretical Basics and Studies in Implication*, Cambridge/London: MIT.

Oddy, Nicholas (2016) "Design Classics," in Clive Edwards (ed.) *The Bloomsbury Encyclopedia of Design*. Volume 1, London: Bloomsbury.

Oliver, Kelly (1993) *Reading Kristeva: Unravelling the Double-bind*, Bloomington and Indianapolis: Indiana University Press.

Olkiewicz, Jerzy (1958) "Przeobrazenia Przestreni," *Projekt* 5 (13): 9–12.

O'Reilly, Karen (2012[2005]) *Ethnographic Methods*, London: Routledge.

Oswalt, Philipp (ed.) (2009) *Bauhaus Conflicts 1919–2009. Controversies and Counterparts*, Berlin: Hatje Cantz.

Otsuka, Marie (2019) "HTML Energy," podcast, Laurel Schwulst (Interviewer), broadcast by *HTML. Energy*, 30 December 2019.

Otsuka, Marie (2020) MICA Design Talks Lecture, Maryland Institute College of Art, Ellen Lupton, 24 November 2020, www.facebook.com/mica.edu/videos/301985177635936/, accessed May 2022.

Özkirimli, Umut (2000) *Theories of Nationalism: A Critical Introduction*, New York: Palgrave.

Paletschek, Sylvia and Bianka Pietrow-Ennker (2004) *Women's Emancipation Movements in the Nineteenth Century: A European Perspective*, Stanford: Standford University Press.

Papanek, Victor (2019[1971]) *Design for the Real World*, London: Thames and Hudson.

Partington, Matthew (2006) "Ceramic Points of View: Video Interviews, the Internet and the Interpretation of Museum Objects," *Journal of Design History* 19 (4): 333–344.

Pearlstone, Zena (2001) *Katsina: Commodified and Appropriated Images of Hopi Supernaturals*, Los Angeles: UCLA Fowler Museum of Cultural History.

Perks, Robert and Alistair Thomson (eds) (2016[1998]), *The Oral History Reader*, London/New York: Routledge.

Petroski, Henry (1992) *The Evolution of Useful Things*, New York: Vintage.

Pevsner, Nikolaus (1956) *The Englishness of English Art*, New York: Praeger.

Piaget, Jean (1972) *The Principles of Genetic Epistemology*, London: Routledge and Kegan Paul.

Piatkowska, Ksenia Katarzyna (2014) "The Corporate Museum: A New Type of Museum Created as a Component of Marketing Company," *The International Journal of the Inclusive Museum* 6 (II): 29–37.

Pitt-Rivers, Augustus (1891) "Typological Museums, as Exemplified by the Pitt-Rivers Museum at Oxford, and his Provincial Museum at Farnham, Dorset," *Journal of the Society of Arts* 40: 115–122.

Podro, Michael (1984) *The Critical Historians of Art*, New Haven/London: Yale University Press.

Polan, Brenda and Roger Tredre (2009) *The Great Fashion Designers*, New York/Oxford: Berg.

Popper, Karl (1990 [1947]) *The Poverty of Historicism*, London/New York: Routledge.

Potvin, John (2014) *Bachelors of a Different Sort: Queer Aesthetics, Material Culture and the Modern Interior in Britain*, Manchester: Manchester University Press.

Pouillard, Véronique (2021) *Paris to New York. The Transatlantic Fashion Industry in the Twentieth Century*, Cambridge/London: Harvard University Press.

Preziosi, Donald (ed.) (2009 [1998]) *The Art of Art History: A Critical Anthology*, Oxford: Oxford University Press.

Prown, Jules David (1982) "Mind in Matter: An Introduction to Material Culture Theory and Method," *Winterthur Portfolio* 17 (1): 1–19.

Prown, Jules David (1993) "The Truth of Material Culture: History or Fiction?," in Lubar, Stephen and David W. Kingery (eds) *History from Things: Essays on Material Culture*, Washington and London: Smithsonian Institution.

Prown, Jules David (1996) "Material/Culture. Can the Cowman and the Farmer Still Be Friends?," in Kingery, W. David (ed.) *Learning from Things: Method and Theory of Material Culture Studies*, Washington/London: Smithsonian.

Prown, Jules David (1997) "The Promise and Perils of Context," *American Art*, 11 (2): 20–27.

Prown, Jules David and Kenneth Haltman (eds) (2000) *American Artifacts: Essays in Material Culture*, East Lansing: Michigan State University Press.

Raento, Pauliina and Stanley Brunn (2005) "Visualizing Finland: Postage stamps as political Messengers," *Geografiska Annaler* 87B (2): 145–163.

Ragland-Sullivan, Ellie (1982) "Jacques Lacan: Feminism and the Problem of Gender Identity," *Substance* 11 (3): 6–20.

Raizman, David (2010) *History of Modern Design*, London: Laurence King.

Ray, Larry and Andrew Sayer (eds) (1999) *Culture and Economy after the Cultural Turn*, Abingdon/New York: Routledge.

Revue FN (1957) "Notre M.A.T. en vedette," *Revue FN* 46 (October): 14.

Revue FN (1958) "A l'Expo de Bruxelles," *Revue FN* 54 (June).

Richins, Marsha (1994) "The Public and Private Meanings of Possessions," *Journal of Consumer Research* 21 (3): 504–521.

Riello, Giorgio (2013) *Cotton: the Fabric that Made the Modern World*, Cambridge/New York: Cambridge University Press.

Riello, Giorgio (2022) "The 'Material Turn' in World and Global History," *Journal of World History* 33 (2): 193–232.

Rihoux, Benoît and Charles C. Ragin (2009) *Configurational Comparative Methods: Qualitative Comparative Analysis (QCA) and Related Techniques*, Los Angeles/London/Singapore/New Delhi: Sage.

Risam, Roopika and Alex Gil (2022) "Introduction: The Questions of Minimal Computing," 16 (2), *DHQ: Digital Humanities Quarterly*, http://digitalhumanities.org:8081/dhq/vol/16/2/000646/000646.html, accessed November 2023.

Ritchie, Donald A. (ed.) (2011) *The Oxford Handbook of Oral History*, Oxford: Oxford University Press.

Ritchie, Donald A. (2015[2002]) *Doing Oral History*, Oxford: Oxford University Press.

Rocamora, Agnès (2011) "Personal Fashion Blogs: Screens and Mirrors in Digital Self-Portraits," *Fashion Theory* 15 (4): 407–424.

Rocamora, Agnès (2012) "Hypertextuality and Remediation in the Fashion Media," *Journalism Practice* 6 (1): 92–106.

Rogers, Richard A. (2006) "From Cultural Exchange to Transculturation: A Review and Reconceptualization of Cultural Appropriation," *Communication Theory* 16: 474–503.

Romero, Elena and Elizabeth Way (eds) (2023) *Fresh Fly Fabulous: 50 Years of Hip Hop Style*, New York: Rizzoli/Electa.

Rose, Gillian (2016) *Visual Methodologies: An Introduction to Researching with Visual Materials*, Los Angeles and London: Sage.

Rosner, Daniela and Jonathan Bean (2009) "Learning from IKEA Hacking: I'm Not One to Decoupage a Tabletop and Call it a Day," in *CHI '09: Proceedings of the SIGCHI Conference on Human Factors in Computing Systems*: 419–422.

Rossi, Catharine (2009) "Furniture, Feminism and the Feminine: Women Designers in Post-War Italy, 1945 to 1970," *Journal of Design History* 22 (3): 243–257.

Said, Edward W. (1978) *Orientalism*, New York: Pantheon Books.

Salinas, Oscar and Ana Elena Mallet (2006) *Clara Porset's Design: Creating a Modern Mexico*, Mexico D.F.: Franz Mayer Museum.

Sandino, Linda (2006) "Oral Histories and Design: Objects and Subjects," *Journal of Design History* 19 (4): 275–282.

Sandino, Linda and Matthew Partington (eds) (2013) *Oral History in the Visual Arts*, London/New York: Bloomsbury.

Schneider Adams, Laurie (1996) *The Methodologies of Art: An Introduction*, Boulder/Oxford: Westview.

Schouwenberg, Louise and Michael Kaethler (eds) (2021) *The Auto-Ethnographic Turn in Design*, Amsterdam: Valiz.

Scolari, Carlos Alberto, Juan Miguel Aguado and Claudio Feijóo (2012) "Mobile Media: Towards a Definition and Taxonomy of Contents and Applications," *iJIM* 6 (2): 29–38.

Serulus, Katarina (2018) *Design and Politics. The Public Promotion of Industrial Design in Postwar Belgium (1950–1986)*, Leuven: Leuven University Press.

Shih, Shu-Mei (2015) "World Studies and Relational Comparison," *PMLA* 130 (2): 430–438.

Simon, Judith (2015) "Distributed Epistemic Responsibility in a Hyperconnected Era," in Luciano Floridi (ed.) *The Onlife Manifesto: Being Human in a Hyperconnected Era*, Cham: Springer.

Slavin, Kevin (2016) "Design as Participation," *Journals for Design and Science*. Available at https://jods.mitpress.mit.edu/pub/design-as-participation/release/1, accessed November 2023.

Sloboda, Stacey (2008) "The Grammar of Ornament: Cosmopolitanism and Reform in British Design," *Journal of Design History* 21 (3): 223–236.

Smelik, Anneke (ed.) (2017) *Delft Blue to Denim Blue: Contemporary Dutch Fashion*, London/New York: I.B. Tauris.

Smith, T'ai Lin (2014) *Bauhaus Weaving Theory: From Feminine Craft to Mode of Design*, Minneapolis and London: University of Minnesota Press.

Smythe, Michael (2011) *New Zealand by Design: A History of New Zealand Product Design*, Auckland: Godwit.

Somerville, Siobhan (ed.) (2020) *The Cambridge Companion to Queer Studies*, Cambridge, New York, Melbourne, New Dehli: Cambridge University Press.

Sontag, Susan (1965) "On Style," in Susan Sontag (1966) *Against Interpretation and Other Essays*, New York: Picador.

Souto, Maria Helena (2011) *Portugal nas Exposições Universais 1851–1900*, Lisbon: Edições Colibri.

Souza Dias, Dora (2018) "International Design Organizations and the Study of Transnational Interactions: The Case of Icogradalatinoamérica80," *Journal of Design History* 32 (2): 188–206.

Sparke, Penny (1995) *As Long as it's Pink. The Sexual Politics of Taste*, London: Harper Collins.

Sparke, Penny (2013) *An Introduction to Design and Culture: 1900 to the Present*, London/New York: Routledge.

Sparke, Penny (2016) "Introduction," in Penny Sparke and Fiona Fisher (eds) *The Routledge Companion to Design Studies*, London/New York: Routledge.

Stake, Robert E. (1995) *The Art of Case Study Research*, Thousand Oaks: Sage.

Stearns, Peter N. (ed.) (1994) *Encyclopedia of Social History*, New York/London: Garland.

Steele, Valerie (1998) "A Museum of Fashion is More than a Clothes-Bag," *Fashion Theory* 2 (4): 327–335.

Steele, Valerie (ed.) (2013) *A Queer History of Fashion: From the Closet to the Catwalk*, Yale: Yale University Press.

Stefanski, Jasio (2018) "Imagining a Solar-Powered Internet: Kris De Decker Low <– Tech Magazine," *Walker Art*, https://walkerart.org/magazine/low-tech-magazine-kris-de-decker, accessed May 2022.

Steffen, Will, Paul Crutzen and John McNeill (2007) "The Anthropocene: Are Humans now overwhelming the great forces of nature?," *Ambio. A Journal of the Human Environment* 36 (8): 614–621.

Stone, Clarence (2002) "Urban Regimes and Problems of Local Democracy," in *ECPR Joint Sessions*. Turin, Italy, https://ecpr.eu/Filestore/PaperProposal/f2ba7f06-75b4-4ea2-9817-1716621efac5.pdf, accessed November 2023.

Studiolabo (2022) "Event 2022 – Design Forever by Elle Decor Italia," *Fuorisalone*. Available at www.fuorisalone.it/en/2022/events/2264/Design-Forever-by-elle-decor-Italia, accessed May 2023.

STYLE BUBBLE (2009) "*Press*," www.stylebubble.co.uk/press, accessed May 2017.

STYLE BUBBLE (2013) "*FAQ*," www.stylebubble.co.uk/faq#comments, accessed March 2017.

Sum, Ngai-Ling and Bob Jessop (2013) *Towards a Cultural Political Economy: Putting Culture in its Place in Political Economy*, Cheltenham/Northampton: Edward Elgar.

Summers, David (2003) "Style," in Donald Preziosi (ed.) (2009[1989]) *The Art of Art History: A Critical Anthology*, Oxford: Oxford University Press.

T+HUIS Website, www.t-huis.info, accessed November 2023.

Tannen, Deborah, Heidi E. Hamilton and Deborah Schiffrin (eds) (2015[2001]) *The Handbook of Discourse Analysis*, Chichester: Wiley Blackwell.

Teunissen, José (2011) "Deconstructing Belgian and Dutch Fashion Dreams: From Global Trends to Local Crafts," *Fashion Theory* 15 (2): 157–176.

The Unheard Archive Website, https://theunheardarchive.com, accessed November 2023.

Thomas, Gary (2016) *How To Do Your Case Study*, Thousand Oaks: Sage.

Thompson, Christopher (2011) "Modernizing for Trade: Institutionalizing Design Promotion in New Zealand, 1958–1967," *Journal of Design History* 24 (3): 223–239.

Thrift, Nigel (2001) "Chasing Capitalism," *New Political Economy 6* (3), 375–380.

Tibbe, Lieske (2013) "Kunstnijverheidsmusea: van techniek naar esthetiek," in Elli-noor Bergvelt, Debora J. Meijers, Mieke Rijnders (eds) *Kabinetten, galerijen en musea: Het verzamelen en presenteren van naturalia en kunst van 1500 tot heden* [Cabinets, Galleries, and Museums: The Collection and Presentation of Naturalia and Art from 1500 to the Present]. Zwolle: Wbooks.

Tight, Malcolm (2017) *Understanding Case Study Research: Small-scale Research with Meaning*, Thousand Oaks: Sage.

Tlostanova, Madina (2017) *Postcolonialism & Postsocialism in Fiction and Art. Resistance and Reexistence*. London: Palgrave Macmillan.

Toms, Steven and John Wilson (2017) "Business history: Agendas, Historiography and Debates," in John Wilson, Steven Toms, Abe de Jong and Emily Buchnea (eds) *The Routledge Companion to Business History*, Abingdon/New York: Routledge.

Trevelyan, George Macaulay (1978[1946]) *English Social History: A Survey of Six Centuries from Chaucer to Queen Victoria*. London: Longman.

Tunstall, Elizabeth (2023) *Decolonizing Design. A Cultural Justice Guidebook*, Cambridge/London: MIT.

Turney, Jo (2004) "Here's One I Made Earlier: Making and Living with Home Craft in Contemporary Britain," *Journal of Design History* 17 (3): 267–282.

Twemlow, Alice (2017) *Sifting the Trash: A History of Design Criticism*, Cambridge/London: MIT.

Tynan, Jane (2022) *Trench Coat*, London/New York/Dublin: Bloomsbury.

Vaid-Menon, Alok (2020) *Beyond the Gender Binary*, New York: Penguin.

van den Berg, Harry (2004) "Discoursanalyse in de praktijk: de discursieve constructie van sociale categorieen", *KWALON* 9 (3): 27–35.

Van Nes, Nicole and Jacqueline Cramer (2006) "Product Lifetime Optimization: A Challenging Strategy towards More Sustainable Consumption Patterns," *Journal of Cleaner Production* 14 (15–16): 1307–1318.

Vansintjan, Aaron (2019) "The Philosophy of Low-Tech: A Conversation with Kris De Decker", *Never Apart*, www.neverapart.com/features/low-tech-kris-de-decker, accessed May 2022.

Varela Braga, Ariane (2020) "Owen Jones, Gottfried Semper et les origines anthropologiques de l'art ornamental [Owen Jones, Gottfried Semper and the Anthropological Origins of Ornamental Art]," *Palíndromo* 12 (27): 34–55.

Vasari, Giorgio (1991[1568]) *The Lives of the Artists*, Oxford/New York: Oxford University.

Vázquez, Rolando (2020) *Vistas of Modernity. Decolonial Aesthesis and the End of the Contemporary*, Prinsenbeek: Jap Sam.

Vincentelli, Moira (2000) *Women and Ceramics: Gendered Vessels*, Manchester: Manchester University Press.

Vogelgsang, Tobias (2017) "Law, Design, and Market Value: Lessons from the Cantilever Chair, 1929–1936", *Enterprise & Society* 18 (3): 536–565.

Votolato, Gregory (1998) *American Design in the Twentieth Century: Personality and Performance*, Manchester: Manchester University Press.

Vyas, H. Kumar (2006) "Design History: An Alternative Approach," *Design Issues* 22 (4): 27–34.

Walker, John A. (1989) *Design History and the History of Design*, London: Pluto.

Walker, John A. and Sarah Chaplin (1997) "Chapter 5. Production, Distribution and Consumption Model," *Visual Culture: An Introduction*, Manchester: Manchester University Press.

Wallner, Theresa Stephanie, Lise Magnier and Ruth Mugge (2020) "An Exploration of the Value of Timeless Design Styles for the Consumer Acceptance of Refurbished Products" *Sustainability* 12 (3): 1–17.

Wang, Han (2023) "Authorship of Artificial Intelligence-Generated Works and Possible System Improvement in China," *Beijing Law Review* 14: 901–912.

Weikle, Brandie (2022) "Gender-fluid Dressing Could Lead To Renaissance in Fashion, Says Advocate," *CBC Radio*. www.cbc.ca/radio/tapestry/gender-fluid-dressing-could-lead-to-renaissance-in-fashion-says-advocate-1.6306160, accessed May 2022.

Weinryb, Ittai (2017) "The Object in the Comparative Context," in Jas Elsner (ed.) *Comparativism in Art History*, London/New York: Routledge.

Weller, Richard, Karen M'Closkey, Billy Fleming and Frederick Steiner (eds) (2019) *Design with Nature Now*, Cambridge: Lincoln Institute of Land Policy.

Wells, Kay (2019) *Weaving Modernism: Postwar Tapestry Between Paris and New York*. New Haven: Yale University Press.

Werbel, Amy B. (2000) "The Foley Food Mill," in Prown, Jules David and Kenneth Haltman (eds) *American Artifacts: Essays in Material Culture*, East Lansing: Michigan State University Press.

Whelehan, Imelda, *"Having It All (Again?)*," Paper given at the Economic and Social Research Council (ESRC) seminar series on new femininities at the London School of Economics and Political Sciences (LSE). 19 November 2004. www.docin.com/p-99447553.html, accessed May 2022.

Williams, Brien R. (2011) "Doing Video Oral History," in Ritchie, Donald A. (ed.) *The Oxford Handbook of Oral History*, Oxford: Oxford University Press.

Wilson, John F., Ian G. Jones, Steven Toms, Anna Tilba, Emily Buchnea and Nicholas Wong (2022) *Business History: A Research Overview*, New York: Routledge.

Winship, Janice (1985) "*A Girl Needs to Get Street-wise*: Magazines for the 1980s," in *Feminist Review21*: 25–46.

Winship, Janice (1987) *Inside Women's Magazines*, London: Pandora.

Wölfflin (1950[1915]) *Principles of Art History: The Problem of the Development of Style in Later Art*. New York: Dover.

Wood, Ness (2016) "'I Would Suggest that You Should Not Think of the Design Centre as a Museum; It is a Live, Active, Moving Thing': Designs of the Year, 1957," in Liz Farrelly and Joanna Weddell (eds) *Design Objects and the Museum*, London/New York: Bloomsbury.

Wood, Summer (2004) "Freedom of 'Choice': Parsing the Word that Defined a Generation," in Leslie L. Heywood (ed.) (2006) *The Women's Movement Today: An Encyclopedia of Third-Wave Feminism*, Westport: Greenwood Press.

Woodham, Jonathan (2005) "Local, National and Global: Redrawing the Design Historical Map," *Journal of Design History* 18 (4): 257–267.

Woodside, Arch G. (2010) *Case Study Research. Theory. Methods. Practice*, Bingley: Emerald.

Woodward, Ian (2007) *Understanding Material Culture*. Los Angeles/London/New Delhi/Singapore: Sage.

Woodward, Sophie (2009) "The Myth of Street Style," *Fashion Theory* 13 (1): 83–102.

Wright, Arthur C. (2019) *Decoding the Bayeux Tapestry: The Secrets of History's Most Famous Embroidery Hidden in Plain Sight*, Barnsley: Pen & Sword.

Yagou, Artemis (2011) *Fragile Innovation: Episodes in Greek Design History*, self-published: CreateSpace.

Yaneva, Albena (2009) "Making the Social Hold: Towards an Actor-Network Theory of Design," *Design and Culture* 1 (3): 273–288.

Yerena Official Website (2014), www.hechoconganas.com, accessed November 2023.

Yin, Robert K. (2018) *Case Study Research and Applications, Design and Methods*, Thousand Oaks: Sage.

Yotka, Steph (2016) "Meet the People, Trends, and Items That Will Rule Fashion in 2017," *VOGUE*, Condé Nast. www.vogue.com/article/2017-fashion-trend-predic tions, accessed March 2017.

Zhou, Feifei (2020) *Models of the Human in Twentieth-Century Linguistic Theories: System, Order, Creativity*, Singapore: Springer.

Ziff, Bruce and Pratima V. Rao (1997) *Borrowed Power: Essays on Cultural Appropriation*, New Brunswick: Rutgers University Press.

Zukin, Sharon (1995) *The Cultures of Cities*, Cambridge/Oxford: Blackwell.

Index

For Product Safety Concerns and Information please contact our EU
representative GPSR@taylorandfrancis.com
Taylor & Francis Verlag GmbH, Kaufingerstraße 24, 80331 München, Germany

www.ingramcontent.com/pod-product-compliance
Lightning Source LLC
Chambersburg PA
CBHW070710280326
41926CB00089B/3528